Praise for
THE BUNKER

"Superb . . . Quite simply the most accurate and terrifying account of the nightmare and its end I have ever read."

—Theodore H. White, author of
The Making of the President

"A riveting, damned near incredible story . . . Nothing I've read on the subject reveals so vividly the psychopaths, quasi-criminals and looneys who made up the entourage around Germany's demon king."

—Gerald Green,
author of *Holocaust*

THE BUNKER

The History of the Reich Chancellery Group

James P. O'Donnell

*This low-priced Bantam Book
has been completely reset in a type face
designed for easy reading, and was printed
from new plates. It contains the complete
text of the original hard-cover edition.*
NOT ONE WORD HAS BEEN OMITTED.

THE BUNKER

*A Bantam Book / published by arrangement with
Houghton Mifflin Company*

PRINTING HISTORY

*Houghton Mifflin edition published November 1978
3 printings through February 1979
Book-of-the-Month Club edition January 1979
History Book Club edition January 1979
Macmillan Book Club edition February 1979
Serialized in* BOOK DIGEST *April 1979
Bantam edition / December 1979*

*The drawing on page 46 and the map on page 271
are by John V. Morris.*

ISBN 0-553-13248-2

Published simultaneously in the United States and Canada

PRINTED IN THE UNITED STATES OF AMERICA

To Marguerite Higgins

While much is too strange to be believed, nothing is too strange to have happened.

—THOMAS HARDY

Contents

Contents

THE BUNKER

Prologue

Even God cannot change the past —ARISTOTLE,
quoting Agathon

THE GAP BETWEEN the generations, unless it is to become
a chasm and make history meaningless, must somehow
be bridged. Each generation owes an after-action report
to the generation that follows. The best I have read was
written by the seventeenth-century Swedish diplomat Baron
von Oxenstierna, in the middle of the Thirty Years' War.
An nescis, mi fili, quantilla prudentia mundus rogatur?
(Do you not realize, my son, with how little wisdom this
world is run?)

Members of my own generation are my witnesses that
1945 was a breathless year, perhaps the most remarkable
on the calendar of our turbulent century. I remember
hearing of the sudden death of President Roosevelt on the
same day, April 12, 1945, as we who were soldiers had
reached the Elbe River and were preparing to cross.
Events, tremendous events, were in the saddle; history
was happening faster than it could be recorded or com-
prehended. *Annus mirabilis*, victory in Europe in May;
annus terribilis, victory in Asia in August, under a mush-
room cloud. Historians are still sorting out that year 1945,
when "Whirl was king."

This report turns the clock back to that April 1945. It
centers on the grisly death of one man only, the man the
ironic Cockneys, trembling in their shelters during the
London Blitz, had called "Little Old Hitler." Most of the

Allied world was waiting for news of his death as it paused to mourn the passing of that jaunty warrior, the stricken American President. Roosevelt and Hitler had both come to power in the same year, 1933, in the middle of a catastrophic world depression. Both left the stage of world history in that same April 1945. But there the parallel ends, abruptly. It was Hitler, not Roosevelt, who radically changed the lives of almost every member of my generation. He was the phenomenon of our time; he was our rendezvous with destiny.

Paltry as a human being, yet a mighty phenomenon. World War II was Hitler's war, and let there be no revisionist cavil about that. A recent biographer, that odd-man-out Englishman, David Irving, maintains that there is no archival document linking the name of Adolf Hitler with Auschwitz. Such casuistry is pernicious. A tyrant who gave the order to burn millions of human beings would know how to give the order to burn documents.*

Paper, we are told, burns at 451° Fahrenheit. In the last pandemoniac weeks of the Third Reich, document incineration became a Wagnerian cult ceremony. More than three quarters of the events narrated in this book have never been "documented." We will hear one of Hitler's orderlies, in a casual conversation, telling how seven foot-lockers of documents were destroyed in a madcap effort to have them flown out of the bunker on April 22, 1945.

Berlin was Adolf Hitler's capital, the bunker his last abode and legal address; his suicide took place there on a horsehair blue-and-white velvet sofa. Berlin may have become his potter's field. His body was cremated, the ashes scattered either in the bleached yellow sand of a remote suburb called Buch, or possibly just east of the city, in Erkner or in Finow. A decade ago, the Russians finally announced that they had cremated Hitler's charred body. They were vague about the exact place. Few living men know, and none is talking.

The city of Berlin is built on alluvial sand. It is located on a flat plain, or geologic end-moraine, formed by the departing glaciers of the last ice age; these left behind the

---

* Perhaps the only proper answer to Irving's preposterous thesis is the one given long ago by the Right Honorable Edmund Burke when confronted with similar nonsense-on-stilts. "No one who is allowed to walk around without a keeper can possibly believe that!"

confluence of two rivers, the Spree, which flows into the Havel, in an ancient river valley. Many men of power have built monuments to themselves on this sand. The monuments topple, the power-handlers vanish, the sand remains. It is political quicksand. The muse of history, that natural daughter of Professor Hegel and the dialectic, collects this shifting sand in her Berlin hourglass.

In German, an hourglass is called *eine Sanduhr*, a sand clock. An hourglass has no hands; that is its fascination. I have such a *Sanduhr* on my desk before me as I write. In the bright Berlin early morning hours, or again in the late evening when the great city falls deathly quiet, I can hear the sand flowing. When I listen closely, I imagine I hear it ticking, softly. I force my thoughts back to the year 1945. I reach for the hourglass, turn it bottom up, reverse the flow. The ghost of Adolf Hitler comes knocking at my door.

*   *

My generation of Americans was destined to celebrate the Fourth of July, that most robustly national of all our holidays, in many distant places, amid alien cornerstones, in the anarchic rubble of war and the aftermath of war. I still have a vivid memory of one such Fourth—in 1945. That was the day, a glorious, inglorious day, of the American military entry into vanquished Berlin. Today the American flag is still flying over Berlin, which is 5000 miles east of Fort McHenry. I often gaze at it fondly, with Baltimore eyes. Still, I must admit it is a strange, an awkward, legacy to an American generation now grown, many members of which were not even born in that faraway 1945.

Our troops had been marking time on the Elbe River for more than ten weeks before they finally reached Berlin that July 4. On April 11, 1945, when the U.S. 2nd Armored Division reached and took Magdeburg on the Elbe, it was then less than ninety miles west-southwest of Berlin, with one last river to cross. Nothing else stood between us and the tottering capital of the Third Reich except an open and beckoning autobahn, a few Brandenburg lakes, scraggy Scotch pine and birch forests, and beaten sadsack German soldiers yearning to surrender. That Berlin autobahn be-

came the road not taken, in our fateful hesitation. It is
not for nothing that Sir Winston Churchill, in his memoirs,
refers to this hesitation as a time of triumph and tragedy.

On that Fourth of July 1945, the lingering exultation of
Allied victory in the summer air was mingled with foreboding. Berlin was now supposed to become the revolving
stage for an exercise in international harmony, Four Power
government. But the stage was full of trap doors. It was
already set for what has since become the most durable
confrontation in post–World War II history. Berlin is a
city in suspense; here, 1945 never really ended. It simply
repeats itself. In a city of three and a third million, which
is still the largest metropolis and industrial city between
Paris and Moscow, life goes on, the decades pass. For
Berliners, life in Berlin is life in an hourglass.

Berlin is a great theater city, and the theater tradition is
Brechtian. Now and then, a shot rings out in the night.
Some desperate soul has tried to cross the smooth-sanded
death strip that today runs through the heart of the city.
This death strip, parallel to the hideous Berlin Wall, was
once a simple borough line. It was drawn up by municipal
planners in 1920, when they incorporated the old boroughs
and suburban communities into metropolitan Greater Berlin, an administrative act. Sometimes this imaginary line
runs down the middle of a street or follows a sidewalk, a
curbstone, a river bank, a canal, a house-fronting.

In 1945, this invisible borough line was adopted by the
four victorious Allied commanders as a convenient, tem-
porary demarcation line for the quartering of troops.
Berlin's twenty boroughs were divided into four sectors,
but Berliners still moved freely throughout their city. All
so casual; a second administrative act. Today, that old
borough line groans under the wall. Sentinels in green uniforms stand guard in tall towers. One third of Berlin has
become a roofless concentration camp.

As at least most Berliners are glumly aware, there is a
perverse element of historical continuity from the brown
bunker to the Red wall. If a visitor stands today on Potsdamer Platz, he can see how the lengthening shadows fall
toward, and point to, the desolate plot where the Hitler
bunker once was. That is perhaps only melancholy symbolism. The real historical link one can no longer see,
though for many years I watched it with foreboding. It was

the long column of gaunt refugees, streaming endlessly through Berlin, east to west, always east to west, as predictable as the diurnal rising and setting of the sun.

That flow of uprooted humanity climaxed in 1961, with more than 3000 escapees in a single day. But it had already begun back in the summer and autumn of the year 1944. Which is to say, as the Red Army first loomed on the frontiers of East Prussia and German Silesia, a steady trek of German refugees was soon seen trudging through Berlin. Now and then there were Latvians, Lithuanians, and Estonians sprinkled among them, the human flotsam of war. Many, at least half and probably more, passed under the Brandenburg Gate, for this familiar landmark stands in the heart of the city, along its thirty-mile East-West Axis. Those wartime refugees had permission to stay in Berlin for no longer than forty-eight hours: one day for trekking, one for rest and recuperation. Bomb-wracked Berlin had no housing for them. They spent the night in camps, then plodded west, at dawn, toward the Elbe.

For anyone with a sense of history, this was a somber historical pageant, the reversal of the momentum of the once-mighty German colonization drive eastward from the Elbe. It had begun deep in the Middle Ages; had led, indeed, to the founding of Berlin around A.D. 1230. This *Drang nach dem Osten*, less a conquest than a colonization, meant to Germans what the winning of the West means to Americans. Adolf Hitler, the Austrian who had so glibly preached a Thousand Year Reich, had, in fact, destroyed the honest work and labor of seven centuries of German pioneers and colonizers.

Nor did that trek, a reversal of the historical newsreel, ever stop, or even pause, in 1945. During all the 105 days that Hitler was mooning about in his Berlin bunker, striking historical poses—from January to April 1945—more than one million refugees from the east were passing in bitter silence through Berlin. Hitler did not see them; they did not see him. The flow was routed around and away from the Reich Chancellery.

The postwar statistic is even more staggering. From May 1945 to August 1961, more than 4.4 million German refugees passed through Berlin, which is to say, a transient number higher than the total resident population. More than one million of these crossed town by the simple step

of taking the subway or the elevated trains. As even Lenin
was forced to admit, refugees are people who vote with
their feet.

This steady post–1945 Berlin refugee drama, a mighty
plebiscite on Communism, is what finally forced the German Leninist Walter Ulbricht to throw up the barbed wire
behind which the hideous wall was built. The refugee flow
has since dropped off to a trickle, a trickle often ending in
shots and pools of blood. *Si monumentum requiris, cir-
cumspice:* if you are searching for my monument, look
around. The wall, and this is its true meaning, is a Hitler
legacy.

But the bunker was still there on that Fourth of July
1945, and it was very much on my mind. That day I also
had reason for private celebration. On July 1, *Newsweek*
magazine had secured my early release from military service. This involved a quick shift from the rank of captain
to civilian correspondent, with no time to change uniform.

My assignment was to establish a German bureau in
Berlin. In the early morning hours of that Fourth, a
Wednesday, I was aloft aboard a U.S. Air Force C–47 as
it headed toward Berlin's Tempelhof airport. Our pilot was
flying a precise, narrow air corridor. He had even more
precise instructions to keep that matter secret. Had I been
more curious, or at least more persistent, I might have had
my first exclusive before landing. Air corridors, corridor
ceilings, air lift, autobahn checkpoints, confrontation—all
words soon to become clichés of crisis; Berlin was already
pregnant with alarming headlines of the future.

But the past, the immediate Armageddon past, was still
omnipresent, overwhelming. We could now look down and
see it in an apocalyptic panorama as our pilot circled the
shattered city before landing. We were flying low over a
stony ocean of monumental rubble, a stalactite desolation
that resembled the vague ideas we Americans then had of
the landscape of the moon. The stricken, prostrate capital
city was no longer smoldering, but a pall of powdery yellow dust lay over it like malignant morning fog.

Still, from the air I could make out a few orienting
landmarks announcing the old capital of Prussia—the
Brandenburg Gate, the charred shell of the ponderous,
gutted Reichstag, the marble-halled New Reich Chancellery. They stood out like derelict hulks that had refused to

sink into that monotonous ocean of ruin. I had a cable in my pocket from Harry Kern, *Newsweek* foreign editor in New York:

PLANNING COVER STORY UPCOMING POTSDAM CONFERENCE STOP MEANWHILE WANT FULLER DETAILS EVENTS IN HITLER BUNKER STOP RECONSTRUCT LAST DAY STOP WHO WAS EVA BRAUN?

I was vibrating on the same frequency. Surely the Hitler bunker story was the first among many still-untold stories under all this appalling devastation. To my disappointment, the bunker had not been visible from the air. It was quite impossible to spot or identify it among several score bunkers, squat, like brown mushrooms, that still cluttered the flattened downtown area. Several haughty high bunkers were visible, but these were former *Flak*, or antiaircraft, towers.

To get from the airport to the Reich Chancellery area as rapidly as possible, I flagged down a passing jeep. It was the only moving object in a sea of static silence, a silence one could reach out and touch. Two paratroopers from General James Gavin's 82nd Airborne Division volunteered to take me to the Brandenburg Gate "if I could show them where it was." On that day, we could have made the three-mile trip faster in a Sherman tank or a bulldozer. We were soon lost in the labyrinth of rubble, winding our way along the only arterial street cleared for vehicular traffic. It was midmorning; the sun was shining.

To my surprise, the scene at the battered gate was a lively, even colorful, spectacle, the first visible Berlin crowd. Here at last is where the people are. This, I soon discovered, was the already flourishing black market. The currency, cigarettes; the Berliners, mostly lean and hungry housewives. What furnished the dash of color was the motley display of Allied uniforms.

The quadripartite experiment, at least at the simple soldier level, seemed to be working out splendidly. American GIs were swapping Mickey Mouse watches ($7.50 at the PX) for sundry souvenirs. One Russian infantryman already had twelve such watches, strapped from his wrist to his elbow. Back home, he said, he could sell them for enough to buy that one milch cow he was allowed down on the old collective.

I moved over to the Reichstag, nearby. Here, a steady flow of Russian officers, in groups of twelve to twenty, were visiting the double ruin of this solid parliament building, gutted in 1933, stormed in April 1945. These were husky combat veterans who had come to conquered Berlin from the German provinces. Like skilled acrobats, many were standing, shoeless, on each other's shoulders. They were inscribing in Cyrillic letters names, ranks, units, and other graffiti on the tall, chipped Corinthian columns. Thousands of their comrades had preceded them. The Reichstag had become, in the Russian mind, the symbol of their recent military conquest of Berlin. This was a political nuance that quite escaped me on that day.

I moved off quickly, heading down the Wilhelmstrasse, passing ruined embassies, toward the Reich Chancellery only some five blocks away. I rather expected to meet up with another large crowd. But the area was a wasteland. I met several German strollers and a few Russians, all, however, heading toward the action at the gate. One Russian was helping Berlin youngsters cut steaks from a dead horse. I saw the cadaver of an ocelot, not a local animal. I surmised that it had escaped from the zoo in the last horrendous bombings, a poor terrified beast yearning for the peace and quiet of its native tropical rain forests along the Amazon.

In the long Parian marble halls of the New Reich Chancellery itself, most of which, to my surprise, was still defiantly standing, I met up with perhaps a dozen uniformed visitors, Russian, British, American, a single pleasant Frenchman with a Midi accent. Nobody seemed to know for sure just where the already half-legendary Hitler bunker was. In our imaginations, perhaps, we were all looking for something vaguely impressive, like Cairo tourists heading for the Giza pyramids. *My name is Ozymandias, king of kings . . .*

On my own, in the far corner of the Old Chancellery garden, now an obscene junkyard, I finally located the obscure entry. I found there a rectangular, unsurfaced tawny-colored cement block, perhaps twenty feet high, with a narrow oblong entrance and indented vestibule. It resembled nothing so much as an old weathered pillbox in the Maginot Line or the Siegfried Line. The whole garden roundabout now looked as if it had been churned up by myriad giant moles. What had once been trees were

now blasted, uprooted stumps. I saw the rusty tail of a dud
bomb poking up from a crater; I treaded warily.

A single Russian soldier, armed but pleasant enough,
stood on sentry duty. At first I feared he might have orders
to turn sightseers away. No, he simply wanted to show
me a snapshot of his Natasha far away, back in Omsk or
Tomsk. He was only a private first class, but he was proudly
wearing the Stalingrad medal. I saluted him in the name of
the common victory and offered him a pack of Camels.
He handed me a yellow kerosene lantern.

Back on the Elbe River in April, however, that lost
April, I had already had enough experience with Russian
soldiery to know they were seldom on duty alone. Sure
enough, at the bottom of the staircase I met his chum, a
corporal. This second sentry was not quite so pleasant or,
perhaps, just more bored. He had set up quarters in a room
where the walls and ceiling were charred, the floor smeared
with gray ash, and the blue Frisian-tile wall paneling
sooted up. (He may not have known it, nor did I at the
time. This was Hitler's study.) He was armed with a submachine gun, but this lay on the table. He was also flourishing a long-barreled .22 caliber German target pistol.
Another pack of cigarettes, my last, and the premises were
open for inspection.

At first I thought I was alone; it was spooky. Soon I
came on three Russian military visitors, officers, who were
moving about silently with pocket flashlights. A few minutes later, we were all quite startled when a staccato shot
rang out. The deadeye corporal had winged a rat and was
now grinning a steel-toothed grin. Other rats, some as fat
as groundhogs, were scooting and slithering up and down
the one long room, the main corridor. They had gnawed
away much of the waterlogged red carpeting.

Worse than the darkness and the dankness was the odor.
Although I could make out, in a separate power room, a
quite modern ventilation machine, it had long since been
closed down. So had the untended latrines. These were
clogged but obviously still in use. From the sickening
sweetness of the strongest stench, I guessed that an earlier
rodent casualty had crept into the ventilation system to die.
There had been suicides down here, but the smell was not
the sweet-sour smell of decaying human flesh. War and
rubble have their distinct malodors. I wondered how this
poor downstairs Ivan could hold out in the Stygian atmos-

phere. I soon noted how that problem was being solved. The two sentries rotated duty every fifteen minutes. They will live forever in my memory as the upstairs and the downstairs Russians.

At some time, a bunker pipe or an emergency red-rubber garden hose had burst. There was thus a shallow, stagnant pool at the far end of the central corridor, some three or four inches of water, muck, and slime. I had to slosh through it to get to the farther reaches of the bunker. Soon I came to a large steel bank-vault door that opened on to an iron spiral staircase leading to what—as I was later to learn—was called the *Vorbunker*, the upper bunker.

I was wary. I still had that former soldier's instinct not to reach for or pick up any stray bric-a-brac or harmless-looking souvenirs. They just might be booby-trapped. The Germans were mean-minded, even sly, about such matters, and this had recently been a military headquarters. However, trudging back through the water, I kicked up by accident what appeared to be a large map. I did pick this up and, wiping away the dripping green slick, found it was a large parchment in faded purple-sepia, a blueprint of a city plan. By lantern light I noticed I was holding not a map of Berlin, for the Danube flowed through this city. In the caption in the corner I read "Grosslinz." This was an architect's sketch for the postwar remodeling and en-larging of the Austrian city of Greater Linz. I let the map and the matter drop.

My mind, at the moment, was on other things. I had now been underground perhaps twenty minutes. I noticed that one of the visiting Red Army officers, less booby trap-conscious than I, and obviously a staff man, had picked up and donned an old German gas mask. That had solved for him the odor problem. As he left, he handed the mask to me. I too had been about to flee up those steep stairs, gasping for fresh air. Now I could move about, room by room. I counted more than thirty cubicles. I was aston-ished by how cramped and small they were—the largest three by four meters, many smaller.

The longer I dallied below deck, the more frankly puz-zled I became. Something in this dungeon did not quite add up. Obviously, the original German occupants had fled in a hurry. They had left behind a mass of military impedi-menta. It was equally obvious that the victorious Russian soldiery had ransacked the place. There was nothing of any intrinsic value, no full liquor bottles, no usable weapons, no blankets or articles of clothing, no dress daggers, radios, or cameras.

Still, the bunker looked like the Paris flea market after an auction sale, and this perplexed me. Everywhere the floors, corridors, and duckboards were littered with glass shards and bottles, rusty picture frames, German Army cheesecake photos, warped gramophone records, scattered sheet music, dented air-raid–warden helmets, empty first aid kits, bloodied bandages, old knapsacks, tin cans, ammunition drums, empty pistol clips, scattered playing cards, film magazines, cigar and cigarette butts, slimy condoms.

But what most caught my eye was the sheer mass of printed and written material—military telephone books and telephone-number pads, looseleaf notebooks, business office files and dossiers, diaries, military manuals, scratch pads, letters. What was so wrong with that picture? Simply this: this Reich Chancellery bunker had been not only an air-raid shelter; it had also served as a military headquarters. During the long war, whenever we American soldiers had overrun a German headquarters or signal center—which had, in fact, been quite seldom—we found that the Germans had been most meticulous in destroying even minor bits of evidence; above all, printed matter. Whenever they had had time, they had usually blown up a signal message center. Bored soldiers make doodles and jottings on paper. This habit can betray a code, a radio frequency, a call sign.

I had had field experience in just this kind of specialized signal intelligence work. We called it "Gutenberg." Once, in the Battle of the Bulge, a German regimental signal officer had slipped up. He had failed to destroy a Belgian wall calendar. An unwary soldier had scribbled a list of code names on that calendar. This helped us break the code of the German 9th Panzer Division three hours before it launched a dawn attack. Because I had belonged to the same trade union, I now asked myself where Red Army intelligence could have been. Or, since the capture of this bunker had taken place in the very last days of the war, political intelligence. This considerable bulk of paper evidence, the scattered printed matter, may have been photographed, although I doubt it. It had never been collected and collated, the most elementary rule of the intelligence game. (The second rule is never underestimate the other fellow's intelligence. There must have been *some* reason for this benign neglect.)

As I now know, one of the documents still lying in the bunker on that July 4 was Adolf Hitler's appointment book (crowded) and Martin Bormann's personal diary (boring). Another, most probably, was a daily battle log. This had been kept by Lieutenant Colonel Klingemeier, the chief of staff to SS Major General Wilhelm Mohnke, the bunker troop commandant. A fourth document, according to my researches, may have been microfilm cassettes of the Goebbels diary, 1923–1945, as well as voluminous writing he had done in the last days. Goebbels had entrusted these to an aide, Herr Otte. After Goebbels' suicide, the wary aide hid them in a packet stuck behind a ventilator.*

What I had stumbled on was glaring evidence that the Russians, for reasons that were to dawn upon me only many years later, had committed an intelligence oversight of major importance. At least five Red Army search teams had been in the bunker the day it fell. They had been looking for one thing only, the body. Operating under instructions from Hitler's great antagonist, Stalin, these NKVD hearties fell over each other to locate it. Otherwise, the death of Adolf Hitler was treated like a non-event, a repeat of the death of Leon Trotsky. By the same Orwellian logic, the bunker from the first day of entry by the Russians was already on its way to becoming a non-place. Hence that steady crowd of sightseers at the Reichstag, the official bus tours. Always to the Reichstag, *never* to the Hitler bunker.

One of the few Soviet historians, even today, willing to talk on this matter disputes this interpretation. Lev Bezymenski, with whom I was recently on a popular West German television panel, insists the original Soviet motive in playing down the Hitler bunker in 1945 was a very genuine fear that it might one day become "a German national shrine like Frederick the Great's summer palace, Sans Souci." In fairness, I record this. We know that Hitler regarded Stalin as a great man; the feeling was indeed

---

* There is still (1978) some dispute as to whether Otte hid these himself or gave them to either Dr. Werner Naumann or SS Captain Schwaegermann to hide. There may also have been duplicates. The recently published set came from East Germany and is incomplete.

mutual. It still does not explain the sloppy intelligence work; for this there was another reason, and we shall come to it.

None of these second thoughts was troubling me that July morning on my underground trip into the past, a ghastly, now already ghostly, past. I did linger some forty-five minutes, despite my fear of rats. I came up out of the bunker. Four flights. I counted forty-four steep steps. With fresh air in my lungs, back in the sunshine, I began to collect my addled thoughts. Suddenly, Grosslinz! I now recalled that Linz was the county seat of Braunau, Adolf Hitler's birthplace. Cursing my own dull reaction, I whipped back to the bunker, down the forty-four steps on the double. Too late. One of those British colonels one usually meets only in the pages of *Punch* had found and was rolling up the map of Grosslinz: "My only war souvenir. It won't look half bad over my fireplace in Kent."*

The story of that blueprint does not end in 1945. Almost a quarter of a century later, in Heidelberg in 1969, I was sitting interviewing Albert Speer, Hitler's former architect, on the occasion of the German publication of his memoirs. I told him about the trivial incident, the blueprint and the colonel from Kent. He confirmed that my lost souvenir had belonged to Hitler.

Ah, yes. On my last day in the bunker, seven days before Hitler's suicide, the nostalgic Fuehrer hauled out that blueprint and began to reminisce. His lifelong dream of rebuilding the Linz of his childhood had been assigned not to me, but to my colleague, Professor Herman Giessler. However, one special building was my design. It was a tall campanile to be attached to the new Gauleiting building, the palace for the Gauleiter. Hitler ordered me to make it taller than the cathedral. I obliged. Although he never said so flat out, I surmised that Hitler wished to be buried there. So, just in case, I designed my granite tower as a cenotaph.

Albert Speer on this occasion—it was the first of seventeen interviews I had with him—went on to say:

At our melancholy farewell meeting on April twenty-third, Hitler talked for almost an hour about Linz. Perhaps this was because it was a mutual link with our own past. In earlier

---

* God bless you, Colonel, if you are still alive and well and living in Kent. The souvenir value of that blueprint today is around £10,000.

and happier days, in Berghof, his chalet above Berchtesgaden,
he would sometimes gaze over into his native Austria and
talk of his dream of retiring there someday. He would build
a house, he said, a few miles upstream from Linz, on the
Danube. This house would have two architect's studios. I
would always be welcome to use one of them. How pleasant
it would be, he said, to watch all the power-handlers fading
away. He and Fräulein Braun would be so happy to entertain
the Speers anytime, as weekend guests.

Speer was remembering a talk with Hitler, probably in
1935 or 1936, high above the clouds in Berchtesgaden,
about retirement in some blissful year that never came for
Adolf Hitler but most likely, in his imagination, was to be
in the mid–1950s. Hitler would have been sixty-five in
1954. Speer's mind was moving back and forth in the
kaleidoscope of time. All bunker witnesses talked this way
whenever discussing Hitler. He was the central experience
in their lives, and it was a traumatic one.

I was at first astonished to hear that Adolf Hitler and
Albert Speer, in the tumult of the last days in the bunker,
had found time for reminiscence, auld lang syne. I asked
about this. Speer replied, "Yes. Reminiscence, perhaps a
more exact word would be sheer escapism, was a bunker
leitmotif. My final visit lasted twelve hours. The only real
event was the flap over a telegram from Goering and his
instant dismissal. Almost all the rest of Hitler's time, at
least while I was with him, was spent in recollection of
things past."

So in fact was Speer's, as he made the rounds and said
goodbye forever to Eva Braun, Magda Goebbels, Ambassador Hewel, Colonel von Below, General Krebs, others.
The place was utterly divorced from any objective reality.
To preserve what was left of his own rationality, Speer
fled.

What Speer said here we will later hear confirmed by
more than fifty witnesses. It is the one point perhaps on
which all agreed. Adolf Hitler told and retold the whole
story of his life during the endless days and nights underground. Arrivals and departures, and there were many,
always touched off some memory of things past. A playwright could not have improved on this.

Speer, of course, is a most exceptional man, able to
articulate his experience. Most of the other bunker men
and women are anything but exceptional. All, I found,

performed remarkable feats of memory about certain bunker events, drew total blanks about others. This was seldom cover-up. Most spoke freely. Almost all were willing to talk about matters passed over in silence for many years. More than twenty of the bunker group were speaking for publication for the first time.

Just how close this composite account comes to historical truth, to the kind of documentation an academic historian insists on, I simply cannot say. Nor is it overly important to my purpose. I am a journalist, not a historian. I ring doorbells; I do not haunt archives. What I was looking for is what I believe most people look for, psychological truth. I am aware that many of the accounts here differ from the accounts—meager, in any case—given in some of the first interrogations back in 1945.

Frau Gerda Christian, the senior of the two blond secretaries who were still with Hitler at the very end, spoke frankly of her 1945 testimony as a "withholding account." I know what she meant. Few of the Allied interrogators in 1945 had a passion for objectivity. Those who did were seldom in a position to frame the right questions. Few of the interrogated Germans were in any mood to volunteer answers that might prove embarrassing. Most were under arrest; all were under duress. It was like asking the shell-shocked to describe exactly the burst of artillery. These people needed time to collect their own thoughts.

In my own account of my July 4, 1945, descent into the bunker, even though I had the help of diary notes and the carbon of the story I then filed, I have no doubt forgotten much, recalled some details inaccurately, distorted, manipulated the lens. I had no clue, then, about the interior layout, which room was which. Was it the upstairs or the downstairs Russian who had the mouthful of stainless-steel teeth, or maybe both? They are dim young figures, gone back to their native steppes. Memory of the rest of that Berlin day has faded.

*   *

Early in 1970, the editors of *The New York Times Magazine*, who had just run my profile-interview with Albert Speer, queried me as to whether there were other major witnesses now willing to reconstruct their personal experience in the bunker. I set out and soon located Professor

Ernst-Guenther Schenck, a practicing physician in Aachen.
He had recently published a moving account of the bedlam
conditions in his own emergency operating room in the
cellar of the Reich Chancellery. Schenck had performed
more than 300 major operations on soldiers wounded defending the bunker.*

In talking to Dr. Schenck, I found that his narrative
alone raised mighty ghosts. It was impossible to handle in
a single magazine article. Schenck is white-haired, sober,
low-key, a believable and honest man.

Schenck, as our interviews proceeded, began mentioning several figures: Major General Mohnke, Professor
Werner Haase, Ambassador Walter Hewel, Gestapo chief
Heinrich Mueller, all of whom he described as playing
critical roles in the last days of the bunker. In earlier
accounts, these names, when mentioned at all, were footnote names among those present. Haase, Hewel, and
Mueller are all known to be dead. But whatever had happened to Major General Mohnke? The story of the bunker
commandant had never been told. And yet on military
matters, Mohnke clearly was the soldier charged with
minding the shop.

Dr. Schenck had lost all contact with General Mohnke
after their release from Russia in 1955. He mentioned that
Mohnke's whereabouts were a bit of a mystery, then
dropped the subject. He did, however, give me the names
and addresses of three other bunker veterans, Major Otto
Guensche, Captain Helmut Beermann, and Sergeant
Rochus Misch. Sergeant Misch turned out to be my first
real windfall. Not only was he in touch with some twenty
old comrades; he also had an accurate, no-nonsense memory. Misch was both a switchboard operator and a valet.
He was also a highly decorated soldier and the last military
man to leave the Fuehrerbunker, an escape at dawn.

Moreover, Misch was and still is a Berliner. Today he
runs a paint-supply shop some two miles away from the
old bunker and only five or six blocks from my office in
downtown West Berlin. This was again most helpful.
Misch, who had manned Adolf Hitler's switchboard for
five years, became my message center for the five years I

* I never located a single surviving patient. Neither has Dr. Schenck.
One of them was the grandnephew of Friedrich Engels.

spent flushing bunker witnesses. He is convivial and gregarious, the type of old soldier who enjoys annual reunions. Yet he, too, had never been able to locate General Mohnke, who once had been his first company commander.

In the summer of 1972, I began to compile a card-index file of bunker veterans. I called it my black box. The rock-bottom basis was Misch's handy list of twenty. Seeking these people out—almost all were in West Germany —I found that most were both willing and able to come up with two, three, even four new names and addresses.

The timing turned out to be most propitious. From the beginning of my long journey down the autobahn into the past, I realized I was operating on the very outer fringes of time and human memory, including my own. Thirty years are a chunk of living in everyone's life. In another decade, many of these witnesses will have reached what the computer registers as terminal status. Or their fading memories will be too clouded to be reliable. General Krukenberg was the oldest I met. He is now over ninety, but still mentally sharp.

Memory always distorts, of course. It re-creates past events in a strange new light. It "alienates" to use the theater word. Yet it also lends to a narrative what Bertolt Brecht called an epic quality. I was struck by how often these witnesses, describing this or that scene, would stand up and act it out, with gestures: "This is how Hitler walked . . ." Brecht would have approved heartily.

Further, and for a variety of reasons not excluding human vanity, I found many of these witnesses far more willing to talk freely than they would have been three, two, or even one decade ago. This, I suppose, is the process of Hitler and the Berlin bunker becoming a part of history. The Germans call this "digesting" their own national past. All of these people did play a role, if sometimes only a spear-holder or walk-on role, in a historical event. They seemed to recognize that the opportunity to tell their story, in pretty much their own words, might never come again. Only two or three reluctant dragons refused to see me— eventually. Of the major bunker witnesses, among those who surived both the 1945 debacle and a decade of Soviet captivity, the only one whose story is still untold is SS Major General Johann Rattenhuber. He was the detective chief of the Reich Chancellery security squad. He died in 1967. Only the Russians have his account, gleaned from extensive interrogations, which they have never published.

I approached Hitler's senior secretary, Johanna Wolf, in Munich, where she had first gone to work for Hitler way back in 1925. She had stayed with him in the bunker until eight days before the end. I already knew, via the grapevine, that two publishers had offered her one million Deutschemarks (more than $500,000) for her story. She had steadfastly refused. This had been interpreted as a case of extreme loyalty to the Fuehrer. Yet she told me simply enough, "Good heavens no, not really. It is just that I was brought up to believe that the first and last duty of a private secretary is to remain private."

In that first year of basic research, which consisted of ringing doorbells, thumbing through provincial telephone books, cross-checking references, I had hopes of locating, at most, perhaps forty or fifty sources. At year's end, to my amazement, I needed a second black box. The first contained more than 250 names, all genuine, still-living witnesses who had been present in the bunker at some time during the last battle in Berlin. My surprise was based, of course, on my own memory of the cramped and limited topography of the bunker proper. What I had overlooked was the maze of tunnels leading into the New and Old Reich Chancellery and other nearby government buildings. The bunker was a small stage, a snakepit. But the comings and goings, in the desperate last days of April 1945, had a Grand Central Station, rush-hour atmosphere.

I pruned my list drastically. From the black box I dropped all mere spear-holder witnesses. With some reluctance, I also eliminated that half of the Reich Chancellery Group, some of whom had been with Hitler long years, who were flown to Berchtesgaden on April 22. This evacuation was called Operation Seraglio. I repeated, in short, the "hiving-off" process that was itself very much a part of the original bunker reality. There was a clutter of witnesses present when the last stand began, but only a relevant dozen at the end.

There were all those who had left with the major ministers, right after Hitler's birthday. That was April 20. Two days later, Operation Seraglio took place. One day later, Field Marshal Keitel and General Jodl departed, trooping off with large military staffs. Officer-couriers began decamping discreetly whenever the chance arose. One general officer even deserted. This was Lieutenant General Hermann Fegelein, Eva Braun's brother-in-law.

The hiving-off process, although interrupted now and again by spectacular arrivals (Goebbels, Speer, General Robert Ritter von Greim, and the aviatrix Hanna Reitsch), is precisely why we have so many published accounts of the beginning of Hitler's Alamo stand, but so few of the very last days and last hours, practically nothing on those more than thirty hours that elapsed between Hitler's death and the dramatic breakout.

I have given that breakout, which was like the last night in doomed Troy, two full chapters. Despite at least four epic movies to the contrary (and Soviet Lieutenant Colonel Klimenko's bogus official account) the Red Army never stormed the bunker. The tale of the bunker is no comedy, but the real story of its capture reads like Aristophanes' *Lysistrata.*

A word on method. This is an interview book. Although I located the names and addresses of more than 250 genuine bunkerees, and communicated with more than 100, I actually interviewed at length only about fifty, concentrating on the Reich Chancellery Group itself. From Chapter III on, each chapter is as seen through the eyes of one or two major witnesses only. The exception is the breakout.

Technically, it was just not possible to have every witness read the final draft of every chapter in this revised and expanded American edition. But all have read any chapter in which they appear or are quoted. All have read the original German version, *Die Katakombe.* Many have made valuable corrections. To maintain credibility, I simply eliminated four or five overloquacious witnesses I knew or believed to be lying, or "spinning," as they say in German.

The others, while they often fall into palpable error or are victims of lapses of memory sometimes verging on amnesia, on the whole did their best to recapture historical truth, or the truth as seen through the Berlin hourglass. By mutual consent, we spared each other many valuable hours by not discussing whether Adolf Hitler was a great man. Some, above all the women, would sigh that the verdict should be left to history, and I went along with the banality of that. It set up the trap door.

Most of my witnesses talked so willingly for a simple

reason not unconnected with human *faiblesse*. They are all getting long in the tooth. In their youth, these Germans all knew Adolf Hitler well. Most worshiped the man. One is young only once. But with luck one is old only once, too. These people are survivors, still clutching their survival kits. Many struck me as chastened, sobered survivors. The long years of secret interrogation lay behind them. So did the bunker. When they talked of present-day politics, as they sometimes did, it was like listening to a group of middle-aged fire-insurance salesmen who had all had a fling at arson in their youth.

From 1972 to 1976, Rosinante to the road again, I had many adventures. Operating out of Berlin, cruising Hitler's old autobahns, I clocked more than 50,000 miles. Sixty months elapsed between my first interview with Professor Schenck and my last with Hitler's secretary Gerda Christian. She agreed to meet me in the home of a third party only after she had read several draft chapters. I had been warned that she might be hostile or at least haughty and difficult. She was, in fact, frank, intelligent, witty—a pleasant surprise. And still a beautiful woman.

I have left for the epilogue, when readers will know them better, an account of where these survivors are today. According to my card-index record, at least 90 percent of those who were in the breakout survived. Ninety percent of these, in turn, managed to endure more than a decade of Soviet prison camps. And of these, more than 90 percent are still alive today. A hardy lot.

* *

Let us go back now to January 1945. January, the bleak month named for the two-faced old Roman god of beginnings. Berlin, chill and cheerless, was still Hitler's capital, the Reichshauptstadt, the hub of the reeling, tottering Greater German Reich. It had become Hitler's hourglass, one he could not reverse. Every frail military front was now wobbling or collapsing. He had just lost his last desperate major offensive in the Ardennes. The American First and Third Armies had defeated and decimated his last two intact panzer armies, two elite armies his harassed generals knew they had needed to defend the capital. Berlin was now being steadily pulverized by 1500–plane saturation-bombing raids. It was sinking into a molten mass.

Fire-storms made a maelstrom of its asphalt and agitated rubble. The groggy big-city citizenry were reduced to a troglodytic existence. During one bombardment stretch, death was falling from the air on twenty-one successive days and nights, by sunlight, by moonlight.

Standing silent amid their ruins, Berliners could also see the even more dismal shape of things to come. A steady parade of forlorn, bedraggled refugees plodded through the city day and night. But now, in mid-January, these derelicts of a lost war had to trudge through snow-drifts more than two feet high. A mighty blizzard had struck between air raids. For many thousands of these trekkers, often peasant families, it spelled the white death. See Berlin and die.

Even the rhythm of nature was disturbed. Berlin in peacetime has many remarkable bird colonies; one of the largest and most visible is the hooded crows, called *Nebel-kraehe*, or fog crows. This migratory breed nests in Poland, summers in Russia, but always winters in Berlin.

These winter Berliners had arrived in November 1944, as usual, and knew their way around town. Their favorite feeding stations were downtown in the heart of the city, in the many spacious parks, whereas the best overnight roosting perches were out in the tall pines, willows, and elders of the Havel lakes on the western outskirts. Of a Berlin winter midafternoon, as the sun fades rapidly toward the northwest horizon, these giant flocks of more than 40,000 birds can be seen assembling, wheeling in the sky. Then slowly they head west in loose but very methodical formation. For one long hour, they blacken the darkening sky.

But this, the last fierce winter of the war, was otherwise. In the daytime, the morning hours, these startled Berlin crows found their familiar feeding plots under steady bombardment. They swarmed, enraged, about the sky, cawing at the larger, mechanical silver birds above them. At night, in their rookery roosts, phosphorous bombs set the trees aflame; the Havel River and the lakes were suddenly ablaze at midnight. The bewildered crows soon became neurotic. When the blizzard hit, the exhausted and baffled birds, hungry and insomniac, deserted Berlin. They flew off into the Mark of Brandenburg in scattered, flapping flocks.

Because of the bombings and the blizzard, and the lack

of ground food, the crows were dying like refugees and the refugees dying like crows. Men, women, and birds starved and fell silently into the omnipresent snow. In the Middle Ages, the mysterious and sudden departure of such large black birds would have been interpreted as a harbinger of death and pestilence, of the coming doom of a Godforsaken city. It was.

There was another harbinger. On January 16, 1945, Commander-in-Chief Adolf Hitler returned from the west, by train, unannounced, to set up his last field headquarters in an obscure and hidden mid-town air-raid shelter. He knew it was a symbolic necropolitical move, the stage-managing of his own approaching death. Hitler had become Germany's underground leader.

CHAPTER I

•

The Caveman

The truth is concrete —BERTOLT BRECHT

ON JANUARY 16, 1945, Adolf Hitler went underground in downtown Berlin. There had been a thousand-plane raid by the U.S. Eighth Air Force that morning. Now, in the bleak afternoon, a pall of smoke hung over the city. The lemon-pale winter sun of North Germany sagged toward the horizon. A few casual passersby may have noticed the Fuehrer's yellow and white standard, which he had himself designed, flying above the New Reich Chancellery. It announced his return to the German capital after several weeks' absence.

Most Berliners simply scurried home—if they were fortunate enough still to have a place called home. They knew the Royal Air Force was due that evening, and, in their sixth wartime winter, they could only pray for dirty weather. Sunny days and cloudless, moonlit nights always brought out the bombers.

No curious passerby could have seen the Fuehrer descending into the safest bunker in Berlin. He moved through an underground tunnel that led from the New Reich Chancellery into and under the garden. The Chancellery garden was a kind of spacious interior court, in atrium style, discreetly shielded from public view. Few Berliners, and only a few hundred Hitler court retainers, knew of the bunker. Aboveground, there was not much to see, anyway—an emergency exit, about twenty feet high in the form of a square blockhouse, and a round pillbox-

23

> "Hitler's eyes, once iceberg blue and lustrous, were now often glazed, the eyeballs sunken and bloodshot. There was often spittle on his lips, and at times he simply drooled or whistled through his teeth."

tower. The latter was unfinished; it was supposed to have been a watchtower. There was also a raised wooden water barrel, or cistern, used by air-raid wardens. Finally, there was a curious trench, designed as a moat, that ran around both the emergency exit and the tower. A part of the permanent outside décor of the bunker drama was a large, abandoned cement mixer; in the general confusion, nobody had bothered to trundle it away.

Adolf Hitler made his last move into the bunker quietly, without fuss, with the aid of a single soldier-valet, who lugged his personal belongings and his toilet kit. The move was from his luxury apartment, in the upper reaches of the Old Reich Chancellery,* into a catacomb fifty-five feet below ground level. The buried roof of this bunker was sixteen feet thick; the exterior walls, six feet wide. The roof was covered with several tons of earth, to a depth of thirty feet. From the moment Hitler moved in, this cement cave became the Fuehrerbunker, his reduced realm, a kind of Third Reich in miniature.

Down under, the interior was ghostlike and bleak. All ceilings were low. The corridors were like the narrow passages in a crypt. A few of the thirty-odd cramped rooms had been painted battleship gray. The rough corridor walls were a rusty brown. In places, the bare cement dripped moisture; the masons had never been able to finish their plastering work. Three rooms, only slightly larger than the rest, ten by fifteen feet, plus a toilet and shower, were Hitler's private quarters. Like monastic cells, they were furnished with a few sticks of furniture. The living room had a couch, a coffee table, and three chairs; the bedroom,

---

* The Old Reich Chancellery had been the traditional residence since Bismarck's day. Hitler kept his apartment there even after he built the New Reich Chancellery in 1938. The old building remained as a wing of the much larger new one.

a single bed, a night table, a dresser. This was now not only the Fuehrerbunker; it was also the Fuehrerhauptquartier (FHQ), the supreme military headquarters of the Third Reich, the last of the thirteen command posts from which Hitler had directed the war. Command posts from which, only three short years before, Hitler the conqueror had dominated Europe and beyond, from the North Cape of Norway to the African deserts, from the Pyrenees to the Caucasus.

The historic moment of Hitler's descent passed unnoticed. He preferred to make his moves unannounced. And the distance from his old to his new bedroom was only about 100 yards. Those who must have seen him, as he shuffled toward the tunnel leading out of the cellar of the Old Chancellery, would no doubt have assumed he was just making another of his inspection tours, minding the shop. Adolf Hitler was, after all, the most familiar sight in the dreary routine of their daily lives. Some were guarding his personal security as head of state; some simply waiting on him; all were serving in his intimate court in some capacity. Most had known him for years. For them, he was less Der Fuehrer than Der Chef, "The boss." One of these loyal retainers, Sergeant Rochus Misch, reported, however, that the soldier-valet who accompanied Hitler that day was Sergeant Arndt, a favorite, if junior, valet in this last period of Hitler's life.

In the last three months of the war, there were an estimated four million military and civilian casualties in Central Europe. Every single day that Hitler hesitated, thousands would die. In the concentration camps, from January to April, 500,000 went to the gas chambers.* Hitler's death in the afternoon, on the last day of April 1945, was only one of twenty million casualties in World War II. His war.

Adolf Hitler was still destined to live another 105 days. But he had spent his last full day aboveground. "To the best of my memory," said Captain Helmut Beermann, one of the SS honor bodyguard (Fuehrerbegleitkommando, or FBK), who attended him during this time, "Hitler never saw another sunrise or sunset after January sixteenth." He worked, slept, took meals and tea, bathed, made his toilet, and finally married and died—all underground. In a world

---

* Auschwitz shut down in January 1945. But other death camps farther west were overrun only in March and April.

where day and night blended into a continuous glare of artificial light, the departure from reality became more evident with each passing week.

There were, though, several breaks, for at least a few hours, in this marathon underground endurance contest. Like a submarine commander coming up for air, Hitler surfaced from time to time, to re-enter and prowl his familiar haunts in the New Reich Chancellery. When there was no air-raid alarm, he would risk a military conference around the great marble table in his old spacious office on the ground floor; only its tall windows had been shattered. In a corner of the old dining room, where he once held daily noontime table for from forty to fifty guests, he sometimes took a snack, alone, or with his dietary cook, Fräulein Constanze Manzialy, a fellow Austrian. Or he would take tea and crumpets with one of the four female secretaries who had accompanied him to the bunker. Most of Hitler's meals, upstairs or downstairs, were now with women—the secretaries, the cook, and, in the last stages, Eva Braun.

Apparently Hitler did make two brief sorties out of Berlin. On February 25, he was chauffeured by his old stalwart behind the wheel, SS Colonel Erich Kempka, to address a secret meeting of Gauleiters just outside the city. This was one of his last political acts, although he was still chief of state and head of the Nazi Party. And on March 15, he emerged from his bunker lair around noon, to make a quick overland drive to the east front, in a Volkswagen, with two military aides. Curtains drawn, they headed along the Frankfurter Allee, the main artery heading east. It runs through one of the large working-class districts of East Berlin. The front was now only sixty miles away, at Frankfurt on the Oder. According to Kempka, the Fuehrer was back in about four hours, before sundown.*

The last formal exception to the underground monotony was his own last birthday party. On April 20, Adolf Hitler was fifty-six. With the Battle for Berlin already on—it had begun four days before—with the city all but surrounded by the Red Army, Hitler still insisted on this last appearance of all the major power-handlers of the Third Reich. This reception was quasi-public, for newsreel cameramen

---

* I interviewed Kempka at his home in Ludwigsburg in the fall of 1974. He died a few months later. He was thus the only major bunker witness who has not checked this manuscript for accuracy in detail.

were there. Although it was held in the traditional spot, the Ehrenhof, or Court of Honor of the Chancellery, it lasted less than an hour. No champagne was served. The party then adjourned back to the bunker for a listless military briefing.

That birthday party was a spectral performance, the guests trying to act as they had in the giddy years of power now so clearly over. This cheerless *Fest* was the last time Hitler ever saw Heinrich Himmler or Hermann Goering or most of his more than twenty ministers. Himmler and Goering vanished from Berlin, Himmler to the north, Goering south. Most of the ministers packed up to join ministries, which had already left.

On this day the newsreel cameramen also captured a second scene, a melancholy vignette with a touch of realism. In the garden, just outside the bunker, Hitler decorated twenty Hitler Youth turned soldiers, all orphans who had come to Berlin from Breslau and Dresden. He was patting the cheeks of one of them, a forlorn gesture. Photos of Hitler in the last weeks are rare. None was ever taken in the bunker proper. That was *verboten*.

From time to time, for a few nighttime minutes, Hitler would venture outside the bunker to walk his Alsatian dog, Blondi. For long weeks on end, this was Hitler's one desultory gesture toward getting some fresh air and exercise. The fact that these short strolls were nocturnal lends credence to the belief, held by many of his intimates, that Hitler's fast-fading eyesight was irritated by sunlight.

Hitler always walked alone with his dog. In earlier years, and from earlier bunkers, he had established this routine, and it continued in Berlin. He had taught Blondi to roll over, fetch a stick, walk to heel. But Hitler was never really alone. Alert eyes constantly watched his halting steps, his shambling gait. The fear that Hitler might collapse on one of these rare excursions to the surface, or that Blondi could pull him off balance, was a genuine worry. For months, he had been complaining of a sudden loss of his sense of balance, and he had a tendency to lurch to the right.

One of these pairs of eyes belonged to Captain Beermann, who remembered the Fuehrer "painfully negotiating those forty-four steps, four steep flights of concrete steps, up to the emergency exit." Beermann and the rest of the SS honor bodyguard were rugged young bucks, chosen, among other things, for their height and good health; the contrast with their leader was appalling. But their customary twelve-hour shift made even them groggy and intensely weary. "We would murmur about this batlike routine among ourselves, part-time prisoners of this cave life. The old life at Berchtesgaden was a perennial topic of conversation. We were all silently hoping that Der Chef would take off. Better to face death in the sunlight, and in the Alps, than to perish like miserable rats in a musty cement tomb in Berlin. None of us ever expected to survive."

At the end of their long tours of duty, they would come up, literally gasping for air. Beermann recalled:

The whole atmosphere down there was debilitating. It was like being stranded in a cement submarine or buried alive in some abandoned charnel house. People who work in diving bells probably feel less cramped. It was both dank and dusty, for some of the cement was old, some new.

In the long hours of the night, it could be deathly silent, except for the hum of the generator. When you came upon flesh-and-blood people, their faces seemed blanched in the artificial light. The ventilation could be now warm and sultry, now cold and clammy. The walls were sometimes gray, some bleached orange; some were moist and even moldy. The constant loud hum of the Diesel generator was broken only when it switched over and coughed. Then there was the fetid odor of boots, sweaty woolen uniforms, acrid coal-tar disinfectants. At times toward the end, when the drainage backed up, it was as pleasant as working in a public urinal.

* *

In the pages to come, we shall see scores of actors entering and leaving the bunker. Some are there but briefly, on purely military missions. Some stay for a few hours only, very important hours in the case of Albert Speer, quite unimportant ones in the case of Joachim von Ribbentrop. Some, like Eva Braun and the whole Goebbels family, arrive quite late but are with Hitler underground for several days and nights running. Yet none endured the subterranean endurance test Hitler imposed on himself.

Eva Braun, for example, in the middle of the Battle for Berlin, went casually strolling in the Tiergarten, the large public park just west of the bunker and the green lung of the city. Eva and several of the young secretaries took daily pistol-practice on an emergency range set up in the yard of the Goebbels' Propaganda Ministry, a ruined hulk of a building just next door. Like all women in the bunker, the terrified secretaries were afraid that even if by some miracle they survived Hitler's death, lusty peasant-style rape would be the Red Army's final order of the day. It was.

Even Hitler's personal secretaries, and such important assistants as Martin Bormann and Major Otto Guensche, Hitler's senior SS adjutant, left the lower bunker at least twice daily for meals. They ate in the upper bunker, in the Old Chancellery dining room, or in the large military mess, from German Army "goulash cannons" (field-kitchen tureens). This army mess was operating after April 16 on the ground floor of the New Reich Chancellery. Smokers nipped up from time to time for a cigarette break. Smoking was forbidden in the bunker proper, on orders of non-smoker Hitler.

Very few, even of the Hitler inner circle, actually slept in the Fuehrerbunker. The only exceptions to this bunking-down rule were the chief valet, Heinz Linge, who moved out when Dr. Goebbels finally moved in; Hitler's personal physician, Dr. Theodor Morell, who was succeeded in the last stages by the surgeon SS Colonel Ludwig Stumpfegger; and Fräulein Constanze Manzialy.* These were all people Hitler might need in a hurry—the valet, the doctor, the cook. Eva Braun, when she arrived in mid-April, had a small suite next to Hitler's. And finally there was Blondi. Blondi even whelped in March.

The presence of Hitler at this very center of things, for all that he is more than fifty feet underground, determined to run his own show to the bitter end, lends to the action a theatrical effect. The leading actor has withdrawn as far away from objective non-Hitlerian reality as his own wish fulfillment can take him, short of that death itself which will close the Hitler book forever. For the prisoners of the bunker, as for the prisoners of Plato's metaphysical cave, shadows become reality. The images they project are strange ones. But random actors and messengers entering the bunker from the outside world—and some come from hundreds of miles away—have the dust, grime, and blood of a different reality on their uniforms and faces. Always,

---

* In the very last days, Frau Gerda Christian also slept in a sleeping bag just outside the Fuehrer's study.

when we listen to testimony, we must make quite clear whether the witness is outside or inside the bunker.

A brave woman, the aviatrix and test pilot Hanna Reitsch, flew into Berlin on April 27, four days before the end, together with General Robert Ritter von Greim. Albert Speer, making his way back to the bunker after a long automobile drive in West Germany in March, was already referring to the bunker and its inhabitants as "The Isles of the Departed." Yet once inside the bunker, Speer spent a long hour with Hitler discussing postwar plans for rebuilding the bombed city of Linz.

Hardbitten front-line veterans like Generals Heinrici, Krukenberg, Weidling, and Reimann, summoned to the bunker, regard it as a madhouse being run by the inmates. On one occasion, General Helmuth Weidling arrived in trepidation. It was April 25, and he had been told that Hitler had just ordered that he be taken out and shot. When General Weidling left, an hour later, he had been promoted to city commandant of Berlin. And yet we shall hear Ritter von Greim, a man apparently in delirium from a painful wound, sending out a cable on April 27 referring to the bunker as a "*Jungbad*," a fountain of youth. He had just been named successor to Hermann Goering as chief of the Luftwaffe, still another surrealist touch.

More than a quarter of a century later, so I discovered, many otherwise rational men and women had trouble explaining their own bizarre actions in the bunker—just as victims of a shipwreck, a train crash, or an earthquake can never quite reconstruct in tranquility the moments of panic and trauma. There will be several bunker suicides even after the Hitlers and Dr. and Mrs. Goebbels stage their barbaric family-suicide pacts. Some of these are of SS stalwarts with extremely guilty consciences; but other suicides seem simply actions of individual despair, induced by the infectious collective hysteria. A few minor actors, like the veterinarian Sergeant Tornow, who was in charge of the bunker kennel, went round the bend. The sergeant was led away in an improvised straitjacket.

Back on that January 16, 1945, Hitler had been in Berlin only about twenty-four hours before he decided to make his permanent descent into the bunker. He had come, via his night train, from the field headquarters known as Adlerhorst, or Eagle's Eyrie. This was one mile north of Ziegenberg, near the spa town of Bad Nauheim, in the

Taunus Mountains not far from Frankfurt on the Main. From here the Fuehrer had masterminded the last desperate, lunging German offensive in the west, an attempt to force a breakthrough from the snowdrifts of the Ardennes to the Meuse River in Belgium, and from there on to the great port of Antwerp. Now known in the annals of the U.S. Army as the Battle of the Bulge, it was at the time—erroneously—headlined as the "von Rundstedt offensive."

All the earmarks of the kind of Hitler *"Feldherr"* operation that had once so dazzled the world were present: the bold use of tactical surprise, the first breathtaking breakthrough successes, which in the end would prove to be strategically disastrous. The born gambler had lost the secret of how to break the bank. And, again like the born gambler, he was seeking a way out by doubling the stakes with chips that were no longer on his side of the table.

There was a direct connection between the Battle of the Ardennes and the Battle for Berlin. It was this shattering setback in the Ardennes that had brought Hitler, posthaste, back to Berlin in mid-January 1945. As the then Chief of the General Staff, Colonel General Heinz Guderian, had repeatedly, if vainly, tried to warn him, the two crack panzer armies Hitler had thrown at the west might have been more wisely employed in stemming the Red Army offensive in the east. The Russians were advancing from the Vistula to the Oder rivers. The Oder is only sixty miles east of Berlin, and the Red Army had reached it in mid-February. By mucking about in the Ardennes against the Americans, Hitler had thrown away whatever slight military chance he might have had to stop the Russians before they reached the Oderbruch, the marshy plain that is the historical gateway to Berlin from the east.

Hitler's descent into the Berlin bunker, for all its symbolic Wagnerian overtones, was thus dictated by the realities of a disastrous military situation, including that war in the air over Berlin so often forgotten in accounts of the fall of the city. Like the avenging furies, U.S. and British strategic bombers were now engaged in round-the-clock saturation bombing. Targets in the west, Cologne, Hamburg, Frankfurt, had long since been reduced to rubbled ruin, in a systematic overkill.

Now, for long months, Berlin had been the prime target of the air fleets, which often numbered more than 1500 four-engine bombers. Two thirds of the total bomb load dropped on Berlin was unloaded in the last three months of the war. Sixty-two percent of Berlin housing was destroyed or badly damaged. In the downtown heart of the city, where the bunker was located, destruction was closer to 85 percent.

The phrase "round-the-clock bombing" now took on a terrifying literalness for the average Berliner, as it did for the pilots flying the planes. Based in the United Kingdom, American daylight bombers, the Flying Fortresses and Liberators, protected by long-range fighter escorts (P–51s), would take off at break of dawn. They could be expected over Berlin by the middle of the morning. They were back in England in the afternoon. The RAF, relying more on saturation techniques, took to the air at dusk. They were usually over Berlin around midnight. More than 1.5 million Berliners had already been evacuated, but three million still remained in the city. Very few had private shelters.

The groggy Berliners had learned to snatch what sleep they could, in heatless, often windowless, bedrooms, during afternoon and early evening hours. From midnight to noontime, many of these hollow-eyed, sleepless citizens burrowed into their cellars or fled to the larger neighborhood shelters. Most Berliners were not even aware that Hitler was back in the capital. The Fuehrer never visited a Berlin public shelter. Nor did he ever tour the ruined city, as Churchill had done so gallantly at the height of the London Blitz.

Perhaps nothing better symbolized Hitler's complete isolation from the great municipality,* the capital of his Third Reich, than the bunker's self-contained utilities and facilities. Water was piped from a nearby artesian well. The sixty-kilowatt generator supplied electricity for lighting, heating, the switchboard, and the water pump. Food, drink, medicine, candles—all were in plentiful supply in the vast storerooms of the New Reich Chancellery and in the narrow corridor that served as the bunker butler's pantry, known as "Kannenberg Alley," after the fat chief steward, Artur Kannenberg. Only the air was Berlin air, and even this passed through a filter system.

---

* In 1925, with 4.5 million inhabitants, Berlin was the third largest city in the world, after London and New York. In 1940, for a short while, it reached five million. By 1945, however, it had dropped from third to eighth in the world scale. More than one million wartime evacuees never returned. They live today in West Germany. Munich has a "Berlin" colony.

Hitler's life would obviously have been endangered had he stubbornly remained aboveground. He was not a physical coward. His Iron Cross first class, which he had won as a front-line regimental courier in World War I, counted as a high decoration indeed for a man of humble origins and low rank. It was earned, and he wore it proudly to his dying day, one of the few authentic touches in his elaborate act. But he was also, in his own mammoth self-projection, the Richard Wagner of politics, a "metapolitician." The Wagnerian hero never dies in bed. What Adolf Hitler really dreaded was not death, but that fate might deprive him of the chance to stage-manage his own departure.

It had been SS General Johann Rattenhuber, chief of the Fuehrer's detective squad, who had urgently advised the Fuehrer to vacate the Reich Chancellery and move both his office and his residence underground. The target of the saturation bombing was now clearly the center of the city. The bombing would probably have been just as intense whether Hitler was back in his capital or not. But the thought that he just might be there spurred the young pilots on. The site of the bunker was, of course, not known to them.*

American and British pilots flying into Berlin from the northwest or west were usually astonished, on their first flight, by the sheer vastness of the German capital.** It covers 240 square miles, including large lakes and evergreen forests. But they soon learned to orient themselves easily by the great wide artery called the East-West Axis, which Hitler had constructed in 1938. It had been the march route of the great victory parade two years later, after the fall of France. This grand avenue ran almost as straight as an arrow, for fifteen miles, directly to the Brandenburg Gate.

The gate is the true center of the city. It is rather small and delicate, a replica of the Propylaea in Athens—much smaller than the Arc de Triomphe in Paris. But, its conspicuous position made it visible from the air. Traffic flow-

---

* For all the many books on the triumphs of wartime espionage, I have come on no conclusive evidence that the western powers or the Soviets knew, for sure, where Hitler was during the last hundred days. They almost certainly did not know about the bunker. This despite the fact that the security measures surrounding the Fuehrer were so cumbersome that they should have been easy for any skilled operator to penetrate.
** The Russians never sent heavy bombers over Berlin. Only in the last week did the Red Air Force appear—fighters and fighter-bombers supporting the ground troops with tactical bombs and strafing runs.

ing eastward through this gate then entered Unter den Linden, Berlin's most famous boulevard, which had become an extension of the East-West Axis.

For a pilot, the last two critical miles of his flight toward the gate would be over the heart of the Tiergarten, which extended along on both sides of the axis. The Tiergarten is clearly bounded to the north by another topographical landmark easily identifiable from the air—the meandering, darkling Spree River. And there was still a third familiar landmark. In the narrow bit of space between the Spree River and the Brandenburg Gate stood a large, isolated square building, the Reichstag. Although gutted since the fire of 1933, this squat edifice was so conspicuous that no attempt was ever made to camouflage it.

The pilot's trained eye would, however, have been even more interested in what he saw just at the edge of the Tiergarten, due south of the Brandenburg Gate. Here lay a huge wedged-shape block bounded by the Unter den Linden in the north, the Wilhelmstrasse in the east, the Hermann Goering Strasse to the west and Voss Strasse in the south. Here the Reich Chancellery stood.

When the 1945 Battle for Berlin began, this governmental area became known as Zitadelle, and its defense was called Operation Clausewitz. The Reichstag was just north of the wedge, and a great traffic circle, the Potsdamer Platz, just south of it. These were also included in the area perimeter defense plans, as was Goering's huge Air Ministry, a block south of the Reich Chancellery.

From the air, the New Reich Chancellery, which Albert Speer had built in 1938, was even easier to identify than the Reichstag, though it was camouflaged. To maximize available space, Speer had designed an extremely long, rather narrow building with a façade running the whole length of the northern side of Voss Strasse, the equivalent of four normal city blocks. The Chancellery somewhat resembled an art museum, although it mounted a good deal more concentrated antiaircraft batteries than any art museum. The building had already received several direct bomb hits, at least a dozen, most of them through the roof. The windows were shattered from blast effect and flying mortar. But on the lower levels, the ground floor and the shelter-cellar, the solid building was still habitable.

For security reasons, all who entered the bunker had to pass through a bewildering maze of controls set up in the

New Reich Chancellery. And those working in the bunker during the day ate and slept in the much larger Chancellery bunker at night. Some were in a second bunker, also large, under the barracks of the SS honor guard nearby. This was at the corner of the Hermann Goering Strasse, at right angles to the Chancellery. The whole area was honeycombed with at least six large bunkers and as many smaller ones. All were interconnected, underground, in what was probably the most elaborate labyrinth built since the cult of the Minotaur in ancient Crete.

Photographs of the only part of the Hitler bunker that was aboveground, the emergency exit and that curious round tower, sometimes convey the impression that visitors entered or left here, but only the security guards themselves were allowed to do this, when they were mounting watch. Even high-ranking generals could enter the bunker only by passing through three separate checkpoints and by showing passes and identity papers. At night, the watch was doubled. They were armed with machine pistols and hand grenades.*

It was not only security, and the pressuring plea of General Rattenhuber, that led to Hitler's decision to go underground. His personal physicians had become increasingly worried, in these last months, about the state of his health. Although he doped himself with sedatives, sleepless nights exhausted him. But Hitler knew, from earlier nocturnal sojourns there in 1943 and 1944, that he could at least snatch some sleep in the bunker. Here the shattering roar of aerial bombardment was muffled and remote. "It felt like a distant artillery barrage on the World War One front," Hitler once said. Only when a two-ton blockbuster landed really close by would the bunker shimmy and shake. The soft alluvial sand on which Berlin is built had a kind of cushioning, shock-absorber effect. Thus, the bunker was even safer than if it had been built on rock or more solid earth foundations, though the trembling made its denizens queasy. The lamps would swing as if moved by a silent underground wind.

---

* It was at the corner of the Wilhelmplatz that the Old Reich Chancellery, although it was a complete ruin by 1945, was connected to the east wing of the New Reich Chancellery. This rather odd location, more in the corner than the center of this large building complex, can be simply explained. The Hitler bunker was a development of an earlier shelter first dug in 1936, that is, two years before the New Reich Chancellery was built.

The bunker really did not solve Hitler's sleep problem; it simply gave him some assurance he would not die an awkward and uninspiring death—in bed. At best, he seems to have managed about four hours of sleep a day, and that was fitful. He seldom retired before 4:00 or 5:00 A.M., or rose before 10:00 or 11:00 in the morning. We know that he spent some of this time reading, with special magnifying reading glasses for his fast-fading eyesight.

"We all knew the man was only fifty-five," said Captain Peter Hartmann, who was a young officer in the FBK, "and those of us who had known him in the earlier years before the war, when he was a human dynamo often bursting with restless energy, now noted, from about nineteen forty-two on, that he seemed to be aging at least five full years for every calendar year. Near the very end, on the day he celebrated his last birthday, he seemed closer to seventy than to fifty-six. He looked what I would call *physically* senile. The man was living on nerves, dubious medicaments, and driving will power. Sometimes, even the will power seemed to slacken. Then suddenly it would flash again, with all the old drive and fury."

To what extent did this unnatural bunker life—Adolf Hitler's "speleological hang-up," as one medical man put it—directly affect, or accelerate, the German leader's failing health? There is an obvious cause-and-effect at play here, although it was probably never as simple as that. Hitler was a notorious hypochondriac from the days of his youth. Even during the peacetime years of his chancellorship, when he was, in fact, in quite robust health, he was constantly changing his diet, experimenting with pills, worrying about his pulse beat, his vocal cords, his potency.

As early as 1938, several members of the inner circle begin reporting remarks by Hitler, usually thrown out as asides, indicating that he had the morose conviction that his years were numbered, that he would never live much beyond fifty. Apparently, these haunting intimations of his own mortality speeded Hitler's aggressive war plans. There was noticeable mounting hectic behavior in his decision-making from 1938 on.

One of the odd reasons he sometimes gave for his war-time retreats into various cavernous headquarters was that he could work better there, "free from fresh-air poisoning." Daylight, fresh air, the morning hours, these had never been his working ambience. "It is always late in the night that I get my most creative ideas," he liked to say.

Part of the riddle was whether Hitler's worries about his health drove him underground or whether, as many suspected, what finally shattered it was his unnatural regimen. It was the classic vicious circle, where psychosomatic, sometimes hysterical, symptoms began, in fact, to erode the hypochondriac's once-vigorous constitution. By the end of his life, Hitler was also suffering from real organic ailments.

If there is disagreement as to what those ailments actually were, it is perhaps due to the Byzantine atmosphere of his court and the rivalry among his doctors. Many among the courtiers strongly suspected Dr. Theodor Morell, Hitler's private physician, of quackery and misuse of drugs. But Hitler regarded Morell as a miracle worker and brooked no criticism of him. Four other doctors were also present in the last fortnight. These were Dr. Werner Haase, Dr. Ernst-Guenther Schenck, Dr. Karl Gebhardt (all three professors) and Dr. Ludwig Stumpfegger.* Dr. Morell left the bunker forever on April 22. Haase, who had first been Hitler's doctor in 1933 and who returned just before the end in 1945, was both Hitler's first and last personal physician in the Chancellery.

Haase was in attendance on Hitler every day until the end. He sometimes came over to the operating room in the New Reich Chancellery cellar to chat with troop doctor Professor Schenck, and often gave him surgical advice. Schenck, by profession an internist, was performing frantic emergency operations on wounded soldiers. Stumpfegger, a real surgeon, spent most of his time drinking with Martin Bormann and was to die with him; his views are not known. But the three professors all made diagnoses. Haase was convinced that Hitler was suffering from Parkinson's disease. Schenck, though he did not see Hitler up close until April 30, took one long look and also came up with this diagnosis. Both Haase and Schenck also suspected that Dr. Morell, himself a morphine addict, had been injecting Hitler with morphine and other detrimental potions. Professor Gebhardt, in a postwar affidavit, did not accept the

---

* A German medical man who also has an academic chair prefers to be called "professor." The distinction here is that Dr. Stumpfegger, an orthopedic surgeon, did not have such a chair.

Parkinson's diagnosis; he tended to defend Dr. Morell. But Gebhardt had political reasons for supporting Morell, *his* protégé.*

Schenck, who met Hitler less than twenty-four hours before the Fuehrer's death, was profoundly shocked by his condition. "Now I knew there could never be a Saint Helena for Adolf Hitler. At best, a brief Elba, even had he been in any condition, or position, to escape his doom in Berlin. This ruined hulk of a man had, at the very best, but one, two, maybe three years to live. He must have sensed this, as the mortally stricken often do. By the time I met him, the Fuehrer's decision to commit suicide in Berlin had already been taken."

Those close to Hitler every day during the last weeks were less shocked than those who, having been away for a while, returned and noted how rapid the falling-off really was, or those who, like Schenck, saw him for the first time. Others, like General Wilhelm Mohnke, the troop commander in the Reich Chancellery, point out that Hitler seemed to have had good and bad periods and that he actually looked better in January 1945 than he had in September 1944.** The composite report, however, is overwhelmingly on the side of progressive worsening.

Hitler's eyes, once iceberg blue and lustrous, were now often glazed, the eyeballs sunken and bloodshot. His brown hair had turned suddenly gray. He no longer stood erect. His walk was more of a shuffle; he dragged one leg behind. His head was bowed, his body bent forward, with a list to portside. He often seemed in danger of losing his balance. Both hands trembled, and he used the right hand to hold the left up close to his body. While standing, he often leaned his left leg against a table for support. When he lay down on his bunker couch, his senior valet, Linge, had to lift his feet from the floor to the couch. In the very last days, there was often spittle on his lips, and at times he simply drooled or whistled through his teeth. His complexion was sallow. Soup-slop and mustard spots now stained his once natty and spotless uniform jacket.

---

* Neither Gebhardt nor Schenck ever examined Hitler in the bunker. Professor Haase, however, may have. He was close to Hitler at the end, and they were old friends. Haase died in Moscow in 1947.
** In September 1944, Hitler had a jaundice attack and was bedridden for a fortnight in Berchtesgaden.

It seemed more like an age than a mere six years since Albert Speer, in honor of the Fuehrer's fiftieth birthday in 1939, had built a forty-foot-long wooden model showing how Berlin, renamed Germania, would look in 1950. Germania would be a city of ten million by then, with a Prachtstrasse, or Street of Splendor, triumphal arches, and a superdome, or Kupferhalle, seven times as large as the dome of St. Peter's in Rome. And there would be, of course, a *newer* Reich Chancellery, called the Fuehrerpalast. In April 1945, this model was still in the Berlin Academy of Arts, near the Brandenburg Gate. Hitler had a secret passageway to the academy. But he did not visit it. In the bunker, he now had a much smaller wooden model of another city—Linz.

Now, in his last bunker in Berlin, Hitler was reduced to one switchboard, one radio, and one radio-telephone to the OKW, the German Supreme Command of the Armed Forces. The telephone depended on a swaying antenna, hanging aloft from a toylike aluminum balloon above the Berlin Radio building in the Masuren Allee. And yet with this puny signals setup, almost a parody of the spider-like electronic network he had once spun out across Europe, Hitler remained in command, underground, to the last day, the last hour.

As Hitler had moved from headquarters to headquarters during the six long years of war, one item of his office-study furnishing always moved with him. It was an oil painting of Frederick the Great. He had purchased this in Munich in 1934. It was packed in a special, rather bulky, crate, and it was one of Chefpilot Hans Baur's chores to see to it that it was handled with tender care. It took precedence in the Fuehrer's plane over passengers, including general officers. This irksome chore often exasperated Baur, a man of flaming Bavarian temperament, because the only available space was in the narrow corridor between the seats of his plane, a Condor. Passengers would sometimes stumble over it, and the wood-and-steel crate scratched the plane's fancy leather seating. Hitler, however, was always mum to Baur's murmurings. The picture, by the painter Anton Graff, was an essential perquisite of the FHQ. And so, after having been crated and flown back and forth across Europe, it too had arrived back in Berlin. The picture went underground with Hitler. It was the only wall decoration in his last study.

Alone, the Fuehrer now spent long silent sessions gazing at his painting. He was looking, he said, for inspiration. The soldier-valet Misch, a minor but often very keen observer of bunker life, once disturbed one of these reveries by accident. He hurriedly and discreetly withdrew. "It was very late, and I thought of course that the Fuehrer had already retired. I went into his study to find something. There was Der Chef, gazing at the picture by candlelight. He was sitting there, motionless, his chin buried in his hand, as if he were in a trance. Hitler was staring at the king. The king seemed to be staring right back. I had barged in, but Hitler took no notice of me. So I tiptoed out. It was like stumbling upon someone at prayer."

The scene is Chaplinesque. Hitler and Frederick the Great! One wonders if this was not another one of his strange premonitions coming true. Hitler had no sense of the absurd, the ridiculous, no self-irony, all things he might have learned from Frederick the Great. Even Chaplin might have hesitated to place the Great Dictator in such a mock-heroic pose, for the historical parallel Hitler was now conjuring with was a familiar event in the drum-and-trumpet history books known to every German schoolboy of his generation.

In December 1762, at a very tight moment toward the end of the Seven Years' War, the King of Prussia found himself holed up in his ruined palace in Breslau, in Silesia. His capital of Berlin was surrounded, his weary Prussian troops greatly outnumbered by those of the Russian, Austrian, and Saxon coalition. In fact, nobody has ever described the grim situation better than Frederick himself, in exquisite French, writing to his friend and minister, the Marquis d'Argens:

> You judge correctly of the whole situation I am in, of the abysses that surround me and, as I see by what you say, of the kind of hope that still remains to me. It will not be until the month of February that we can speak of this, and that is the term I contemplate for deciding whether I shall hold to Cato—Cato and the little glass tube I have—or to Caesar's *Commentaries* and the best fight one can make . . .
>
> What would become of us without philosophy? I read a good deal. I devour my books, and that brings me useful alleviation. But for my books, I think hypochondria would have had me in bedlam before now. In fine, dear Marquis,

we live in troublous times and desperate situations. I have all the properties of a stage hero; always in danger, always on the point of perishing!

Voilà un homme! This is the spirited letter of a real king to a real marquis, an aristocrat to an aristocrat. It breathes the lofty, if skeptical, humanity of eighteenth-century civilization at its best. The bantering, manly tone is something that Adolf Hitler, the nobody from Braunau, could never understand, not if he sat the whole night through before a whole gallery of paintings of noblemen. Like Frederick, Hitler was in a parlous situation. Like Frederick, Hitler had indomitable will power.

There the parallel ends, abruptly. For this great king was a highly civilized man, a soldier and statesman who really knew how to show grace under pressure. He jests at the prospect of his own death. He remembers Cato's advice about suicide, but he goes on reading Caesar, for there are always two possibilities. He blames none of his generals, smiles at his own hypochondria, pens a lighthearted, stylish letter that must have charmed the marquis. The king sees himself, realistically, in a desperate but at the same time ludicrous position. The fact that he could see this—the ludicrous in himself—made him every inch a king, born to the purple even in his prose style.

All that Adolf Hitler had inherited from the tradition of Frederick the Great, other than the oil painting, was another desperate situation before the gates of Berlin. Frederick had been saved, early in 1763, by a "reversal of alliances." But the grand alliance against Adolf Hitler was a much more formidable affair than that which had almost cornered the embattled King of Prussia. On January 16, 1945, when Hitler finally returned to his capital, the three Allied wartime leaders were already assembling their staffs and packing their bags for their last Big Three wartime rendezvous at Yalta.

President Franklin D. Roosevelt came by cruiser and by plane, Prime Minister Winston Churchill by plane, and Premier Stalin by train to the resort town in the Crimea on the shores of the Black Sea. The code name of the rendezvous was Argonaut, in memory of those earlier bold voyagers to the land of the Golden Fleece. When Hitler learned of the locale of this secret Allied powwow—as he did—he must have winced and groaned. For the Crimean peninsula had been in German Army hands from 1942 to April 1944. It had been evacuated nine short months before. Had things gone according to the Fuehrer's plans, Yalta might have made an ideal location for one of his own headquarters.

CHAPTER II

•

The Thirteenth Bunker

Only in the last moment of a life can a balance
be struck.

—WILHELM DILTHEY,
The Methods of History, 1910

THE BERLIN BUNKER had now become the final FHQ, the
last of the command posts from which Adolf Hitler had
personally directed every aspect of the war. The Allied
wartime propaganda picture of the tyrant of Berlin, sitting
in his Chancellery in the Reichshauptstadt, the capital of
the Greater German Reich, was absurdly wide of the mark.

Strange as it may seem, even in retrospect, Hitler had
seldom been in Berlin, after 1941, for any lengthy period.
The capital of the Reich had become for him a mere place
to visit. Most of the summer of 1942 the Fuehrer was not
even inside Germany. He was deep in the Ukraine. Most
of the years 1943 and 1944 he spent in East Prussia. East
Prussia was the remotest corner of the Reich—both his-
torically and geographically. Rastenburg, the FHQ in the
East Prussian lake country, was as close to Leningrad as
it was to Munich. Now, from mid-January 1945, the
Fuehrer was leading the embattled nation from *underneath*
his capital, at a level twenty feet lower than that of the
municipal sewage system.

This lifestyle was not, however, anything new. This was
Adolf Hitler's thirteenth FHQ. Almost all of these had
been giant bunkers, and at least half were underground.
The Fuehrer's staff, although they grumbled or suffered in

> "The Fuehrer enjoyed upstaging field marshals and ordering them around as if *they* were lance corporals. There was more than a touch of Walter Mitty in Adolf Hitler."

silence, had slowly inured themselves to this troglodytic life. As early as 1940, we hear Fräulein Christa Schroeder, Hitler's bright, pert, speed-typist, complaining about the clamminess of Felsennest (Rocky Nest), the Hitler hideaway in the remote Eifel Mountains. From here the Fuehrer had conducted the opening stages of the *Blitzkrieg* into the Lowlands and France. Felsennest was, in fact, the first of his long line of underground headquarters; the embattled bunker in Berlin, the last.

The patent absurdity of much of the action that follows, the turgid atmosphere and snapping nerves of most of the actors, came, in part anyway, from the paradox that this last "field headquarters" was located in the middle of Berlin. By returning to Berlin so late in the game, Hitler found that he had painted himself into a corner.

For hitherto, Hitler had always managed to remain linked with Berlin, with the ministries, for example, by a superb communications system. On July 20, 1944, he was able to put down the officers' revolt without leaving his bunker in Rastenburg. Rastenburg was in a dark pine forest more than 400 miles northeast of Berlin. Colonel Stauffenberg's assassination plan reflected his own keen appreciation of the real source of Hitler's power. In a letter to a confederate, written in June 1944, Stauffenberg insisted, "Hitler in his bunker, that is the *real* Hitler."

This, too, is why Stauffenberg was determined to kill Hitler in his bunker, and not in the Berghof above Berchtesgaden. He sensed that power depended on control of communications. The failure of Stauffenberg's hesitating co-conspirators to seize the vital Berlin end of Hitler's communications was even more disastrous to their cause than the fluke failure of the bomb to kill Hitler in Rastenburg. Stauffenberg's friends did seize control of the military-signals net. In Paris, on July 20, the plot succeeded with almost ridiculous ease. Leading SS, Gestapo, and other Nazi officials were rounded up, disarmed, and held prisoner for almost twenty-four hours in the Hôtel Continental. Had the conspirators in Berlin been as active and successful as their opposite numbers in Paris, even the living Hitler would have been isolated in his bunker, with no phone or radio link to Berlin. It was that close.

Now, in the Berlin bunker, from January 1945 on, there was no such elaborate communications system. This irony is explained by the fact that, with the Fuehrer back in his capital city, the builders of the bunker had assumed he would no longer need extensive electronic communications. He could simply tie in with the great grid of large signal centers, military and civilian, already within Berlin or just on the outskirts.

At Zossen, for example, only fifteen miles due south of Berlin, there was Amt 500 (Central 500), military code name Zeppelin, the largest long-distance central board in Germany and, most probably, in all of Europe. The seat of the German General Staff was also near Zossen. Central 500 was in a bunker at least seven times as large as the Berlin bunker. It was forty feet underground and had been operating since 1939.

Central 500 was directly linked to, and serviced, the OKW, plus the army, navy, and air force headquarters, all of which had duplicating, if smaller, signal centers inside the city—as did most of the major ministries. Central 500 handled long-distance calls, military and civilian. It had a direct line into the New Reich Chancellery, but *not* into the bunker.

In mid-January 1945, when they first heard that Hitler was descending into the bunker, both Field Marshal Keitel and General Jodl, Hitler's senior military advisers, who, of course, knew the Zossen layout well, tried in vain to induce Hitler to move there. He would, they reasoned, be safer, away from the constant Berlin air raids and at the very center of a giant communications war room. But here Hitler's political instincts prevailed, early evidence that he was thinking beyond the purely military situation. He was already planning his own death—as a symbolic act.

Adolf Hitler may have come from the provincial town of Braunau near Linz, but he had no intention whatever of dying in Zossen, a small, almost unknown Mark of Bran-

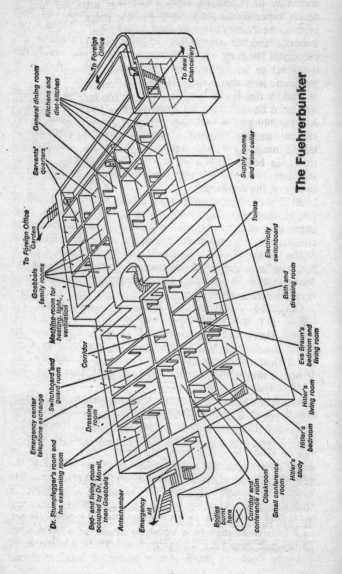

The Fuehrerbunker

To Foreign Office

To new Chancellery

To Foreign Office
Garden

General dining room

Kitchens and diet-kitchen

Servants' quarters

Goebbels family rooms

Supply rooms and wine cellar

Machine-room for heating, light, ventilation

Corridor

Toilets

Switchboard and guard room

Electricity switchboard

Emergency center telephone exchange

Dr. Stumpfegger's room and his examining room

Dressing room

Bath and dressing room

Eva Braun's bedroom and living room

Bed- and living room occupied by Dr. Morell, then Goebbels

Hitler's living room

Hitler's bedroom

Antechamber

Hitler's study

Emergency exit

Corridor and conference room

Cloakroom

Small conference room

Bodies burnt here

46

denburg hamlet. That clearly did not suit the shooting script. Hitler always thought big; even the very monumentality of the Berlin rubble probably attracted him. It was a superlative backdrop, a flaming stage. He thus dismissed the Zossen idea as unworthy of the unfolding historical drama. Death in a place called Central 500 was not for Adolf Hitler.*

It had to be Berlin, and this is what created the real problem. In a single room of the bunker, which was also shared by the guards on duty, a new, modern switchboard had been hastily wired up in November 1944. It even had a scrambling device, used for Hitler's private calls to Munich and Berchtesgaden and for highly classified military messages. But this switchboard was not large. It had a plug-in board with place for only a single operator. It had been designed by the Berlin Siemens firm for a wartime division headquarters, or a peacetime medium-sized hotel. The operator could reach Central 500 only over a relay link to Central 200. This was another large and busy central, in the tall *Flak* tower by the Zoo railroad station, about a mile from the Berlin bunker.

The operator most familiar with this switchboard was not even a professional. He was Sergeant Rochus Misch. Misch had learned to handle a similar small board in earlier years at Berchtesgaden. In the last fortnight in the bunker, the normal Berlin municipal telephone system began to falter. In the last days, it went dead silent in several Berlin borough exchanges as these fell into Red Army hands. Harassed staff officers would often use this board, just before briefing Hitler, to call up old friends around town, asking if the Russians had already arrived and, if so, with how many tanks.**

Sergeant Misch, like many of the low-ranking soldiers now trapped in the bunker, had worries outside, in the great city. Until Operation Clausewitz began on April 16, he had been living with his wife in a small rented house in

---

* Zossen was vague name to German civilians, though not, of course, to professional soldiers. For them it was a kind of West Point. Hitler, when he wished to denounce the General Staff, would rage at "the Spirit of Zossen."

** According to Berliners, the municipal exchange never shut down completely. This is one of the factors that made the battle within the city surrealist. On one occasion a Red Army officer, who was already occupying an office in Siemenstadt, found Goebbels' unlisted number in the notebook of a Siemens manager. He dialed it and was put through, to his own astonishment—and that of Goebbels.

Karlshorst, one of the first eastern boroughs of Berlin to fall to the Russians. On Misch's wedding day, in 1943, Adolf Hitler had given him fifty bottles of vintage Rhine wine and told him to cellar it down until the war was over. Misch had buried the cases in a corner of his small garden. On duty in the bunker, he had not had a chance to retrieve the wine cache, so he now wrote it off. That was a small problem. He then decided to call his wife and tell her to move, with their infant child, to the more southern Berlin borough of Rudow, where her father had a small garden house.

The next day, he tried to phone through to Rudow, which was about ten miles away. He could not make a connection. He became frantic. It was the middle of the night. The guards were snoring on cots nearby. Fooling around with the switchboard to pass the time, Misch found that he could still get through, easily enough, to Munich and to Berchtesgaden.

"While I was telling my old chums down there my problems, the Munich switchboard operator—who may or may not have known that I was phoning from the Fuehrer-bunker—cut in pleasantly to say that she still had a line open into Berlin-Rudow. I could hardly believe this; but in ten seconds she had put me through. That was the night I learned my father-in-law had just been killed while running for the air-raid shelter. My wife was still holding up, but sobbing. I told her I hoped to be with her in a few days." But Misch would be captured and sent to Russia. The few days turned out to be ten years.

In this same room in the middle of the lower bunker, where Sergeant Misch had his switchboard, there was also a German Army medium- and long-wave radio trans-mitter, but it had no short wave. For the radio-telephone linked up to it, it needed an outside antenna. This was hastily improvised by signalmen dangling a wire suspended above the bunker. Before the end, this emergency antenna was twice knocked out by artillery fire. When the land line leading to the switchboard was also hit by shellfire, as it finally was on Friday, April 27, the switchboard, too, was out for critical hours until new wire could be laid.

Here we have the reason why, in the climactic days of the Battle for Berlin, military couriers, with their hectic arrivals and departures, played such an important role. It is also why—a minor but delightful irony—Adolf Hitler, in the last days of his life, was getting his world news roundup from BBC broadcasts, as edited by Pilot Hans Baur. It was thus that Hitler, on April 28, learned of the defection of Heinrich Himmler.

*   *

Adolf Hitler's eccentric conception of wartime leadership was a marked reversal of his own peacetime practice and form. Der Fuehrer, the charismatic, unforgettable figure of the Nuremberg Party Day rallies, stimulated, and was stimulated by, mass hysteria. After delivering a speech loaded with verbal explosions, the man was both exhausted and relaxed. He had always regarded oratory, and not the written word, as the very wellspring of political power. Yet Hitler the orator gave relatively few speeches during the war, and these were usually before small audiences. Major political addresses became even rarer after 1941. Goebbels, the Gauleiter of Berlin, did remain in the capital. It was he who slowly took over the role of the Nazi tribune of the people, the man who made the Berlin Sportpalast rock with his frenetic appeals for total war.

The wartime Hitler had consciously adopted a new role, *Feldherr*, the great captain, the military leader of the nation. This is why he always wore the simple gray uniform tunic, the black trousers, the visored cap, the Iron Cross. Other reasons have been suggested: the heightened wartime security problem; his hypochondriac fear of infection, "fresh-air poisoning"; his fascination with the Spartan appeal of life in the field, surrounded by maps, generals, daily briefings, snappy young adjutants and aides-de-camp. Finally, no old soldier who knows the psychology of one-stripe lance corporals can fail to see how hugely the Fuehrer enjoyed, one world war later, upstaging aristocratic field marshals and ordering them around as if *they* were lance corporals. There was more than a touch of Walter Mitty in Adolf Hitler.*

Hitler had a deep-seated aversion to aristocrats, an aversion that extended also to their architecture, for it

---

* Although it has been printed 1000 times and more, Hitler never did make the rank of corporal in World War I, not, at least, in the American sense of that word. A U.S. Army corporal wears two stripes. Hitler's rank was *Gefreiter*, or one stripe—in our terms, a private first class. The British Army equivalent, however, is lance corporal, and thus he is usually referred to as Corporal Hitler in English accounts of his early days.

reflected their way of life. He heartily disliked castles, palaces and country houses; he seldom entered them. There is no better illustration of this than the fate of Adlerhorst, the only FHQ that Speer actually designed and built for him.

> Just before the outbreak of war, in the summer of 1939 [Speer remembered], he sent me off to find a spot for a head-quarters somewhere near Frankfurt on the Main. As a hiker in my youth, I was familiar with the Taunus Mountains, roll-ing hills really, and with Ziegenberg, a charming out-of-the-way place about seven miles from Bad Nauheim. The youth-ful Goethe had spent many idyllic hours there. My staff and I soon found a large *Gut*, a kind of manorial country house. It was on a knoll, about a mile north of Ziegenberg, at the end of a grassy meadow. We requisitioned it. It was ideal for camouflage purposes—a large house, stables, barns, a great courtyard. We reconverted it. Knowing, by now, Hitler's habits, I redesigned everything so that he could live at least as pleasantly as at Berchtesgaden, while his military staff could be housed inconspicuously in Ziegenberg, the surround-ing villages, and the spa town of Bad Nauheim. In fact, I was rather proud of this bit of trickery, building a head-quarters into the landscape so that it would attract a mini-mum of attention, even from the air. All suspiciously military installations, of course, were in underground shelters, with cows grazing over such things at the subterranean garage.
>
> Hitler came back to Berlin, fresh from the Polish campaign, late in September 1939. We took off together to inspect his new western headquarters. Imagine my chagrin when he re-fused to stay in the place even overnight. It was too luxurious, he fumed, not his style, too grand, "something for a horse-loving aristocrat."* In wartime, he said, he as Fuehrer must inspire the soldiers at the front with the Spartan simplicity of his daily life. And so, with a lofty gesture of disdain, he turned this headquarters over to Field Marshal Gerd von Rundstedt, the Commander-in-Chief West. The Fuehrer or-dered a new headquarters, Doric in its total lack of decora-tion, to be built in the Eifel Mountains. To be precise, in an old cave in the Eifel. I was flabbergasted.

As Speer pointed out:

> The Lacedaemonian, simple-life pose may not have been completely insincere in Hitler, at that time, but it fell rather flat on those of us who now had to calculate the staggering

---

* Heine one defined German aristocrats as "jackasses who live in the country and raise horses," one of the few of Heine's thoughts with which Hitler would have agreed.

cost of duplicating the installation. It had cost five million Reichsmarks [$2 million]. Many hundreds of miles of cable had to be relaid, the expensive electronics reduplicated, and all on a crash-program basis. Hitler was still hoping, at this stage, to launch his great offensive in the west in October or November of nineteen thirty-nine.

This was the time of the so-called Sitzkrieg, the *drôle-de-guerre*, autumn of 1939. There were two more FHQs built in the west. The first was in the side of a mountain at Rodert, about ten miles from Muenstereifel in the Eifel Mountains near the Belgian border. This was Felsennest. It was here that Hitler's personal staff got their first grim foreboding of the underground shape of things to come. This FHQ was in a bat-infested natural cave, the walls dripping with November fog. When the wind came whistling round the mountain in the Eifel, it was penetrating. Hitler spent only a few weeks here, the first time round. When the autumn invasion had to be called off, he spent most of the winter in Berlin and Berchtesgaden. He was back in Felsennest in the spring, however, for the big push.

The other large FHQ in the west, which Hitler was destined never to occupy or use (although he did visit it), was built at this same time, 1939, in the Black Forest. It was under a mountain called Kniebis, west of Freudenstadt. Its code name was Tannenberg. It was also underground. One mentions it here as a historical curiosity. The Black Forest is in the southwestern state of Baden, facing French Alsace across the Rhine. The German military problem, at the time, was to crack and pierce the Maginot Line, which the world had been told was impregnable. Here is a hint for historians that there must have been an alternative plan to turn the flank of the Maginot Line in the *south*, near Strasbourg. The breakthrough, when it came, was at Sédan, 200 miles north and west.

Already being built—in fact, it was to become one of the largest of the FHQs—was still another underground installation at Berchtesgaden, under the Obersalzberg. The Berghof was all that was ever visible from the peaceful valley below. But now the whole mountain, on instructions from his private secretary, Martin Bormann, was hollowed out and honeycombed with giant installations. Moreover, many of the major satraps—Bormann himself, Goering, Himmler—built residences on the nearby hills. These, too, all had underground bunkers.

When the big drive into the Lowlands and France finally came, in April and May of 1940, Hitler was again at Felsennest in the Eifel. Things were moving so fast that after the breakthrough at Sédan in May, he moved quickly to Brûly-de-Pesche, a Belgian village just behind Sédan, close to the French border. It was here that Hitler danced that strange St. Vitus' jig at news of the French capitulation.* It was from here too that Hitler flew into Paris on June 26, in the early morning hours.

A permanent installation, designed as an FHQ, was also built in France, in the summer of 1940. It was underground, at Margival, just north of Soissons. From here, Hitler had intended to direct Operation Sea Lion, the invasion of England. He inspected this headquarters, but once again he never used it. Had his troops ever landed near Dover to march on London, Hitler planned to move up to still another headquarters built into the chalk cliffs above Calais. The French use this today for growing mushrooms.

As in September 1939 in Poland, the spring of 1941 found Hitler aboard his special train. Mussolini's troops had got bogged down in Greece, forcing Hitler to rush to his aid, via Yugoslavia. This train operated out of Moenichkirchen, in Austria, and was linked with still another new FHQ near Wiener Neustadt.** (There were two Fuehrer trains, code names Brandenburg and, curiously, Amerika.)

In the steadily mounting list, we come now to one that was to become far and away the best known—Rastenburg, in East Prussia, code name Wolfschanze, or Wolf's Redoubt. In all the others, Hitler had spent, at best, only a few weeks. Here he was destined to spend almost three years. As described by General Alfred Jodl, a dour soldier not usually given to colorful phrases, "Rastenburg was a cross between a cloister and a concentration camp."†

This FHQ was *not* underground, but its walls were twenty-two feet thick, and no sunlight could enter. From

---

* A jig much magnified by British trick-film photographers. The Germans saw the original film in the weekly newsreel and noticed nothing unusual. The film, as released in London and shown in the U.S., was doctored.
** The code name, once again given by Hitler, was Fruehlingsstorm (Spring Tempest).
† He used this phrase, of course, in his Nuremberg interrogations *after* the war. One seldom spoke of concentration camps in the FHQ or in Hitler's presence.

the outside it looked like some primitive sarcophagus. It was a great block of concrete without windows, with no direct ventilation except when the iron doors swung open. The roof was sixteen and a half feet thick. The thickness of the walls and roof, in terms of cubic feet, exceeded the habitable, usable cubic feet they enclosed—an architect's nightmare. It was first built in 1941 and greatly enlarged in 1944.

Rastenburg was in a forest in the country around the Masurian Lakes. General Jodl's reference to a concentration camp refers to the barbed-wire military encampment that surrounded the FHQ. Although there were pleasant lakes nearby for such fishing devotees as Hans Baur, for most of the Reich Chancellery Group Rastenburg was an ordeal. It was icy cold in winter, mosquito-infested in summer. Lusty bullfrogs croaked through the sultry night. Once, in an attempt to control the giant mosquitos, Hitler's staff poured kerosene on the nearby lakes. This killed off all the frogs, much to Hitler's exasperation. He said the frogs serenaded him to sleep. So more frogs had to be fetched, the next year, from more distant lakes.

After the first months in Rastenburg, which is 400 miles northeast of Berlin, the German panzer armies had slashed so deep into Russia that this FHQ was already more than 900 miles behind the front by the critical autumn of 1941. East Prussia was the easternmost province of the Reich proper. We now find the Fuehrer moving out of Germany altogether, to Vinnitsa in the Ukraine (code name, Werewolf). Here, he was actually closer to Moscow than to Berlin. Hitler spent the better, summery part of 1942 in Vinnitsa. Once again, the FHQ was in a coniferous forest. But this time, at least, Hitler was living in a wooden blockhouse. He was, however, back in Rastenberg late in 1942, just before the Stalingrad debacle, and remained in residence there until November 1944.*

There had been, of course, occasional trips back to Berlin, Berchtesgaden, Munich. One anniversary date that Hitler always kept was November 9 in Munich, in the beer hall where the 1923 *Putsch* had begun. In 1943, in the pleasant Munich suburb of Pullach, Martin Bormann

---

* February–March 1943 also found him in Vinnitsa. By this time, there were partisans active in the woods.

ordered the building of still another FHQ, "in case the Fuehrer is there during a bombing raid and cannot get back directly to Berchtesgaden."

The meaning of all this, in terms of mass movement of personnel, was graphically described by Baur. "When the war broke out, I had a Staffel Baur [*Staffel* means staff] of two pilots and six transport planes. At Rastenburg, in nineteen forty-four, this had swelled to twelve pilots and more than forty planes."

The harassed Baur was beginning to earn his pay as a lieutenant general. The really happy flying days, when he tumbled through the clouds with his friend the Fuehrer, were over. He was now so essential to the Hitler operation that he flew only when the Fuehrer flew. He groaned under the administrative load of Staffel Baur.

It was, as Baur put it on another occasion, "government by shuttle." Hitler had run into Nemesis in the form of Parkinson's Law—it took more and more people to accomplish less and less. The Reich Chancellery Group, his entourage, was, by the middle of the war, five- or sixfold what it had been in 1939. One section was always physically present wherever the Fuehrer was, for example in Rastenburg; a second section was backstopping in Berlin; a third was in Berchtesgaden; and, again according to Baur, "a fourth was on leave or on the move back and forth between the FHQs or off on various Fuehrer missions."

The list of FHQs just reviewed totals eleven. When one day I showed my list to Speer, simply to check for accuracy, he smiled wanly and commented:

You have missed the one FHQ that was, and by far, the largest of these underground catacombs. It was quite probably the largest ever built in World War Two. The work began in nineteen forty-four, in Silesia, in the small spa town of Charlottenborn. There was then still some hope that the Red Army could be stopped before it reached this highly industrial, exposed area of the Reich. Its code name, appropriately enough, was Riese [Giant]. It also was never used, either by Hitler or anyone else. It cost one hundred and fifty million Reichsmarks [around $60 million], that is, four times as much as even Rastenburg, and tenfold the cost of Pullach.

According to Point Eighteen of the Fuehrer Protocol, the daily record of Hitler's conferences, I reported, on June twentieth, nineteen forty-four, to the Fuehrer, "At the moment a good twenty-eight thousand workers are building additions to the various FHQs."

A memo I sent him on September twenty-second, nineteen forty-four, gave the cost-breakdown. These nineteen forty-four projects required three hundred and twenty-eight thousand cubic yards of reinforced concrete, two hundred and seventy-seven thousand cubic yards of underground passages, thirty-six miles of roads, with six bridges, and sixty-two miles of plumbing pipe . . .

Giant in Bad Charlottenborn alone consumed more concrete than the entire German civilian population [seventy million] had at its disposal for air-raid shelters in nineteen forty-four. It was ten percent of the total cement-tonnage we released to the civilian economy for that same year.

Speer came up with some additional information about still another 1944 project, along the lines of Giant, for a FHQ in Thuringia, in the heart of Germany. But since it was never built, I have not included it.* A curiosity of my research was that among members of the Reich Chancellery Group so privy to so many of Hitler's secrets, which were then also secrets of state, I found only two—Speer and Baur—who could name from memory the complete FHQ list.

Baur knew of all of those he had operated out of, since he always had the task of locating a nearby airstrip. But even he had apparently never heard of Giant. This unused FHQ, never completed, was blown up late in 1944 by German engineers. It was never discovered by the advancing Russians. Several years after the war, the Poles located it. (Silesia in 1945 had become part of the new Poland.) All German workers on this top-secret project had, of course, been sworn to secrecy, then evacuated. The German peasantry of this area, many of whom must have seen the building operation, were themselves driven out in early 1945.

It is a long, giant, lizardlike trail, winding through frozen oceans of poured cement, back and forth across the map of wartime Europe. But what about the building of the

---

* Its code name was Olga, and thereby hangs a tale. When the U.S. First Army rolled over this installation, in mid-April, an overalert wire-service reporter, spotting the name "Olga" on one of the rooms, jumped to the conclusion that this was probably the room reserved for Hitler's mistress. To embellish the story, he also assumed that the lady in question was Russian, White Russian. The story made headlines. Eva Braun's name and status were then unknown to the world. In these same days, mid-April, she had just moved into her quarters in the Berlin bunker.

Berlin bunker itself? This is the last, wry irony of the whole astonishing Hitler bunker hang-up. With twelve abandoned FHQs now stretched across Europe, from Soissons in France, across the Black Forest to Silesia, to Vinnitsa in the Ukraine, finally we find Adolf Hitler, at bay, in a ridiculously small cement command post designed neither for permanent living nor as a proper FHQ. The lower bunker looked like an air-raid shelter designed as a place for perhaps a dozen people to spend a not too comfortable night, or day, in a city under steady bombardment. There were several score larger bunkers in Berlin.

Johannes "Hannes" Hentschel was the chief electrician in the Reich Chancellery. He is the man who was in charge of the *Maschinenraum* (engine room), with its Diesel motor, which powered most of the bunker utilities during the hectic last stand—air, electricity, water.

As Hentschel put it, "In that last desperate fortnight, I had to run electric-light cables strung out on the floor in the corridor. I used fire hoses as an emergency substitute for water piping, and one of these hoses sprang a leak. With all of the comings and goings, these wires and hoses got as tangled as spaghetti."

He went on to admit that there were two woefully wobbly links in this whole improvised system. The first was that the tunnel passage from the New Reich Chancellery to the upper bunker was not nearly deep enough, little more than a meter, plus perhaps ten centimeters. This shallow structure was finally hit directly, by artillery, in the last week of April 1945.

"As you passed through," Hentschel remembered, "you could look up and see daylight, or the nighttime sky, through two or three jagged, gaping holes. Hitler probably never knew about this, for I don't think he used this passage in the last days."*

The second weak link became, during the Battle of Berlin, a life-and-death problem. The casualty station set up in the cellar of the New Reich Chancellery had woefully inadequate ventilation for its 500 to 750 wounded soldier-patients.** Handyman Hentschel hastily rigged up

---

* Apparently he did, at least once, on April 27 or 28, 1945, according to Hitler's SS adjutant, Major Otto Guensche.
** The idea of converting this Chancellery cellar into an emergency field hospital was Hitler's. Minimal surgical equipment had to be brought in hastily from Hohenlychen, ninety miles northwest of Berlin.

a Rube Goldberg system for blowing air out of the Hitler bunker and back into the New Reich Chancellery cellar. This, in turn, put a heavy overload on his single Diesel engine.

I first learned from Hentschel that, contrary to what I had so often already heard, the ventilation in the Fuehrerbunker itself never broke down. The reason so many bunker people complained of stuffiness or headaches from stale air was that Hitler had given orders to Hentschel to turn off the ventilation in the conference room during military briefings. These powwows usually dragged on for two or three hours, in a room crowded to begin with. The Fuehrer claimed that the air passing through the blower system produced excessive pressure. Smoking was never allowed. The military did not walk out from these conferences; they staggered out. It had the same soporific effect on Hitler, but he was apparently too stubborn to admit it.

As Hentschel said, "When you hear bunker veterans talking loosely about the generator coughing, or seeming to break down, that was just me, Old Hentschel in the machine room, switching the generator over now and then to serve its new dual purpose. The more chaotic things got in the bunker, the more I felt the most useful thing I could do was pump water toward those wounded and dying young soldiers."

Hentschel is the best eyewitness authority on the successive stages in which the Berlin bunker had been built. This is, in part, because he himself attended to all of the wiring, and also because he was able to watch the progress of the bunker work from a window in his own private flat. Most people on duty in the bunker and Chancellery, until the last fortnight anyway, were not resident there. They had private flats around town. But Hentschel lived in a curious pavilion-style house that stood with two others in the Chancellery garden, only a half-minute walk from the bunker emergency exit. The second was called the Kempka House, after its resident, Erich Kempka. Heinz Linge occupied the third small dwelling. Even when this whole area was drastically re-landscaped, in 1938, Hitler, acting on some conservative whim, said he wanted these three old houses to remain.

Hentschel had come to work in the Old Reich Chancellery in the summer of 1933, when he was twenty-six.

This was the building that had served every German chancellor from Bismarck to Bruening and Hitler. He got the job quite by accident. Something had gone wrong with the wiring in the old building. An exasperated Hitler sent one of his aides, Wilhelm Brueckner, out into the street to locate the nearest electrician. Hentschel was working nearby in the Wilhelmstrasse and answered the frantic call.

> Actually, it was just a routine short circuit, but it was making quite a bit of black smoke. I let it fume and billow for a while, then repaired it. Hitler liked my work and offered me a permanent job, on the spot. He didn't even ask me if I was a party member, which I wasn't. I was a newlywed then, looking for a roof over my head. Soon, my wife and I were living in what later came to be called "the Hannes House." When a man who is running your country offers you a fairly well-paying job, in the middle of a worldwide depression, you don't say no. I thought I had things made for the rest of my life.

According to Hentschel, the first bunker air-raid shelter was a rather modest affair, with walls less than a meter thick. It was about thirty feet underground and was dug early in 1936. This was the same year German rearmament began—officially. This bunker was to serve the Old Reich Chancellery, since the New Chancellery was yet to be built. This is why, even at the end, one finds the Hitler bunker, above all the so-called upper bunker, or "foreshelter," so close to the surface, just under the Old Chancellery garden.

This distinction also helps to orient us on the difference in location between the Old and the New Reich Chancellery, which pops up so often in this narrative. Basically, these two key buildings stood at right angles to each other. The old building, once called the Radziwill Palace, faced the Wilhelmstrasse and the Wilhelmplatz. The new building, however, was around the corner. It ran the entire length of the Voss Strasse. However, they met—and were internally connected—at the Wilhelmplatz corner. Hitler's private flat, for example, always remained in the old building, with a connecting corridor into the new. In short, the two buildings dovetailed.

According to Hentschel, the place where he saw the first digging back in 1936 was, naturally enough, the garden—

before it was so greatly enlarged in 1938. This, too, helps explain what must be a puzzle to many—namely, why the Hitler bunker seems so off-center, almost in a corner of the vast complex. It is because of the special relationship of the two buildings, erected at different times. The Old Reich Chancellery was a baroque building in the shape of an H—that is, the original eighteenth-century building plus four later wings. A part of the west wing of this structure was originally directly over a part of the upper bunker (until this west wing collapsed into rubble in 1943). One originally entered the first bunker not through any tunnel, but simply by way of a staircase in the cellar of the west wing of the Old Chancellery. This first bunker, later to be called the *Vorbunker*, was only about fifteen feet below cellar level.

The New Reich Chancellery was built in 1938. In itself, it had no bunker, but Albert Speer had designed the cellar in such a fashion that it could easily be converted into bunkers. (This is just what happened in 1943, in the middle of the war.) A tunnel, more than ninety feet long, but only five feet underground, was bored to connect the New Reich Chancellery to the upper bunker of the Old Reich Chancellery. Hentschel believes this was done either late in 1939 or in 1940. This was the situation before the real air war began, when the largest British bomb weighed only about 200 pounds.

As the war progressed, tunneling toward the Fuehrer became a kind of government game. Soon both Ribbentrop's Foreign Ministry and Goebbels' Propaganda Ministry had tunnels into the Old Reich Chancellery, hence underground access to Hitler. What grew up was a kind of downtown governmental labyrinth. Officials and messengers could pass for whole city blocks, always underground, to arrive, ultimately, at one of the underground entrances to the Fuehrerbunker.

Hentschel went on with the story of the building of the bunker.

In nineteen forty-three, a Berlin private-construction firm, Hochtief, was called in to reinforce the upper bunker as larger bombs began to fall. But it was not until late in nineteen forty-four that the same Hochtief people came back again to build, this time much deeper and with solider walls, what now became known as the lower bunker, the Fuehrerbunker proper. Its roof was more than sixteen feet thick, the walls at least six feet. Tons of earth were piled on top of it all. The lower bunker never was completed, as far as permanent facilities were concerned.

(This accounts for that lonely cement mixer, one of the permanent props in all pictures of the bunker.)

This lower bunker was safer, of course. When we hear bunkerees speaking of bunker events involving Hitler, we can be sure they are always talking of this lower bunker, for Hitler seldom changed levels, as all others did, even Eva Braun, Bormann, and Goebbels. One of the reasons for this is that there was a convivial mess, operating around the clock in the last days. It was in the corridor of the upper bunker. The only description we ever get of Hitler just outside the lower bunker is on the last night, when he said goodbye to a group of nurses. He had emerged from his study and come to the vestibule entrance. But he did not change levels.

These two bunker levels were connected by a wrought-iron staircase, ten to twelve steep spiral steps. A bulkhead and a steel door on the lower level separated the two areas. There were always two armed sentries posted just before the bulkhead. With Hitler always in the lower bunker, the upper bunker became a kind of servants' quarters, with storage space for provisions. The kitchen was here, the pantry, the oak-table communal mess, the refrigerator, the wine cellar.

Before I met Johannes Hentschel, I had already heard so many complaints about the ventilation that although I accepted his technical explanation, I did query him, yet once again, about the filter system. Was he sure that it was always functioning? I had my reason for this question, but did not let Hentschel know it at the time. He lives today in a pleasant small house in Baden, on the edge of the Black Forest. Perhaps it was the wonderful clear air sweeping through the fir trees that allowed me to pop the filter question so innocently.

He thought it over, then replied:

Yes, there just may have been some malfunction with the filters—although they were quite new. Back in February nineteen forty-five, in that long lull before the storm, Hitler had come to me and asked how often the filters had to be changed, and whether I could check and see that they had been properly installed. Then, the next day, or maybe it was the day after, Minister Speer spoke to me about this same matter. I had known Speer, of course, since the days when he had been Hitler's architect. We had often consulted, in the past, about just such minor technical problems. He was one of the few National Socialist big wheels who was also a naturally friendly man. He knew how to talk to a worker without talking down to him.

Together, Speer and Hentschel went to take a look at the air-intake. It was half-concealed behind an iron grill, which was itself obscured by a low juniper bush. Speer casually suggested that Hentschel remove the old filter for the time being and look around for a replacement, and this Hentschel agreed to do.

A trivial, routine happening. Except that it set up the last of at least nine serious assassination attempts.

CHAPTER III

•

The Bunker Brutus

We should never have trusted that fellow Speer.
He was a second Brutus.

—HERMANN GOERING,
in the Nuremberg jail

A LATE WINTER LULL prevailed through February. Along
the Oder, an unexpected thaw slowed all movement by
the Red Army. The Yalta Conference was meeting. Every
evening, a triumvirate of old Hitler cronies—Martin Bormann, Dr. Joseph Goebbels, and Robert Ley, boss of the
Nazi Labor Front*—met for a regular parley in the
bunker, from 7:00 to 9:00 P.M. Later, at a midnight conference, a glum Hitler would listen in silence to news of
how the British and American armies, though still west of
the Rhine, were slogging forward on a broad front. They
had not yet reached Cologne, the largest Rhineland city
and a communications center. But it had become increasingly clear that nothing could stop them.

Hitler had still not abandoned his hope that another
counterattack was the ticket. Nor, as a Central European,
could he be unmindful of what was now looming in the
Danube regions. The same two German panzer armies that
had been so badly mauled in the Ardennes in December

---

* Ley was the by now almost forgotten functionary. Only by sticking
around in Berlin, and appealing to Hitler's sympathies, did he manage
to achieve this late prominence. He was a buffoon. Even Hitler knew this.
But now he somehow enjoyed Ley's company and ideas for new wonder-
weapons.

> "What Speer really had in his thumping heart that evening was the decision he had taken that same afternoon. He was preparing to murder Adolf Hitler and his three bunker cronies by filtering poison gas into the bunker."

were now hastily regrouped, resupplied with new Tiger tanks still rolling out of Ruhr factories, and committed before Budapest. His old friend SS General Sepp Dietrich led this desperate action. It was repulsed. Budapest fell on February 12.

As is perhaps too often forgotten, in February 1945 the most active front was the vertical "third front," the air war over the Reich. Hitler and those in the bunker at least could not forget this. Spring was announcing itself early, by mid-February. The clear skies now meant that Berlin would be bombarded for twenty-one consecutive days and nights, often daytime and nighttime. This is why these early evening Nazi bull sessions were always in the bunker, in the hours after the U.S. Air Force had left and before the RAF arrived.

Berlin was now the major, but by no means the only, target of the bombers. The Anglo-American supersaturation raid on Dresden, from February 12 to 14, was a grim classic in overkill. At least, as originally planned, the sudden assault on this "open city" was an attempt to destroy Hitler's two panzer armies as they passed by rail through Dresden, shifting from the western to the southeastern front. In fact, both armies had already passed through, in the first week of February. This intelligence did reach England, but too late to reverse the major air operation. The result was the appalling slaughter of at least 35,000 civilians, mostly refugees, and the utterly unnecessary destruction of a beautiful city.

March came. For the Russians, now on the Oder, it was a month of thaw and steady buildup. Here they were assembling three mighty army groups, called Fronts. In the north, around the port of Stettin, was Marshal K. K.

Rokossovsky with his 2nd White Russian Front. In the center, near Frankfurt on the Oder, Marshal Georgi Zhukov was now commanding the 1st White Russian Front. To the south, near the confluence of the Oder and the Neisse, was Marshal Ivan Koniev and his 1st Ukrainian Front. Zhukov and Koniev were rivals. Stalin would play on this rivalry when the big push began.

Fremde Heer Ost, German Army counterintelligence, gave Hitler a quite accurate estimate of the extent of this Red Army buildup—2.5 million men, 6250 tanks, 7500 tactical aircraft. This meant a superiority of at least 3 to 1 in manpower, 4 to 1 in airpower, 5 to 1 in tanks, and probably at least 10 to 1 in artillery, the Russian specialty. The Germans did not have the precise artillery figure. After the war, the Russians said it was more than 20,000 fieldpieces.

On the east, Hitler had but one army group to meet this onslaught. This was Army Group Vistula. It consisted of two infantry armies, the Ninth and the Twelfth, both undermanned, and only remnants of the German Third and Fourth Panzer Armies. He did have a second army group, under Field Marshal Schoerner, but this was engaged down on the Czechoslovakian border. It was thus too far away to affect the coming Berlin action.*

Most of the month of March, events again directed Hitler's attentions westward. General Eisenhower's three army groups, comprising seven armies, was now advancing rapidly to and across the Rhine on an extremely broad front. It now extended from Holland to Alsace and the Swiss border. Cologne fell, after a hard fight, on March 6. The first American troops crossed the Rhine on March 7,

---

* Given this situation, there would seem to be some validity to the argument later raised by Marshal Vassily Chuikov, in his 1967 memoirs, that he had been in a position to mount an armored thrust and reach Berlin several weeks earlier than he in fact did. Chuikov, then the general commanding the elite Eighth Guards Army, the victors of Stalingrad, had reached the Oder in strength in the first days of February, before the thaw. He pleaded with his superior, Marshal Zhukov, to give him the order to keep rolling. This is the natural urge of all tank generals, but in this case Chuikov seems also to have sensed, correctly, that the German forces between the Oder and Berlin were a good deal less formidable than had been generally assumed. He puts the blame on Zhukov and his "broad-front strategy." Which is to say, he was raising precisely the same argument against Zhukov that, in the west, Field Marshal Montgomery and Generals Simpson and Patton were soon to raise against Generals Eisenhower and Bradley. It is only fair to record this echo from the east, since it adds another dimension to the long-standing debate, a dimension often ignored in the west. Thus, the Red Army also passed up an open chance to get to Berlin much more quickly.

exploiting to the full the unblown railroad bridge at Remagen. A week later, General Patton, roaring out of the Palatinate, slipped across the Rhine at night at Oppenheim near Mainz. In the third week of March, Field Marshal Montgomery's whole Twenty-first Army Group, aided by an airborne operation, crossed the Lower Rhine at Wesel.

The one intact German army group still in this area, General Model's Army Group B, now received orders from Hitler to hole up in the Ruhr Pocket. Here they were later double-enveloped. Now, for two of Montgomery's armies, the British Second and the American Ninth, the way to Berlin was a 300–mile open road. One armored corps, given preferential logistic support and supplied by air, could have barreled into Berlin in less than a fortnight.

A rather special authority for this statement is General Guderian. As he later put it, almost diplomatically, "I was then Hitler's senior briefing officer in the bunker. When he asked me why the British and Americans had opted for such a slow, broad-front strategy, I could give no valid, purely military answer. But war is often like that; generals do not always know what is on the other side of the hill. I, of course, knew how absurdly thin our forces were between Wesel and Berlin, since I had now at last convinced Hitler we must shift all we could east."

General Guderian gave a graphic description of the doubletalk atmosphere of those March 1945 bunker briefings.

All his life, Hitler was fascinated by maps. He knew how to read them. Moreover, from his earlier political days he had an intimate relationship, a strong liking or dislike, for every major German city. Now he would listen in stony silence as the Luftwaffe briefing officers read off the lurid litany of the mounting fury of the air war—Nuremberg, Hamburg, Hanover, Munich, all tumbling into rubble and ruin.

In our army briefings, almost every day we too had to announce the fall of some major German city, now Cologne, now Mainz, or Muenster, Frankfurt, Mannheim, Aschaffenburg. We often did this simply by dropping them from the previous day's situation map. We were using large-scale grid-coordinate maps. As a city disappeared, so would a map.

By the end of March, Guderian had had enough of these spectral war games. The abrupt circumstances of his departure have been described in his own and others' memoirs. The scene is memorable as one of those very rare occasions when somebody really did talk back to Hitler.

The date was March 28. Hitler, in a vile mood, started out to blackguard his generals. The object of his wrath was General Busse, commander of the hard-pressed Ninth Army, the one that was doing most of the fighting outside Berlin. Guderian vehemently came to the younger general's defense. The slanging match got so hot that Guderian's aide, cavalry Captain Berndt von Boldt, had to hold his general back by the tunic. Guderian, to everyone's amazement, was shaking his fist in the Fuehrer's face. Hitler was, of course, astonished. When he recovered, he played the affair very coolly. The Fuehrer adjourned the briefing. An hour later, he quietly suggested to General Guderian that he take a six-week vacation—"after which time your services may be even more urgently needed."

What had got into the usually contained, stiff-upper-lip Guderian? Hitler apparently never knew, but the answer serves for a bit of welcome bunker comic relief. On this particularly early spring day, Hitler had suddenly canceled his usual noontime conference, whereupon Guderian and an officer-friend had gone off to a luncheon being given by one of the few major ambassadors still in Berlin, the Japanese Hiroshi Oshima. Oshima, in his student days at the University of Freiburg, had developed a taste for Black Forest *Kirschwasser* (cherry brandy). He still had a plentiful supply in the Japanese embassy, which was in the Tiergarten. Guderian, too, had a fondness for cherry brandy. He was also probably enjoying this rare noontime above ground. It did not last long. A call soon came in that the briefing had been rescheduled, for 2:00 P.M. Thus, Guderian arrived in the bunker with a good deal of warming brandy in his belly, and in the mood to get a few things off his chest.

So in these waning days of March, Hitler dispensed with the services not only of Guderian, but of the only other voice in the bunker, courageous enough to tell him to his face that the war was lost. That second voice belonged to his minister for war production, Albert Speer, the architect who had once been the Fuehrer's most trusted confidant.

Speer was the one prominent member of the old entourage who had deliberately distanced himself from the court—though in terms of Berlin municipal geography, he was only four blocks from the bunker. He was working and living in the last surviving corner wing of his own bomb-shattered ministry on the Pariser Platz, next to the Brandenburg Gate. Speer hated the bunker and its squalid atmosphere. He both worked and lived these days in his ministry, partly because he himself had been bombed out of the modest home he had built in the suburbs, but more to be physically present in the heart of Berlin, the center of reality, however fearsome.

From time to time, Speer ascended a nearby *Flak* tower, in the middle of the raids, to watch hurtling bombs smashing to smithereens the Berlin for which he had once been named city planner. It was a title he still retained. His emergency office had few windowpanes left; it was heatless, lightless; the minister worked by candlelight. His living quarters were in the same building. Here he was attended by his family cook, Klara, and his dog. This latter was a huge shaggy Landseer, a British black-and-white breed resembling the St. Bernard. Discreetly, he had sent his wife, Margarete, and their six children to Berchtesgaden.

Like Hitler, Speer was still operating from the same building, including the air-raid shelter, that had been the scene of his earlier triumphs. As minister for war production from 1942 to 1944, Speer had doubled, and in some instances tripled, German arms production. September 1944 had been the peak month, but also the month in which the graphs of Speer's team of 300 crack technocrats spelled out the doom to come. The production of fighter planes had reached 3000 a month; Tiger and Panther tanks, 900 a month; construction of submarines had been narrowed from nine months to less than two. The production of synthetic gasoline, however, had plummeted by 70 percent. U.S. Air Force strategic bombers had, finally, got to the great Leuna and I. G. Farben hydrogeneration plants.

As a young and ambitious architect in quest of a patron, Albert Speer eagerly bartered his soul to the devil. His mundane motive was decent enough; he wanted to build. When Hitler, in his one brilliantly intuitive appointment, put Speer in charge of armaments, to succeed Dr. Fritz Todt after the latter had been killed in a plane accident early in 1942, the devil outsmarted himself.

Once Speer became minister, the sheer pressure of work

and the realities of the war estranged him from the court, and thus from his youthtime idol, Adolf Hitler. As architect, Speer had always been treated by Hitler as an equal; as a minister, only as one among several, a subordinate. Hitler himself, once war began, became the prisoner of his own court. Speer did not. His job now brought him back into daily contact with one of Germany's true elites, the industrial managers, the technocrats and the more intelligent and rational among the military.

Speer, moreover, had always had a deep streak of patriotism in him, less the tub-thumping chauvinism of the National Socialists than the more old-fashioned, almost poetic devotion to the hills and valleys, the rivers and streams, the forests and heaths of his native land. There was a touch of the Wandervogel in him, that earlier and idealist German youth movement for which he had been born half a generation too late. As an architect, Speer could describe the nave and transept of every cathedral in Germany. But as a technocrat, he knew that the romantic fatherland of the past, the Germany of cathedrals and lyric poets, now lived in the highly industrial present. Postwar Germany, whatever the military decision, would have to export or perish. Although he had not yet read Edmund Burke,* Speer would have agreed, emphatically, with Burke's thesis that no one generation has any right to play at ducks and drakes with the destiny of a nation.

Human beings are seldom moved by single, linear motives, least of all mature men trapped in a convoluted historical situation. Speer had long been torn, as was shown on July 20, 1944, between his residual personal loyalty to Adolf Hitler and his deeper feeling of responsibility for the nation. Speer had six children; Hitler had none. Speer took his title of "Reichsminister" seriously. Like most technocrats, he had, for far too long, displayed a shocking moral obtuseness about "living so carelessly among murderers." During the earlier years of the war, Speer had managed to convince himself that the fate of Germany, for better or for worse, was linked with the person of the Fuehrer. But, this also implied that Hitler would have the same feeling of responsibility. Now, however, in the last months of 1944 and early 1945, Speer had filled memo-

---

* He did later, in Spandau prison.

randum after memorandum on the mounting hopelessness of the supply situation. He had constantly stressed the imperative of making peace. Hitler, in the various bunkers, filed these in his safe. Some he had even refused to read, as he told General Guderian and as Guderian, in despair, had told Speer.

Neither before he met Hitler, nor after, had Speer ever read *Mein Kampf*. Once, on a quiet weekend above Berchtesgaden, he had started to wade through it, but the author told him that "it is quite outdated." Then, in his office in Berlin in mid-February 1945, Minister Speer received a visit from one of his close friends, the white-haired, seventy-two-year-old Dr. Friedrich Lueschen. Lueschen was a senior industrial manager of Siemens, the spokesman for the German electrical industry, and, in this latter capacity, an honorary member of the staff of the Speer ministry—a kind of dollar-a-year man. Dr. Lueschen *had* read *Mein Kampf*, and he now quizzically asked Speer, "Are you aware of the passage in *Mein Kampf* that is most often quoted by the public nowadays?"

With this, he handed Speer a slip of paper with the following quote:

> The task of diplomacy is to ensure that a nation does not heroically go to its destruction but is practically preserved. Every way that leads to this end is expedient, and a failure to follow it must be called criminal neglect of duty.

No sooner had Speer read and absorbed this than his friend presented a second similar slip.

> State authority as an end in itself cannot exist, since in that case every tyranny on this earth would be sacred and unassailable. If a racial entity is being led to its doom by means of governmental power, then the rebellion of every single member of such a folk is not only a right, but a duty.

The elderly man then departed, without saying a word.

Nation . . . Tyranny . . . Folk . . . Duty. There was no doubt about the author. Seldom had the pages of *Mein Kampf* been quoted with better effect. This, after all, was precisely what Speer had been brooding about for months, what he had been iterating and reiterating in his oral and written reports to the Fuehrer.

For long hours of the rapidly fading Berlin afternoon, Speer paced the floor of his bleak office. Through one of the few remaining panes in the window he saw Berliners scurrying home to spare, cold-cut suppers, in dreary unheated homes or cellars. There was still a foot of snow on the ground. On the *Flak* tower in the distance, he could see the awkward ballet of the ack-ack crews, rehearsing for the coming air raid. That would be about midnight, by the light of the moon. Finally, Speer was triggered into action. The time was shortly after 7:00 P.M. At this hour, Speer knew, Hitler would be palavering in the bunker with Goebbels, Bormann, and Ley.

Clad in the warm long overcoat he had been wearing in the office, Speer now put on the visored cap he wore when driving and went down into the underground garage. As a minister, he was entitled to a limousine, chauffeur, and bodyguard. Instead, and as usual, he preferred to take the wheel alone.

Soon he was moving up out of the underground garage near the Brandenburg Gate. Glancing down Unter den Linden, which was almost deserted, he saw a few early evening couples heading for the bar of the Adlon Hotel. He rounded the Adlon corner and was in the Wilhelmstrasse, the old, once-swank diplomatic quarter, now Germany's boulevard of broken dreams. There was little traffic, but he drove slowly, for the Wilhelmstrasse was like a slalom-run. The rubble was piled neatly, but it had toppled here and there into the street and snowdrifts. In Berlin one got inured to rubble. There was some wan consolation in seeing that Dr. Goebbels' Propaganda Ministry was smashed, as well as Foreign Minister von Ribbentrop's palace, except that both had been quite beautiful buildings, of another century.

As he reached the Wilhelmplatz, Speer glanced up at the balcony, built onto the extension of the Old Reich Chancellery, one of the first small jobs Hitler had given him, back in 1934. Now he wheeled briskly into the Ehrenhof. The posted guards recognized the familiar figure; "*Guten Abend*," they said, and waved him on. Adolf Hitler had given his protégé many privileges; one of these was that he could park in the courtyard, as he had been doing ever since the days when he was building the place.

It was now perhaps seven-thirty, and the winter evening was dark; the moon had not yet risen. Speer did not enter the underground tunnel, as he normally would have done had he been reporting to Hitler in the bunker. Instead, he sauntered out into the Old Reich Chancellery garden, which now looked less like a garden than a dump. He headed straight for the blockhouse that served as an emergency exit, passing the water barrel and the cement mixer. Soon he was strolling along the narrow gravel path where Hitler, when he did emerge from his catacomb, walked Blondi. Speer's mission, on this particular evening, was to inspect the air-intake of the bunker ventilation system. He had designed and built almost everything else in this area, but *not* the bunker.

If anyone had stopped him at this point—a most unlikely prospect, since he was an old familiar on the premises— Speer would simply have answered that Hitler had been complaining about a possible malfunction in the ventilation system, which was true enough, and had asked Speer to talk to Cheftechniker Johannes Hentschel about the possibility of changing or cleaning the filter. But what Speer really had in his thumping heart this evening was the decision he had taken that same afternoon. He was preparing to murder Adolf Hitler and his three bunker cronies by filtering poison gas into the bunker. Hence this silent nocturnal reconnoitering expedition.

Desperate times call for desperate measures. The element of murder that made Speer shudder was the fact that the gas inevitably would kill not only the Hitler foursome, but the guards, the telephonist, perhaps the cook. These were innocent people, but certainly no more innocent than the thousands of humans dying every day and every hour the was was prolonged.

The architect found the air-intake pretty much where he had expected it—at ground level, within easy reach, only partly hidden by a scrawny evergreen, and covered by a removable iron grill. Examining it more closely with the help of his flashlight, Speer could make out the filter. No problem, really. The gas he had in mind was a deadly new nerve gas called Tabun. One grenade of this gas, which could penetrate any filter or gas mask, would do the job. The bunker, closed off as it was, would become a gas chamber. Speer winced.

Tabun had been invented to make the conventional gas mask useless. Instead of vaporizing, it broke up into tiny, death-bringing particles that easily penetrated any known

mask or filter. Only a few drops, properly dispersed in the
open air, would kill an infantry platoon. Hitler himself had
spoken with great glee of the lethal properties of this gas.

Speer remained at the bunker only about ten minutes.
He did not enter it, nor did he intend to be present at the
second staff conference scheduled, as usual, for midnight.
Instead, he drove back to his office, ate a snack alone, and
went to sleep. The problem was how to procure the gas
without arousing suspicion. For months now, even in his
own ministry, Speer knew that there were at least two
men, planted in responsible positions, who were reporting
to the Reichssicherheitshauptamt (the RSHA, the secret
service under Himmler). The trouble was, Speer could not
be sure just who the two informers were.

The irony of the situation was that Speer, as minister
for war production, would have had no trouble ordering
up a bomber, a Tiger tank, even a V–2 rocket; Admiral
Doenitz could probably have sent him a submarine through
Germany's excellent canal system. But, and above all since
Colonel Stauffenberg's attempted assassination in Rastenburg, any unusual request for bombs, grenades, or gas
canisters could arouse suspicion. Thousands of defense
workers had daily access to Tabun. The powerful war production minister did not.

Whom could he trust with the tricky mission of procur-
ing Tabun? Two or three evenings later, this nagging problem solved itself. Around midnight, with the Berlin air-raid
sirens again sounding alarm, Speer descended into the
small shelter reserved for high officials of his ministry.
The only other senior aide still in the building at this hour
was Dieter Stahl, the head of Speer's Munitions Division.
In peacetime, Stahl had been the owner-manager of a
machine-tool plant in Bernau, about ten miles northeast of
the Berlin city limits. In wartime, as Speer knew, this plant
had been converted to the manufacture of artillery shells.
Here was the ideal man to make inquiries without arousing
undue suspicion. Dieter Stahl's own plant might well want
to conduct experiments with gas shells.

Although he had known Stahl for less than a year, there
was good ground for mutual trust. The previous June, Stahl
had been arrested by the Gestapo for "making defeatist
remarks"—that is, he had stated flatly that the war was
lost. Speer had had to use all of his persuasive influence
with the Gauleiter of Brandenburg to free Stahl, and then

had to persuade the young industrialist to remain at his post in the ministry. It was from this incident that Speer had learned of the Himmler "spooks" in his own shop. Since then, the two men had become close friends. Speer and Stahl had spent several weekends together at the latter's lakeside cottage in Bad Wilsnack, near the Elbe.

Still, Speer moved cautiously. As the bombs rained down, and the small cabin-shelter shuddered, Stahl himself gave an opening. He grabbed Speer by the arm, lamenting, "This is madness, and the end is going to be frightful, frightful."

Speer launched a few leading questions about Tabun and how to procure it. A rather unusual request. But Stahl took it in stride, as if Speer had asked him for a cigarette or a light. Perhaps he was reading his minister's mind. Finally Speer, shocked at his own frankness, told Dieter Stahl flat out: "It is the only way to bring this war to an end. I want to try to conduct the gas into the Fuehrer-bunker."

Stahl showed neither undue surprise or shock, nor did he flinch from the implications. He promised to scout about discreetly for ways to obtain the gas. The date of this remarkable conversation, in the air-raid shelter under the Brandenburg Gate, was February 20.

For the next days, Dieter Stahl had to move just as cautiously as Speer. He went to see his friend Major Soyka, in the Army Ordnance Office, telling him he was interested in experiments in remodeling artillery shells in his own Bernau plant—to deliver Tabun, for example. In the course of the technical discussion, he discovered to his consternation that his cover story was too good. Tabun became effective only after it had been exploded in a shell or a hand grenade. But such a grenade, introduced into the bunker, would, of course, have shattered the thin wall air ducts. Stahl reported this disappointing news to Speer, meanwhile promising to continue his search for one of the conventional gases, such as mustard. February was fading into March.

While awaiting the Tabun, Speer had, on at least three other occasions, repeated his nocturnal prowling of the bunker area. He found Hitler, Goebbels, Bormann, and Ley meeting, as usual, and at the same hours. On one of these lonely clandestine strolls, he met Hentschel. Realizing now that he would have to use mustard gas, he casually spoke to Hannes about removing the filter of the ventilation system. Hentschel did this, a bit too promptly, for two nights later Speer found that the filter had been replaced. This was a minor obstacle. When the mustard gas arrived, he would simply have Hentschel repeat the performance.

Considerable time had, however, now elapsed. It was March 7 before Speer got the news, from Stahl, that mustard gas was on the way and would arrive the next day. Yet once more, Speer made the short journey at 7:00 P.M., from the Brandenburg Gate to the Reich Chancellery. Once again he parked in his special corner lot in the Ehrenhof and headed, on foot, through the short passageway directly toward the bunker.

Now, as he entered the Chancellery garden, Speer found, to his astonished dismay, that he was walking directly into a garish glare of searchlights. They were mounted atop the bunker and were serviced by four armed SS guards of the FBK. In the light he could make out that the searchlights were playing on a round metallic chimney, about ten feet tall, that rose from the ventilator air-intake which was his destination. Speer froze in sheer terror. At this moment he was convinced that somewhere along the line his plot must have been discovered. "I stood there, flat-footed, feeling guilty, as all conspirators do. I thought I must have been betrayed. Or that, by my own surreptitious activities, I had betrayed myself—perhaps the look on my face these past three weeks. I stood motionless, silent, for long seconds, before I even dared turn around. There was cold sweat on my brow and running down my spine. At this moment, I half-expected a tap on the shoulder, to turn around to face Heinrich Himmler, Ernst Kaltenbrunner, or Gestapo Mueller calmly waiting in the shadows to arrest me."

But all was silent. Nothing happened. Even the mounted guards took no notice of the nighttime lone intruder. They were about forty feet away and higher up, and could not see him in the darkness. They themselves were in the glare of the lights, whereas Speer had stepped back into the shadow. When he finally did turn around, nobody was there. Slowly, Speer began to recover his composure. He soon surmised the triviality of what had happened. Since January, Hitler had been complaining not only about the ventilator, but also about the fact that the bunker was unfinished when he had first moved in. Hitler himself, one of the mustard-gas victims of World War I, knew that this gas was heavier than air. Therefore, he must have ordered the chimney as a routine antigas precaution, and handyman Hannes Hentschel had installed it.

"On that evening, as I left the Reich Chancellery," Speer remembered, "I felt like one of those desperate gamblers who had just played Russian roulette—and won. I was completely frustrated in both my poison-gas schemes, for there was, now, no practical way to bring gas into the bunker. Inwardly, I was also—strangely—relieved. My mind quickly shook off all brooding ideas of assassination. I now began to feel it was better, on balance, to attempt to frustrate Hitler's 'scorched-earth' plans."

The spooky near-murder just described, one of the lesser known of at least nine serious attempts on Adolf Hitler's life, is cited by many who believe that one of Hitler's uncanny qualities was a sixth sense about danger looming for his own person. Switched planes, revised speaking schedules, a bomb in a cognac bottle in his plane that failed to tickoff, Stauffenberg's briefcase, which was accidentally moved only four minutes before it exploded—the list is, indeed, uncanny. A sixth sense or sheer luck. The several narrow escapes he himself was aware of Hitler, with lofty blasphemy, always attributed to "Providence."

*   *

The end was not yet. By the time Albert Speer had pushed from his mind the thought of killing Hitler—and had canceled the mustard-gas order—it was already the second week in March. The U.S. 9th Armored Division was now across the Rhine, and the Red Army might cross the Oder at any moment. Budapest had fallen; Vienna was besieged. Hitler was preparing to execute his scorched-earth or so-called Nero orders.

On March 15, 1945, Albert Speer, using the green ink that was the prerogative of a minister, sat down to draft the most courageous memorandum ever penned in the Third Reich, and the most important historical document ever to be delivered to Hitler in his Berlin bunker. Not without a touch of irony—Speer had a far more educated feel for history than anyone else in the Hitler court—he composed the first draft on the back of the copy paper on

which his secretary had typed out the two quotations from
Mein Kampf that Dr. Lueschen had written one short
month before. Speer wrote to Hitler:

> In four to eight weeks the final collapse of the German econ-
> omy must be expected with certainty . . . After that collapse
> the war cannot be continued . . . We must do everything to
> maintain, even if only in the most primitive manner, a basis
> for the existence of the nation to the last . . . We have no
> right, at this stage of the war, to carry out demolitions which
> would affect the life of the people. If our enemies wish to
> destroy this nation, which has fought with unique bravery,
> then this historical shame should rest exclusively on them.
> We have the duty of leaving to the nation every possibility
> of ensuring its reconstruction in the distant future.

In the last fortnight of March 1945, Albert Speer was
to use every ruse, invoke every friendship, manipulate
every string he had learned to pull in his once high-riding
days as the fair-haired prince of the Hitler court. If the
technocrat had been living all too casually among born
intriguers, toadying yes-men, all the doubletalkers and
doublethinkers of the Third Reich, he now employed their
methods to play off one satrap against another. For he still
held one of the very highest of court cards in his hand—
his sophisticated knowledge of the complicated psyche of
Adolf Hitler. But he was also in the perilous position of
the poker player drawing, again and again, to an inside
straight.

He knew that if Hitler read the memorandum of March
15 in one of his black moods, the Fuehrer would, at the
very least, fire Speer and probably have him placed under
house arrest. This was the same week Hitler had ordered
four Wehrmacht officers shot for not having blown the
bridge at Remagen on the Rhine. Speer's "eyes and ears"
in the bunker, with orders to stick as close as possible to
the Fuehrer, was Luftwaffe Colonel Nikolaus von Below.
Von Below, an intelligent and courageous man, had, from
1938 to 1944, been Reichsmarschall Goering's liaison man
in the FHQ; he was now performing the same job for
Speer. Von Below was given a typed copy of the memorandum by Speer and was told to give Hitler a verbal
briefing. He was advised to choose a moment of relative
calm. An experienced courtier, he carried out this risky
assignment with the utmost skill.

Strange is the role of sheer chance in what follows. Albert Speer's birthday was March 19. The Germans make a great thing of birthdays, and seldom had any man approached the threshold of forty with less assurance that he had a fair chance to live to be forty-one. Within the inner circle of the Reich Chancellery Group, Hitler always remembered birthdays. One of the most prized gifts was an autographed photograph of the Fuehrer, framed in solid silver with gold-inlaid swastika, mounted in a red leather case. It had always been a status symbol, much sought after by eager-beavers anxious to improve their standing and precedence. It was also a sentimental bit of *grossdeutscher Kitsch*. Speer had always been too proud to ask for one—above all because, since the bunker, Hitler had taken to handing them out like boxtops or Crackerjack tokens. Now, however, Speer approached Hitler's personal adjutant, SS Major General Julius Schaub, to drop the hint that he would not mind being given such a framed photograph.

Thus, on March 18, the eve of his birthday, Speer headed once again for the bunker, less than a fortnight since he had abandoned his poison-gas mission. He had the original of the twenty-two-page memorandum under his arm. Before the routine midnight conference, Hitler, in a fairly cordial and relaxed mood, came into the conference room to greet him. "Ah, you know, Speer, your beautiful architecture is no longer the proper frame for the situation conferences."

During the conference itself, however, Hitler's mood darkened. The chief topic was General George S. Patton, Jr.'s, Third Army, its armor now rampaging through the Saar and the Palatinate, hell-bent for the Rhine and Main rivers. At one point, Hitler turned to his armaments minister and said, "Speer, explain what the loss of the Saar means to our production."

"It will speed the inevitable collapse."

Most of the conference participants were startled at the bluntness of Speer's answer, which bordered on lèse majesté. There was a shattering silence. But Hitler let it pass. Before the conference broke up, however, the Fuehrer unleashed one of his Nero-like orders: all Germans west of the Rhine River were to be evacuated forthwith. This involved a population of some eight million. Field Marshal Keitel, without protesting, drafted the order. Such a pell-mell evacuation, under battlefield conditions, meant certain death for countless civilians.

The conference broke up around 2:00 A.M. It was now March 19, Speer's fortieth birthday. Before the conference, he had planned to fly to besieged Koenigsberg. Now he changed his mind, reversed direction. He decided to fly to the Palatinate, where the danger of scorched-earth tactics and mass evacuation so clearly loomed. Partly to deliver his March 15 memorandum personally, partly to receive the birthday present, but mostly to say goodbye to the Fuehrer, Speer requested a private audience. For many reasons, it might be the last.

When Albert Speer had first met Adolf Hitler, it was in the Fuehrer's private apartment, in 1933, on the Prinzregentenstrasse in Munich. Speer was then twenty-eight years old; Hitler, forty-five. The handsome, rather shy, young architect had come to bring Hitler some sketches of designs to decorate a party rally. Hitler was seated alone, and remained so, cleaning his revolver. He received and dismissed Speer in silence, except for a laconic "In order." Yet at this moment a career was born, one of the strangest in history since the day that another handsome young man, Joseph, caught the eye of the pharaoh. Now, in the bunker, it was past midnight, both on the clock and in the careers of these two men. Although the scene is not free from a certain mawkish sentimentality that is a constant bunker refrain, still one would like to see it dramatized, one day, by some second Shakespeare, some second Brecht. A scant two weeks before, this same Albert Speer had been standing outside the bunker, preparing to play a mustard-gas Brutus to this most malignant of the world's long line of Caesars. Now he was asking for an autographed picture.

Hitler rang for his valet Fehrs to fetch the framed picture, as requested. His hand trembled as he handed it over. Tears were welling in his glassy blue eyes.* He mumbled a friendly felicitation. Since the gift was enclosed within a leather case, Speer first put it casually aside, laying it down on the Fuehrer's desk; he intended to open it later. Hitler began to fumble with his nickel-rimmed spectacles, murmuring apologetically, "Lately it

---

* Valet Heinz Linge was now giving him cocaine drops several times a day.

has been hard for me to write even a few words in my own hand. You know how it shakes. Often I can hardly complete my signature. What I have written for you came out almost illegible."

Happy birthday, and remembrance of things past. At this hint that he should open his present, Speer did so, and, as Hitler had warned, he was barely able to decipher the scrawled handwriting, as familiar as it must have been to him. The dedication was, however, warm and friendly, thanking the architect and minister for his past work, and pledging enduring friendship. Nothing catches the ambivalent nature of the relationship between these two antithetical men better than this nostalgic moment. How often, alone together on the terrace of the Berghof, with the full moon or the northern lights playing on the magic mountain, the Untersberg, had the all-powerful patron and his architect heard the Berchtesgaden village chimes, those echoes of an earlier faith, calling others to worship. Hitler and Speer both saw themselves as modern men, freed from superstition. And so they planned their heaven-defying buildings of the future—that monster Berlin dome seven times the diameter of St. Peter's. Now they were standing in a room that measured ten by fifteen feet.

Was the Hitler of this Speer-birthday moment sincere? Rather obviously, he was. His warm relationship with Speer, the "fellow artist," was always something special, and it remained so. Adolf Hitler, after all, had a right to be proud of this minister—his discovery, his protégé, his surprising choice for high office. Speer, at this moment, was seeing the pleasanter side of Hitler the dreamer. How fine it would be to have more time to sit upon the ground, under the Lombardy poplars along the Danube, at Linz, discussing Callicrates and Phidias, Vitruvius and Palladio, the Vienna Ring Strasse, Garnier's Paris Opéra. Perhaps, then, Speer would get his chance to explain why the Place des Vosges, in Paris, is really better than the Place de la Concorde. And why the Sainte Chapelle is a finer piece of architecture than the Sacre Coeur.

Speer's midnight epiphany in the bunker, on this his birthday, recalled those happier days, those fireside dreams of a future never to be. Hitler was touched by the corny request for the autographed photo, from the same man who had come to tell him officially that his Third Reich was tumbling down. Hitler was sincere; but he was also, still and as always, the inveterate actor. He was hoping to soften Speer's resolve.

The tottering tyrant had reached the stage where he could no longer endure, or even register, unpleasant news. He reached for any and every opportunity to retreat from reality. He might or might not have read the Speer March 15 memorandum, but he knew well enough what it contained. Why could not Speer, at least on his birthday, forget these dismal production figures, relax, and talk about the good old days? Why had he not brought a fresh set of crackling blueprints? On this normally festive occasion, Hitler would gladly have spent the whole night poring over blueprints; the more, the better. Speer knew this.

At this moment, Speer recently admitted, "I almost flinched." Except that he knew Adolf Hitler far too well. He also had in his mind's eye a harrowing vision of the world of catastrophe outside the bunker—the mute columns of trudging refugees, the strafed cadavers along the roadside, the frozen, shoeless children, the holocaust of martyred Dresden, the bedraggled, ridiculous Volkssturm (the home guard), the bomb-pocked autobahns one could now drive only at night, the blown bridges, the beaten Wehrmacht veterans tramping in constant retreat, the rail chaos on the Reichsbahn, chaos of supply, chaos of communications.

He therefore now handed Hitler the memorandum. To break, somehow, the long and ugly silence that ensued, as casually as possible Speer informed the Fuehrer that he had changed his mind about his own plans. Instead of flying to Koenigsberg, as he had announced earlier, he would be leaving by car for western Germany. Discreetly, he then left the Fuehrer's office.

But while Speer was still in the bunker, telephoning for his car and driver, Hitler summoned him back. "I have thought it over. It will be better if you take my car and have my chauffeur, Kempka, drive you."

Hitler had thus not taken long to fathom Speer's mind and purpose. The military conference just held had made clear to him that Speer had switched plans and was heading west for the Rhineland and the Palatinate to block industrial destruction. This sinister little matter about the car and chauffeur meant that Hitler wanted to control Speer's activities, outside the bunker and outside Berlin.

He was using Erich Kempka as a personal spy on his own minister. Speer at first protested. A compromise was reached. Speer could take off in his own car, Hitler said, provided he took Kempka along as chauffeur.

The atmosphere in the bunker had become icy. The friendly birthday warmth had dissipated. Once again, Hitler had undergone one of those rapid shifts in mood, from the manic to the depressive. Speer was already at the steel door, coolly and brusquely dismissed, when Hitler again addressed him in a tone he seldom used, even to awkward valets. "This time you will receive a written reply to your March fifteenth memorandum."

There was a pause, and then Hitler let loose with all the Vandal vehemence of which Speer knew him to be capable when the black mood was on. "If the war is lost, the people will be lost also. It is not necessary to worry about what the German people will need for elemental survival. On the contrary, it is best to destroy even these things. For this nation has proved to be the weaker, and the future belongs solely to the stronger eastern nation. In any case, only those who are inferior will remain after the struggle, for the good have already been killed."

This blatant Social Darwinism, the law-of-tooth-and-claw survival of the fittest, was hardly a new pattern in Hitler's mental cosmology. But here he was not just sounding off, as many thought he was doing in *Mein Kampf*, getting rhetorical mileage out of one of the more dubious nineteenth-century ideas he had picked up in his brooding years in Vienna.

Speer recalled this moment more than a quarter century later. "It shook me to the core. It did then, and it does today. I can still hear that Attila voice ringing in my ears."

Even Erich Kempka, for all the moral sliminess of his stool-pigeon mission, was happy at this moment to leave the fetid atmosphere of the bunker and to come up into the early spring air of nighttime Berlin. Like his chum Hans Baur, Kempka belonged to the higher ranks of the coterie of cronies in the inner circle of the Reich Chancellery Group, which Speer derisively called the "Chauffeureska." Like Baur, he had been faced, for long weeks now, with technological unemployment. In the past three months, he had driven the Fuehrer perhaps five or six times. Kempka held the rank of colonel in the SS.

Speer and Kempka had only two things in common—
their personal relationship with the Fuehrer, and a mutual,
almost boyish, fascination with fast automobiles. Auto
buff Speer insisted on keeping the wheel of his own car—
it was, after all, now his birthday. Kempka yielded grace-
fully, promising to relieve him from time to time. The car
was a six-cylinder, three-liter, souped-up BMW cabriolet.
Kempka sat in the seat next to the driver. Colonel Manfred von Poser, a young aristocrat who was Speer's liaison
man to the General Staff, sat in the rear. It was an odd
trio. As they left Berlin on the autobahn, destination Bad
Nauheim, RAF Mosquito bombers were out. Speer snapped
on the car radio, tuned in on the air-warning signal. He
dimmed down to parking lights whenever enemy planes
were announced in their grid pattern. When all was clear,
with amber foglights and the jacklamp in operation, Speer
threw in the supercharger and roared on through the
night. Dawn came in a blissful fog, which grounded the
prowling fighter planes. The trio reached Bad Nauheim in
time for late breakfast.

Here, Field Marshal Kesselring, only recently brought
back from Italy to succeed von Rundstedt, was now the
Commander-in-Chief West. At his headquarters, Ziegenberg, the field marshal was drinking a pleasant birthday
toast to the minister. Suddenly, a U.S. Ninth Air Force
Thunderbolt strafing attack, bombs and machine-gun bullets, sent the whole party scrambling, through broken glass
and mortar dust, toward the shelter. This was Adlerhorst,
the same headquarters Speer had designed as a FHQ back
in the balmy peacetime summer of 1939, and Hitler had
rejected.

For the next forty-eight hours, most of them spent without sleep, Speer covered a fair amount of German geography. He was now in the Rhineland area that had become
the western front—the Palatinate, his native North Baden,
and the Westerwald, which is just across the river from
Bonn. He even managed—still on his birthday—to visit
his parents in Heidelberg, just before it was to fall to the
rapidly advancing Americans. Otherwise, he was zooming
about, talking to generals, plant managers, mayors, anybody and everybody in a position to block or forestall the
scorched-earth decrees soon to come from the Berlin
bunker.

Once again, it was a deadly duel of communications,

the very field in which Hitler himself had once been such
a sovereign master. Now, because the Fuehrer had isolated himself in Berlin, he was utterly out of touch with
public opinion. Nor did he give a rap for it. Even in a
dictatorship, public opinion is somehow always there; it
cannot shout, but it mumbles and murmurs. The prevailing mood was now of galloping defeatism, *sauve qui peut.*
Millions of chastened Germans, going down in a sea of
white flags, were already snugly behind the ever-advancing
American lines. Millions more—not least the three million
Berliners—were quietly hoping for a similar beneficent
fate. The tattered, battered remnants of the Wehrmacht
tried, here and there in the west, to make a stand.* The
citizenry would send out the Buergermeister to ask, *Bitte
sehr*, would the troops mind moving on to the next town
or village? Even several Gauleiters, once the brown-granite
pillars of the Nazi state-within-a-state, were now wobbling. In the Palatinate, General Patton was a lot closer to
the local Germans than was Martin Bormann in Berlin.

True, Bormann still had formal control of the Gauleiters.
His problem was, he now had no henchmen in the field to
discipline reluctant Gauleiters. They were supposed to be
the first and last guardians of the National Socialist state,
but who could control the guardians? This is one of the
oldest, recurring questions in every tyranny. *Quis custodiet
ipsos custodes?* The German Fuehrer was becoming a remote figure in remote Berlin.

Speer, who still had the nimbus and power of a minister, was also a well-known, still-respected figure, as Bormann was not. Only the Gauleiters knew how powerful
Bormann really was in the Hitler court. Speer's effective
power was outside the bunker, out where the awesome
reality was.

In both cases, the power was derivative—from Hitler.
If Speer stayed out of the bunker one day too long, the
ultimate in disaster loomed. So he cagily returned to Berlin, every second or third day, to protect his own shoulder
blades. Bormann's problem, in this den of court intrigue,
was even more thorny. He knew very well what Speer was
doing, for Bormann was getting daily reports (although
sometimes the reports were curiously delayed).

---

* This was the almost universal mood in the west. The mood was the
opposite in the east.

Roving around the Palatinate, Speer discovered, happily, that the mass-evacuation order was being ignored. The three Palatinate Gauleiters whom he met in Mainz all assured him it was now too late to carry out any demolition orders. Because he knew the people on the spot and they knew him, because he was there so close to the collapsing front, Speer's communications net and his authority were thus able to trump Bormann's. Speer had his man in every important factory, and a staff of technocrats in every industrial city, the so-called shock committees.

While he was at Field Marshal Model's headquarters in the Westerwald, however, on March 20, Minister Speer received the telegraphed answer to his March 15 memorandum. Hitler was replying with a written text, as promised. The long and short of the message was that Speer was stripped of all power to advise or interfere in the destruction program. The power was handed over directly to the Gauleiters, under Bormann.

Hitler, in the most savage of his decrees, now ordered "the destruction of all military, transportation, communications, industrial and supply facilities, as well as all resources within the Reich."

Every previous Speer order—for example, the one for crippling rather than destroying the industrial infrastructure—was thus explicitly revoked. Speer received this Hitler directive while sitting in Model's Army Group B headquarters in the Ruhr Valley, the most concentrated industrial complex in Europe or, for that matter, the world. The literal carrying-out of Hitler's order meant that within less than a year's time, even as peace came, the life of the Ruhr miners would be thrown back to the anthropological level that once prevailed here along one of the Ruhr tributaries, the Neander. The Ruhr *Kumpel* (miner) would become a modern, more wretched version of his museum-piece ancestor, the Neanderthal man.

As Speer put it not long ago, "The consequences would have been inconceivable. For an indefinite period there would have been no electricity, no gas, no pure water, no coal, no transportation. All railroad facilities, canals, locks, docks, ships, and locomotives were to be destroyed. Even where industry had not been demolished, it could not have produced anything for lack of electricity, gas, and water. No storage facilities, no telephone communications—in short, a country thrown back into the Middle Ages."

Now he was in the Westerwald, a mixed forest of deciduous trees and evergreens that carpets the pleasant rolling hills lying just east of the Rhine and south of the Ruhr, a wood where Beethoven often hiked as a young man. When he received the March 20 order, the first thing Speer did was to go for a long walk. It was the eve of the vernal equinox, in a year in which the winter had been retreating rapidly, as if it were part of the Wehrmacht. Spring had already come; the forsythias were in bloom, the willows greening.

Weary and distraught, I feel into a sleep in a friendly farmer's house. A few hours later, I wandered across the fields and came to the top of a hill. Below me lay a village, wrapped in a mantle of mist, basking peacefully in the spring sunlight. Beyond and far away, I could make out the Sauerland, which lies between the Sieg and the Ruhr rivers. How was it possible, I asked myself, that any man should desire to turn this landscape into a desert? I lay down in a field of sprouting fern. Everything had an air of unreality. Yet a spicelike lush fragrance was rising from the soft soil, the first optimistic green shoots of plant life were thrusting toward heaven. As I returned to the farmhouse, the sun was setting. I had made my decision. Hitler's scorched-earth orders must be blocked. I canceled my scheduled Ruhr interviews, for it was better now to sound out the situation in Berlin.

The last breath of German Romanticism still lingered in the haunted soul of Albert Speer. To understand the irony of this passage, itself so familiar in the writings of such authors as Moerike, Novalis, and Eichendorff, one must comprehend the piquant irony involving the man, the time, the place. Those pushing ferns might have been found in a Romantic lyric. They were, however, growing just off the autobahn that runs through the Westerwald from Cologne south to Frankfurt on the Main.

As noted earlier in this chapter, on this day, March 20, 1945, U.S. Army armored reconnaissance teams had broken out of the Remagen bridgehead. When they reached this autobahn, they might have captured Hitler's armaments minister had they turned north instead of south. Driving back to Berlin in this wildly fluid situation, Speer was skirting what was soon to be known as the Ruhr Pocket, where Model and his Army Group B would sit atop the coal mines until the last days of the war.

Seven hours on the road, and Speer was back in Berlin. En route, he had quietly torn up all the notes of his interviews. At one stop along the way, he saw that the torn scraps were still clinging to the running board. He kicked them into the roadside ditch.

It was the afternoon of March 21, the first day of spring, when Speer reported back to the bunker. Hitler asked for a briefing, not from Speer but from Kempka. Technically, Speer was still minister, but he had been stripped of all effective power in the only field that really mattered. Hitler invited him to the briefing that evening, but Speer decided not to show up. He sent instead his deputy, Karl Saur. One of the truly giddy topics of this meeting was a long discussion of the military prospects of "Greek fire." This wonder-weapon was invented by Callinicus of Heliopolis— in the year A.D. 688.

*   *

On March 24, the day Field Marshal Montgomery's Anglo-American Twenty-first Army Group crossed the Rhine at Wesel, just north of the Ruhr, Speer again left Berlin for the great industrial basin, once the first arsenal of the Reich. At least half of his ministry's field teams were still based there. Even as late as September 1944, when the western Allies had reached the Siegfried Line, or West Wall, the German border in the west, these Speer men, operating in shock committees, had still been able to rearm and re-equip forty German divisions thrown back from France and the Lowlands. Most of the heavy weapons used in the Ardennes offensive of December 1944 had been stamped out that autumn in the Ruhr. Although badly bombed, Ruhr factories were still functioning at 91 percent capacity. Militarily, the Ruhr was now about to be cut off from the rest of Germany by a classic double-envelopment operation. The encirclement and by-passing of the Ruhr Pocket was about to put both the Ruhr and Germany out of the war.

Now, for the first time, Speer ran into real resistance. It came from the three Ruhr Gauleiters. As minister, Speer had been stripped of his power to forbid scorched-earth measures. His cunctatory tactics, doubletalk and delay, were patent defiance of Hitler's orders. Despite this handicap, Speer was still able to softsoap two of the hesitant

Gauleiters into waiting at least for "implementation orders."

The third, however, Gauleiter Florian of Duesseldorf, was determined to order the total evacuation of his city. He threatened to put the torch to every factory and every building. A part of Duesseldorf, the suburb of Oberkassel, which lay west of the Rhine, had already fallen to the U.S. Ninth Army. The terrified Duesseldorfers could gaze across the Rhine every day and see Americans.

Florian was finally told, by cooler heads in Duesseldorf, that the pyromaniac idea of burning a city might lead an enraged citizenry to the ardent idea of burning a Gauleiter. Had a workers' uprising ever come in Nazi Germany—an unlikely event for many reasons—it would probably have been sparked right here. The tergiversating Gauleiters were now caught between fear of Hitler's wrath and fear of the possible explosion of the populace.

On March 25, in Schloss Landsberg, near Essen, a castle that the Nazis had confiscated from the steel baron Fritz Thyssen,* Speer summoned an emergency meeting. Demolitions were scheduled to begin within twenty-four hours. At this meeting, in addition to the Speer ministry staff, were some twenty top Ruhr industrial managers. Speer proposed three measures: (1) In the coal fields, all dynamite, blasting caps, and fuses were to be thrown into the sumps of the mines; (2) Submachine guns were to be issued to workers and factory police in the power plants, with instructions for them to use the weapons in any showdown against the Gauleiters' demolition squads; (3) All available trucking in the Ruhr—transport still came under the Munitions Division of War Production—was to be distributed to the troops, who could be counted on to defend them. Or the trucks were to be driven out of the Ruhr by night, east and southeast, to use up most of the available gas. All of these orders were carried out. It amounted to open revolt; these were quasi-revolutionary measures.

Before returning to Berlin, Speer took a last quick swing south, to Baden. He was in Heidelberg when the Berlin order came through to blow up every waterworks

---

* Thyssen was, at that moment, in Dachau. Once a Hitler supporter, he had been arrested in 1939 for sending a telegram of protest against Hitler's attack on Poland.

and public utility in Baden. He suggested that all these orders be dropped into a mailbox about to be overrun by American troops. On at least two occasions, Speer was driving and weaving his car *between* the advancing Americans and the retreating Germans. Only his knowledge of the backroads of the Odenwald, his childhood tramping grounds behind Heidelberg, saved him from capture.

Speer was back in Berlin the next day, March 26, having arrived around midnight after a strenuous drive. He was physically and nervously exhausted as he approached the inevitable confrontation and showdown in the bunker. The first news he got, from his own liaison man, Colonel von Below, was that the Fuehrer had just dismissed General Guderian, Speer's last real ally and fellow spirit in the bunker. Hitler, after the midnight conference, now received Speer alone and came directly to the point. "Bormann has given me a report of your conferences with the Ruhr Gauleiters. You pressured them not to carry out my orders and declared that the war is lost. Are you aware of what must follow from that?"

Had the culprit been anyone else but Speer, the choice might well have been between shooting and hanging. Or if Hitler had got the least wind of suspicion of the poison-gas affair, it would have meant strangulation while suspended from a meathook. But the tension soon seemed to lessen. He merely said, calmly and rather matter-of-factly, "If you were not my architect, I would take the measures called for in such a case."

The magic word had fallen, like an incantation. Speer was an architect, a creator, *ein Kuenstler*. In the murderous game of one-upmanship in the Hitler court, this and this alone is what Speer had going for him. This is what he had over the paladins and hierarchs, over Bormann, Goering, Goebbels, Himmler. In the Hitlerian vocabulary, there was simply no higher word of praise.

Speer refused to flinch. "Take the measures you deem necessary and grant no consideration to me as an individual."

Hitler countered, solicitously, "Speer, you are overworked and ill. I have therefore decided that you are to go on leave at once." They were the identical words he had spoken to Guderian, just a few hours earlier.

"No, I am perfectly well," Speer replied. "If you no longer want me as your minister, dismiss me. I cannot

keep the responsibility of a minister while another is acting in my place."

At this point, and for the first time, Speer added the
conciliatory note "I cannot, mein Fuehrer."

As the conciliatory phrase fell, there was a lengthy, relaxing pause. The Fuehrer sat down. So did Speer, un-
asked, a real breach of established court etiquette. Now
Hitler began again, this time almost pleading. "Speer, if
you can convince yourself that the war is not lost, you
can continue running your shop."

The request was simple enough in its emptiness. It was
a request for lip service, the real language of the unreal
world of the bunker, the *lingua franca* of self-deceivers.

Speer, too, had now taken his cue, and modulated his
earlier tone of calm defiance. But he did not capitulate.
He had often, in the past months, warned Hitler that he
was surrounded with "nodding donkeys," so why should
he, Speer, suddenly start to bray? Hitler would see through
that.

"You know I cannot be convinced of that. The war is
lost, *verloren*."

Verloren, the word Hitler just could not take. He
launched into his broken-needle recitation, variations on
the theme of never-say-die, Leonidas at Thermopylae,
Horatius at the bridge, Frederick the Great in 1762, his
own incarceration in Landsberg prison in 1923, the 1941
stand before Moscow, the 1942–1944 miracle production
figures of Speer's own ministry. For a long while Hitler
seemed lost in his own monologue-reverie, which ran on
and on for perhaps twenty to twenty-five minutes. Then:
"Speer, if you could believe that the war can still be won,
if you could at least have faith in that, then all would be
well."

Hitler's thespian ability, his skill at pulling out all the
stops, had not deserted him. Speer by now knew the act
pretty well, but he was by no means unmoved by this plea
for pity. Yet he also remembered that he was talking to
Martin Bormann's boss, and the boss of Goebbels and the
others. He also had not forgotten the cardinal issue at
stake. Now he used an even stronger animal image than
the nodding donkeys one. "I cannot, with the best will in
the world. And after all, I do not want to be one of the
swine in your entourage who tell you they believe in victory without believing in it."

The strong word here is *Schwein*, much stronger in German than it sounds in English. Hitler knew exactly whom Speer meant—Bormann, Goebbels, Ley, Keitel, General Burgdorf. But since it was not aimed directly at him, he let this irreverent slur pass.

Hitler said, "Do you still *hope* for a successful continuance of the war, or is your faith shattered? If you could at least *hope* that we have not lost. You must certainly be able to *hope*. That would be enough to satisfy me."

Speer still refused to answer. The bunker silence was now intense. It finally snapped Hitler, the pleader, back into the authoritarian tone with which this showdown session had begun. "Speer, you have twenty-four hours to think over your answer. Tomorrow let me know whether you *hope* the war can still be won."

There was no handshake. Speer was dismissed. The time was once more an hour after midnight.

Standing up to Adolf Hitler had exhausted Speer, as it had the very few others who ever did so and lived to tell about it. He emerged from the bunker like a frogman surfacing for fresh air. It was the middle of the silent Berlin night. There was a bright moon overhead. He wondered idly why the RAF had failed to put in an appearance.

Speer drove again down the deserted Wilhelmstrasse, to his bachelor's flat in the ministry. He tried to sleep, but sleep came only fitfully. Sitting on the edge of his cot, he began drafting a handwritten letter to Hitler. It was twenty-four pages long, a mixture of honey and vinegar, a long philosophic review of how, why, and when the war had been lost. It ended with an earnest plea to Hitler to be manly, to end the insensate destruction.

Some time in the early morning hours Speer must have fallen asleep, for it was late afternoon before he sent the letter over, by courier, to Johanna Wolf, Hitler's senior secretary, to type up on the special block-letter Fuehrer typewriter. Hitler, meanwhile, had anticipated Speer's likely action; he had ordered his secretaries *not* to type up any more Speer letters. He said he wanted to see his minister in person.

Once again it was close to midnight as Speer drove toward the bunker. The twenty-four-hour deadline was lapsing. All the trenchant points he had so neatly rehearsed in the personal letter suddenly became a vast blur in his mind. He entered the Fuehrer's study unsure of what he was going to say. Without shaking hands—when Hitler was rude it was always intentional—the Fuehrer greeted him with one terse word: "Well?"

"Mein Fuehrer," Speer said, "I stand unreservedly behind you!"

At first, this sounds like a capitulation. For the moment, the Fuehrer did not even answer. Then, slowly, he shook hands, his own hand trembling. His eyes welled up with tears of gratitude. "Then all is well." It was a mellow moment and a melancholy reminder of the old days now vanished forever. Hitler had what he wanted and apparently needed, a lachrymose profession of mouth loyalty. Now Speer moved deftly to nail down what he in turn needed, like a poker player asking the dealer for one card. "Since I stand unreservedly behind you, then you must once again entrust me, instead of the Gauleiters, with the implementation of your decree."

The operative word here is "implementation." Hitler authorized Speer to draw up a document that, he said, he would sign at once. He did not really budge an inch in principle, but he allowed Speer to smuggle in the loophole clause that "the same effect can be achieved with industrial installations by crippling them." Speer had retreated upstairs into an empty room of the New Chancellery to work up this draft. When he came back, Hitler initialed it in pencil.

These initials—A.H.—spelled restored power. Speer rushed back to his ministry, gathered up all the available cars and motorcycles, and whipped off for the printing plants in the Kochstrasse, Berlin's Fleet Street. As dawn broke over Berlin, Speer, with his revived ministerial authority, was out to restore the situation as it had existed before the Hitler decree dated March 19. Each of the printed orders that he now sent out, posthaste, stressed that "precise implementation orders will follow."

As Speer said recently:

I had no intention of ever sending out any such orders, and the key people at the receiving end all knew this, like laughing Roman augurs. But now they were covered. They were, so to speak, in the position of carrying out my orders *not* to carry out my orders. Perhaps only bureaucrats can fully understand what the fateful word "implementation" means. In the nineteen days from March eighteenth to April seventh, nineteen forty-five, no less than twelve contradictory decrees had been issued, either from the bunker or my ministry. This, of course, created a chaotic command situation. According to Professor Parkinson's famous first law of bureaucratic behavior, the more orders issued from on high, the less chance anything will ever happen. This was precisely the quandary I had wanted to create.

To end the account of this amazing episode—all that was at stake was at least $200 billion worth of industrial plant—Speer also managed to wring from Hitler, when he caught him a few days later in a relaxed mood, the common-sense admission, "Perhaps, after all, the scorched-earth idea has no point in a country of such compact topography as Germany. It can fulfill its purpose only in vast spaces, such as Russia." Speer made a quick jotting of this last word on the subject by the Fuehrer. From here on to the end, he used it with telling effect.

CHAPTER IV

•

The Mountain People

April is the cruelest month . . . —T. S. ELIOT,
The Waste Land

FOR BERLIN IN 1945, April was indeed the cruelest month. On April 23, the ultimate military alert was proclaimed for the city under siege. Operation Clausewitz, a hasty, ill-prepared plan for a last stand within the city, went into effect. Around noontime on that day, a Monday, Waffen SS Major General Wilhelm Mohnke and his battle group of some 2000 combat troops marched seven miles from their Lichterfelde barracks into the cellar of the New Reich Chancellery.

One week before, at dawn, the 1st Ukrainian Army Front under Marshal Georgi Zhukov had begun moving out of its bridgehead between Frankfurt on the Oder and Kuestrin and were now storming across the Oder River in force. The Oder, which flows south to north, is only sixty miles east of Berlin. The Russians, who had come from the Volga and the Don, across the Dnieper and the Vistula, had now bridged the last river barrier on their 2500–mile march to Berlin.

Thus another forlorn hope, to which most of three million Berlin civilians had still been clinging, was about to be dashed. For weeks, Berliners had been eagerly following reports of the extremely rapid advance east of the U.S. and British armies after their Rhine crossing in March. Twelve days earlier, on Wednesday, April 11, advance units of the spearhead U.S. Ninth Army under

"Martin Bormann is not only present; he is omnipresent. Stocky, bullish, drinking heavily when off duty, Bormann is literally at the Fuehrer's elbow, wheeling and dealing madly in what is left of the Nazi power game."

Lieutenant General William H. Simpson had reached and crossed the Elbe River at Magdeburg, which is only ninety miles west southwest of Berlin.

Military men in the bunker, who knew that the autobahn from Magdeburg to Berlin was now free of any large German combat units,* also calculated that elements of the U.S. 2nd Armored Division and the U.S. 83rd Infantry Division would be arriving in Berlin within twenty-four to forty-eight hours; that is, at least two full days before the Russians stormed across the Oder. Americans now had an open road to Berlin.

Although it is not directly the theme of this book—it is well worth a book in itself—this historical event, more strictly speaking this historical nonevent—is still a matter of much dispute today. What was the real reason for this strange American halt, in effect a pull-back order by General Eisenhower to allow the Russians to become sole conquerors of Berlin?

This writer and several thousand other American soldiers were eyewitnesses not of events in Berlin, but of just what was happening on the Elbe River. I was, at that time, operations officer of the 137th Signal Radio Intelligence Company. I had attached four of my radio-intercept platoons to Combat Command B of the 2nd Armored Division. This was the unit that had captured Magdeburg on April 11. Sometime before noon on Thursday, April 12, we were all set to cross the Elbe River. There was no visible opposition as combat engineers strung out a pontoon bridge and brought up amphibious "ducks." We heard that ten

---

* This was the same strip of autobahn destined to make so many post–1945 headlines.

94

miles to the south of us units of the 83rd Infantry Division were also preparing a crossing.

Just before noon—it was a warm, cloudy day—we received from on high (Ninth Army headquarters, in Brunswick) sudden countermanding orders. This baffled us. By radio we were told that no American soldiers were to cross the Elbe; if any were already across, they were to return immediately to the west bank of the Elbe. Soon, by field telephone, I got an even more peremptory order, delivered in the otherwise pleasant Mississippi drawl of the Ninth Army signal officer: "Drag ass backwards, and don't ask me why."

Orders, as they say, are orders. To clear up part of the popular mythology relating to this vignette of world history, it is just not true that any American soldiers, at least any whom I knew or met, were particularly eager to roar into Berlin as conquering heroes. Three-day passes for Paris were much more in demand; for the first time in weeks I was able to issue them. Berlin, for us, was the great unknown. We assumed it was heavily defended. We knew it was a rubble heap.

Moreover, as far as daily military tasks were concerned, my own operation could function almost as well from the west bank of the Elbe River. Our radio mission then was to establish, by wireless intercept and direction-finding devices, the precise German OB (order of battle)—or what was now left of it. For we were now no longer able, by the usual means, to identify German Army units we had been tracing and tailing since the Normandy beachhead. On the other side of the Elbe, between us and Berlin, the German front seemed to be disintegrating into battle groups. Most messages we were able to intercept were now in clear text—always a sure sign of utter military confusion. Most of these battle-group units were at first heading west, that is, in our direction, then east, and then, like phantoms, they vanished from the air waves.

It was only during my research for this book that I finally established to my own satisfaction what was really happening in that chaotic military situation around Berlin and in the Mark of Brandenburg in mid-April 1945. The answer is simple enough. While Hitler in the bunker was girding for Armageddon, determined to defend his capital to the last man, last building, and last cartridge, cooler heads among the German General Staff, above all Colonel

General Gotthardt Heinrici, the last commander of Army Group Vistula, had other, saner ideas.

German generals and other senior officers active in the field, at long last able to ignore or fudge orders coming from Hitler, were out to help their troops—plus the gigantic flow of German civilian refugees—elude Russian captivity. Most of the refugees were women and children trekking west, hoping to reach the Elbe. Thousands even swam it, in order to reach the area now occupied by the British and Americans.

General Heinrici, like the Roman Fabius of old, was able to do this by clever maneuvering—and by poker-faced doubletalk whenever he had to report to the Fuehrerbunker. This took courage. The two battered (that is, *more* than decimated) German armies now trapped between the Oder and the Elbe were the Ninth Army under General Busse, east of Berlin, and the Twelfth German Army under General Wenck, west of the city and east of the Elbe. Heinrici so maneuvered these two armies that while creating the appearance of falling back to defend Berlin—Hitler's persistent order—he was, in fact, quietly telling General Wenck to collapse the front in the west; to move east to support General Busse's disengaging efforts, and then to head west again.

Heinrici thus created a corridor through which both the battered German units and the civilian refugee flood could by-pass Berlin, both to the north and to the south. In the final stages, they could make a dash for the Elbe, to surrender to the British and the Americans. Under the circumstances, it was an eminently sensible decision. By these delaying tactics, General Heinrici also quietly hoped that American armor would use this corridor for a quick dash into Berlin. But here foxy General Heinrici had outsmarted himself.

Another quite unexpected event on this same fateful Thursday, April 12, was the sudden death of President Franklin D. Roosevelt in Warm Springs, Georgia. Death struck around noon, Eastern Standard Time. The startling news, picked up by radio-monitoring of a BBC Reuters flash, reached the Berlin bunker around 11:00 P.M., Middle European Time. This was just before Hitler's second, or midnight, situation-briefing. Any urge in the bunker to celebrate was more than slightly dampened by a mighty RAF raid then in progress. This was the night when both the Old Reich Chancellery and the Foreign Office went up in flames.

Just after midnight, Joseph Goebbels, en route by motorcar from a visit to the Oder front, arrived at his residence, to get the news at the door. According to one witness, "his face lit up—partly from the news, partly from the reflection from the burning city." The propaganda minister now invited his aides and some members of the German and neutral press into his study. Goebbels was soon on the phone to the Fuehrer, some five blocks away. Parts of this conversation were overheard by several of Goebbels' aides, who have since reported the gist of what was said. "My Fuehrer, this is the 'miracle of the House of Brandenburg' we have been waiting for, an uncanny historical parallel. This is the turning point predicted in your horoscope!"

The reference to the "miracle" is easy enough to explain —although Goebbels in his malignant ecstasy got the quotation wrong. Back in February and March, he had spent early bunker evenings reading to Hitler from the one-volume German edition of Thomas Carlyle's *History of Frederick the Great*. The highlight was the account of how the beleaguered King of Prussia had been saved when his sworn foe, the Czarina Elizabeth of Russia, died in 1762 and was succeeded by her nephew, Peter III, a friend of Frederick's. This had led to the sudden "reversal of alliances" in 1763 that saved Frederick and ended the Seven Years' War.*

Goebbels at this moment of ridiculous euphoria was certainly aware of the hypnotic effect the portrait of Frederick had on the Fuehrer. Hitler could see it as he talked on the phone. Apparently because of the bombing raid, Goebbels did not go personally to the bunker, as one might have expected. Perhaps he was simply not invited. Only Sergeant Misch, who was at the switchboard, could recall Hitler's reaction. "He said something to the effect that, with this remarkable turn of events, the U.S. and the Red Army might soon be exchanging artillery barrages over the roof of the Reich Chancellery. I didn't quite fathom just how he meant that."

Rochus Misch, often an unconscious humorist, was not really a political animal. What Hitler obviously meant—

---

* The "miracle of the House of Brandenburg," in fact, referred to an event that took place three years earlier, in 1759.

or at least yearned for—was the sudden breakup of the
alliance between the western powers and Stalin. He knew
it was in the cards; he was simply a few months off in his
timing.

Goebbels also made a curious reference to the Fuehrer's
horoscope, which requires explanation. We find it in the
diary being kept by Count Lutz Schwerin von Krosigk,
Hitler's finance minister and a former Rhodes Scholar at
Oxford. Fatuously aware that he was now recording historic events, the count noted in his diary that he had had
a chat at this time with Goebbels about a Hitler lifetime
horoscope drawn up on January 30, 1933, the day Hitler
became chancellor. It had predicted "the outbreak of war
in 1939, amazing victories until 1941, a series of setbacks
in early months of the year 1945, to be followed by an
overwhelming victory in the second half of April 1945 . . ."

The count went on to add that Goebbels had the horoscope broadcast the next day. This was Friday the 13th,
another fine nuance for the superstitious.

Does this mean, as the quite credulous Schwerin von
Krosigk implies, that Goebbels himself believed in any of
this claptrap? Goebbels' mind was much too sharp and
realistic. Moreover, it is highly doubtful that Hitler ever
believed in astrology, either. Stories to the contrary are
usually based on the fact that SHAEF (Supreme Headquarters Allied Expeditionary Force), in London, did indeed employ a full-time British professional astrologer on
its staff. His odd military assignment was to figure out just
what German astrologers might be telling the Fuehrer. In
my researches, I never came across a single witness, including some otherwise fairly credulous souls, who did
not, when asked, scoff at this astrology story.

The real source and custodian of the Hitler horoscope
was Heinrich Himmler, who *did* believe in astrology. It
was he who had ordered the Hitler horoscope cast, and for
years kept it in his own safe. He had recently sent a copy
to Goebbels (most likely, via Schwerin von Krosigk) and
Goebbels was now using it as a convenient propaganda
ploy. The propaganda minister was also aware, of course—
he had heard this from his editors throughout the Reich—
that millions of German newspaper readers, during the
catastrophic last months, had turned to the astrology
columns.

The appearance and actions of Goebbels in this ma-

calm, flaming midnight scene—the telephone call was followed by a champagne party celebrated in his study—helps us locate one of the major actors in the developing bunker scenario. Actor, and at times director. The little doctor was not, as yet, holed up in the Fuehrerbunker, nor would he be for another ten days. As Gauleiter of Berlin, he was always where the action was—now visiting the battle front, now giving bitter-end speeches, still writing his weekly column, still holding daily press conferences.

Hitler, meanwhile, spent the rest of the evening on the telephone to Vienna. The city fell the next day, April 13. Hitler hated Vienna, but as an Austrian and Central European he was acutely aware of its historic, geographic, and symbolic significance. In 1683, the Turks had been thrown back at the gates of Vienna. In all of Eastern Europe, the only capital still in German Army hands was Prague.

*   *

By mid-April, just one day before the Battle for Berlin was to begin, who was present in the bunker? We meet several members of the Hitler court already mentioned, as well as others soon destined to play major roles in the developing action. Johannes Hentschel is at his post in the machine room. Sergeant Misch is at the switchboard, working the shift with one relief man, Corporal Exmann. Some thirty members of the FBK, under Lieutenant Colonel Franz Schaedle, are mounting guard. Major General Rattenhuber, chief of the security squad, is present with at least a dozen of his detectives, all of them in their SS uniforms. The military proper have not yet moved in to take up battle stations. They first file in on Monday, April 23.

The busiest retainer at this moment is pilot Hans Baur. Der Chefpilot has not flown the Fuehrer for long months, not since December 1944.* But he is still in charge of considerable air activity in and around Berlin. He spends about half his working time in the bunker. He is also often out in the city, straw-bossing construction of an emergency airstrip near the Brandenburg Gate, or inspecting the small fleet of planes he still has in the underground hangar at Tempelhof airport.

---

* When he flew Hitler from Rastenburg to Berlin, Hitler then went west, by train, for the Ardennes offensive. Baur went to Bavaria on holiday, returning to Berlin in mid-January.

One of Baur's aides, copilot Colonel Beetz, is already moving about the bunker, compiling a list for the flight called Operation Seraglio. On this list are the names of all those of Hitler's staff who have been chosen to fly to Berchtesgaden as soon as the Fuehrer gives the word. Whether Der Chef will fly with them or not is still a moot question. The list contains the names of half of the permanent personnel present. (This has led some historians to insist that Hitler, at this stage of the game at least, was still considering a possible flight to Berchtesgaden for a last stand in the so-called Alpine Redoubt. In General Eisenhower's headquarters, the chief of staff, General Walter Bedell Smith, was convinced, in fact overconvinced, that Hitler had already fled Berlin or would soon decamp.)

"I think," said Bauer in retrospect, "that this whole flight idea was much more Martin Bormann's than Hitler's. Anyway, it was always Bormann, not Hitler, who kept nagging me about that list, about the condition of my planes, and progress on the emergency airstrip." One notes here, and it is reflected by most other bunker veterans, Baur's sharp hostility, even loathing, of Martin Bormann.

Martin Bormann is not only present; he is omnipresent. Stocky, bullish, drinking heavily when off duty, Bormann is literally at the Fuehrer's elbow, wheeling and dealing madly in what is left of the Nazi power game. In terms of physical proximity, although not of course of power or influence, there is, however, one man who is often to be found even closer to Hitler. This is Major Otto Guensche, the tall rugged soldier of twenty-seven who is the Fuehrer's senior SS adjutant. Guensche is a kind of bunker Man Friday.

There are some dozen women present in the Fuehrerbunker, and more in the Reich Chancellery and the barracks. Fräulein Constanze Manzialy, the mousy forty-year-old Austrian vegetarian cook, is always on duty in or near the upper bunker. Fräulein Else Krueger is secretary to Martin Bormann,* and there are three or four German Army signal corps women, or Blitzmaedel, running messages back and forth from the bunker to the Reich Chancellery.

All four of Hitler's permanent women secretaries are

---

* She has said that she was less the chief secretary than the "Berlin coordinator" of his typing pool. Bormann, the paperwork man, kept *six* secretaries busy.

also still with him. The eldest is Fräulein Johanna Wolf. In her mid-forties, "Wolfie" has been with Hitler since 1924. The second unmarried secretary is Fräulein Christa Schroeder, thirty. The two youngest—and best-looking— are in their mid-twenties, both married. Frau Gerda Christian, once engaged to Erich Kempka, is now married to Luftwaffe Major General Eckard Christian. Frau Gertrud Junge is a recent widow. She married a corporal in Hitler's honor bodyguard, the FBK; he fell in 1944 on the Russian front.

Ambassador Walter Hewel, the liaison officer from the Foreign Office, is an old friend of Hitler's from the 1923 Munich beer hall *Putsch* days. Hewel was with Hitler for a short while in 1924, in Landsberg prison. Kempka, now in charge of the Chancellery garage, is usually in or about the bunker—as are Heinz Linge and some half-dozen other minor charges. Ernst Kaltenbrunner, of Himmler's RSHA, and Heinrich Mueller, chief of the Gestapo, move in and out of the bunker frequently, but they are not stationed there.

Finally, there is SS Lieutenant General Hermann Fegelein, Eva Braun's brother-in-law. Liaison man between Himmler and Hitler, Fegelein usually appears in the bunker at least twice every day at briefing time. But he is spending most of his hours in a bachelor-style flat in the Bleibtreustrasse, just off the once-fashionable Kurfuerstendamm. He is keeping a lady friend there—a naughty liaison that will have some wildly dramatic consequences.

Thus, the men and women known today to historians as the Reich Chancellery Group are pretty much the old familiar court, or rather the remnant of it still with Adolf Hitler in his last bunker. Artur Kannenberg, Hitler's major domo, had already slyly decamped, and a few other old familiars are on duty elsewhere. SS General Sepp Dietrich is commanding troops retreating from Vienna; Lieutenant Colonel Richard Schulze-Kossens, who set up the FBK, was now commandant of the SS officer candidate school in Bad Toelz, south of Munich. With a small company-size battle group called the Nibelungen, he will even attempt to march north in mid-April, but he will never reach Berlin. The Nibelungen were captured by American troops in the Leipzig area.*

---

* He has since become an occasional guest lecturer at West Point.

When interviewing various members of the Reich Chancellery Group, I noted that while they often used this term to describe themselves to me, it was not, in fact, the way they spoke of themselves at the time these bunker events were happening. They then called themselves "*die von dem Berg*" (the mountain people). Those, that is, who had also served Hitler in Berchtesgaden.

This cozy, familiar phrase also accounts, I believe, for the extraordinary amount of otherwise listless bunker hours, day and night, spent in reminiscence. Whenever I was checking out just exactly what this or that witness was doing on a specific day, at a given hour—or, for that matter, what Hitler himself was doing—I invariably ran into evidence of these marathon talk-sessions about the happy, happy days on the Obersalzberg. The mountain people all knew Berchtesgaden well.*

The Reich Chancellery Group in 1945 included two ministers, Speer and Goebbels, though rarely in their official capacities. Speer enters the inner circle as an architect; Goebbels, as prophet and raconteur. The group also includes Bormann, who may not have been a minister but who was as powerful as any. But it did not include von Ribbentrop, the foreign minister; he was represented by his subordinate, Walter Hewell. Neither Goering nor Himmler belonged; they were off running their own courts. Goering's man at the Hitler court until 1944 was Colonel Nikolaus von Below. General Fegelein was Himmler's liaison man. Although we meet them often enough in the bunker, neither Field Marshal Wilhelm Keitel nor Colonel General Alfred Jodl really "belonged to" the Reich Chancellery Group. Present twice every day to conduct briefings, they always leave and go to their own headquarters just outside Berlin. But Generals Hans Krebs and Wilhelm Burgdorf, destined to remain in the bunker until the end, *did* become late members of the group. As did Major General Mohnke, the two doctors, Professor Werner Haase and Colonel Ernst-Guenther Schenck, and Reich Youth leader Artur Axmann.

*   *

---

* One exception was Johannes Hentschel. His permanent duty kept him in Berlin. But even he spent several vacations in Berchtesgaden.

At the time the New Reich Chancellery was built, in 1938, Albert Speer also threw up, in nonornamental, strictly utilitarian style, two large barrackslike structures at right angles to the show-piece Chancellery, on the Hermann Goering Strasse. This helped to close off the whole Chancellery site from the nearby Tiergarten. The architect thus also betrayed his knowledge that Hitler was not only running a court, but that this court was, by now, a far cry from the relatively small, chummy group of personal retainers with whom Adolf Hitler had first entered the Old Reich Chancellery, in 1933. These two military-style *Kasernen* could have housed a regiment. They were the occasional quarters for the military members of the Reich Chancellery Group, Hitler's Praetorian Guard.

Its official military designation was Leibstandarte Adolf Hitler. (Leibstandarte means "lifeguards.") The LAH had begun as an honor guard about the size of a platoon. The recruits were all tall, all young, all volunteers. This guard was first set up in 1934 by Sepp Dietrich. In a very few years, it became part of what was later to be called the Waffen SS, grew to battalion-size before the outbreak of war, and in 1940 was already a motorized panzer regiment. Its home headquarters was in Berlin's large Lichterfelde cadet barracks. (The Reich Chancellery barracks were used only when Hitler was in Berlin.) By 1941 the LAH had become the first of the elite divisions of the Waffen SS. Major General Wilhelm Mohnke, its last commanding general, had begun the war as a captain and company commander. Kampfgruppe (Battle Group) Mohnke was largely composed of LAH veterans. Most were wounded men with front-line experience; this explains their presence, in early April 1945, back at the Lichterfelde barracks. German elite divisions, like the British guards, always maintained a home base, their old peacetime barracks. They rotated personnel *within* units.*

Although the Leibstandarte, like so much in the Third Reich, had vastly outgrown its original function, it still retained its body guard role and its personal link to the Fuehrer. It was the only division that bore his name. From its members were recruited the Fuehrerbegleitkommando,

---

* That is, a wounded soldier, on recuperation, could count on returning to his unit. This is an important morale factor in all elite formations. The LAH trained at Marburg on the Lahn River.

the FBK. This consisted of a detachment of some forty
men, ten officers and thirty enlisted men, most of them
handsome and strapping SS stalwarts, many highly decorated. Hitler used the enlisted men not only for normal
guard duty, but also as orderlies, valets, waiters, couriers.
The officers supervised the mounting of the guard. Often
service tended to rotate, that is, from the FBK to the LAH
at the front, then back again. But when Hitler took a
special, personal interest in one of these young soldiers,
particularly those who had been wounded, the job could
become permanent. The enlisted men, who served him personally, were thus usually much closer to the Fuehrer than
the officers.

The FBK, however, never did have charge of Hitler's
personal security. This was a job for professionals drawn
from Dienststelle I (Post I) of the Reichssicherheitsdienst
(Reich Security Service, or RSD) under SS Major General
Johann Rattenhuber. These were professional police officers
and plainclothes detectives. Friction between the two groups
was, of course, constant. The detectives tended to be "dick"
types, older and more experienced hands, and they regarded the FBK as "parade soldiers and skirt-chasers." This
is perhaps just another way of saying that the younger
FBK men were more successful with the ladies of the
Fuehrer's entourage. An FBK captain, rather than marry
Eva Braun's promiscuous sister Gretl at Hitler's request,
volunteered for the eastern front. A corporal who seduced
one of Hitler's upstairs maids at Berchtesgaden was called
to task by the Fuehrer and told to do right by the girl. "How
the devil can I marry on a corporal's salary?" was his
cheeky defense. Hitler smiled, promoted him to sergeant,
and then told him to name the nuptial day. The sergeant
did. This incident, trivial in itself, gives a whiff of the
tolerant intimacy that prevailed in this group.

Hitler was aware of most, if not all, of the hanky-panky
in the Reich Chancellery Group. He rather encouraged it.
Hitler was part pander, part avuncular father-confessor—
boys will be boys and girls will be girls, as he said. The
bachelor Fuehrer, in his more mellow, less lonely moments,
regarded these personal retainers as part of his family. He
seldom fired anyone, security from gossip about goings-on
in his own shop being one of his pragmatic motives.

Hitler was also a great tease. He spent several years
actively trying to promote a match for his old friend Walter

Hewel, the shy bachelor. Hewel was one of his several candidates for the hand of Gretl Braun, a matter of some urgency when Gretl became pregnant. This problem was solved, to the Fuehrer's relief, by SS Lieutenant General Hermann Fegelein, always a fellow for the main chance. Hitler's special interest in marrying off his mistress's sister was, of course, to make Eva Braun socially acceptable. When, in June 1944, Eva became the sister-in-law of General Fegelein, Hitler could present her at parties and diplomatic receptions—except that the time for parties and diplomatic receptions was, by 1944, fading fast.

In addition to the FBK and the RSD detectives, there was a third mixed bag of uniformed men in the Fuehrer cortège. This was a group that was expanding steadily even before war came: the personal adjutants, aides-de-camp, and a cluster of liaison officers. They were attached either to Hitler personally, or assigned to the Reich Chancellery Group by the armed services and the ministries. They came first under General Stumpff and later under General Burgdorf, Hitler's chiefs of personnel. This, too, is another infallible sign of court government. Not even the ministers, the heads of the armed services, or the major party functionaries really knew what Hitler, the chief of the government, was thinking, saying, or plotting to do next. Thus, all insisted on having at least one set of eyes and ears as close to the center of omnipotence as possible. A sharp liaison man, of course, would keep his ears tuned to the frequency that most concerned his boss. A casual approving or disapproving word or phrase from the Fuehrer could rock a ministry. It also helped the ambitious to keep book on just who was who in the murderous Nazi pecking order.

Once the war began, there came an interesting alien penetration into the Hitler inner circle. Until 1939, it is safe to say that anyone within the Reich Chancellery Group was an ardent National Socialist, although not everyone was a party member. The few who may have been genuinely nonpolitical were, nonetheless, admirers of the Fuehrer. But this was not true of some of the younger military adjutants and field officers who now began to appear. Several of them were aristocrats. Most were decorated front-line officers. Some had admired the earlier Hitler, some not. Suddenly assigned, by chance, to the Fuehrerhauptquartier, they found themselves caught up in the swirling intrigue and sordid selfishness of the whole Hitler crowd. Most were appalled. The von Belows, von Freytag-Loringhovens, von Posers, von Boldts, all came from ancient, usually honorable, German families. Many had brothers and relatives who had already fallen at the front.

These young men from the nobility were shaken by the vulgarity, the banality, of the Hitler court. While there was a rather lofty class-attitude in this, the place was certainly crying out for a bit of class, something more than that supplied by that lonely oil painting of Frederick the Great.

In part, anyway, we owe it to this small elite group that the others have not been able to cover up some of the outrageous conduct of Hitler himself—or that of Goebbels, Bormann, Burgdorf, Keitel, and Fegelein. Listening to several of these adjutants, one is reminded that the Reich Chancellery Group contained many of the selfsame types the Roman satirist Juvenal ticked off in his savage indignation at an earlier court. "Yesterday they were nothing but village ruffians, today they are the arbiters over life and death, and tomorrow they will wind up as keepers of the public lavatories."

*   *

In the years of ascendancy, there was a kind of pattern of court ritual, and every member was well advised to adjust his personal routine to that of Hitler. As we have seen, he invariably arose late, around 10:00 or 11:00 A.M. It was often noon before he first looked into his office, usually a brief visit to chat with the secretaries, glance at the fan mail, peruse the press summaries. By 2:00 P.M. some forty or fifty guests were gathering for luncheon in "The Merry Chancellor's Restaurant." Hitler first greeted them in his reception room, showing up when he pleased. Most were party people or visiting Gauleiters, along with the familiar faces of about a dozen regulars of the Reich Chancellery Group—Baur, Sepp Dietrich, Goebbels occasionally, the senior adjutants, Speer. This sitting seldom broke up before 4:00 P.M., often later. Hitler then might or might not whip back to his office, depending on his interview schedule, or on whether Speer had brought along another rolled-up set of enticing blueprints.

Shortly after 5:00 P.M. came the tea ceremony, sometimes with the secretaries, sometimes with two or three guests. The Fuehrer's work-style was unorganized, lackadaisical. Except during real crises, Hitler had a Bohemian flair for avoiding routine. By constitution, or perhaps by early habit, he had become definitely an *Abendmensch*, a man who first really came alive after the sun went down. German suppers are cold, rather tasteless affairs, and supper in the Reich Chancellery was no great splash. The evening guests tended to be more from the Berlin entertainment milieu than from the political or governmental world. Every night, two movies were shown.

Then, around midnight, when most of the guests had already departed, Hitler would gather around the fireplace, usually with old cronies—Dr. Ley, Dr. Morell, Hewel, Baur, sometimes Goebbels. These were, invariably, reminiscence sessions, less about the topics of the day than about the exhilaration of the early days of struggle in the 1920s. Except when Goebbels came, these fireside sessions tended to be monologues. But Goebbels, and sometimes Hewel, had the raconteur's knack of relaxing the Fuehrer, getting him to listen. Goebbels could always be counted on to come up with the latest gossip, a tidbit of Berlin scandal, now and then a good political joke—against Goering, for example. Except in the deep of winter, dawn comes early to Berlin, announced by a shrill, chattering chorus of black thrushes. This serenade was long over before Hitler, reluctantly, said good night to the last lingering, weary guest, around four or five in the morning.

It was a highly idiosyncratic style of government. Such satraps as Hermann Goering, Heinrich Himmler, Joachim von Ribbentrop were notably absent. They were all off running their own satellite courts, as was Goebbels in his own way. Hitler was able to parcel out vast domains of power precisely because he had no real rivals as Fuehrer. The rivalry, and it was intense among the paladins, was *always* for the Number Two, or crown prince, slot. Hitler encouraged this rivalry. The whole preposterous wrangle over the succession reached its dizzy climax in the last days in the Berlin bunker. It was won, if won is the word, by Martin Bormann and Joseph Goebbels at the expense of Goering and Himmler.

Hitler had, without doubt, a fair amount of executive ability. He reserved all the big decisions for himself, often retiring to Berchtesgaden to brood before making one. But

he certainly was no organization man. It was not until the
arrival of Bormann, in 1938, that the amorphous Reich
Chancellery Group was whipped into shape. Bormann was
the bureaucrat personified, with a yen for administrative
paperwork, and he gave scrupulous attention to detail. His
very appointment as Hitler's private secretary was a court
maneuver. Bormann for years had been secretary to the
rather hapless Rudolf Hess, whose title, Secretary and
Deputy to the Fuehrer, was imposing but hollow. By 1938,
Hess, a real oddball, realized he had fallen from grace in
the Hitler court. He sent Bormann to the Fuehrer to repre-
sent his interests.

If Adolf Hitler is a unique phenomenon in the long
pages of history, the Bormann type is a hardy perennial.
When Edmund Burke remarked that "ambition can creep
as well as crawl," he was thinking of Robespierre, but he
could have been describing Martin Bormann, out of the
womb of time. Bormann's ambition was of the silent,
smarmy, self-effacing kind. He had, however, a real gut
instinct for the realities as distinct from the trappings of
power. More intelligent than Himmler, more hard-working
than Goering, more stolid than the too-clever Goebbels,
Bormann also was well aware that he had all the necessary
humdrum qualities the Fuehrer himself so conspicuously
lacked. Hitler loathed anything with the inartistic odor of
routine—administration, paperwork, filing, programming
—the whole smell of castor oil on the ballbearings of
bureaucracy. Hitler did not even enjoy firing anyone. Once
a cook at Berchtesgaden fiddled the marketing accounts;
Hitler gave her her walking papers, but with reluctance.
Until the arrival of Bormann, the Reich Chancellery Group
was anything but a disciplined outfit. Anybody could go
directly to Der Chef and, if he caught him in a soft mood,
get pretty much what he wanted—a raise, a vacation, an
autograph for the kiddies. To this inner circle, Hitler was
no ogre.

Martin Bormann, the take-charge man, changed all that.
He was universally hated and feared by almost all in the
Reich Chancellery Group, including his own brother Alfred,
who was one of Hitler's personal adjutants.* By placing
his own desk in the anteroom to Hitler's office, Bormann

---

* Alfred Bormann finally left the bunker on April 22. He is today a
businessman in Munich, and was one of the few who refused to talk with
me.

could control access to the Fuehrer. Except for three or four ministers and the high military, no one could now report to the Fuehrer directly. Bormann also processed all nonmilitary papers before they crossed the Fuehrer's desk.

Finally, by his custody of the Fund of the Friends of the Fuehrer, which he had set up for the purpose of gouging industrialists, Bormann had access to a vast slush fund, which he used for boondoggles and for bribing Gauleiters. This fund also financed the building of the bunker. All this increased mightily his personal power. As Hitler, from 1939 on, began to concentrate almost exclusively on military affairs, Bormann was building his own power base within the party.

One otherwise trivial incident told by old FBK members shows what, as the war progressed, had happened to the once rather comradely spirit of the mountain people. One of Hitler's oldest and most faithful retainers was Bruno Gesche, a roistering, pistol-packing type who had been with Hitler since the Munich storm-trooping days. Gesche rose slowly in the SS and the Leibstandarte until, by 1942, he had become the commanding officer of the FBK, with the rank of Obersturmbannfuehrer (lieutenant colonel).

At a wild Christmas party in 1944, in the officers' mess at Felsennest—it was during the Battle of the Ardennes—Gesche got roaring drunk, apparently at the bad news coming in from Bastogne. A deadeye marksman, around midnight he whipped out his P–38 Parabellum pistol and shot out all the mess-hall light bulbs. Bormann insisted that Gesche stand before a court-martial. Hitler refused to intervene. Gesche was broken to the rank of corporal and exiled to the Italian front. The old hand said goodbye to the Fuehrer like Falstaff taking leave of Prince Hal. Bruno Gesche had heard the chimes at midnight once too often.*

There was, however, one person in the court who made no bones about her loathing for Bormann. This was Eva Braun. The rest of the Reich Chancellery Group often counted on her to get their message through to Number One. She told Hitler about Bormann's sycophancy in pretending, in the Fuehrer's presence, to be a nondrinker, a nonsmoker, even a vegetarian, while keeping a whole salami hanging from the back of his cot. "And besides,"

---

* Today, Gesche is alive and living in Hanover. His successor, SS Obersturmbahnfuehrer Franz Schaedle, committed suicide in the bunker.

as Eva put it, "the girls all tell me he is an oversexed toad."
Whether Bormann ever took a pass at Eva Braun is doubtful. He did at just about every other female in the entourage. For Eva Braun, in a cloistered lifetime loaded with
humiliations, not the least embarrassing moment was when
she had to go to Martin Bormann to beg for pin money.
From 1943 on, Bormann's takeover operations included
his handling of the Fuehrer's personal finances.

Little Eva was no du Barry, no Pompadour, not even a
Lola Montez. Perhaps for this very reason she fitted rather
snugly into screamingly petit-bourgeois atmosphere of the
Hitler court. Hitler fondly called her "Tschapperl," a Bavarian dialect word for "honey bun" and a trifle belittling.
When Goebbels once penned a pompously long article
stressing that Adolf Hitler, the Fuehrer of all the Germans,
had "no private life," Eva came up perkily with a great
anti-Goebbels line: "Just call me Fräulein No-Private-Life."

There is perhaps no better definition of the loose Reich
Chancellery Group, a most banal elite, than Erich Kempka's: "those of us who were really in the know about Eva
Braun." The number, all told, of those who were privy to
this rather harmless, yet best-kept, secret of the Third
Reich must have been at least 200, and probably closer to
300. Whole books have been written about Hitler's alleg-
edly bizarre sex life. These books usually throw more light
on their authors than on the humdrum private life of Adolf
Hitler. All courtiers testify that his relationship to his
mistress was normal, almost respectable. The affair was
about as exciting as the mating of fireflies in a wet summer.

The Berlin weekend that began on Friday, April 13, was
still one of anxious anticipation—manic hope, depressive
fear—just before the battle. This was the day of that
obscene champagne party in the small hours at which
Goebbels and company celebrated the death of President
Roosevelt. On Saturday, in the Reich Chancellery, Colonel
Stumpfegger's medical corpsmen could be seen setting up
the emergency field hospital they had just transported in
from Hohenlychen.

Sunday, April 15, also brought a new VIP arrival as
resident in the lower bunker—Eva Braun. Eva had been
in Berlin since mid-March, living in her private apartment
in the Reich Chancellery, which was, miraculously, still
undamaged. Now several people saw her supervising

soldier-valets as they trundled her bed and dresser down from the apartment into the lower bunker.

Gerda Christian described the scene. "Her arrival was greeted in silence. We all knew what it meant. The day before, Saturday, I had gone walking with E.B. Two or three other girls were with us. We talked about taking pistol practice. None of us talked about what was on every woman's mind, sometimes called the fate worse than death. We talked around it. We were still wondering whether the Fuehrer would leave for Berchtesgaden. I was now convinced Der Chef would never fly off to the Obersalzberg. Berchtesgaden, in the person of Eva Braun, had come to Berlin."

An SS enlisted man in the canteen put it more bluntly. "*Der Todesengel* has arrived."

Todesengel. The angel of death.

Albert Speer, in those early April days, kept up his shuttle-visits from the front to the bunker and back. With the front moving closer and closer, this was easier to do. He could be in Hamburg at noontime, and back for the bunker séance at midnight.

With General Guderian gone, General Hans Krebs took over as briefing officer. Krebs, the last Chief of the General Staff, was a fairly decent man and no fool. Yet night after night, Speer listened in utter astonishment as he moved German armies, corps, and divisions that simply no longer existed. He was playing phantom wargames on the Fuehrer's bunker briefing map. And every night the Fuehrer, as of old, would give orders for this or that division not to yield an inch, or for this or that city to be defended to the bitter end. But Frankfurt fell, and Kassel, Hanover, and Brunswick. The next night there would be no mention of these cities, just quiet, often belated "situation adjustments" on the war map. Hitler was now deploying ghost divisions around Potsdam with the same imperial arrogance with which he had once moved real divisions through France or along the Volga and the Black Sea.

In the second week of April, Hitler summoned Field Marshal Kesselring, still Commander-in-Chief West, to the bunker. The field marshal's headquarters had long since moved from Adlerhorst, and was now somewhere in the Thuringian Forest. One day Speer overheard the Fuehrer trying to sell Kesselring on a counterattack. American armor had just taken Eisenach. Hitler wanted to "throw in several hundred tanks" to blunt the spearhead, a second Ardennes offensive. Kesselring at first demurred, but in a few minutes was nodding in agreement. Speer was flabbergasted.

> I knew he no longer had hundreds of tanks, or ever a hundred, or even fifty. In fact, in the Eisenach area, we probably had hardly more than two or three tank companies, and these very short on gas.
>
> But, as I thought it over, I was not perplexed for very long. I knew that neither Krebs nor Kesselring was a dunderhead. Nor were they nodding military-lackey types, like Field Marshal Keitel. They were playing these ridiculous wargames just to keep the Fuehrer occupied and distracted. Every day gained was a day closer to the end, and the end had to come any day.

One morning that week—it must have been on or about April 18—Baur was shaving in his heatless, windowless, unfurnished emergency flat. He heard a loud explosion nearby, somewhere in the already ravaged trees of the Tiergarten. At first he took it for a delayed-action bomb—he had heard no planes in the air—or possibly a parachuted land mine, dropped by a British Mosquito. The sound was new to the pilot, yet somehow familiar. A second followed, and now Baur recognized it for what it was—Russian field artillery, the 17.5 centimeter gun. When, around noon, he nervously reported this news to the Fuehrer, Hitler was instantly convinced that the Soviets must have had a railroad gun on or near the Oder. They were, in fact, a good deal closer.

Hitler's haunted imagination was harking back to World War I days, when the German "Big Bertha" hammered Paris from more than seventy miles away. He also was beginning to express his morbid fear that these Russian shells, when they were aimed directly at the Reich Chancellery, might deliver poison gas. This obsession came naturally to Hitler. In the closing weeks of World War I, he himself had been gassed on the Somme and temporarily blinded. In fact, on November 11, 1918, Lance Corporal Hitler was a patient in the military hospital of Pasewalk, a small Pomeranian garrison town about 140 miles northeast of Berlin, near the estuary of the Oder. At this very moment Pasewalk had already been overrun by the Russians. That did not escape Hitler's notice.*

Friday, April 20, brought a strange interlude. It was the Fuehrer's birthday, since 1933 a national holiday. It was celebrated, as in former years, in the New Reich Chancellery. Speer, who was now living at Bad Wilsnack, about 100 miles northwest of Berlin, drove to Berlin for what he believed would be the last time. This was also the last appearance of such other major figures as Hermann Goering and Heinrich Himmler. Most ministries had already been evacuated, and their moving vans were clogging the arterial roads. Luftwaffe Colonel von Below told Speer by phone that most of the court, sparked by Martin Bormann, was still trying desperately to convince Hitler that he must leave for Berchtesgaden. Hitler had, to this point, kept this option open; but he had agreed to send half of his staff there, just in case. They would fly out sometime on Monday. Von Below himself now told Speer he believed "Hitler will never leave the capital."

It was at this time that Speer learned that his friend Dr. Karl Brandt, Hitler's personal physician since 1936, was in peril. He, too, had been caught up in the murderous net of court intrigue.** Brandt had quietly allowed his family in Thuringia to be "overrun" by American troops. Hitler, when he heard this, ordered Brandt court-martialed, and himself presided over the handing down of a death sentence. Hitler's blood lust, as he now lashed out in every direction, jeopardized Speer, too. The Third Reich was ending as it had begun—in terror.

Speer spent Sunday, April 22, at Bad Wilsnack. For the first time in his life, he had begun to train himself with a

---

* Poison gas was one of the few instruments of total war not employed in World War II. Mutual terror, the two scorpions in the bottle, had kept this threat in its canisters and shells. Hitler was not the only wartime leader who dreaded that gas might yet be released in the final stages of the war. The Germans, in addition to such deadly new nerve gases as Tabun, had also developed one that was not lethal. It merely made victims unconscious for twenty-four hours. German Intelligence believed that the Soviets had a similar gas—though in fact they did not. This was the "secret weapon" Hitler feared most, one that would render him unconscious so that he could be taken alive "like a stunned animal in the zoo."

** Brandt was the victim of a double intrigue, medical and political. He had begun to complain about the pills and shots being administered to his patient by his rival, Dr. Theodor Morell. He was also a close friend of Speer and the Speer family. Bormann, therefore, sided with Morell and helped undermine Brandt's standing with Hitler. Morell had the advantage of being present in the bunker (until April 22), whereas Brandt was not.

pistol, shooting at targets on the lake. Geographically, he was a good deal closer to the British and American troops, now bivouacked on the west bank of the Elbe, than to the Fuehrerbunker. Late that afternoon, he received a guarded telephone call from Colonel von Below. All hell had broken loose in the bunker—"The Fuehrer has had a nervous crackup."

CHAPTER V

•

Farewells

It is tragic to see the Fuehrer cutting himself off
from life and leading such an unhealthful daily
routine. Seldom does he breathe any fresh air; he
never finds relaxation. He sits there in his bunker
fiddling about, mumbling and grumbling. If one
could only get him to try some other environment.
But he has convinced himself that he must direct
the war in his own peculiar, Spartan manner, and,
as far as I can see, there is no changing the man.
—JOSEPH GOEBBELS, to his
press aide Rudolf Semler,
March 1943.

THE PROPHET was not wrong, and he knew his man. All
through the war, Goebbels had been trying to get Hitler
back to Berlin, away from the remote bunkers. Now, on
Sunday, April 22, 1945, he himself finally moved into the
Berlin bunker, with his wife, Magda, and their six children.
The most loyal of the retainers was now moving close to
his Fuehrer with all he had left in the world.

To bunker veterans, the sudden arrival of the whole
Goebbels clan could have only one meaning. Like the
arrival of Eva Braun just a week before, it meant that the
end was near. Even insane optimists knew it must be but
a matter of days.

In the week just passed, the Red Army had swept from
the Oder to the outskirts of the city. On this day, it had
entered the boroughs of Koepenick and Spandau. Some
advance tank elements were reported *west* of Berlin. The

"Hitler had long been accusing the German Army of betrayal; the SS was no longer immune from the charge."

city was closed on three sides; only one road to the south and one to the west were still open. On the Elbe, neither the British nor the Americans had budged. So ended another forlorn hope. The day before, Hitler had ordered a counterattack by SS General Steiner's Panzer Corps just northwest of Berlin. This battered force had fewer than 11,000 men and less than fifty tanks, at least half of which had run out of gas. Steiner could not possibly attack; even his last chance to retreat was rapidly vanishing.*

But to the embattled Hitler, now mesmerized by his own maps, a panzer corps, above all an SS panzer corps, still must have three elite divisions. But as reports reached the bunker of Steiner's utter inability to attack—a whole Red Army group was moving in on him—the Fuehrer's anger mounted. He had long been accusing the traditional German Army of betrayal; since the fall of Budapest, the SS was no longer immune from the charge. By the midday conference on the 22nd, Hitler had lost all control. He blurted out, "The war is lost!"

This was not only his first open admission of the obvious. It was also the signal for his first serious crackup. Even when he had exploded at Guderian, Hitler had managed to keep relatively cool. Now he turned chalk white, then blue in the face. He was silent for long minutes. Flopping back into his chair, trembling, he ordered the startled conference room cleared of all save his four senior generals (Keitel, Jodl, Krebs, Burgdorf) and Martin Bormann.

The whole flock of adjutants and aides retreated in a hushed flutter. This main conference room was split down the middle by a thin plywood partition, and most tried to eavesdrop from the other side. Some felt sure that Hitler had had a stroke or a heart attack; others, that he was simply suffering from exhaustion. All were convinced that this time the man was definitely not play-acting. As the

---

* All Steiner had were remnants of the 7th Panzer Division and the 25th Panzer Grenadier Division, plus a few Luftwaffe ground troops.

senior generals stumbled out, a half hour later, the adjutants button-holed them and managed to piece together a garbled story of what had happened. Then they rushed to their telephones.

The gist of what Hitler had said, before dismissing his generals, was this: the war was lost; he would give up the supreme command, sending both Keitel and Jodl to direct resistance in the south; he would remain to conduct the Battle for Berlin; he would not surrender, could not physically fight, and hence he would commit suicide; anybody who now wanted to leave the bunker could do so; all the women would be flown to Berchtesgaden. He asked everybody to clear the room and leave him alone.

Twenty minutes later, Hitler emerged and asked Major Otto Guensche to fetch his senior adjutant, SS Major General Julius Schaub. It was Schaub who had the matching key to the safe in Hitler's study. Together, they began sorting out Hitler's private papers. A few he kept and entrusted to Schaub.* The rest, Schaub, with two valets, began lugging up the steps of the emergency exit into the Chancellery garden, where they were burned in an incinerator. When Schaub returned, he found Hitler fondling his large Walther pistol. This, too, had now been removed from the safe. It was later placed on the dresser in his bedroom. Schaub retreated, feeling this might be the moment. But soon Eva Braun appeared, stayed for ten minutes, and left. Hitler—it was now almost 5:00 P.M.—put in a call to Goebbels.

It was the familiar baritone voice of his old friend that seemed to calm Hitler completely. Either Hitler had abandoned all idea of immediate suicide, or Goebbels talked him out of it, probably both. Instead, Hitler gave his propaganda minister the order Goebbels had long been waiting for, even pleading for. He was to announce over the Berlin radio that "the Fuehrer is in Berlin and will die fighting with his troops defending the capital city." This was the first news Berliners had had that Hitler was in their midst.

Like other Germans, Berliners had last heard Hitler's voice on January 30, 1945. It was his final radio address. He did not say where he was. The Goebbels broadcast of April 22 went out within half an hour of the Fuehrer's

---

* Schaub flew alone on a special flight to Berchtesgaden twenty-nine hours later.

request. It clinched his triumph over Hitler's battery of
bunker advisers. All (except Speer) had been advocating
decamping to Berchtesgaden. At last Goebbels was ready
to go underground.

In the bunker it was now tea time, in Hitler's life a
ritual hour. Fed up with the men around him, above all
the generals, he tried to find as much time as possible for
the women in his entourage. This Sunday afternoon he was
joined by the two younger secretaries on duty, Gerda
Christian and Gertrud Junge, and by Eva Braun. At first
he repeated his order that all three were to fly away—
"Girls, the situation is hopeless." But he was not unhappy
when the trio pleaded to stay. According to Gerda Christian, he said, like a pasha, "Ah, if only my generals were
as brave as my women." Then he stood up and kissed Eva
Braun on the lips. "It was the first and only time we
ever saw him do that," Christian remembers. "E.B. was
radiant. Hitler's eyes were moist and weepy." The silent
soldier-valet Corporal Schwiebel poured tea. Hitler passed
the crumpets and chocolate éclairs. There was no more
talk of suicide.

Goebbels, meanwhile, had been busy putting out the
broadcast. He spent all afternoon in his residence near the
Brandenburg Gate, for his office was now in his residence.
At five-thirty, the minister called his staff together and dismissed them abruptly, telling them they would have to join
in the coming battle or fend for themselves. His aides had
already helped him burn his own papers; one had been
busy for days microfilming his diaries.

Two Mercedes limousines, one Goebbels' official bullet-
proof model,* had been standing for the last hour before
the entrance. He packed his wife and their children into the
unarmored limousine and stepped into his special vehicle.
He rode alone beside his chauffeur, Rach. Several Berlin
passersby saw the departure. The two cars headed toward
the Chancellery; they moved slowly, like a funeral cortège.

Yet there was something precipitate in all this, in
Goebbels' last actions aboveground. He was saying goodbye to Berlin. He had certainly expected and welcomed
the Fuehrer's invitation. They had talked this over before,
as part of the dramaturgy of the end. But not even toilet

---

* Hitler had presented it to Goebbels after an assassination attempt in
Berlin in 1941.

articles had been packed for the children. Each was clutching a single toy. Magda Goebbels had but a small valise and one extra dress; Goebbels, two pearl white shirts. This seems evidence that Goebbels had some reason to expect the Russian breakthrough to come much more quickly than it actually did. By persuading Hitler to postpone his suicide, Goebbels had extended the bunker melodrama by eight days.

The arrival of the Goebbels family on this hectic Sunday coincided with a mass departure just about to begin. Hans Baur was waiting for nightfall to launch Operation Seraglio, the mass escape to Berchtesgaden. Goebbels himself moved into the lower-bunker room just deserted by Dr. Morell, one of those scheduled to leave. Magda was assigned a separate room in the upper bunker, with three small rooms for the children. The corridors were crowded with some forty members of the Reich Chancellery Group and their luggage. Departures began at sundown and lasted until midnight. Hitler spent much of this time seeing them off: it was clear to everyone that they would never meet again. This party included Johanna Wolf and Christa Schroeder, his naval aide, Admiral Karl-Jesko von Puttkamer, his adjutant Albrecht, and Martin Bormann's brother Albert.

It was Baur's job, not that of the Luftwaffe, to get this Gypsy-like show airborne. He had a gaggle of ten transport planes available, some of which he had already shifted from Tempelhof to Gatow airport. They were loaded with files, personal possessions, and other valuables. Between the hours of 9:00 P.M. and midnight, nine of the ten planes successfully got off for Munich. The tenth plane, piloted by the veteran Major Friedrich Gundlfinger, was somehow jinxed. Engine trouble delayed it an hour in Berlin. This delay was critical, for the morning air in South Germany would be swarming with U.S. Air Force fighters. At dawn, when this last plane was reported more than an hour overdue, Baur began to worry. All the other planes had landed on schedule, although at least one of them had run into German flak over Nuremberg.*

Baur got a few hours' sleep, but when he awoke on the

---

* Baur hotly disputed this later, but I got it from two of the passengers (Frau Hentschel and Fräulein Schroeder). He denied it, I believe, because he had taken a somewhat foolhardy risk in dispatching these planes unannounced.

morning of April 23, there was still no word of the missing
plane. Baur told Hitler, and the Fuehrer broke down in
tears. "It would have to have been *that* plane, with Sergeant
Arndt aboard, and all the footlockers." Arndt was the
youngest and one of the newest members of the Reich
Chancellery Group, and had become a favorite of Hitler's.
A twenty-year-old wounded veteran, Arndt had taken over
some of Rochus Misch's routine valet duties when Misch,
in the last weeks, began working regularly at the bunker
switchboard. Baur hastened to assure Hitler, who feared
the worst, that Major Gundlfinger was an experienced pilot.
Baur felt that there had probably been a recurrence of the
original engine trouble and that the major had made a
forced landing.

The possible death of Arndt was not the only reason
why Hitler reacted to the news with such dismay. Aboard
the lost plane were ten large footlockers full of all the
shorthand stenographic originals of his "Table Talks" for
the years 1943–1945. They must have added up to two or
three million words, for the footlockers, Misch estimated,
weighed at least half a ton.

I was aware that a few months of the "Table Talks" of
1942 and a short period of February 1945 had been discovered and published several years after the war. The bulk
was thus missing. The usual explanation is that Bormann,
who had charge of this operation, had ceased, after 1942,
to bring in the male secretaries and hide them behind the
arras while Hitler was spieling off his metapolitical musings.
This explanation had always sounded a bit thin. Most
bunker veterans say several male secretaries were present
in the headquarters throughout 1943 and 1944.* Moreover,
why should Bormann have suddenly revived the old practice in February 1945? He did not, of course, and the fate
of the missing documents became linked with that of the
plane.

For the occupants of the bunker, there would be no
further word about the mysterious disappearance of the
tenth plane. But it had, indeed, crashed in Bavaria; all
aboard had been killed instantly and their bodies burned.
The remains were buried in a nearby cemetery. All docu-

---

* One of them, Berger, was killed on July 20, 1944, in Rastenburg by
Colonel Stauffenberg's bomb.

ments aboard were apparently burned, too. The search work was done by the Luftwaffe Graves Registration organization some years after the war. Several country people remembered the noise of the crash. But there was no one who claimed to have been an eyewitness of the critical time just *before* the crash; the cause will never be known.

For those readers who like detective stories, that is not the only question that remains unsolved. As all police reporters know, documents have a way of surviving crashes in which humans are cremated. While even metal melts, a book or a notebook does not burn easily, above all when it is packed tightly into a container excluding oxygen. Paper in bulk tends, rather, to char at the edges. In the case of Hitler's "Table Talks," whether some notebooks were reduced to ashes, and others not, many have depended on the packing.

So one is left with the nagging thought that some Bavarian hayloft, chicken coop, or even pigsty may well have been waterproofed and insulated with millions of words of the Fuehrer's unpublished, almost ineffable utterances, simply hauled away at dawn as loot from a burning German transport plane.

*　　　*

The departure of so many familiar faces changed the mood of the bunker, from a hectic one to a new stillness after midnight. Captain Helmut Beermann of the FBK explained how this affected his duties.

We veterans of the bunker called this day Blue Monday because, with the departure of half of our comrades and the arrival of the whole Goebbels family and Eva Braun, everyone could now read the handwriting on the wall. The last act was about to begin. My own dream of again seeing Berchtesgaden vanished. Colonel Schaedle, my commanding officer, insisted I stay, since I was by now an old hand in the FBK. Previously, I had enough officers and men to be able to work out shifts, twelve hours on, twelve off. Now, every hand was assigned to his task for the duration, which might be for two days or for two weeks. I issued sleeping bags, so that some of my key men could sleep at or near their stations. The old spit-and-polish discipline was all shot to hell. Many soldiers were not even saluting anymore.

One of the few civilians present, Johannes Hentschel in the machine room, also remembered this Monday with mixed emotions.

> On the one hand, this was a happy day for me. I had managed to get my wife aboard one of those shuttle planes to Bavaria. You didn't have to believe everything Goebbels said to know that rape was probably on the program when Berlin fell. My wife, Gretl, was terrified, and so was I. For me as a husband that was one big worry off my mind, half the battle.
>
> Now I had to worry only about myself. The safest place still seemed to be the bunker. So, I lugged my personal effects from my garden house down into the machine room. On the other hand, one of the FBK sergeants who had been relieving me had also left, so now I was on my own, with no relief. No one else was familiar enough with the complicated technical controls.

Back on the Elbe River, Albert Speer made his snap decision to head east again to Berlin. That afternoon he had heard from von Below of Hitler's breakdown. He had also been told of the arrival of Goebbels and of the departures of Field Marshal Keitel and General Jodl. The last stand had begun.

At dawn, with Colonel Manfred von Poser beside him, Speer set out to drive from Bad Wilsnack to Berlin. This trip normally would have taken less than two hours. Now, with the main highways north and west out of the capital clogged by fleeing vehicles, it took the pair more than ten hours to cover under 100 miles. Around noon, forced to abandon hope of reaching their goal by land, they headed for the Luftwaffe base at Rechlin.

En route from a German division headquarters in Kyritz, Speer was able to get through a telephone call to Berlin. He was still anxious about the fate of his friend Dr. Karl Brandt. Speer's last information had been that Brandt was being held in house arrest in Dahlem, a Berlin suburb. But he now heard, to his relief, that Dr. Brandt had been moved out of Berlin to North Germany—on Himmler's orders. This meant comparative safety, since it was Bormann, not Himmler, who had been intriguing against Brandt and demanding his head. Speer had reason to believe that the intrigue was directed at least as much against him as against Brandt. It was.

Speer made a second telephone call to another old friend, Dr. Lueschen. He was trying to persuade the elderly industrialist to leave Berlin while there was still time. Of the 6000 Jews and half-Jews still living in Berlin, Dr. Lueschen had concealed several hundred in his AEG plant by classifying them as "essential war workers."* Goebbels had got wind of this and was demanding that they be "winkled out." The call got through, and Speer asked Dr. Lueschen to come to the Reich Chancellery that evening.

For Speer, there were other personal reasons for his sudden return. "The driving motive," he admitted, "was to say goodbye to Adolf Hitler. I had left his birthday party, only three days before, like most of the other ministers, without even shaking hands, without a formal goodbye. We all just faded away. It nagged my conscience, and I wanted to make amends."

At Rechlin, while waiting to be flown with fighter escort to Gatow airport on the western rim of the city, Speer and von Poser encountered Major General Eckard Christian, the senior Luftwaffe liaison man in the FHQ. The general had left the bunker shortly before noontime. He was now waiting to take off for Berchtesgaden to join his chief, Hermann Goering.** General Christian filled Speer in on the exodus of the military high rank from the bunker. Admiral Doenitz, he said, had headed north to Schleswig-Holstein on Friday. Field Marshal Keitel and General Jodl had both checked out of the bunker that morning. Keitel had a headquarters near Potsdam-Eiche, but had gone instead to the Twelfth Army headquarters of General Wenck, near the city of Brandenburg. General Jodl had gone just twenty miles south of Berlin to his OKW headquarters in Zossen. These two old familiars never saw Hitler again. Nor did they get to fly south to Berchtesgaden, as Hitler had ordered. The Fuehrer had created a Northern Command under Admiral Doenitz. He wanted the Southern Command to be under Jodl and Keitel, *not* under Hermann

---

* Two years before, in Berlin in 1943, Albert Speer's old acquaintance Karl Hanke, later Gauleiter of Breslau, began to talk out of school. Hanke had warned Speer to stay away from a Polish town called Oswiecim (in German, Auschwitz). There was something going on there, he hinted, far worse than the usual tales of atrocities coming from the east. Speer had taken Hanke's advice.

** Goering had left the vicinity of Berlin two days before from his estate, Karin Hall, which he had dynamited. Placing his hefty foot on the plunger, Goering was overheard to remark, "Well, it's the kind of thing a man has to do—once in a lifetime."

Goering—even though the Reichsmarschall was already on location in the south.

There is a bit of bunker gossip connected with the departure of General Christian, the former ace who was also the husband of Hitler's best-looking secretary, Gerda Christian, née Daranowsky. He had won "Die Daran's" hand back in 1943 over an earlier rival, Erich Kempka. This was the reason that he was still assigned to the Fuehrer's headquarters. Now the husband was leaving, though he knew his wife had opted to stay with Hitler. True, Hitler had told Christian that he could leave to join Goering, but it was apparently the kind of permission he hoped would be rejected. At this point, however, survival apparently meant more to Christian than his wife. Her comment was, "Well, he went his way and I went mine. But that ended our marriage. I couldn't forgive that kind of desertion. I'm glad I survived, just to be able to divorce the lout."

After their chat with General Christian, Speer and von Poser were flown from Rechlin to Gatow. The fighter planes that had escorted them then peeled off to attack the Russian tanks already on the outskirts of Potsdam. At this time, the highway from Gatow to downtown Berlin was still open; Speer and his aide could easily have driven to the bunker. Instead, sparked by the curious spirit of adventure that had inspired this whole junket, the pair gladly accepted lifts in two Fieseler Stork planes that the Luftwaffe placed at their disposal. Ten minutes later, these small artillery-observation craft landed both men at the Brandenburg Gate. They hailed a passing army vehicle and asked the surprised driver to take them to the Reich Chancellery. Even flight inside the city had become dangerous. The Russians were aware of the flight pattern and had mounted antiaircraft batteries parallel to it. Speer asked the two pilots to stand by. They were to spend the next twelve hours playing Skat, a kind of German pinochle, with Hans Baur's Luftwaffe ground crew at the gate.

As he entered the Reich Chancellery, Speer saw that it was being hit here and there by long-range Red Army artillery, but was not much damaged. The earlier bomb damage had been far more extensive. Speer clambered over a hurdle of burned beams as he headed for the adjutant's office to announce himself. Here he stumbled into the middle of a drinking party.

Everywhere, he saw signs of relaxing discipline. In these

elegant rooms once inhabited by Bismarck, where Speer himself had spent many evening hours with Hitler in the early years of his chancellorship, disarray now reigned. Beer and wine bottles, messkits, stale sandwiches, Wehrmacht musette bags littered the marble floor. Retainers whose faces he did not recognize came in and out. Three or four minor charges and Nazi Party members were sleeping it off in armchairs. The whole Chancellery atmosphere had suddenly changed over the weekend.

Speer was happy to see the florid, smiling features of one of Hitler's senior adjutants, Schaub. As he well knew, one could always read the Fuehrer's mood on Schaub's moonlike face. He had been an adjutant as long as Speer had known him, since 1933, and was a hard-drinking, rowdy member of the Chauffeureska. Although Speer had made a point of telephoning ahead, it was obvious that Schaub was surprised at his turning up. Schaub left, returning five minutes later to say the Fuehrer was ready to receive Speer.

Speer went alone through the upper bunker and down the spiral iron staircase to the lower chambers. He was half wondering whether ascent would be as easy. At the bottom of the staircase he met another, far more important courtier, Martin Bormann. Bormann, too, was all smiles. In fact, he was oozing cordiality and bonhomie. Nor did it take Speer long to discover why. "Speer," Bormann said, "when you talk with the Fuehrer, he is certainly bound to raise the question of whether we should stay here in the bunker or leave for the Obersalzberg. It is my feeling that it is high time he now took charge of things in South Germany. These are the last hours in which such a necessary move is still possible . . . Please use all your powers of persuasion to induce the Fuehrer to fly out and away."

This was a moment of minor personal triumph for Speer over a man he had always feared and hated. He had no intention whatever of telling Hitler this. Bormann probably realized his plea was fruitless. Speer rather enjoyed having the born bully at long last reduced to wheedling.*

---

* From a historical point of view, this Speer evidence, in substance the same as that which he gave in his 1945 interrogations, should have ended all speculation that Bormann, in the last days in the bunker, might have been scheming to defect to the Soviets. If that had been the man's game, Berchtesgaden was just about the worst conceivable goal, logically or geographically. It was about to fall not to the Red Army, but to the U.S. Seventh Army.

Speer entered Hitler's study. There was no warm greeting, no handshake, nor was he even asked to take a chair. This last meeting between Adolf Hitler and Albert Speer, in marked contrast to their previous long discussion on the eve of Speer's birthday, was neither emotional nor particularly cordial. Hitler did not seem to be impressed or flattered that his old friend had returned. Speer was at first relieved. He knew, at least, that his life was not in danger. Yet he was also more than a bit crestfallen. The hazardous, foolhardy trip had really counted for nothing in Hitler's book.

Speer, still standing, studied Hitler's face and demeanor. He seemed strangely empty, burned out, more shadow than substance. This last time they talked little about architecture, except when Hitler pulled out the blueprint plan for Greater Linz.*

The first businesslike question Hitler asked of Speer was his opinion about the leadership qualities of Grand Admiral Doenitz. From this, Speer deduced correctly that Hitler was at long last about to name his only successor. Speer spoke well of the admiral, but was careful not to lay praise on too thick. From long experience with Hitler's suspicions and whims, he knew that overpraise could have an effect opposite that intended. Later, in Spandau prison, salty old Doenitz was to spend ten years belaboring Speer for having "fingered" him on this occasion. "You, Speer, got me into all my trouble."

Soon Hitler abruptly changed the subject. "What's your opinion, Speer? Should I stay here in Berlin or fly to Berchtesgaden? General Jodl has told me I now have, at the most, twenty-four hours to make my final decision."

"My Fuehrer, it seems to me much more advisable, if it must be, that you end your life here in the German capital as the Fuehrer, rather than in your weekend vacation chalet," Speer replied.

Hitler's response seemed both sincere and in character. "I, too, have resolved to stay here in Berlin. I only wanted to hear your view once more."

---

* Although Speer apparently did not know this, others who were present in the bunker have said that his colleague and rival, Professor Hermann Giessler, had made a wooden model of Linz, and that this was located in a room in the New Reich Chancellery. One of Hitler's last trips out of the bunker—at tea time in late March or early April—was to show this model to his secretaries and Eva Braun. He pointed out the house in which he had lived with his widowed mother, Klara, before he left for Vienna in 1907.

With two old friends and senior ministers as different as
Albert Speer and Joseph Goebbels strongly urging him to
stay and die in Berlin, with only lesser personalities like
Bormann, Jodl, and Baur still touting the flight to the Alps,
the issue was already a foregone conclusion—if, indeed, it
had ever been an issue. Willful and erratic as he now was,
Hitler never completely lost sight of his historical image.
He knew that both Speer and Goebbels had the same image
in mind.*

Speer, still closeted with Hitler, noted how listless, how
subdued his manner had become. His glaucous eyes were
glazed; his left hand trembled as if he were an old man
with palsy; his face was puffed, part yellow, part gray. The
man seemed to have aged in what had been only weeks.
His voice was now soft, low-pitched, clear but a monotone.

"I shall not join in the battle personally," Hitler announced. "There is always the dangerous prospect that I
might merely be wounded, and thus fall into Russian
hands while still alive. I do not want to give my enemies
any chance to mutilate my corpse. I have already given
orders that my body be burned. Fräulein Braun has expressed her desire to end her life with mine; I intend to
shoot Blondi before I die . . ."**

Then, in an almost stoic mood, Hitler added, "Believe
me, Speer, it is easy for me to put an end to my life. One
brief moment, and I am freed of everything, liberated from
this painful existence."

---

* I spent considerable time questioning all knowledgeable bunker witnesses on the whole Alpine Redoubt scheme. It was taken seriously—in
retrospect, far too seriously—in SHAEF. Above all by U.S. Intelligence;
less so by the skeptical British. This in turn may have influenced General
Eisenhower's decision, at this time, not to march on a possibly Hitlerless
Berlin (he did not want to send American troops on to the German capital
only to discover Hitler had decamped to Bavaria). An enticing suspicion
here is that U.S. military intelligence had some inkling of Operation Seraglio. One single agent in either Berlin or Berchtesgaden, more likely in
Berchtesgaden, would have done the trick. Such overinterpretation of solid
information often happens in wartime. Once U.S. Intelligence knew of
such a flight, directly from Berlin, with passengers out of the bunker, it
would not have been wild fancy to assume Hitler might be aboard. Such
an intelligence break, of course, would have had to be made at least a
fortnight before the flight took place, for the order to halt on the Elbe
came on April 12. Neither Baur nor anyone else could remember just
when he received instructions to prepare this flight. "It could have been
in the first week of April, certainly not before, maybe a few days after."
** That Adolf Hitler could blithely mention both his mistress and his
dog in one and the same sentence is, again, quite in character. Since Hitler
did in fact have Blondi killed five days later, according to plan, his reference here to Eva Braun as Fräulein or "Miss" Braun would seem to
indicate that no serious thought of marriage had yet crossed the Fuehrer's
mind. E.B. had lived with him, and Hitler at this point said she was ready
to die with him, not as Mrs. Hitler but as plain Miss Braun.

He had, seemingly, given up again. Not, as on the day before, after a violent emotional explosion, but calmly, with the plaintive overtones of resignation and self-pity. At this point Speer, his own emotions frayed, blurted out how he had been frustrating the demolition orders since mid-March. This was something Hitler surely knew, anyway. Hitler just stared at him morosely and vacantly. Speer, stammering, uttered words to the effect that he was willing to stay in the bunker with the Fuehrer "to the bitter end." Hitler did not even answer.

A merciful interruption came at this point, giving Speer time to recover his emotional balance. General Krebs appeared to announce that he was ready to give the military-situation report.

Speer is not the only bunker witness who observed that Hitler, on this Monday afternoon and early evening, was in a relaxed, almost philosophic mood. There may, however, be a simple medical explanation for these placid hours. Among the some fifty who departed during Operation Seraglio was Dr. Morell. Everybody in the court knew that Morell had been treating Hitler with frequent injections and mysterious pills. The suspicion of some was that, at best, these were very strong tranquilizers; at worst, morphine. Before departure, realizing he would not be attending his star patient for at least several days, Dr. Morell might well have given him "farewell booster" shots and a supply of pills. This could account for the period of calm —and for the emotional outbursts, symptomatic of withdrawal, which followed. Morell did not confide to either of his medical successors in the bunker, Colonel Stumpfegger or Professor Haase, the nature of these "parting shots." He may or may not have told Hitler.

Speer noted how Hitler, in the military conference that followed hard on the melancholy soliloquy about his own suicide and cremation, was once again all aglow, exuding sheer optimism about the military situation. Yet there was nothing in the military situation on this day calling for any optimism. Every soldier in the conference room was aware of this. But this is the kind of rapid shift of mood, from low to high, often induced by drugs.

This military conference was brief; it ended around five-thirty. Outside the door, in the long reception lobby, Speer next met Dr. Goebbels, who had moved into the room vacated by Dr. Morell. In Goebbels, too, Speer noted that flight-from-realism that so soon overtook all bunker residents. Goebbels told Speer, "Yesterday the Fuehrer stopped the fighting in the west so that British and American troops can now enter Berlin unopposed."

There was no truth to this. Hitler had never given such an order. The idea was General Heinrici's, as Speer already knew and as Goebbels may have heard on his trips to the collapsing front. Nor did Goebbels, according to Speer, pursue this mirage for long. He himself had nothing to expect from the British and Americans. Speer also later reported that Goebbels, the fresh arrival in the bunker, was, in marked contrast to Hitler, in good health and was still very much in control of his nerves and emotions. He was nattily dressed, with clean shirt, white gloves, polished boots.

Still in the long lobby, Speer next met Colonel Stumpfegger, the lanky SS doctor, who told him that Magda Goebbels was now his patient and that she was bedridden in the upper bunker. She was suffering from frequent heart palpitations. Speer sent off word by an SS orderly that he would like to be received. He wanted to talk to Magda Goebbels alone. Less than a week before, he had visited her at Schwanenwerder, the small woody peninsula on the Havel River where Goebbels had his summer house. Through his ministry, which commanded a whole fleet of river barges, Speer had secretly released one to rescue Magda Goebbels and her children. The plan was to hide them aboard the barge, with ample provisions, then quietly float the self-propelled barge, at night, west to the Elbe— to the Americans. This was the last call.

Speer never got his chance to broach this daring escape plan. At Frau Goebbels' door he met her husband, the little Herr Doktor. Goebbels almost certainly knew what Speer had in mind, so the conversation with Magda was limited to a polite inquiry about the state of her health. Speer saw that the woman was close to hysterical collapse. Only toward the end of their talk did she confide that "I'm happy Harald is at least alive."*

Speer believed, even thirty years later—as did several other bunker witnesses, especially the women—that Magda Goebbels was suffering not only from heart palpitations,

---

* Harald Quandt was her son by her first husband. Eighteen and a soldier at the time, he was safe in a prisoner-of-war camp in Canada.

but from the remorseless emotional blackmail of her own husband. Long estranged, they held their marriage together on Hitler's orders only. This miserable couple hated each other.

Speer, because of his close friendship with Karl Hanke, who was also his suburban neighbor, had long been privy to the more lurid details of the Goebbelses' marital break-up, the hushed scandal of 1938–1941. In 1938, Goebbels, who had the reputation around Berlin as a great but rather casual lover, had fallen deeply in love with the Czech film actress Lida Baarova. And she with him. It was a torrid affair. His wife, in turn, was having a passionate affair with Hanke, one of Goebbels' bright young men. At first Hitler tolerated this. Goebbels, after all, was in the best position to keep it out of the newspapers.

But a public scandal was something Hitler could not tolerate. The Goebbels family, with five children then, had been built up as the First Family of the Third Reich; the Goebbelses' villa was the Fuehrer's substitute home. More-over—this was the year the Munich crisis was brewing—Goebbels' beloved was a Czech. Just such a public scandal had threatened at the 1938 Bayreuth summer festival, where many members of the international press were present. Hitler was there, as the house guest of Winifred Wagner. The Goebbelses, in turn, were his guests one night at a performance of *Tristan und Isolde*. Magda broke down weeping in the stalls. She confided to Hitler that she was about to file for divorce. Hanke, the importunate lover, had not helped matters at this time by sending a cheeky letter to Hitler asking for Magda's hand.

Next morning, in Bayreuth, Hitler sent Goebbels packing back to Berlin. He had ordered him to break off his relationship with Baarova and send her back to Prague. Goebbels, confronted now with a choice between the Great Man and the Great Love, at first—surprisingly—opted for the Great Love. He told Hitler he intended to marry Baarova and would give up his job as propaganda minister. He asked to be sent abroad as the German ambassador to Japan.

This simmering crisis had clearly become highly political. It clouded the relationship between Hitler and Goebbels for the next three years. Hitler finally forced Goebbels to knuckle under, and to say goodbye forever to Lida, late in 1938. Hanke, Goebbels dismissed. When war came in 1939, Hanke volunteered to go to the front. Heidi Goebbels, born in 1942, was known to Berliners as the "reconciliation child." No reconciliation ever really took place. The marriage was shattered, Goebbels still carrying a torch for his "Lidushka," Magda for Karl Hanke.*

Evidence of how deeply husband and wife loathed each other came from a surprising source. General Mohnke, the bunker commandant, in his last conversation with General Rattenhuber, the chief detective, was told by this bunkmate that Magda Goebbels, with her five children, had tried to flee the Third Reich in the spring of 1941 by automobile. She was arrested near Bregenz, on the old Austrian-Swiss border, and flown to Berlin under arrest. It was Rattenhuber who received her when she arrived at the Reich Chancellery. Hitler, realizing there was no political motive, freed Magda, forgave her, and made her promise to behave. He reminded her that there was a war on. Hitler's relations with both Goebbelses were at an all-time low. Goebbels was not back in favor until the fall of Stalingrad, early in 1943.

The timing of what would have been a most spectacular flight seems to have been just before or just after the Rudolf Hess flight of May 1941 to Scotland, and in either case just before the invasion of Russia. Hitler thus had imperative reasons for hushing the matter. Like the Hess flight, the Magda Goebbels escapade would have made world headlines at the time.

As Albert Speer left Magda Goebbels' room, he saw the three older Goebbels children: Helda, Hilde, and Helmut. They were romping up and down the corridor, playing with a ball and a hoop. The three younger ones were already in bed. Although he knew them all by name and liked them, Speer did not interrupt the game to say goodbye. He simply nodded to them quickly and went below. Speer, the father of six children, all born into the Third Reich, could not face any of these six, whom he had tried to save but was now abandoning. "I just did not have the gumption to intrude on them. I might not have been able

---

* Hanke would be forgiven. Hitler made him Gauleiter in Breslau in 1943. He also would name him in his will as the successor to Heinrich Himmler.

to control my emotions. What could I have replied if they
had asked me—a natural question—about the whereabouts
of my own children?"

*   *

Eight in the evening. The calm of Monday afternoon had
been broken. From Berchtesgaden, a telegram had just
arrived from Reichsmarschall Hermann Goering. It was
addressed to Hitler, inquiring whether, in line with the
1941 law of succession, he, Goering, should not take over
the leadership of the Reich "if you my Fuehrer are now
hindered in your freedom of action or decide to remain
in Fortress Berlin." Given the grim situation, it was a
sensible if somewhat fatuous request. Martin Bormann,
however, roared into Hitler's office, accusing Goering of
treason and coup d'état plans. Albert Speer—and here his
account differs from most extant earlier versions—said that
even this news did not arouse Hitler from the apathy that
had been his prevailing mood all afternoon. Speer had
followed Bormann, more out of curiosity than any active
interest in the dwindling power game. He thus became the
only eye-and-ear witness of just how Bormann did, finally,
succeed in knifing Goering.

   Bormann had two obvious motives for eliminating
Goering. The first was to induce Hitler himself to take off
for Berchtesgaden. That, after all, was exactly what had
been on his mind when he pleaded with Speer just a few
hours earlier. Bormann had not yet given up. His second
motive was even more personal. It really had less to do
with the truly mad "succession problem" than with Bormann's own status. Despite the high-sounding title of
"Reichsleiter," his only real job was secretary to the
Fuehrer. He was not a minister, not a general, not even
a Gauleiter, although he controlled the Gauleiters, in
Hitler's name. If Hitler were to die intestate, if he did not
draft a political last will and testament before his suicide,
then Bormann would suddenly have no status—and no
powerful friends. Even the fifty-odd Gauleiters would
switch loyalty either to Heinrich Himmler or, possibly,
Goebbels, who was the senior Gauleiter. Had Hitler, as
threatened, in fact committed suicide twenty-four hours
previously, by law Hermann Goering would already be
Fuehrer and chancellor. One of his first acts would have

been to order the arrest of Bormann. The military and others would most gladly have obliged him.

Speer's version of Goering's downfall concerns not the first but a second telegram, and he documents the case with a duplicate copy, which some careless signal officer left lying about. Speer—who hated Goering—simply pocketed it as a souvenir of this historical moment.* Goering's fatal blunder was not his first telegram, which was addressed, properly enough, to Hitler, but the second one. It was addressed to Foreign Minister von Ribbentrop, who had been staying, for the last week, in a special suite in the still-standing major wing of the Adlon Hotel.

> I have asked the Fuehrer to provide me with instructions by 10:00 P.M., April 23. If by this time it is apparent that the Fuehrer has lost his freedom of action to conduct the affairs of the Reich, his decree of June 29, 1941, goes into effect, according to which I inherit all his offices as his deputy. If by twelve midnight, April 23, 1945, you receive no other word either from the Fuehrer directly or from me, you are to report to me in Berchtesgaden by air.

Despite the meticulous legalities in which this telegram is phrased and hedged, and the care we can be sure went into the drafting of it, Goering had badly blundered. Bormann, this second time around, was able to convince Hitler that Goering was now dealing in "ultimata" and was thus guilty of "treason." Goering's double mistake was to have set time limits; above all, such short ones. Worse still, he had communicated directly with Hitler's top official** rather than with the Fuehrer himself. That did it.

Martin Bormann was out for blood. He suggested that Goering be shot forthwith. Hitler was not willing to go quite that far. But, whipped into high fury by Bormann's masterful use of innuendo—treason to Hitler's person was the important word here—the Fuehrer now stripped Hermann Goering of all rank and office and demanded that he resign instantly for "reasons of health." Bormann's one decisive advantage in this showdown was that he was still at Hitler's side. He was expert at waiting for moments

---

* The rivalry between Speer and Goering, from 1942 on, concerned control of the aircraft industry.
** He had sent identical telegrams to at least three others, Goebbels, Keitel, and Krebs.

when he could knife a rival. Even a rival as formidable as the portly Reichsmarschall. Meekly, before midnight, Goering complied with Hitler's orders, proof positive that he was engaging in no conspiracy, no usurpation.

I could find no convincing reason why Goering at his end or Hitler in reply conducted this whole affair by tele-gram. It was fast enough, as was shown in the event. The telephone lines, according to Rochus Misch, were still func-tioning between the bunker and the FHQ in Berchtesgaden. Perhaps Goering was in another building. More likely, he flinched from speaking directly to the Fuehrer on such a touchy matter. Misch heard, by phone from Berchtesgaden, how Goering had been arrested by the SS that same eve-ning, but had been freed within a few hours by his own escort of paratroopers. If Hermann Goering had really wished to pull off a coup d'état, he was in a position to do so. His problem was that Hitler was still living.

Albert Speer, normally no friend of Hermann Goering, nonetheless realized that the man, until this moment the second most powerful in the Reich, had been rashly, un-fairly judged. But Speer discreetly refrained from inter-vening, as he well might have done, had this power struggle had any real meaning. As he looked on, Hitler had an outburst remarkably similar to the explosion of the pre-vious day. He began to rage in a wild fury, with manic expressions of bitterness, betrayal, self-pity, and despair. His face was flushed crimson, his gray-blue eyes glaring, and his mustache, now white, was twitching.

He ranted on and on, as if talking to himself. "None of this is anything new to me," Speer remembered him saying. "I have always known that Hermann Goering was lazy. He let the Luftwaffe fall apart. The man was a monumental crook, and his bad example let corruption flourish at lower levels. He has been a drug addict for years. I have known these things all along."

A moment of truth, indeed. Hitler *had* known these things all along, but had done nothing about it. As far back as 1942, Speer himself, Goebbels, and General Milch had all tried to convince Hitler that Goering had become incompetent and was a drag on the war effort. Yet Hitler continued to defend Goering, one of his first followers, less perhaps out of old-time loyalty than of concern for his own image. Goering was popular, and he had been part of the Hitler legend from the earliest days of the struggle.

If the dramatic and sudden downfall of Hermann Goering this day in the bunker was a real historical moment, the arrival and departure of another senior minister, Joachim von Ribbentrop, had elements of farce in it.

It happened shortly after the Goering episode. Speer was back in Hitler's study. The Fuehrer, he noticed, had again dropped back into his listless, weary-with-it-all mood. Speer, therefore, took advantage of the occasion to request Hitler's approval for a flight west of Czech industrial managers still in the Skoda works in Prague. The Czechs wanted to escape the Russians and establish contact with the Americans in Munich. A minor if touchy matter, Speer broached it as casually as possible. A short fortnight ago, he would not have dared to sponsor such a plan. Hitler voiced no objection, initialing the flight permission.

At this point there was another interruption. Bormann bustled in to remind Hitler that von Ribbentrop had been waiting several hours for an audience. He had come to the bunker some time before Speer's arrival. "Bormann," Hitler said, "how many times do I have to repeat that I just don't want to see that man?"

"Ribbentrop says that he won't move away from your doorstep. He will wait there like a faithful old hound dog until you relent, mein Fuehrer."

As Bormann knew, the dog ploy was always a good one with Hitler, who now relented. Speer left, and Ribbentrop waddled in. During their short talk of ten minutes or so, Hitler must have told the foreign minister about the Speer scheme to airlift the Czech managers. For later, as he left Hitler's office, Ribbentrop buttonholed Speer. He began to insist, querulously, that such a project needed *his* approval. Speer reminded him that it was the Speer ministry, not the Foreign Office, which had the available plane. "Well," said Ribbentrop, "I shall be satisfied if the document says 'Approved by the Fuehrer at the suggestion of the foreign minister.' "

Speer yielded on this absurd point of bureaucratic punctilio. The whole point, after all, was to help the Czechs. Ribbentrop left the bunker around 11:00 P.M. and was driven by his chauffeur to Hamburg, where he intended to go into hiding in the apartment of his mistress. Thus, he departed from the bunker and Berlin forever, just an hour or so before another 1000–plane RAF bombardment began.

As one reconstructs this last appearance of Albert Speer in the Fuehrerbunker, one continually notes a distinct change in the atmosphere on this day. The lower bunker was no longer crowded; there was much less hustle and bustle. The corridor lounge, where Speer met Bormann and Ribbentrop, was empty. Just a few days before, it had been crowded. This is explained by the departure, the day before, of most of the high military, which radically changed Hitler's daily routine.

Previously, during these long weeks underground, life in the bunker had been pretty much dictated by the priority Hitler himself gave to his two daily military conferences. Hitler slept—when he could sleep—in the hours between these formal sessions. Bunker routine revolved around this rigid program. Bormann, too, slept when Hitler slept, as did the senior adjutants. Those on regular duty, the FBK and Rattenhuber's security detectives, worked twelve-hour shifts.

The departure of such military luminaries as Hermann Goering, Field Marshal Keitel, and Grand Admiral Doenitz meant an emptier stage. Goering, in particular, always had brought an entourage with him, arriving and departing with a clutter of attendants, aides, adjutants, briefing officers, perhaps a dozen or more. Keitel and Doenitz had almost as many. Those minor actors would often gather in the outer corridor lobby at least an hour before briefings began. Thus, except for a few quiet midmorning hours, and again in early evening, the lower bunker was usually overcrowded. A dozen chauffeurs were also in attendance, waiting upstairs in the Chancellery.

Hitler's military conferences and shorter briefings, while still taking place, could now come at any hour and had more of an ad hoc nature. He had, in fact, abandoned the Supreme Command of the Armed Forces to Keitel, Jodl, and Doenitz. He was no concentrating his attention on the area around Berlin. The other senior military man in the bunker, in addition to General Krebs, ws General Wilhelm Burgdorf. Others who came and went were the city commandants, Generals Reimann and Weidling. In command in the Reich Chancellery area itself, reporting only to Hitler, was Major General Wilhelm Mohnke. He was not usually in the bunker proper. His command post was in the cellar of the New Reich Chancellery.

Women had been in the bunker from the beginning, but now their presence became more apparent and of increased importance. Although Johanna Wolf and Christa Schroeder had left, Eva Braun and Frau Goebbels had arrived. The active and excited Goebbels children created a problem the women were best able to handle. Frau Goebbels herself was in no conditon to attend to her children and this gave both Gerda Christian and Gertrud Junge something to do. They were soon joined in their task by Eva Braun. These three childless women did their best to mother the young-sters. In a few days, they would be joined by the aviatrix Hanna Reitsch, who wanted to fly the children out. Among these women, the fate of the children was often talked about, if only in whispers.

Adolf Hitler—it was part of his general withdrawal from political reality—was spending more and more of his time in female company. Many of his meals he took alone, from a tray. But at tea time he usually invited Gerda Christian and Gertrud Junge to join him. Since January, in fact, he had seldom dined with men, nor had them to tea. In this last week, even Constanze Manzialy was invited to join the tea group. Frau Goebbels was not invited, probably for reasons of protocol. Neither was Eva Braun. Hitler preferred to keep his female admirers in distinct categories. The mild flirtation that was going on here—again accord-ing to bunker gossip—was between Hitler and his young-est, recently widowed, secretary, Frau "Trudl" Junge.

But for the most part, Frau Christian recalled, Hitler would drink his tea and eat in silence. It was "a silence broken by reminiscence, recriminations, or some bleak comment on the events of the day. The general themes were all too familiar—Berchtesgaden days, the loyalty of women, the disloyalty of Prussian generals, the breeding of dogs. We just listened glumly. We had heard it all before."

*   *

It was now after midnight in the bunker. Albert Speer, who had gone upstairs into the Chancellery to have still another last rendezvous, this time with Dr. Lueschen, was not able to induce him to leave Berlin. Speer returned to the lower bunker. Hitler, he found, had already retired. This was

still another break in the Fuehrer's routine, since the usual
midnight conference had been discontinued. Once the
busiest of hours, there were few souls about now in the
lower bunker. So ended Blue Monday.

Eva Braun had not retired. She sent an orderly to invite
Speer to join her in her combination bed-and-sitting room.
Speer had been waiting for this invitation. He braced himself for still another farewell meeting. It was already Tuesday, April 24; he had been up and about since 4:00 A.M.
the previous day.

As Speer entered Eva Braun's cramped quarters, he saw
how bulky the familiar dresser now looked. He had designed it, back in 1938, for a much larger apartment. He
had woven the initials E.B. into a four-leaf clover design
in the woodwork. Now it looked grotesque. The young
woman's first words were casual, spontaneous, quite in
character.

"Albert, you must be hungry!"

In the general orgy of selfishness and self-pity in the
bunker, no one had as yet offered Speer so much as a
sandwich. He himself had been too busy, perhaps too distraught, to take time out for a meal. Eva now managed to
hustle up a postmidnight snack, cookies and sweets. And,
for old times' sake, she opened up a bottle of Moët et
Chandon champagne.

The twelve-year friendship between Hitler's architect and
his mistress was purely platonic, and this last of half-a-
hundred tête-à-têtes was almost as pleasant as ever, despite
overtones of *tristesse* and the somber setting. Speer was a
South German gentleman with a touch of the cavalier.
Hitler played the Austrian cavalier, perhaps, but without
the manners of a gentleman. Speer was always aware of
this distinction. Eva Braun was not.

Moreover, Albert Speer belonged to that big world of
affairs that the Fuehrer's mistress did not know. It was the
Berlin world of tingling power. But, from his days as rising
young architect and frequent Berghof weekend guest,
Speer and his wife, Margarete, also belonged to Eva Braun's
world. For they, too, were mountain people, skiers, nature
lovers. Thus, here in the bunker, Albert Speer by his very
presence was not only an emotional link with Eva's own
past; he was also a last visible link between the Berlin and
Berchtesgaden worlds.

Speer was soon aware that, however incongruous, Eva Braun at this moment was perhaps the only bunker inmate who seemed even remotely happy. She radiated a quiet serenity that was not merely play-acting. It was a serenity, Speer felt, not unmixed with exultation on the part of a woman who, if only in a morbid pact, like that of Tristan and Isolde, complete with poison potion, was finally going to get her way with the man she loved.

While serving up the midnight refreshments, Eva Braun confirmed what Speer had already heard, from von Below and others, about the turbulent events of the bunker weekend just past. "You know, Albert, you almost arrived too late to see any of us. Only yesterday [she meant, of course, Sunday, April 22] the military situation outside Berlin seemed to have collapsed. There was much talk of the imminent arrival of Red Army troops. The Fuehrer was really ready to give up and take his own life. But then over came Dr. Goebbels. He managed to persuade the Fuehrer to carry on. Goebbels pulled him out of the deep doldrums. This is really the only reason any of us are still alive and still here."

During this conversation in Eva Braun's boudoir—it lasted almost two hours—Adolf Hitler had either retired or, as is more likely, had fallen asleep on his cot. His room adjoined Eva's. Speer was quite aware of this as a potentially embarrassing situation. One also notes here, in passing, that this evening the Fuehrer and his mistress were neither keeping the same hours nor sharing the same bedroom.

Eva next told Speer, with obvious pride, about how Hitler in an avuncular way had tried to induce her, only the week before, to leave for Munich; how she had categorically refused; and how this stubborn show of loyalty had so pleased him. (And confirmed one of his constant forebodings.) Then she let drop a remark that, however casual, Speer instinctively sensed was loaded. It was a shuddering reminder that as long as Hitler was still alive, neither Albert Speer nor any other human being was completely safe in this concrete shelter.

"How glad I am, Albert, that you have managed to find your way back here to the bunker. The Fuehrer had come to believe that you were working against him . . . Ah well, now that you are here it proves just the opposite, doesn't it?"

Speer, stunned, made no reply. He knew that his presence in the bunker this night proved nothing of the sort. A naïve Eva Braun might, touchingly, believe so, but Adolf Hitler was no naïf. It is not that Albert Speer, at this moment, suspected the Fuehrer's mistress of duplicity, least of all against him. But in her almost breathless innocence, she had let a black cat out of the bag. This sounded too much like the direct echo of some hot dispute with Bormann, in Hitler's presence, about the ambivalent conduct of Minister Speer.

Only a fortnight ago, as Speer now uneasily remembered, Hitler had cleverly manipulated Eva Braun into trying to make him betray his own intentions. Hitler had prompted her—as Eva later admitted—to inquire about the whereabouts of the Speer family. "How are the folks—and where are they?"

Speer had parried this question with a suave, bland lie. He told Eva, simply, that his wife and children were staying with his industrialist friend Dieter Stahl, who had a lakeside cottage between Berlin and the Elbe River. In actual fact, Speer on April 6 had moved them from Berchtesgaden, where he had first sent them, to the remote shores of the Baltic. This was far to the north, but still between the fronts, and it by no means protected them from possible reprisal.

"Why do so many people have to be killed?" Eva Braun continued. "It is all for nothing."

It was now 3:00 A.M. Hitler, in the next room, was up and stirring, so Speer sent in word that he would like to come over to say goodbye. He had now been in the bunker for twelve hours. One pilot was still waiting for him at the Brandenburg Gate, and Manfred von Poser, who was upstairs in the Chancellery, was lining up a second flight from Gatow. The pilots were naturally anxious to fly before dawn, now only ninety minutes away.

"So, Speer, you're leaving? Good. *Auf Wiedersehen*."

No thanks, no handshake, no present, no good wishes, no greetings to the family, no nice-having-known-you. Speer, dog-tired and overwrought, again mumbled some banality about his willingness to stay until the end. Hitler simply turned away. Speer had risked his life to come to the bunker. He got this curt, rude put-down. On this tawdry, unworthy note ended one of the strangest friendships of the twentieth century.

It was still pitch black outside the bunker. The new moon had long since set with the evening star. The desultory nighttime rumble of the battle building up was now ominous, now still, a quiet broken by random shell bursts. Speer knew that his pilots were impatient to take off. But he had one last goodbye to make, to a building to which he had devoted one of the most intense years of his life—the Neue Reichskanzlei, his 1938 showplace.

The day before, he had passed through the building on his way to the Fuehrerbunker. He had seen how much damage this monumental half-ruin had absorbed since his previous visit. But he took pride in the fact that his most ambitious completed building, for all of the criticism of his modernist friends, was built well, or at least solidly. Now it was standing up to the distant artillery potshots, much easier to shake off than the bombs of the saturation air raids. Only part of the roof had caved in; several ceilings had collapsed of their own weight. Smashed windows, charred galleries, broken beams, huge jagged trunks of truant marble, somehow still recalled former pomp and majesty.

It was dark, and Albert Speer walked alone, careful not to stumble. In the blackout he could not see where he was going. But, as the architect, he always knew where he was. He was standing in the very middle of what, in younger days, he had named the Ehrenhof, the Court of Honor. One of the problems he had faced, back in that crash-program year of 1938, was how to muffle the inevitable street noise that must be combated when one builds in the heart of a great metropolitan city in the automotive age, a noise that penetrates through walls and windows at every hour. Now, in the nighttime heart of Berlin, all was ghostly, silent, as still as the graveyard. For long minutes, even the echo of the still-distant battle faded. It was, as Speer was to write many years later in a memorable phrase, "like a night on the mountain . . ."

Speer, joined now by Manfred von Poser, walked to the Brandenburg Gate. Soon they were airborne. The perky little Fieseler Stork put-putted along through the night. Speer, with the eyes of the city planner who knew almost every street in Berlin, spotted, vaguely, many familiar outlines, dim lakes in the mist, campfires of the Hitler-jugend, who were defending the great Frey Bridge over the Havel, the waters of the Wannsee and the string of lakes around Potsdam.

Even the noise was distant, unreal, rumbly. As they approached Gatow, a few pale silver, fingerlike searchlights scanned the predawn German horizon. Albert Speer had left behind him, forever, the Berlin bunker. At Gatow, the change to a fighter plane was made quickly. Then, twenty minutes later, he was landing at the great Rechlin fighter base, still in operation. Dawn was breaking across the Mecklenburg lakes, where Speer in 1930 had spent his honeymoon boating. Migrating geese were heading north.

*   *

Blue Monday had been equally hectic for Hans Baur.

During the early afternoon [he recalled] I had to move my three medium-range Condors from the emergency strip at Kladow, near Gatow across the Havel River, on the western rim of Berlin. I had them flown to our Luftwaffe base at Rechlin, ninety miles northwest in Mecklenburg. There I also had three Junkers–Three-nineties, the long-distance transports. Then I came back to my quarters in the basement of New Reich Chancellery. Next day, Tuesday, very reluctantly, I reported this last Berlin close-down for the large birds.

"I am sorry, my Fuehrer, Kladow is now under Russian artillery barrage, and one of our three remaining Condors has already been destroyed in its hangar. The Red Army is not yet visible from the control tower, but its reconnaissance troops cannot be far away. There are gaping craters in the runway, which make it most difficult to take off in daylight hours and quite out of the question at night."

The Fuehrer took the news without visible emotion. He simply said, "Baur, take off yourself while there is still time. There is no urgent need for you here. What we need now are more *Panzerfauste* [bazookas] for the street fighting and the last stand. If you find you cannot land, then drop or parachute them in. For myself, I shall stand or fall in Berlin. This decision is irrevocable. You can serve my cause much better from outside Berlin."

"My Fuehrer, there are now only about twenty of us left from your old Chancellery Group. You know, I am sure, that I am not the type to fly out and off in your hour of supreme peril. I still have several plane crews out at Rechlin who can transport those bazookas and other supplies. And I know I can still be of some use and loyal service to you here."

And so Adolf Hitler gave in, nodding in friendly resignation. "All right, Baur. It is your decision and of course you have my permission."

And, at that moment at least, the man seemed at ease.

In Berlin on Tuesday, April 24, toward evening, the last overland highway out of Berlin was finally cut. Thus from this time her last links with the outside world were by air only.

With Kladow and Gatow under artillery fire—they went out of operation three days later—even the air link was now restricted to hazardous takeoffs and departures from the emergency strip near the Brandenburg Gate. Only small planes, Fieseler Storks and trainers coming in from Rechlin, could land here, often under rifle, artillery, and antiaircraft fire. As dangerous as this flight to the center of the city was—and the danger grew with each passing day—several visitors could and did enter and leave the bunker by air. From Rechlin they would take off to whatever airports, most in South Germany, were still in German hands.

*　　　*

Cumulative evidence from all other witnesses had convinced me that Adolf Hitler never considered flying out of Berlin after Sunday, April 22—if, indeed, he ever seriously considered such a flight before that date or at any time. When, therefore, Baur kept persisting—"Right up to the last day, I could have flown the Fuehrer anywhere in the world"—I tended in my mind to dismiss this as the kind of wild-blue-yonder talk pilots are given to—pilot romanticism, and the dogged loyalty to the Fuchrer of the kind Baur had so often indulged in during our conversations. In some ways, it was. But one day, more or less out of idle curiosity, I asked, "General Baur, even if you had ever reached that long-range transport at Rechlin, the Junker–Three-ninety, where would you have flown your Fuehrer? It was, after all, rather late in the game."

"Anywhere he wanted to go," Baur said. "I had maps and flight plans for Greenland, North Africa, Madagascar, Tibet, even Manchukuo."

Out of this world! But Hitler knew that it was patently absurd. Tibet and Manchukuo, while not exactly neighbors, were equally remote, halfway round the world from the

Berlin bunker and hence attractive goals for a daring pilot like Baur. Pilot Baur's harping may even have inspired Hitler to remark sardonically, a couple of nights earlier, "Once out of Berlin, I would be like a Tibetan lama without his prayer wheel." Nor did he put much stock in all the loose talk about an Alpine Redoubt. Hitler was still clear-minded enough to recognize that there was, in fact, no Alpine Redoubt, only the refuge at Berchtesgaden, which had underground bunkers larger than, but similar to, the cluster in Berlin.

Why, then, would Soviet Intelligence spend literally years grilling Baur on this long-range flight plan, a flight that had most obviously never taken place? Why did Baur himself return to the theme so often, and keep insisting that "right up to the very end in Berlin, the last hours of his life, I was ready and able to fly Adolf Hitler anywhere he wanted to go."

The answer finally dawned on me. A skilled pilot such as Hans Baur, if only he could once reach Rechlin, could, indeed, have flown Adolf Hitler almost anywhere. And if not Adolf Hitler, then anyone else escaping from the bunker. For example, Martin Bormann.

Baur, so I discovered, is really the critical witness when we later come to the story of the attempted flight of Bormann. But, before that, we must consider the eight long days of ordeal that followed Blue Monday in the bunker.

CHAPTER VI

•

Casualty Station

Is there no balm in Gilead; is there no physician there?

—Jeremiah 8:22

EVEN WHEN OUTSIDE THE BUNKER—and he is one of the few of its inhabitants who was, every day—Baur did not see much of Berlin in its death throes since he always went directly to the Brandenburg Gate, only a half-mile away. In normal times, this was a lively area, the very center of the city, but now 92 percent of it was bombed. Few Berliners lived here anymore. Fewer and fewer had to report to work; the ministries had been evacuated. The great department stores were closed; most had been bombed and looted. No restaurants, no theaters, no movie houses. Buses, street cars, the subway, were no longer running. Many street cars had been loaded with boulders and tipped over, to serve as tank obstacles.

The flow of normal traffic had stopped. The streets were graveyards, strewn with giant blocks of fresh rubble. Only the military and high officialdom still had gas-ration cards. One of the few shops that remained open, in the Wilhelmstrasse, was a small bakery. The baker, who seemed to have had an emergency cache of fresh flour, stayed on the job through it all. He was baking away when the first Russians stormed in. He offered them white bread, something few of them had ever eaten.

A second strange oasis still in operation was the cellar bar of the once-posh Adlon Hotel, most of which was still

> "Liquor, profligacy, fear, despair, the handiness of weapons and poison vials, all played their suggestive role among lost souls. All were now waiting for Hitler to shoot himself. It became an obsession."

standing, in the shadow of the Brandenburg Gate. Now—on Ribbentrop's orders—it was the exclusive preserve of the few diplomats still accredited to the Third Reich—those from Mussolini's rump Italian Republic, the Japanese, Eastern European satellite governments-in-exile, like Tiso's Slovakia, and some French Vichyites, who had discreetly not gone back to France. These derelicts of diplomacy were not only drinking at the Adlon; when the bar closed at midnight, many slept there. Their embassies had been bombed.

Baur talked very little about what he saw aboveground. This is symptomatic of the bunker mentality, which he shared with all of the Reich Chancellery Group, the mountain people. They knew little if anything of what was happening in the big city above them. The Berliners, though they had now heard that Hitler was in town, did not know where he was; the bunker was not visible from the street. Nor did very many care. Baur was moving between two utterly different worlds. The Berlin he had once known well had vanished. There was, however, a second man who emerged often from the subterranean depths. This was Professor Dr. Ernst-Guenther Schenck.

He was operating in the emergency casualty station—*das Bresthaus*—in the cellar of the New Reich Chancellery. A wartime colonel, he was the only officer who had actually volunteered his services. Schenck spent the first week of the siege aboveground in Berlin, the last seven at the operating table.

The doctor described the scene there. "Most of my working hours had been spent over the emergency field-surgery operating table. Casualties were now tumbling in from the fierce street fighting just three blocks away at the Potsdamer Platz, and from the larger battle now raging for the Reich-

stag. This was only four or five blocks from us. From time
to time, soldiers who were still conscious and could talk,
told me of their hopeless battle. The younger ones, many
under sixteen, were terrified, bawling."

The Red Army had by now reached the Berlin inner
ring, the Zitadelle. Most of the German casualties had been
inflicted by artillery-fire shrapnel. Now, more were from
rifle and smallarms fire, grenades. This meant there was
close combat by tank and infantry forces. Russian planes
and artillery were now hitting the area of the Chancellery
and the bunker. The battery lamp over Dr. Schenck's operating table swung like a jerky pendulum.

Dr. Schenck commented, "Only madmen, of whom there
were still several around, in uniform, would have called
this a military situation, the kind of battle I had known as
a medic at the front in the earlier years of the war. If
there was still what could be called a 'front' in Berlin, few
combatants on either side knew just where it was . . . Over
our heads we could hear not only Russian shells bursting,
but, to our chagrin, the deadly German Eighty-eight twin-
purpose gun."

What had happened? The Russians had fought and captured Tempelhof airport on Wednesday, April 25. The
next day, they turned the captured guns on the Germans.
Because Berlin is built on alluvial sand, every shell burst
had a crunching side effect.

As Professor Schenck put it: "Sometimes, I felt as if I
were standing in a shot-put pit. Red Army massed artillery
was spraying us like conscientious gardeners. I was reminded of the bitter barrages at Leningrad, with the roles
now painfully reversed."

The massive artillery barrage just described took place
on the evening of Friday, April 27, and the early morning
hours of Saturday, April 28. The artillery of General
Vassily Kasakov was located about two miles off, on the
northern edge of the Tiergarten. Some shells were probably coming from the captured German guns at Tempelhof, a bit farther away and to the south.

The Red Army artillery had two prime targets. Target
105 was the Reichstag; Target 106, the Reich Chancellery.
Both massive buildings loomed invitingly on the horizon.

The Russians were not firing directly at the Fuehrerbunker, which they could not see, and the precise location
of which they did not know. Still, the noise of exploding

shells gave the inhabitants of the bunker, including Hitler, once again the grand illusion that they were at the epicenter of things, that the whole vast capital city was under similar bombardment. It was on this night, according to Colonel von Below, that Goebbels made the most grandiloquent of his bunker pronouncements: "When we leave this stage, then will the planet tremble."*

Colonel Schenck himself knew better. When he went in desperate search of medical supplies now in such short supply—bandages, splints, iodine, morphine, plasma—he found that while many boroughs of Berlin had been occupied with little or no fighting, others had simply been bypassed by the Russians. With one commandeered Wehrmacht truck driven by his adjutant, Captain Max Mueller, Colonel Schenck went weaving between the municipal battle lines, raiding familiar hospitals and supply depots. This was a perilous mission. Baur's excursions out of the catacomb of the Reich Chancellery took him back and forth along the same short linear route to the Brandenburg Gate; he did not see much of the rest of the city. Professor Schenck, on the contrary, was acutely aware of the appalling human tragedy all around him.

> In one abandoned hospital in Berlin-Steglitz, in the basement where I was prowling about with a flashlight in search of supplies, I suddenly came on some dozen very elderly, moaning women. When this hospital had had to be evacuated, two days before, they had been left behind. Apparently there was just no transport. When I entered their basement ward at midnight, they thought I was the first Russian. They began screaming like Valkyries. I made the familiar bedside rounds, gave each patient a few placebo pills. Then I, too, had to abandon them to their fate—hungry, distraught, forlorn. It was ghastly. I simply had to leave them alone in the midnight dark.

Schenck's truck had to follow one main artery, the Schloss Strasse. It was all that was still passable. Most Russian artillery fire now did no more than pulverize rubble. This Berlin rubble was gigantic, obscene. Some was old and molding, sprouting rare spring wildflowers; some was still fresh and smoldering, like angry lava. Lilliputian loco-

---

* A quote from the Athenian tragedian Phrynichus, a contemporary of Aeschylus. Milton translated it, "When I die, let the earth be roul'd in flames."

motives on toylike narrow-gauge tracks, brought to Berlin
from the Ruhr mining valleys, chugged and puffed along
what once had been broad streets and now were canyons,
piling up 110 million square meters of debris—brick, concrete, mortar, shards of glass, limestone, sandstone, head-
less caryatides from pompous old Berlin Jugendstil portals
and balconies. The Reichsbahn, the national railway, estimated that there was enough rubble to fill four million
freight cars. Or, if piled all in one place, to make an artificial mountain higher than the tallest peak in the Harz
Mountains (the Brocken, 3747 feet above sea level).*

More than ten square miles in the center of the city were
flattened; less than one third of all private dwellings escaped
destruction or were classified as even half-habitable. Intact
windows were a rarity.** More bombed-out Berliners were
living with relatives, friends, or strangers than were
living under their own roofs. Kitchens had become communal, mostly those with old-fashioned wood-burning
ranges. There was no gas; electricity was available only at
odd hours.

Yet almost to the end, life staggered on with a ludicrous
façade of normality. Six hundred thousand Berliners still
had essential wartime jobs; they could be fined for being
late. The factories, even in mid-April 1945, were producing
at 74 percent of top capacity. Absenteeism, even among
foreign workers, was negligible. All Berliners were groggy.
No one had had enough sleep for long weeks. Most beds
were slept in relays around the clock. Managers and shop
stewards moved cots into their offices. Nerves were frazzled,
not only from constant loss of sleep, but from lack of
fresh vegetables or vitamins, meat or fresh fish, real coffee
or tea. What served as coffee was made from acorns; cigarettes were made of dried dandelions. Only in the last fortnight were Berlin rations suddenly doubled. These were
called Himmelsfrahrt (Ascension Thursday) rations, "announcing the end."

Dr. Schenck, on his forays outside the bunker, also
shuddered at the familiar stream of silent refugees passing
through Berlin in the dark. From January 1 to April 15,
1945, 672,000 had already trooped through the city. They

---

* After the war was over, this rubble was eventually piled into seven
heaps inside the city. Once quite flat, Berlin now has seven hills, equipped
with planetaria, ski lifts, radar stations, and swimming pools.
** People removed the dangerous glass and substituted cardboard.

had permission to linger but one night and one day. Pass on. It was a somber parade: 80 percent were women of all ages; the rest, either men over sixty-five or children. None had autos or buses. A lucky few had bicycles, wagons, carts, horses, cows, poultry, pigs. Many were peasants in traditional dress. A silent parade, like a black etching from a page of Grimmelshausen and the Thirty Years' War or Kaethe Kollwitz. To even the most callous of Berliners, it also spelled out the shape of things about to come.

Dr. Schenck had had a nationalist, patriotic upbringing, but he had enough sense of history to know that what was happening was the reversal of 900 years of steady German colonization to the east. It had begun on the Elbe and was now flowing back there. Berliners did not have to hear harrowing tales of trekkers. They were written on thousands of silent, wrinkled, *Mutter Courage* faces. Grandmothers clasped their ravished, mutilated granddaughters in ox carts, and vice versa. Many of the refugees transported their recent dead in homemade coffins. Berlin health authorities insisted on immediate burial. They confiscated the coffins for reissue. The black-market price on coffins had soared. The three city crematoria were no longer allowed to burn them. It had become expensive even to die.

Dr. Schenck returned to his account of his surgical labors.

On the operating table itself, and while making visits to my two wards nearby, I came across a medley of uniforms. In addition to my old unit, the LAH, there were veterans and young recruits from such strange outfits as SS Panzer Nordland Division, made up almost entirely of Scandinavians, the Fifteenth SS Latvian Fusilier Battalion, SS Denmark Regiment, the Charlemagne Division [French volunteers], SS Flanders Storm Brigade, Belgian Flemish, even a few stragglers from the old Spanish Blue Division. Few of these units were familiar to me; most had been thrown together in the past months.

The strangest, most gaudy uniforms Schenck saw on his operating table were fancy brass-buttoned, blue-and-gold parade uniforms of German Navy sea cadets and midshipmen from Kiel, Rostock, and the Baltic island of Fehmarn. Two battalions had been airlifted into Berlin on April 24 on Admiral Doenitz's orders. Few had had any infantry training, least of all for the kind of street fighting now going on. Yet they had been thrown in to support infantry troops defending the Reichstag. Almost to a man, or boy, they were slaughtered. (I was able to locate but one survivor.)

Dr. Schenck recalled, "All of us were now living a waking nightmare. We had lost any sense of clock or calendar time. Even today I often remember, in turbulent dreams, a kind of spectral hourglass: the sand in the upper glass never empties; the bottom glass never fills. Life and death were then the only grim realities, not transient and deceptive time. Many a wounded soldier died, in horrible anguish, on the blood-smeared table as I operated. These were bewildered young men dragooned from half of Europe. I was up to my elbows in entrails, arteries, gore."

Sometimes, indeed, the mortal blunder with the scalpel was Dr. Schenck's. He was not a surgeon, but an internist and a nutrition expert. He was almost as groggy at times as a punch-drunk boxer, keeping going on nerves and reflexes, with little more than his general knowledge of anatomy, and some field experience he had had at the front. Toward the end, the last two or three days, the casualty station ran out of bandages. The staff had to rip blood-soaked rags and casts off the unburied dead.

Dr. Schenck observed, "Yet a doctor's first instinct is to save human life, to put some meaning into this metastasis of mounting meaninglessness. I just had to carry on, for at the end I was the only doctor present still able to stand on his feet. I got much valuable surgical advice from Professor Haase. All told, in seven days, we did some three hundred and seventy operations, most of them major. Minor casualties, the walking wounded, soldiers shot in the hand or the foot, were not even allowed to leave their assigned combat posts. Those dragged to us, or trundled in on stretchers, were usually unconscious."

The operating room itself, very primitive, was equipped with no more than basic surgical instruments. Nearby, on the same level in the cellar of the New Reich Chancellery, were two fairly large emergency wards, with camp cots. This was the middle section, two compartments of the vast cellar, roughly the same underground area where General Mohnke had already set up his command post. This long cellar ran parallel to the Voss Strasse, under the main entrance. The upper and main floor of the New Reich

Chancellery, including Hitler's abandoned study, was now being used to store several tons of bulk provisions, adequate supply for a six weeks' siege.

These stores had been rounded up in the city by Dr. Schenck, on General Mohnke's orders, during the third week in April. Mohnke and Schenck had known each other since the beginning of the war, when both were captains in the LAH in the Blitz campaigns in Poland, Belgium, and France. It was this first food-requisitioning mission that had, in fact, brought Dr. Schenck to the Reich Chancellery, on Monday, April 23, 1945, that Blue Monday when Albert Speer had paid his farewell visit.

Professor Schenck is a man of background and education somewhat similar to Speer's. His father had been a professor of classics and humanities at Muenster University in Westphalia. Like Speer, Schenck had also become an ardent Hitler follower in his student days during the late 1920s, the last years of the Weimar Republic. Now, in 1945, he shared with Speer an almost total disillusionment with the National Socialist movement. Yet he had, at least when he entered the Reich Chancellery, a lingering loyalty to the person of Adolf Hitler.

Since Dr. Schenck arrived on the scene just as Speer was departing forever, in a sense he picks up the story where Speer left off—a civilized man's comment on the final descent into barbarism. His having come to the Chancellery and the Fuehrerbunker from the outside was always his measuring stick as he described the last days and his own actions and reactions.

Doctors, from the beginning, were in short supply. Dr. Karl Brandt had been arrested in early April and hauled away in handcuffs. Dr. Theodor Morell flew off on April 22. Professor Karl Gebhardt, a lieutenant general and Himmler's top medical adviser (later hanged), did appear once, on the afternoon of April 23, but left within the hour. He had come to ask Hitler to confirm his appointment by Himmler as president of the German Red Cross, a fatuous request that Hitler scornfully granted.* To underline Gebhardt's cowardice (according to Gerda Christian), Hitler turned to his secretaries and others present and said, "Any woman here who wants to fly off with Professor

---

* Gebhardt succeeded Professor Ernst Grawitz, who had committed suicide in Berlin the day before. Inviting his wife and two children to supper, he tossed two hand grenades under the table and blew all to eternity.

Gebhardt may now do so." No one volunteered, though there were at least four women in the room. Gebhardt departed, sheepishly, with his aide.

That left but two doctors present and on duty. One was Colonel Stumpfegger. He had been called in, a fortnight before, to replace Dr. Brandt as Hitler's attending *Leibarzt*, or private physician. But as soon as Professor Werner Haase arrived, on April 21, he in turn replaced Stumpfegger. Hitler knew Haase was a far better doctor, and it was Haase, not Stumpfegger, who was closest to Hitler in the last days. Schenck had, perhaps, another important role in the bunker story. Symbolically, and certainly without being aware of it at the time, Dr. Schenck was playing a kind of surrogate role for hundreds of Germans of his upper-middle-class background, education, and generation. These were people who had followed Hitler blindly, although what should have been their better instincts could clearly have warned them. Once again, one is reminded of Albert Speer and his statement of youthful enthrallment: "Adolf Hitler was my destiny."

Ernst-Guenther Schenck, too, perhaps as politically naïve at the time as Thomas Mann's Hans Castorp on the Magic Mountain, had been a loyal Hitler admirer and convinced National Socialist for what he then called idealistic reasons. He dropped a very promising medical career as *Chefarzt* in Munich to volunteer for front-line service as soon as war came in 1939. "I then felt it was a distinct honor to serve in the only division that had permission to use the Fuehrer's name in its unit designation, and on its armband."

I also suspect that it was probably "residual loyalty" once again that had brought Dr. Schenck to the Reich Chancellery on April 23. He had been ordered to retreat to Bavaria. But he considered it his duty as a doctor to remain in beleaguered Berlin. When General Mohnke put in a telephone call to him, he came. Seven days later, viewing close up what was left of the Nazi leadership, Dr. Schenck was completely cured of any residual loyalties. He was, so to speak, denazified by events.

Professor Haase was one of the stranger apparitions to appear in the bunker at the end, yet another ghost out of Adolf Hitler's past. Back in 1933, Haase had been the first *Leibarzt* in the Reich Chancellery; at his own request he was replaced by his student, Dr. Brandt, in 1936. Haase, who wanted to continue his career in surgery, simply went

back to his clinic in the Ziegelstrasse, only a few blocks
from the great Charité Hospital and not far from the Reich
Chancellery.

He had remained on friendly terms with Adolf Hitler
and was always present at such formal ceremonies as the
Fuehrer's birthday party. In fact, he had attended the last
one, on April 20, 1945, although by that time he was a
patient in his own clinic, where he was dying of tubercu-
losis.

It was apparently on this occasion that Hitler asked
Haase to come over to replace the now disgraced Dr.
Brandt, or perhaps Haase volunteered. In any case, Haase
hustled over. He had only part of one lung left. Often
gasping in the foul air of the casualty station and in the
phosphorous fumes of a capital city burning down, Haase
on most cold days could not stand on his own feet for more
than twenty to thirty minutes.

As a good surgeon he had, nonetheless, been able to give
Professor Schenck valuable advice on critical operations.
Lying on a nearby cot, panting for breath, he would spell
out the trickier aspects of stomach, heart, and even spinal
incisions, and of treating delicate head wounds. Schenck
would have been lost without him. Himself he could not
save, but others he helped. Haase, tall, silver-haired, and
fiftyish, emerges as a somewhat noble if desperate figure at
the center of a macabre and sordid story. It may be that
his colleague (and fellow National Socialist) Dr. Schenck
idealizes him a bit, but his performance in *das Bresthaus*
speaks for itself.

Dr. Schenck later reported:

The day I arrived in the Chancellery the vast place was already beginning to crowd up like a railway terminal. I was
assigned sleeping quarters with some nine other new arrivals.
We were in a cramped cubicle with iron air-raid cellar double
cots. Most of these newcomers were high Nazi Party functionaries, clad in gaudy uniforms and decorations not earned
on any wartime front.

These functionaries, most portly and middle-aged, former
storm troopers, I suspect, had nothing to do except bemoan
their fate and lost privileges. Nor could I induce them to
volunteer to do anything, even make their own beds. None
would help in my casualty station; that was beneath their
rank and dignity. One told me, haughtily, "I simply cannot
stand the sight of blood." Not one of these worthies would
venture out into the city with me in the evening, to forage

for medical supplies. After two or three nights, exhausted as I was, I could not even sleep because of their noisy strutting about and the sodden drinking bouts. When they began dragging stray whores in, I got General Mohnke to shift my bunk assignment, and I moved in with his troop officers. I slept on the floor in a sleeping bag.

*　　　*

Two of the last arrivals in the bunker could also fairly be called dramatic apparitions, airborne ghosts out of Adolf Hitler's past. Even he was astonished to see them. One was General Robert Ritter von Greim,* whom he had ordered to report to him immediately after the dismissal of Hermann Goering on April 23, Blue Monday. It was now the evening of Thursday, April 26. Hitler wanted to promote the pilot-general to field marshal and name him successor to Goering as commander-in-chief of the Luftwaffe.

Pilot Hans Baur commented: "Admitted, the Fuehrer could have done this easily enough by telephone or telegraph, since Ritter von Greim was stationed at Neubiberg, near Munich. But Hitler said he wanted to do this personally . . . When the general did not show up on Tuesday or Wednesday, I feared he had been shot down en route. The air around and over Berlin was swarming with Russian fighters. Many Luftwaffe pilots were refusing to fly into Berlin from Rechlin."

But when Baur later heard that General Ritter von Greim had his mistress, Hanna Reitsch, with him, he braced himself for anything. Hanna was a wartime test pilot who had flown many hot planes and even the V–1 flying bomb. "If anyone could sneak a plane into Berlin, she was the lady."

This whiff of crazy romance in the technical age, fool-hardy as it was, makes Ritter von Greim look slightly less the jackass than he otherwise was. He would need Hanna. His flight from Munich to Berlin had been delayed by a bombing at the Munich end. Finally reaching Rechlin, by a night flight, he had hoped to fly into Berlin in a *Hub-*

---

* The apparition aspect of the appearance of Ritter von Greim is this. Back in 1920, at the time of the Kapp *Putsch* in Berlin, he had tried to fly Adolf Hitler, then Munich-based, into Berlin. It was Hitler's first flight. They had to make a forced landing in Jueterbog, forty-five miles southwest of Berlin. According to Hans Baur, it was this experience that had put Hitler off flying for years.

hrauber, the German version of the helicopter. None was available; the last had been strafed and burned near the runway. The pair were thus stranded at the great Luftwaffe base all day Wednesday.

Finally, the same sergeant pilot who had flown Speer out of Berlin in a Fieseler Stork now volunteered to fly Reitsch and von Greim in a Focke-Wulf–190. Twenty fighter escorts were laid on. The Focke-Wulf was a two-seater, and this presented a problem. So Hanna Reitsch, as petite and wiry as a small tigress, crawled into the back of the fuselage. Ritter von Greim did not know she was there until they were moving down the runway. It was a fast flight of only twenty minutes. Half the fighter escort was shot down, a high price for heroics. There were bullet holes in both of the plane's wings. Fortunately for Hanna, there was none in the fuselage.

When they landed at Gatow, the pair had difficulty in getting through by phone to the Chancellery. Finally, Colonel von Below came on the horn and told them flying was still safer than driving overland; the road was now cut in two places. Spotting a Fieseler Stork, the general himself now took the controls. Hanna Reitsch was crouched in a half-standing position behind him; luckily, as things turned out. At treetop level, they flew over the Havel River and the Gruenewald. South of the Olympic Stadium, the floor of their light trainer was shot up. Ritter von Greim, wounded in the right foot, soon fainted from loss of blood. The fuel tank was punctured. Reitsch reached over her lover's shoulders, grabbing both the throttle and the controls. She flew the last ten minutes to a bumpy but safe landing just before the Brandenburg Gate. It was the most daring stunt-combat flight of a remarkable career.

Hans Baur drove both to the bunker. Hitler was elated to see them—"Miracles can still happen!"—and he promptly named Ritter von Greim field marshal (his last), and boss of what was left of the Luftwaffe. Von Greim was then carried off to undergo surgery by Colonel Stumpfegger, and Hanna Reitsch moved into the upper bunker to help the other women in entertaining the six Goebbels children. She told tales of flying and taught them all how to yodel. Two nights later—one half hour before his wedding to Eva Braun—Hitler sent this strange pair of lovers off again into the night on still another perilous flight. Their wild mission this time was to denounce "that traitor Heinrich Himmler."

The departure of Ritter von Greim and Hanna Reitsch was even more spectacular than their arrival—and even more dangerous. Two full days had passed; the Russians had moved considerably closer. Colonel von Below and Hanna had to help the new field marshal up the steep steps. He was on crutches. At each of the four landings of the emergency exit staircase, the smell of sulphur and smoldering embers, mixed with powdery particles of plaster and rubble-dust, choked their throats and burned their eyelids. When the three, at midnight, finally reached the Voss Strasse, they found it a yellow-red sea of flame and billowing smoke. They were hustled into an armored vehicle and whisked along the Hermann Goering Strasse to the Brandenburg Gate.

Russian-manned searchlights pierced the night. They were criss-crossing the whole length of the East-West Axis. Nonetheless, the same courageous pilot who had flown the couple into Gatow two days before in a Focke-Wulf–190 had managed to sneak in again, this time in an Arado–96. This was a light artillery-observation plane. It was a two-seater, so again the indomitable Reitsch had to be bundled in behind the pilot's seat.

For this last departure, in order to outfox businesslike Russian antiaircraft artillery, the young pilot boldly took off with the wind, directly toward the Brandenburg Gate. He just cleared the Quadriga, the lady charioteer with her span of four bronze horses atop the gate. Searchlights soon picked up and pinpointed the small plane. Tracer bullets whizzed past the wings. It was a slow plane, but it kept mounting steeply. Salvation was a cloudbank at 4500 feet. As this strange trio of Germany's best pilots, a field marshal, a sergeant, and a lady test pilot, finally zoomed into that fortunate cloudbank, burning Berlin vanished. So did the roar and din of battle.

Wartime pilots of the smaller planes, although none had the literary grace of an Antoine de Saint-Exupéry, were sometimes far enough away from the battlefield to be able to evoke a terrible, poetic beauty. They were the last romantics of the prenuclear age. Hanna Reitsch later described the scene, high over Berlin and Brandenburg, sometime between midnight and dawn on Sunday, April 29,

1945. "The top of the cloudbank below us was a fleecy, cumulus white, like a giant quilt over the flaming and lost city. High above us was a silent, springtime half-moon, just beyond zenith. All was still, serene, idyllic. Soon we spotted bright streamers, the Havel and its chain of silvery lakes, through black breaks in the clouds. Then, winging our way to Rechlin, we saw the war again. What at first looked like huge harvest bonfires were, in fact, flaming villages, all put to the torch. Some thirty, perhaps forty. They marked the line of Russian advance." And the wrath of a peasantry in uniform against a peasantry in thatched cottages and huts. Russia had come to Europe, with vengeance in the heart for what Europeans had done in Russia. Like most acts of vengeance, it was indiscriminate.

In the Reich Chancellery, more than 2000 Germans were now crowded into the Chancellery cellar—the fighting soldiers, the wounded, the Nazi Party "*Bonzen*," many Berlin women who had either fled thither for safety or had been brought in by their boy friends in the FBK or Kampfgruppe Mohnke. Although the word "orgy" is perhaps a bit too lurid, the combination of free-flowing liquor, distraught, terrified women, the impending doom of the great city, and the Nazi Goetterdaemmerung mood was having its effect. I had already heard several accounts of the wild parties building up, which were to climax in a *Hexensabbath* on the day the Fuehrer finally committed suicide. Since Professor Schenck had proved a most sober and meticulous witness, I felt that his version would be the most reliable, so I asked him about this.

He answered, "Yes. I saw enough of that with my own eyes and heard a lot more about it later in captivity, from participants and survivors. At the time, of course, I was far too busy and just too dog-tired to observe much, except out of the corner of my eye as I passed to and from my casualty station."

It was only in later years, when Dr. Schenck had time to think back on those days, and when his medical attentions turned to a scientific study of stress, that the bunker bacchanalia began to concern him professionally. Stress is one of the serious medical problems of our century, and the 1945 situation in the Reich Chancellery and the bunker was almost the ultimate in stress situations. One could never reconstruct it in any experimental laboratory.

Schenck said:

Individuals in the bunker reacted in varying ways, depending on their character, physical stamina, and moral integrity. Some went completely to pieces; others did not. Sometimes even generals cracked up, while simple private soldiers kept cool. Often the women showed more courage than the men. Many bunker inmates had little or nothing to do. There were long hours of *Angst*—simple waiting and brooding. So, many took to drink. Drink in turn relaxed inhibitions, releasing primitive animal instincts. During the breakout, I escorted four women out of the bunker. Gertrud Junge told me that only the arrival of the Goebbels children had kept her from "going up the palm tree." It finally gave her and the other girls something worthwhile to do. Fräulein Manzialy, who was also in my escape party, had kept herself busy in the kitchen. She was calm, very brave.

Liquor explains many of the more sordid actions. Contrary to popular belief, alcohol is not a stimulant, but a depressant. From time to time, I myself took a stiff shot of cognac in order to keep going at the operating table. But usually I tried to stick to coffee and a few tranquilizers, and to get as much sleep as I could. From time to time I had to leave a patient on the table while I took a five-minute break in the fresh air—to calm my nerves and to steady my scalpel hand.

There was a kind of contagious mass hysteria seeking a group outlet. Many of the same wild, red-eyed women who had fled their Berlin apartments, in terror of rape by Red Army soldiers, now threw themselves into the arms, and bed rolls, of the nearest German soldiers they could find. And the soldiers were not unwilling. Still, it came as a bit of a shock to me to see a German general chasing some half-naked Blitzmaedel [signalwoman] between and over the cots. The more discreet retired to Dr. Kunz's dentist chair upstairs in the Chancellery. That chair seemed to have had a special erotic attraction. The wilder women enjoyed being strapped in and made love to in a variety of novel positions.

I was skeptical as that story made the rounds. But then one of the women involved, drunk and hysterical, gave me the clinical details. I dosed her with sedatives. She told me she had been twice raped before fleeing to the Chancellery, took to drinking, could not hold her liquor. Toward the end, she lost all inhibitions. Another diversion was group sex, but that was usually off in the dark corners.

All of this was going on in the Reich Chancellery and those two neighboring barracks buildings in the Hermann

Goering Strasse. There was a lot more room there, and a lot
more people, than in the cramped quarters of the bunker.
But don't forget, some of the bunker people—Bormann,
Stumpfegger, Burgdorf, Kempka—would cruise out from
time to time. They were in on the binge.

It was also in this saturnalian atmosphere that the morbid talk of suicide kept mounting. This was once again a
clear case of infectious group hysteria. Liquor, profligacy,
fear, despair, the handiness of weapons and poison vials,
all played their suggestive role among lost souls. All were
now waiting for Hitler, still the center of the bunker melodrama, to shoot himself. This, too, made suicide the foremost topic in almost every group conversation. It became
an obsession.

*   *

Late Saturday, April 28, it was Goebbels who, in his capacity as Gauleiter of Berlin, had to hustle up a minor
official with notary and registrar powers to preside at the
Hitler marriage ceremony. He quickly managed to locate
one Walter Wagner, a fiftyish, quite bewildered municipal
bureaucrat now serving with the Volkssturm. He wore an
armband over his brown Nazi Party uniform. *Nomen est
omen.* This most minor of Wagnerians made a very brief
appearance on the stage of world history, a spear-holder
with a ludicrous walk-on role.

The man was not lacking in a kind of crazy midnight
dignity. Wagner had been told to hustle through the ceremony, and no nonsense. Hitler and Eva Braun were actually
married as a "war couple." But Wagner could not legally
by-pass the formality of asking the bride and the bridegroom whether each was a third-generation Aryan. At the
close of the zip-zip ceremony, with a glance at his watch,
Wagner also noted that it was just after midnight. So, with
a pedantic scribble, he changed the date on the marriage
certificate from April 28 to April 29, 1945. *Ordnung muss
sein* (Things must be in order).

Walter Wagner, a born Berliner, lingered for some twenty
minutes at the reception, meeting his Fuehrer for the first
time in his life. He munched a liverwurst sandwich, had
one or two glasses of champagne, chatted with the bride.
He then was ushered out of the bunker and back into the
night. Walter Wagner was dead a half hour later, shot on

the Wilhelmstrasse on the way back to his foxhole post in the vaults of a famous eighteenth-century wine cellar on Unter den Linden.

The wedding formalities had taken place in the small conference room, or *Kartenzimmer,* sometimes called the map room. Because this was one of the smaller rooms in the lower bunker, only Joseph Goebbels and Martin Bormann were present. Both had to sign as witnesses. At Goebbels' gala wedding to Magda, back in 1931, in Parchim in Mecklenburg, Adolf Hitler had been best man.

The bunker bride wore black, appropriate enough in the funereal atmosphere. It was a short-skirted silk taffeta afternoon dress with two gold clasps at the shoulder straps, Hitler's favorite in her wardrobe. Afterward, at the reception in Hitler's study, a larger room, a dozen bunker veterans moved in and out—Magda Goebbels, Gerda Christian, Gertrud Junge, Dr. Werner Naumann (Goebbels' state secretary), Ambassador Walter Hewel, Generals Krebs and Burgdorf.

I asked Professor Schenck if he had ever met Goebbels. He answered:

Yes, once he came over to inspect our casualty station, one of the few top people from the Fuehrerbunker who did. He acted with dignity, chatting with many of the wounded soldiers, asking how the battle was going. He thanked my two nurses for their noble work. Then, a few days later, I saw him in the gangway of the upper bunker. He was clutching the back of a chair and giving a talk about the Ostrogoths before Rome. Only his single aide was still listening. By this time I had heard the rumor that he planned to kill his children. I thus found the rhetoric on this occasion both high-flown and repulsive. The stoic dignity with which he had visited my patients had yielded to a cold fanaticism that was the opposite of dignity.

Almost a week passed, from Monday, April 23, to Sunday, April 29, before Dr. Schenck entered the Fuehrerbunker proper. He describes his first bunker meeting with Hitler in this way:

It was under rather dramatic circumstances. Although I did not then know what day it was—it was actually Sunday evening—I had retired around midnight. It had been a very exhausting day; more wounded than ever coming in. I soon fell into a deep sleep. But less than two hours later I felt a hand on my shoulder, shaking me. It was the man who was by now my friend, the surgeon I had been working with all that week, Professor Werner Haase. Haàse had just walked over from the lower bunker. He said that Hitler wanted to see me and my two attendant nurses. I looked at my uniform, which I had not taken off for two or three days. It was torn, crumpled, and caked with dry, brownish blood—not mine.

We wound, Indian file, through the underground passage into the upper bunker, a distance of about a hundred and fifty meters. Professor Haase, puffing painfully while he walked, led the way, since it was very familiar to him by now. The two nurses followed. We passed through the central gangway of the upper bunker, which was still crowded at this hour with some twelve to fifteen bunker night owls. There was a long oak table here, laden with ample food from the pantry, cognac, wine, and beer in bottles. Several present were sleeping with their arms crossed on the table.

Then the two doctors descended the spiral staircase leading to the lower bunker, which one entered through a steel bulkhead. A guard was posted here, since it led to the Fuehrer's sanctum. Hardly had the small party entered than they saw Adolf Hitler standing before them alone, just outside his quarters. Haase made the formal introductions.

Schenck remembered, "My first reaction on meeting Adolf Hitler face to face, although the man was relaxed and friendly enough, was to snap to attention and salute. I was a mere colonel in a not very presentable uniform; he was still Fuehrer, chancellor and Supreme Commander-in-Chief of the Armed Forces. My whole body seemed to freeze. A chill went up and down my upper spine. I imagine it was my uniform—and his—that made me snap to attention."

Soon, however, Professor Schenck was looking at Hitler with a doctor's clinical eye. He knew he was gazing at the end—*le néant*. He was a bit shaken himself, since he had never seen his Fuehrer before, except from an admiring distance. Schenck was standing within three feet of Hitler. The pathetic man he saw bore little resemblance to the old, mesmerizing idol of the masses so familiar to millions.

He observed:

I knew, of course, that this was Adolf Hitler and no *Doppelgaenger* [ghostly double]. Hatless, he was still wearing the familiar, once-spotless, natty pearl gray tunic with green shirt and long black trousers, the simple uniform he had donned on the first day of the war. He wore his golden party badge and his World War One Iron Cross on his left breast pocket. But the human being buried in these sloppy, food-stained clothes had completely withdrawn into himself. I was still standing erect, on a kind of concrete step above him. As I glanced down, I could see Hitler's hunched spine, the curved shoulders that seemed to twitch and suddenly to tremble. Somehow his head seemed withdrawn into his shoulders, turtlelike. He struck me as an agonizing Atlas with a mountain on his back. All of these thoughts must have raced through my mind in thirty seconds or so, not more. This pause came because Hitler seemed hardly able to shuffle the two paces forward to greet us. Which he now did.

Professor Schenck's description is not only graphic; it is also precisely clinical and is leading up to a diagnosis. Professor Schenck is here describing Adolf Hitler less than fifteen hours before his death.

His eyes, although he was looking directly at me, said nothing. They did not seem to be focusing. They were like wet pale-blue porcelain, glazed, actually more gray than blue. They were filmy, like the skin of a soft, ripe grape. The whites were bloodshot. I could detect no expression on his vapid, immobile face. Drooping black sacks under his eyes betrayed loss of sleep, although Hitler was not the only one suffering from this bunker malaise.

Today I can see him there still, although the whole scene lasted only about four, maybe five, minutes. Deep folds ran down his rather large, pulpy nose to the corners of his mouth. This mouth was set firmly, his lips nervously pressing each other. The cold-fish, flapping gesture with which he shook my hand was listless. It was really only a jerky reflex, although it was meant to be amiable enough. As he mumbled his thanks, perfunctorily, I was at a loss to make any coherent reply. He then apologized for having summoned us at such a late hour. I must have uttered something trivial, probably *"Danke schoen, mein Fuehrer."*

I was profoundly shocked, and reacted, I suppose, as any doctor would have, not without sympathy. And yet it was far too late, in more ways than one, for any mortal doctor. At fifty-six, the Fuehrer was a palsied, physical wreck, his face wrinkled like a mask, all yellow and gray. The man, I am sure, was senile, without the dignity of silver hairs. As he moved past me toward my Red Cross nurse, Sister Erna, this usually stolid woman broke down completely and began to sigh and moan. "My Fuehrer, keep up your faith in final victory! Lead, and we shall follow!"

One notes here in passing that, to the bitter end, right
here, the old Hitler mystique could still fascinate German
women, young and middle-aged. Sister Erna's pathetic
outburst, however, may only have been hysterical reaction
from her long hours in surgery. She had been a kind of
German Florence Nightingale, standing in a clutter of
amputated arms and legs, and entrails, which she later
stuffed, like slop, into ashcans. The orderlies could bury
the fallings from the operating table only during the spells
when artillery let up.

According to Dr. Schenck, Hitler, in response to Sister
Erna's lamentation, replied calmly, "One must not, like a
coward, seek to avoid one's own destiny." Once again, the
stoic, resigned mood reported by others on this same day,
his last.

Dr. Schenck continued:

There were five of us present, our little party of four and
Hitler. But his words seemed not aimed at anyone in particular. He was just summing things up; speaking, as it were,
for the ages. The four of us were still standing at that moment just inside the lower bunker, a little above his level.
Now, turning around slowly, he made a gesture to Professor
Haase. He was to follow; we others had been dismissed. We
were still standing there, speechless, as an orderly opened the
door leading to Hitler's private quarters and the two shuffling,
very sick men disappeared in silence. It was then about two-
thirty A.M. on Monday, April thirtieth, the last day.

With my two nurses, I began to head back toward my quarters and bunk. However, as we passed again through the
upper bunker, we saw that the convivial table there had
meanwhile become much more alive. I was invited, very
democratically, to join the party. SS Major Otto Guensche,
whom I knew, introduced me to the others. The party included, among others, General Krebs and General Burgdorf,
the pilot Hans Baur, SS Major General Rattenhuber, Artur
Axmann, Ambassador Hewel, Admiral Voss, Linge, the
chauffeur Kempka. Neither Doctor nor Frau Goebbels was
present, nor Martin Bormann. I cannot recall General Mohnke
being there, either.

I remember that it was quiet overhead. British and American planes had not put in an appearance that week, and the
fearful Russian artillery barrage had let up hours before. I
recall General Krebs remarking that it was his guess that the
Red Army would want to wait another twenty-four hours,
until May Day, "so that Marshal Zhukov can present the

big prize, Berlin, to Generalissimo Stalin like a shaslik—on
a spit." This touch of General Staff gallows humor drew
rather hollow laughs.

Almost all of this group were new faces to Professor
Schenck. He soon gathered that they were the Fuehrer's
inner circle. He sat there for a long while, dumfounded;
they were talking about old, happy, far-off things, the
piping days of peace before 1939. They compared notes on
the beauty of various Bavarian lakes, reminisced about the
luminous, ocher light of Munich in autumn, or the bank-
less beauty of the Weser River, the Wartburg at twilight,
the Zwinger in Dresden, the Rhine waterfall at Schaff-
hausen, the Romanesque loveliness of Worms cathedral,
a kind of nostalgic Baedeker trip far, far from the Berlin
bunker.

After a half hour or so, just as I was moving to leave, three
quite good-looking young women joined us, coming up the
staircase from the lower bunker. One was Frau Junge, one
was Fräulein Else Krueger, Bormann's secretary, and the
third, a lithe, well-dressed strawberry blonde. Someone leaned
over and whispered to me that this was Frau Adolf Hitler,
the bride of a day. I had never heard of the lady or of her
special relationship to our Fuehrer. On any other occasion,
it might have been a mildly titillating moment for me; this
night I was just not in the mood.

I must say, I felt an awkward outsider in this chummy
group, once the exalted Obersalzberg circle. I was a little
fish, wriggling in the same big net, and I knew it was closing
on us all. Bu they kept talking on and on about life in
Berchtesgaden, of how they had lived up there, enthroned
like Wagnerian gods, above the clouds that encircled the
foothills and cut them off utterly from other Germans, all
other lesser mortals. Eva Braun, now Frau Hitler, came
from this world. It was probably her only world. I began
observing her as if from afar. If this young woman knew
the desperate situation she was in—and one can hardly doubt
that—she gave no visible sign of it. Once in a while, I thought
I detected a slight tremor in her lisping voice, but that may
have been only alcohol. She was not drunk, but was well on
the way, tossing her glass back regularly. She was seated
at the head of the long oak table in the gangway and was
the real life of the party—like a Rhineland carnival queen.
I was at the other end.

A small social note in this woman's sad life. With the exception of the champagne wedding breakfast, just twenty-four hours before, this seems to have been the only table at which Eva ever presided as Frau Adolf Hitler. But without the bridegroom.

The Fuehrer's bride talked away, in a chirpy, rather pleasant Bavarian accent, to this audience of some fifteen or sixteen men and women. It was all small talk, gossip, rather pointless anecdotes. What she looked like, today I only dimly recall. But what I do remember vividly is that she did not seem to share one bit in the general demoralization that had overcome almost everyone else and was now seeping into the bunker from every corner.

My impression was that she was fighting back hysteria, and this exaltation was, in a clinical sense, a prolonged manic phase. I just don't know enough about her case history to go into such matters as sublimated death wish, but she was not the sweet, simple women she seemed to be. She was deeply neurotic. And she did not strike me as particularly intelligent. She was banal.

Just how many goblets of hock Dr. Schenck tossed back, he does not say, but it did lead to one pressing human problem. Although there were normally two toilets in the bunker, the upper one was now clogged, and these party people were using the john at the other end of the lower bunker. This meant that they had to descend and march past Hitler's quarters, an unthinkable intrusion at any earlier time.

Schenck went on:

The two FBK security guards who always manned that bulkhead door must have wandered off. There was, on this evening, a boisterous party going on over in the enlisted men's canteen. In short, I had to answer nature's call, so I headed down the spiral steps and entered the lower bunker again. Now I had a better chance to look around. I was amazed at how small Hitler's private quarters were. Doors led off left and right from the central corridor. In a kind of vestibule before his bedroom, sitting at a small round table, were Hitler and Professor Haase. They were engaged in an intense conversation. Luckily, they did not even notice me. I whipped past the Fuehrer and into the latrine. While doing what I came to do, I noticed, in a corner, two Alsatian shepherd dogs. They were whining and growling at my intrusion.

Strolling back, almost on tiptoe, Professor Schenck shored up his courage and decided to have another look at the ghostly scene. It fascinated him. The two men were talking, or rather whispering, so intensely that, once again, they took no notice of the intruder.

For the second time within two hours I could observe Hitler, this time *without* his observing me. It was pitiful. His flabby left hand, in which he was clasping his steel-rimmed spectacles,* was also clutching the table. His whole left arm, up to the shoulder, was trembling and, now and then, shuddering. This arm kept tapping the table rhythmically. To brace himself, he had wrapped both his left calf and foot around one leg of the table. This leg was throbbing, shaking. He could not control it.

Now, most doctors would agree with me, I think, that these are the classic symptoms of paralysis agitans, what in English I believe you call Parkinson's disease. If my quick diagnosis was correct [and it was later confirmed by Dr. Haase], this meant that Hitler, even had he lived, would in a very few years have been a hopeless cripple, able to gaze only at the ground.

Professor Schenck is not the only able doctor who has made this diagnosis without having actually examined Hitler. Others have reached the same conclusion. Its importance here is not only that Schenck is a competent doctor, but was a competent doctor on the scene on Hitler's last day. The Fuehrer was to be dead in about eleven hours.

Dr. Schenck added, "It was now obvious to me, on this second meeting, that Adolf Hitler had found his last physician. In the end, Adolf Hitler had definitely turned again to his old friend and first *Leibarzt*, Haase. It was with him and him alone that the Fuehrer discussed the manner and method of his own suicide. I know this because Professor Haase told me, later that day—after the suicide. They also were discussing the problem of how to destroy the bodies."

It was now about 4:00 A.M. Outside, the first streaks of predawn April light fell on Berlin. And, a trivial point perhaps, but one probably already noted by Sherlock Holmes fans, the two dogs (Blondi and also Gerda Chris-

---

* The glasses were, in fact, nickel-rimmed, according to those who knew Hitler better than Schenck did. This, however, is the term Schenck used when, in 1973, he described the scene.

tian's Alsatian) were still alive, in the corner of the toilet. They had growled.

Professor Schenck, when answering the call of nature, had just missed, probably by a matter of minutes, an event described by Major Otto Guensche. Guensche clearly has his timing wrong, for he says "around midnight." But he must have entered the lower bunker a little later than Dr. Schenck. He reported the following:

> When I entered and headed for the familiar toilet, I found it occupied by Professor Haase and Sergeant Tornow, Hitler's veterinarian and dog trainer. Haase was holding in his hands an ampule, or vial,* and a pair of pliers. I had heard Hitler say, earlier that evening, that he wanted to test the poison because it had been given to him by Himmler, "and one could no longer be sure of Himmler." Blondi, Hitler's dog, was poisoned in the toilet. I saw it happening. Tornow forced her mouth open and Haase reached into it, crushing the ampule with his pliers. The cyanide poison acted almost instantly. Soon after that, Hitler showed up and went into the toilet to make sure Blondi was dead. He did not say a word or betray any emotion. A moment later, he disappeared into his study.

Sergeant Tornow, in order to destroy Blondi and the other dogs in his kennel, had got himself crocked. With his pistol, he now shot Blondi's four puppies, who had been born in the bunker in March, plus the dogs of Eva, Gerda Christian, and his own dachshund. Tornow now roared over to the enlisted men's canteen, shouting, "The Fuehrer is dead and it is now every man for himself." Good advice, but premature. The sergeant was ripe for a straitjacket. But these were now in short supply, too.

In this last climactic week, the Berliners, groggy as they were, had noticed a change in the air over Berlin. The British-American air bombardment had stopped—forever. The last American daylight raid had been on April 21, one day after the Fuehrer's birthday. It was followed by the three hundred and twenty-seventh all-clear siren of the long war. It did not take long to figure out why. It stopped as Red Army divisions reached the outskirts of the city.

---

* It was in a cylindrical container, similar in shape to a lipstick. There was a blue band on the container. The ampule was translucent plastic. It fitted into a leather holder and could be worn as a scapular.

Danger still dropped from the air, however; the Red Army had massive artillery, the spectacular Katyushas, or "Stalin organs." Berlin kids stood around in awe of this whooshing multibarreled new weapon.

Those in the inner boroughs, like the Londoners in the summer of 1944, had suddenly to learn a new behavior pattern. Bomb shelters were no defense against V–1, V–2, or artillery, unless one took up permanent residence in them. This is just what most families now did, moving into the shelters and the subway tubes for the duration. Most Berlin men, however, still had jobs to do aboveground; for example, the 11,000 policemen. Many fell victim to the unfamiliar shrapnel that gave no warning.

Civilians soon learned that artillery fire is at least directed—at bridges, crossroads, tank obstacles, and troop concentrations. A German fighting unit backed up into a residential area was less than welcome. The soldiers were often asked to move on and continue their defense of the fatherland from the next block, *Bitte*.

A Volkssturm unit, erecting a cumbersome tank barrier along the Hohenzollerndamm, was told by one caustic bystander, "It will take the Russians only two hours and four minutes to knock that thing down."

Q. "Why so precise?"

A. "The Ivans will stand there two hours roaring with laughter. Then, they will bring up one gun and knock it galley-west."

Most Berliners were now in cellers. Some of these had been converted into impromptu cafés. In one of these cellars, in working-class Kreuzberg, a new song was born:

> I'd rather have a Russian on my belly
> Than a British bomb on my noggin . . .

It captured a passing sentiment. The unknown chanteuse may or may not have changed her mind a few days later.

In that last week, more than two thirds of the Berliners were behind the Russian lines, and only residents of the inner boroughs were inside the fast-closing iron ring. The telephone exchanges were still functioning spasmodically. This led to many bizarre conversations. The most frequent topic was how to face the first Russian soldier as he burst upon the scene.

Reports varied, for the conduct of the individual soldiers and the military units also varied markedly. In the daytime, some of the more playful Russian soldiers were "liberating" bicycles and motorcycles, even boats and canoes on the lakes. Others were fascinated with flush toilets, which they assumed were machines for washing potatoes. The bidets baffled them, too, so they took footbaths in them, a fairly sensible idea for men who had marched such a long way.

But nightfall was another story, and a harrowing one. The best advice was to hide all liquor and all women, even grandmothers. Younger women took to using lipstick to make a rash of little red dots on their faces, simulating scarlet fever. Many telephone conversations with suburbia ended abruptly. A Russian had picked up the phone.

So many records were destroyed in the last days that even today there is no official German figure on Berlin civilian casualties. Unofficially, 52,000 died in bombings (from January 1, 1945). Hospital records show 22,000 heart attacks in April 1945, half of them fatal. There were 6400 suicides. Twenty-one thousand civilians were killed by shrapnel or in the street fighting. In addition, several bewildered Berlin men were taken out and shot for the possession of "concealed weapons." They had forgotten to turn in the children's air rifles and BB guns.

The unofficial estimate of civilian dead runs to more than 125,000. But this figure does not include casualties among the hundreds of thousands of Berliners who fled the city or had been evacuated and died elsewhere in Germany —or among the refugees, except for those who happened to die in Berlin hospitals.

During the month of April 1945, more than eight million German civilians were on the move west from East Prussia and Pomerania, Posen, the lands along the Oder, and Silesia. All strong-arm official efforts to direct the flow around and past Berlin broke down in the general chaos. Almost three million passed through Berlin, a number at least as large as the resident population, and perhaps a bit more. Many died in Berlin, the old from exhaustion, the young from rampant epidemic diseases. As they do in all wars, the refugees tended to haunt the roads and the railroad tracks, knowing that they must lead somewhere. Thus, more than other civilians, they were particularly vulnerable to bombs and strafing. My own estimate, from discussions with municipal officials who remained in Berlin and survived the war, is that civilian casualties far outnumbered those of the German military, perhaps by as much as 5 to 1.

Victims of rape are a rather special kind of wartime casualty. No account of the fall of Berlin can ignore completely the much-disputed figure. An official Berlin figure does exist, but it has never been published. In 1948, under the airlift, Mayor Ernst Reuter once let it slip in a private conversation long after midnight. He put the figure at 90,000, but he soon extracted from me a promise never to print this during his lifetime. Reuter had spent part of his youth in Russia (1917–1919) and had a great admiration and affection for the Russian people. He did not want the Berlin rape story to become an issue in the cold war.

The figure, I believe, can be accepted as a rock-bottom estimate. It includes only hospitalized cases and those who reported to doctors and therefore appear on medical records. Many women were too humiliated or too exhausted to stagger to doctors. Rape was only part of the general horror, to some women the worst, to others only one among many. Maybe the most fortunate were those who opted quickly for a Russian lover and stayed close to him for at least a fortnight. The Roman Catholic bishop of Berlin, Cardinal Preysing, gave Catholic doctors permission to perform abortions. This is rare in church history, a grim indication of how high the number of victims must have been.

Rape, and the fall of cities. "What theme had Homer but original sin?" So asked Yeats in one of the passionate lyrics of his old age. The answer, of course, is that the abduction of Helen was not the real theme of the *Iliad*, the first great book at the beginning of western civilization. It was only the excuse the Greeks conjured up for that expedition to Troy. If the world civilization has any meaning —and it certainly does—it means the building, not the destruction, of great cities. The fall of Berlin fascinates for the same reason as the fall of Troy. Those flames upon the night—and here Yeats got it right—spring from the resin in the human heart. The veneer we call civilization is always very thin.

*　　　*

To backtrack for a moment: on Sunday, April 22, before the noontime conference, Hitler had formally placed the government area, including the Reich Chancellery and the bunker, under the command of SS Brigadefuehrer and Major General Wilhelm Mohnke. Mohnke had just moved in with his troops from the Lichterfelde barracks.

Hitler told him, "General Mohnke, you are a professional soldier, and you already wear the highest award a German soldier can win on the field of battle [the Knight's Cross, or Ritterkreuz]. My life is now in your hands. We have known each other since nineteen thirty-three. As soldier to soldier, I have one last request to make as I now give you the command of the Zitadelle . . ."

This mixture of chumminess and formality was typical of Hitler whenever he was speaking to soldiers. Mohnke, thirty-four, had been a young lieutenant in the FBK when he first met the new chancellor of the Reich, back in 1933. He had risen to major general and last commander of the elite Leibstandarte Adolf Hitler, the LAH, and had served on almost every front in the long war, because the LAH was a kind of "fire brigade" division. It was also the parade division that had marched before a triumphant Hitler as he entered Linz, Vienna, Prague, Danzig, Warsaw. In the great 1940 parade for the victory over France, celebrated not in Paris but in Berlin, the then-Major Mohnke had marched at the head of the lead battalion along the East-West Axis, redesigned in 1938 as a Via Triumphalis.

Hitler continued, "Frankly, I had hoped to be able to remain alive and in Berlin at least until May fifth. There are historical reasons . . ." A pause. May 5 sounded still an eternity away. Mohnke wondered. Hitler did not elaborate.

"However, General, under no circumstances can I risk being captured alive. Whenever you feel the military situation to be such that you can no longer hold for more than twenty-four hours, you must report this to me, in person. I shall take the consequences. This is a personal request. It is also an order."

Mohnke, a man not given to loquacity, said nothing. He simply saluted. Hitler returned the salute and shook hands. Here again we hear a calm Hitler, resigned to his fate, in a meeting only a very few hours *before* his nervous explosion and crackup that same Sunday midafternoon. He was already relaying to Mohnke the suicide-in-Berlin decision he did not give his senior generals until that afternoon. It is added proof that this resolve was no snap decision or a result of the crackup.

Unlike other German general officers who were outside the city, and thus able to operate pretty much on their own, Mohnke had become what he ironically called "reichsunmittelbar," a medieval word (and hence humorous, in this context) describing the link between a noble liegeman and the Emperor. What it meant was that Mohnke was the last general in direct command of troops who was still at Hitler's immediate beck and call. He could not conveniently get lost.

Given that unique situation, the conduct of this seasoned combat general did not really differ so much from that of his fellow generals. On the Potsdamer Platz, he went into classic hedgehog position with his remaining 1000 or so veteran soldiers. Sweating out the inevitable end, he gave orders of the day that were very simple: dig in, take cover, hunker down, don't draw fire.

Here is how he makes his afternoon report:

> The Russians made only one heavy attack on our position in and around the Potsdamer Platz. That was on Friday, April twenty-seventh. It was a bad blunder from their point of view. They came on at dawn with tanks and infantry. Their tanks were highly unmaneuverable, blocked by rubble, and were sitting ducks in this classic street-fighting situation.
>
> Even young boys and old men, or women, for that matter, armed with bazookas and heroic despair, could get at them from point-blank range, usually under fifty yards, often from a cellar to the middle of the street, thirty yards or even less.

The bazooka General Mohnke here mentions was the German *Panzerfaeust*. It was a cheap, almost primitive, strictly one-shot affair. The weapons were still being manufactured in Berlin factories and machine shops, and were delivered to the "front" in carts and wheelbarrows. They were handed out freely, on Goebbels' orders, like extra bread rations. And they were deadly. Berlin was a death trap for the tank. Kampfgruppe Mohnke only had five tanks; the men dug them into fixed-firing positions.

General Mohnke related, "The Russians had brilliant tank commanders who had learned their business against us out on the steppes and in the open country. Even in city fighting, for example, in Stalingrad or Warsaw, they had never come up against hostile, armed civilians. They realized their mistake only belatedly, after they had lost hundreds of tanks.* On the Potsdamer Platz, after that first frontal assault, they got smarter. They simply pulled back and plastered us with artillery, of which they had a plenitude. They never tried to storm our position again."

It was now a long week since General Mohnke had taken over his battle post; Sunday, April 29. The artillery cannonading of the two previous evenings had suddenly been cut off. Hitler's midnight briefing had been short, desultory, uninformative. General Mohnke had returned to his command post in the cellar of the New Reich Chancellery, which was also his sleeping quarters. He had turned in around 1:00 A.M. Now, at 6:00 A.M.—April 30, 1945— the jangling field telephone beside his cot rudely awakened him.

Sleepily, Mohnke recognized a familiar and friendly voice at the other end of the line. It was Sergeant Rochus Misch, who had once been a private in the company of the then-Captain Mohnke at Moldin, in front of burning Warsaw, in September 1939. Long, long ago.

"General," Misch said, "the Fuehrer wishes to see you alone in his quarters. Please come over immediately."

General Mohnke asked, "Sergeant, as an old Leibstandarte hand, please tell me the unvarnished truth. What temper is the Fuehrer in? Is he as down in the dumps as he was last evening? Who else is there?"

Misch replied, "No problem, General. Der Chef is now in a calm and relaxed mood. No one else is with him. I don't think he has been able to sleep at all this whole long night. Twice within the last hour he has come out to chat with me. Just a moment ago he said he wanted to have a talk with his old friend Mohnke. He tod me to ring you."

The general was now fully awake and much relieved. His adjutant and chief of staff, Colonel Klingemeier, was at this hour on duty in the command post.** Mohnke

---

* This admittedly high tank loss—admitted, that is, by the Russians— is still another statistic that built up the illusion of the great Battle for Berlin. Marshal Koniev speaks of the loss of more than 800; Zhukov, of 1200. Several official Soviet histories place the figure higher. The figure one would like to know, the relevant figure, is how many were lost in tank-to-tank battle, or to infantry and artillery, and how many were knocked out by the highly unorthodox *Panzerfaeuste* in the hands of civilians. This figure may be as high as 500.
** One of Colonel Klingemeier's duties was keeping an hour-by-hour battle diary. He either lost it or destroyed it during the breakout.

gulped a quick cup of coffee with Klingemeier, combed his hair, buttoned up his uniform collar, and left on the double.

Passing through the tunnel from the Chancellery to the Fuehrerbunker, the general noticed for the first time that either shrapnel or a bomb had pierced the roof, which was only five feet underground. He examined it more closely. Shrapnel. He had not noticed this break the night before, but now bright shafts of the dawn sunlight pierced the jagged aperture. He made a note to have this repaired. Mohnke was a stickler for just such details.

As he strode briskly the some 160 yards, General Mohnke recalled the standing order the Fuehrer had given him a week back—the twenty-four-hour notice, the man-to-man request that was "also an order." True, his battered troops were still clinging, surprisingly well, to their positions on the Potsdamer Platz. The Reichstag had not yet fallen. But tomorrow was May 1, the great Soviet political holiday. One last Red Army storm assault, and that would be it. Today was the day Mohnke finally had to give Commander-in-Chief Adolf Hitler the bad news. *Der Tag.* His word of honor as an officer, soldier to soldier. This, he now surmised, must be what Hitler's otherwise quite unusual summons was about.

There was, too, that curious matter about May 5. Why not May 1 or 10 or 15? A date that meant something to Hitler, obviously. Maybe just another Hitler tick. His mother's birthday, perhaps. There had been many such nostalgic whims during this last week. Mohnke had been curious, but he had not asked.

Now the general had arrived in the lower bunker. Hitler usually received Mohnke formally, either in the small conference or map room, or, in more recent days, in his private study. These rooms were now empty in the early morning hours. Mohnke had noticed a few retainers sleeping in the upper bunker. But there was nobody in the lower bunker except for Sergeant Misch at the switchboard and two snoozing FBK guards. Mohnke looked again and saw that the study was not quite empty. Gerda Christian was there in her sleeping bag, on the floor. She was not awake. Sergeant Misch saluted his old CO snappily and said, "Der Chef told me he wants to receive you informally in his bedroom."

Highly unusual. As Mohnke entered, he found Hitler

sitting on the edge of his bed. He was wearing a black
satin morning robe over his pajamas, which were white
with blue piping. He had on a pair of seemingly new soft
patent-leather boot-slippers. Hitler rose politely to greet
Mohnke. He moved himself from the bed to the only
chair in the room, then motioned to Mohnke to take a
seat on the bed. The general now noticed that the bed, a
single cot, had not been slept in. At least, the blankets were
not rumpled.

The two men were within three or four feet of each
other, in half-profile. Hitler's chair was near the head of the
bed and the night table. For most of the time, he gazed
straight ahead, past Mohnke toward the wall. Mohnke, in
turn, looked past Hitler, his eyes on the door. He recalled
that Hitler had made the quick move without clumsy effort.
The Fuehrer's left arm was trembling now and then, but
only slightly. He was grasping the arm of the chair and
used his right arm freely to gesture.

As usual, Mohnke began with a brief situation report.
Hitler listened for five minutes or so in silence. The Russians had reached the Wilhelmstrasse, in the area of the
Adlon Hotel, about four blocks away . . . Red Infantrymen
had penetrated into the subway tubes under both the
Friedrichstrasse and the Voss Strasse . . . Most of the vast,
wooded Tiergarten was now in enemy hands . . . Russian
assault troops had all but encircled the German positions
on the Potsdamer Platz. Here they were only 300 meters
from the Reich Chancellery. Mohnke droned on, listlessly.
Hitler took it all in, intently, calmly. He posed no questions.
There was no wall map. Nor did Hitler even have the tattered filling-station map of Berlin he had been carrying
these last days in his tunic pocket. No need. He knew the
local geography even better than Mohnke did. Almost a
historical moment—the next to last of several thousand
FHQ briefings since 1939. Endgame in Berlin.

The silence, according to the usually taciturn Mohnke,
"was palpable. You could reach out and touch it." To
break the extreme awkwardness of the moment, the general raised the matter of his pledge. "My Fuehrer, as soldier
to soldier, true to my oath to you, I no longer can guaran-
tee that my exhausted, battle-weary troops can hold for
more than one more day. I now expect a frontal, massed-
tank attack tomorrow at dawn, May first. You know what
May first means to Russians."

Hitler said, "I know. Let me say that your troops have fought splendidly, and I have no complaints. Would that all the others had fought as tenaciously—Heinrici, Steiner, Holste, Wenck, Busse. Too bad, really. I had sincerely hoped to make it until May fifth. Beyond that date, I have no desire to live."

General Mohnke was still curious about this seemingly minor Fuehrer obsession. Hitler apparently sensed this puzzlement, and answered the riddle himself, with a trace of a wan smile. "General Mohnke, May fifth is a red-letter day all soldiers should remember and circle in their diaries. Napoleon died on St. Helena on May fifth, eighteen twenty-one. Another great career that ended in total disappointment, disillusion, betrayal, despair. The fickle Europeans did not really understand the French emperor and his great plans, as they have not understood me and mine. We were both men born before our times. Well, so much the worse for Europe. History will be my only judge."

Hitler's admiration for Napoleon came only after his own war in Russia. In the Reichstag in 1939 Hitler had dismissed Bonaparte as "that Corsican adventurer." Live and learn. But Mohnke, at this peculiar moment, was less interested in collecting historical phrases than he was in keeping the Fuehrer in as calm a mood as the one now prevailing.

And it did prevail, for most of what turned out to be a long sitting. It soon became clear that Hitler had called Mohnke over for no particular reason, had no special orders, only one small mission. The Fuehrer, it seems, just felt the need for an audience, preferably a soldier, and Mohnke was the very model of his ideal SS officer. Mohnke was tall, rangy, with a craggy face, square wrists. He had that panache of a front-line officer that Hitler truly admired. Mohnke was wearing his Knight's Cross, with oak-leaf cluster.

Adolf Hitler and General Mohnke were not really close friends, and both preferred keeping it that way. Mohnke, for example, had seldom if ever been a guest at Hitler's table. In this sense at least he was a new, fresh listener for old themes. One supposes that this is the most likely reason for Mohnke's odd summons at this dawn hour.

General Mohnke did not later say so—and it is to the man's credit that he did not—but he was at this moment in almost as parlous a situation as was Hitler himself.

Mohnke was in better health and much younger, but what now loomed before him was death in battle, suicide, hanging, or long imprisonment. As a realist he knew this.

Wilhelm Mohnke was a family man; his wife and two children were at this moment in Luebeck, on the Baltic. But there was no mention of this in a conversation that was to last nearly a full hour. No mention of the breakout that Mohnke would soon have to plan and lead. Not even a decoration. (Hitler may have felt such a gesture superfluous, since the Knight's Cross was already the highest military decoration.) He did thank Mohnke for his loyalty, but he did not give him a farewell present.

At 4:00 A.M., so Schenck reported, Hitler had been trembling so badly that he had had to wrap his left leg around the table to support himself, to keep his balance. Now, only a short time later, and without having slept more than a wink, Hitler was sitting fairly calmly by the bed with Mohnke. The general noticed only an occasional twitch. One suspects that Haase had given Hitler a shot of morphine. Or at least a very strong tranquilizer to face the end.

Years later Mohnke commented:

Obviously Hitler was in very bad health, and had been for months. We all knew this. But on this last day, my memory is that his control over his nerves and emotions was far better than just eight days before, the Sunday of the blue-faced explosion at the noontime briefing. Nor did he look quite so sallow, so pasty-faced, as he had on many occasions in the past year. That he was suffering from Parkinson's disease, as Dr. Schenck has said, is news to me. That Adolf Hitler was in no condition to carry a rifle or march in any breakout, I, of course, agree.

Throughout the whole talk I was seated almost at his side, perhaps three or four feet away. But he was either gazing at the wall or looking down at the floor. After the first ten minutes, our talk ceased to be a conversation. It became a monologue. Hitler was sitting a bit bowed, his shoulders bent forward. He sometimes grasped the chair arm, sometimes had both elbows on his knees.

The monologue began with a bitter denunciation of the west. "The western democracies are all decadent, feeble. They will all fall one day to the more virile, vigorous people of the east, who have shown themselves to be the stronger, and for whom the rigid system of Communism is the proper one!"

Then he began a review of his whole career, what he called his dream of National Socialism and how and why it had failed. The German people had, in the end, proved unworthy, just not up to the supreme challenge. His spirit lifted when he reminded me of his old triumphs, like the tumultuous receptions, in nineteen thirty-eight, in Linz and Vienna. I, too, had participated as a member of the FBK. Then he spoke of the many exultant victory parades in which I had marched with the LAH. He was, so to speak, cheering himself up.

When he spoke of the war, he insisted that it had been forced on him by Anglo-American plutocracy, the Marxist-Bolshevik world conspiracy, Jewish international finance, the Freemasons, the Jesuits, all the familiar enemies and scape-goats from "the days of the struggle." He said that he had had to attack the Soviet Union in nineteen forty-one because he knew that Stalin was about to attack Germany. We could have won in Russia, he insisted, but for the sheer failure of our own generals. Never had a national leader been stuck with more incompetent professional military men. The German General Staff, once a truly mighty instrument, had become a haven of reactionary aristocrats. They simply did not know their jobs; maybe they were even out to sabotage his grand plans . . .

Finally—and now Hitler's gorge was rising—he went on to complain woefully that he had not been spared even the humiliation of treason and betrayal within his inner circle. Goering, corrupt and degenerate, had made a mess of the Luftwaffe and had exposed the Reich to massive air raids. Now Goering had had the insolence to try to replace the Fuehrer! Himmler was even more of a wretched traitor, actively negotiating with the west. Speer had left him.

Enemy espionage, he insisted, seemed to know of every secret order he gave—twenty-four to forty-eight hours after he gave it. His own FHQ, he could prove, was not secure. It leaked vital information like a sieve. There was a spy some-where, either in the bunker or the Reich Chancellery. Secu-rity leaks, everywhere he turned. As he said this his voice rose, his fists clenched, his face turned white. It was obvious to me that the thought or reality of treachery almost drove him up the wall. When he used the word *das Leck* [the leak], he was almost screaming. This leak in the FHQ, as I knew, had been concerning him, especially during the last two weeks. He gave it at least as much time as his some half-dozen other major problems. Hitler had begun to suspect every face he saw about him.

CHAPTER VII

•

The Lady Vanished

Those of us working in the psychological-warfare branch never knew too much about this mystery woman. Our shop code name for her was Mata O'Hara. She was operating in Berlin, had intimate contacts in high SS circles, including the Hitler entourage. We used her inside material for Soldatensender Calais, our effort in the field of black propaganda. But when our troops and military intelligence people got to Berlin in nineteen forty-five, they found our most successful lady agent had vanished. The cream of the jest is that she was not English. She was Irish. She should have got the Victoria Cross. Someday she probably will.
                                        —RICHARD CROSSMAN,
                                        British M.P. and journalist,
                                        in a 1955 conversation
                                        with the author

Das Leck! The leak! It was a woman. The story is as old as that of Samson and Delilah. This bunker report is not a detective story, but the matter of *das Leck*, the security leak in the bunker itself, suddenly took on great significance. General Mohnke was at least the fourth of my present-in-the-last-days bunker witnesses to stress this.

I had first heard the leak story from Albert Speer, but did not then tumble to its import. Speer, after all, had left the bunker forever in the early hours of Tuesday, April 24; much had occurred thereafter. How, I asked myself, could Hitler be worried about some annoying security breach when his whole world was crashing about him?

> ## "Himmler a traitor! Heinrich the true! When Hitler got this shattering news, pandemonium broke loose. The delirium of treason now engulfed the bunker."

I was wrong. Later, several other witnesses, ones who were there until the end, confirmed what Speer had said. Hans Baur, Kempka, Guensche, even Misch, returned to the theme often. They insisted that Hitler, surrounded by what he kept calling the phenomenon of general treachery, was also nagged by a specific security leak, something he was aware of but could not locate.

As Speer had first put it:

In those last weeks in the bunker, a special phenomenon of Hitler's mind was a kind of trigger reaction. When he started in on the *nous-sommestrahi* theme, he would usually remark, "This all began with that loony idiot, Rudolf Hess." He would then couple Hess's defection with the July twentieth Staufenberg conspiracy, which was, of course, an utterly different affair. Then he would tick off such things as the Rote Kapelle, which was a Communist espionage ring uncovered by the RSHA [Himmler's secret service]. We also knew about two signal communication links in both the Armed Forces and Wehrmacht Supreme Commands [OKH and OKW], by which military information was going from Berlin, via Switzerland, to both England and Russia.

Speer was speaking here of the highly successful agent Rudolf Roessler. The OKH and OKW leaks were two anti-Nazi daughters of retired German officers, working in the signal center. Both young women leaked tapes and codes to one or more opposition groups, including Roessler's.

Speer continued:

But in that last fortnight, when Hitler mentioned *das Leck* he knew what he was talking about, a steady flow of information out of his own shop. For example, he told me of an order—I believe it was a rather routine promotion list—that he had for some reason pulled back and *not* sent to the

OKW or the OKH. Yet within forty-eight hours, he complained, the news of these "promotions" was on the British radio.* Hitler could thus no longer blame this kind of security breach on either the OKW or the OKH. It utterly exasperated him. Hitler on this matter was not just imagining things. I, too, am still convinced there was such a penetration, but I never heard the explanation.**

During my last visit to the Fuehrerbunker, on April twenty-third and twenty-fourth, I recall Hitler mentioning that he had at last called in both Ernst Kaltenbrunner of the RSHA and Gestapo Chief Heinrich Mueller to make a thorough probe of bunker internal security. Kaltenbrunner, I believe, left for South Germany about the same time I went north. Hitler had sent him on another important mission, but as you have noted, Mueller was in the bunker until the very end. He was not normally a member of the Hitler inner circle. He was there because he had one specific job to do.

Hans Baur, who usually went out of his way to disagree with and contradict Speer whenever he could, made the same point. "In his last talk with me, midmorning of April thirtieth, Hitler said, 'Baur, you can write on my tombstone, "He was betrayed by his generals." ' This was a familiar, blanket indictment. But then he got specific. He said, 'My God, even my own HQ has been penetrated.'" Again Baur, quoting Hitler, used the word *das Leck*.

From Sergeant Rochus Misch, certainly no high-level source but often close to Hitler, I heard, "During that last fortnight, when Hitler talked to me, he would sometimes ask, 'Misch, what do you think of so-and-so? Can we be sure he is secure?'"

Misch recalled another occasion when Hitler mentioned a suspect. "It was the case of a janitor over in the Old Reich Chancellery. He had been there since nineteen thirty-three. His name was Ziegler. He was a kind of sour fellow, or anyway a constant grumbler. One day Hitler said to me, 'Misch, I want you to keep your eye on Ziegler. He is an odd bird—*ein schraeger Vogel*. I just don't trust the look in his eyes. I am having him investigated.'"

---

* Speer is right here. The promotion list was of SS officers in Sepp Dietrich's Sixth Panzer Army. When they failed to hold Budapest in February, Hitler in his wrath held up the promotion list.
** A year after this 1974 interview, I showed Speer the probable explanation, which is the subject matter of this chapter. He accepted it as "the mostly likely solution" to what he had long regarded as a major bunker mystery, though, he said, he never met the woman in question.

Couldn't Hitler fire anyone he wanted to? Misch answered that question. "It was something about the German civil service. He said it was easier to fire a field marshal or a minister than it was to fire a janitor. However, Ziegler disappeared, some time in the last week. I think he took off on his own. But you never know."

How does all of this connect with the mysterious Fegelein affair? The sketchy outline of this case has been known for a long time, but opinion has been inconclusive—as expressed by Hugh Trevor-Roper in *The Last Days of Hitler* (1947): "The real causes and circumstances of the execution of Fegelein provide one of the few subjects in this book upon which final certainty seems unattainable."

Hermann Fegelein had been blessed by good fortune in his career. When he was a young man, his skill as a jockey had attracted the attention of Christian Weber, the Nazi boss of Munich, who thereafter helped him to advance. Fegelein joined the Waffen SS, rose to the command of a cavalry division, and enjoyed several military successes on the eastern front. In 1944, he was assigned as Himmler's liaison officer with Hitler and, as noted previously, made his opportunistic marriage with Eva Braun's sister Gretl. He was definitely a part of the favored inner circle in the bunker.

On Wednesday, April 25, Fegelein left Berlin by car to visit Himmler's headquarters at Hohenlychen. On the 26th, with the roads cut by advancing Russian troops, he made his way back to Berlin by air. He did not report in at the bunker, and his absence was finally noticed on the 27th. On the night of the 27th he was found in his flat, brought to the bunker, court-martialed, and executed within twenty-four hours. The charge, according to Hans Baur, had been desertion. These are the bare bones of the Fegelein case. But as I started to investigate, that case began to take on some astonishing features.

Hans Baur, one of the prime sources for the Fegelein story, gave, essentially, the version related above. Baur and Fegelein shared quarters in the so-called adjutant's wing of the New Reich Chancellery and Baur was sitting in the room late that Friday evening when Fegelein staggered in. Baur had heard of Hitler's mounting wrath and so he asked the other where the devil he had been. Fegelein replied woozily, "Well, if you feel that way, just take me out and shoot me."

Just then, General Mohnke appeared, ready to conduct his drumhead court-martial. Baur left the room—but, later, he saw four angry generals frog-marching the cursing, wheedling Fegelein toward Mohnke's command post. Still a little later, Baur saw the prisoner being led away "in handcuffs toward the Gestapo cellar," after his court-martial for desertion.*

General Mohnke, however, hotly denied to me that such a court-martial for desertion ever took place. If Mohnke was right, then logic dictated that the man must have been executed for some other reason. (That Fegelein was killed almost twenty-four hours after his return is generally agreed, though there are no eyewitnesses—or, at least, none willing to talk.)

Here is General Mohnke's surprising version of what really happened, or did not happen:

General Baur describes the return of Fegelein accurately enough, but Baur soon left the scene. I believe he was concerned that, as a general officer, he might have to sit on the ad hoc panel. Fegelein had a right to trial by his peers. To get around that technicality, Hitler, as commander-in-chief, had already reduced Fegelein to the ranks—he was now an SS private. That action, in my book, was illegal.**

That night—it was now Friday, April twenty-seventh—I had the bad luck to be present in the lower bunker, by chance, when Hitler got the word that defector Fegelein had been hauled back to the Reich Chancellery. Hitler ordered me to set up a tribunal forthwith. I was to preside over it myself. Since his action in stripping Fegelein of all rank was irregular to say the least, I myself decided the accused man deserved trial by high-ranking officers. The panel consisted of four general officers—Generals Burgdorf, Krebs, Rattenhuber, and me. Reich Youth leader Artur Axmann and Colonel Peter Hoegl [Rattenhuber's second-in-command] were present as observers.

Baur is accurate when he says he saw us leading Fegelein away, going off down the corridor toward my command post. We did, at that moment, have every intention of holding a trial. But when Baur says he saw Fegelein being led away

---

* This secret Gestapo cellar was an emergency headquarters set up in the crypt of the ruined Dreifaltigkeit Church on the Mauerstrasse. Mueller (and probably Ernst Kaltenbrunner, as well) had his office there. Baur knew about the place from Mueller—the two had a bond as former World War I pilots.
** The problem bothering Mohnke was Fegelein's high rank—that of SS lieutenant general. Only Generals Krebs, Burgdorf, and Baur were his peers. Mohnke was only a major general.

in handcuffs an hour or so later, he was jumping to a plausible yet quite false conclusion. He also went about the bunker spreading this ugly story. The fact is, however, that no such trial ever took place.

I was quite taken aback at this startling new Mohnke version. It was at variance with everything I had previously heard, not only from Baur but from Linge, Kempka, Frau Christian, and others.* It also flatly contradicts all previously published accounts.

On the other hand, I had long made up my mind that General Mohnke would know more about the Fegelein affair than any other living bunker witness. (Rattenhuber knew even more, but he died in 1966, after his return from Soviet captivity. He may or may not have told Mohnke all he knew.) I also was by now fully aware that the bad blood I had detected between Mohnke and his critics almost always traced back to this mystery-enshrouded Fegelein matter.

My dossier of bunker rumors was heavy with a variety of lurid versions. I cite but two:

1. General Mohnke, after presiding over the court-martial, had shot Fegelein, on Hitler's orders and in Hitler's presence.

2. An even more macabre version. In the presence of Bormann, Mohnke, and Guensche, Hitler had reached for his own pistol and shot Fegelein dead.

The first rumor was possible, if improbable. The second, I dismissed out of hand. A Hitler who knew he could not trust his trigger finger to destroy himself could not shoot to kill across a crowded room, much as he may have loathed the man Fegelein, a coward and traitor.

For the historical record, General Mohnke's statement is this:

What really happened was that we set up the court-martial in a room next to my command post. Someone located a green baize cloth and spread it over a long table. I was determined to carry out this distasteful assignment by the book. We military judges took our seats at the table with the standard German Army *Manual of Courts-Martial* before

---

* One exception is Otto Guensche. He was silent on the matter. Apparently he wanted me to get the story from Mohnke directly. Guensche, who was always on duty in the Fuehrerbunker proper, was *not* an eyewitness.

us. No sooner were we seated than defendant Fegelein began acting up in such an outrageous manner that the trial could not even commence.

Roaring drunk, with wild, rolling eyes, Fegelein first brazenly challenged the competence of the court. He kept blubbering that he was responsible to Himmler and Himmler alone, not Hitler [a droll view, under the circumstances]. Fegelein had a right to defense counsel but rejected it. He refused to defend himself. The man was in wretched shape —bawling, whining, vomiting, shaking like an aspen leaf. He took out his penis and began urinating on the floor. He really was drunk; he was not acting.

At this point, as I am sure you have read in earlier accounts, I am supposed to have informed General Fegelein that the Fuehrer had degraded him to simple SS soldier. Also, that I tore off his epaulets and decorations and threw them in his face.

Well, quite the opposite is true. Fegelein tore off his own shoulder pieces and threw them to the floor. He called us all a collection of German assholes.*

I was now faced with an impossible situation. On the one hand, based on all available evidence, including his own earlier statements, this miserable excuse for an officer was guilty of flagrant desertion. It was "desertion in the face of the enemy" in the literal sense of that phrase. In every army in the world, the penalty for such is both summary and severe. Adolf Hitler, as commander-in-chief, was well within his rights in ordering this trial. He was in no mood to tolerate in an SS general what he could not tolerate in a simple soldier. Nor were the rest of us.

Yet the German Army *Manual* states clearly that no German soldier can be tried unless he is clearly of sound mind and body, in a condition to hear the evidence against him, and able to aid and understand his own defense. I looked up the passage again, to make sure, and consulted with my fellow judges. I felt I had no alternative but to adjourn and dismiss the court. In my opinion and that of my fellow officers, Hermann Fegelein was in no condition to stand trial, or for that matter even to stand. I closed the proceedings.

I needed all my available soldiers for the battle in progress. So I turned Fegelein over to General Rattenhuber and his security squad. I never saw the man again.

Assuming that Mohnke's description of Fegelein's state of inebriation is not exaggerated—and all actors in this turgid drama agree with him at least on that—then many

---

* *Arschloecher*, a strong word even in the Waffen SS.

readers have probably already spotted a slight flaw in his version of events.

Granted, the atmosphere is hypertense and malignant; suspicion in the bunker, by April 28, had peaked to panic proportions. Artillery shells poured in, knocking the mortar from the thick cement walls. We are not dealing with normal, rational, or even sober people. Still, one almost always detects a method in their madness, a sheer self-interest in their calculations. This was above all true of the Fuehrer, often calmer now than he had been just one week earlier. If Hitler was so determined to have Fegelein tried for desertion—and that had been his expressed desire and peremptory order around midnight on Thursday, the 26th—then in his meeting with General Mohnke the next morning surely Hitler would have said something to this effect: "General Mohnke, since you are such a stickler for going strictly by the book, sober up the accused, reconvene your panel, give him a fair trial, and *then* shoot him."

The evidence is overwhelming that Hitler, on this particular day, could reason and react rationally—when he so chose.

We know this did *not* happen. The question is, why? Any drunkard can be sobered up in twelve hours, by the simple method of keeping him away from the bottle. The Gestapo had other quicker methods, and we know that by this time the hapless Fegelein was a prisoner in Heinrich Mueller's cellar chamber in the nearby Dreifaltigkeit chapel. Here he spent all that very warm day of Saturday, April 28, under intensive interrogation. He was probably beaten and tortured. Such a long session in Gestapo hands was seldom just an information dialogue.*

Fegelein before the court was still in the custody of the Waffen SS, a branch of the military. He was no longer a general officer, but he was still a soldier-prisoner. The martinet Mohnke, so otherwise meticulous, even hair-splitting, about legal procedure, would not normally have

---

* We know this by inference: (a) Mohnke said he was handed over to Rattenhuber, and Rattenhuber came under Mueller's orders; (b) Baur identified the Gestapo cellar in the vault of the chapel; and (c) late Saturday afternoon, the 28th, Captain Gerhard Boldt happened to see Fegelein "being brought down the Voss Strasse and into the New Reich Chancellery." The assumption is that at about this time the twelve-to-fourteen-hour Mueller grilling had ended, and Fegelein (now sober) was being brought back to await his fate. He probably asked to see Hitler, a request almost surely denied. Guensche, Christian, and others would undoubtedly have known (and talked) about any such last Hitler-Fegelein meeting.

turned any soldier over to Rattenhuber. It wasn't done.
Rattenhuber, though he held the same rank as Mohnke
—each was a SS Brigadefuehrer, or major general—was
not really a soldier, least of all in the eyes of a professional
military man like Mohnke. Rattenhuber, as head of Dienststelle I in the Reich Chancellery, was responsible for the
personal safety of the Fuehrer.* He was now also reporting
to his superior, Gestapo Mueller.

Mohnke, I believe, was telling the truth; he did hand
over Fegelein to Rattenhuber. But, once again, not the
whole truth; he had concealed something. Why did he turn
a soldier-prisoner over to the security spooks?

"Yes, that was unusual, I admit. Fegelein was my prisoner. But you see, General Rattenhuber had just hotfooted
it over from the Fuehrerbunker and demanded custody. I
gladly yielded it. Rattenhuber later was to tell me that the
fate of Fegelein was decided and handled internally in the
hour before the Hitler–Eva Braun marriage."

In plain language, "handled internally" is a euphemism
for "executed." It happened more than twenty-two hours
after Mohnke turned him over. This is thus a midnight-to-
midnight black melodrama, from about midnight on Friday, April 27, to nearly midnight on Saturday, April 28.
Around midnight on Friday, Hitler, by giving the court-
martial order to Mohnke, had wanted Fegelein to pay the
supreme penalty for desertion, clearly a military offense.
One hour later, however, Hitler must have changed his
mind, for he now brought in General Rattenhuber. This
has to mean that in this short interim Fegelein, in Hitler's
eyes, had become a security problem. He was not only a
deserter, which was glaringly obvious, but a suspected
traitor in the bargain. Something important had been uncovered in this critical hour that put an even grimmer face
on the matter. This was known to five or six insiders in
the lower bunker—Bormann, Mueller, Rattenhuber, Hoegl,
Guensche, and maybe Goebbels. It was not, however,
known to General Mohnke.

Here we must take into account what Baur said of the
last time he saw Fegelein. Baur, as Mohnke had already
pointed out emphatically, was wrong in assuming that a
court-martial had taken place. But under the lurid cir-

---

* He was analogous to an FBI man or, more strictly speaking, a Treasury man; it is the U.S. Treasury that carries out this function in the
White House—protection of the chief of state.

cumstances, this was a very human, quite rational error. Baur, one must repeat—personal motives are all important here—really had but two basic human interests. As for Fegelein, whom he still called "*Flegelein*" (lout) thirty years later, he really could not have cared less. But he did care very much about Eva Braun, Fegelein's sister-in-law. For the next long hours Baur, on the quiet—for he now had little else to do in the bunker—was reporting in to Eva Braun. He confided all he knew or could hear about the fate of Hermann Fegelein.

The pilot's second motive was far less altruistic. It was shared by most of the other mountain people in the bunker. The murderous wrath of the Fuehrer, just unleashed against Fegelein, could lash out tomorrow at any member of the dwindling band of courtiers and retainers. Including Chef-pilot Hans Baur.

Baur described one of his meetings with Eva Braun in this way.

> While I was still shaving early the next morning [Saturday, April 28], Eva Braun came over from the lower bunker and knocked shyly on my door. This was one of her rare trips outside the lower bunker. The girl was sobbing, and said she now feared her lover would be savage and ruthless with Fegelein. She reported Hitler was now in a mood to shoot even his own blood-brother. Her deepest regret was not so much for the unworthy Fegelein, who had cravenly deserted us all. She said he had cooked his own goose. It was rather for her poor sister Gretl, down in Munich, who was now eight months pregnant. Eva even said with a sigh that she hoped it would be a boy—"for the Braun girls were born into this world under an unlucky star."*

On balance, and although he was wrong about the court-martial, I feel the rest of Baur's story is correct. General Mohnke said that he handed Fegelein into the custody of Rattenhuber. There is no reason to doubt this. Obviously at this time, or very shortly afterward, Rattenhuber in turn must have delivered Fegelein to Mueller. For, as Baur reported, "It was only about an hour later that I saw

---

* A girl was born in May 1945 and named for Eva. Gretl was pregnant in 1944 when she married Fegelein, perhaps as a result of a liaison with Captain Fritz Darger. There may have then been an abortion (Dr. Morell was often employed among the mountain people for such a purpose), though my informants were mum on this point. In any case, Eva was a second child and most likely was Fegelein's. She committed suicide in 1975 after an unhappy love affair.

Fegelein being led off in handcuffs toward the Gestapo cellar."

Hans Baur is the only major bunker witness who really knew about this Gestapo cellar. Since he gave me a quite precise description, I surmise that Baur must have been there, at least once. Then, too, as one who entered and left the Chancellery often, Baur recognized the Gestapo operators, and not only from their brown leather jackets. He would not have mistaken Rattenhuber's detectives, all of whom he knew well,* for Gestapo hoods. Der Chef-pilot was an eagle-eyed observer of just such matters.

The point is not trivial. General Mohnke was responsible for the miltary aspect only of Fegelein's fate, and this phase had now definitely passed. Exit Mohnke. Ratten-huber, true enough, was in charge of internal security in the Reich Chancellery and Fuehrerbunker, since both in-volved the person of the Fuehrer. The higher-ranking Mueller was responsible for *external* security. But Mueller had originally been summoned to the bunker with the one specific mission of investigating *das Leck*. We also know that the prisoner Fegelein had now passed into his hands, for a cellar-grilling that was to last more than fourteen hours. Ergo, two conclusions at this point are patent:

1. Fegelein's military desertion had become a secondary matter. The Gestapo did not concern itself, was not inter-ested in, purely military matters.

2. There was now, almost surely, a link with the security-leak matter, for it was, one repeats, *das Leck*, which had brought Gestapo chief Mueller into the Fuehrerbunker one week back, that now brought him into the Fegelein affair. If this had not already been established down in the Fuehrerbunker, at least a strong suspicion had built up.

As we know, on Wednesday, April 25, three days before, Fegelein had left Berlin at dawn that morning for Hohen-lychen, Heinrich Himmler's last headquarters. It is about ninety miles northwest of Berlin, in Mecklenburg. General Fegelein was chauffeur-driven in his staff car. After the short visit in Hohenlychen, he set out for several head-quarters in the same area—Field Marshal Keitel at Waren, General Jodl at Krampnitz, and the SS headquarters at Fuerstenberg. Some time during that afternoon, the road back to Berlin was cut off. Red Army tank patrols had

---

* Security of the Fuehrer's fleet of planes was their common problem.

suddenly appeared on the main road between Nauen and Berlin. Nauen is only twenty miles west of the German capital.

Fegelein was having trouble moving about on these Mecklenburg and Mark of Brandenburg country roads. The Nauen-Berlin highway is the same arterial road Albert Speer had found so clogged as to be impassable forty-eight hours before. It was then blocked by the great week-end exodus of panicky Berliners, those who still had access to wheels and gasoline. Their timing was just under the line. On this day, in the morning, the traffic flow had abated. Russian patrols were sighted some time in the early afternoon. All German traffic ceased.

Fegelein had to take to the air. He made his last visit to one of the headquarters in an Arado–96. Normally, Lieutenant General Fegelein did not have quite enough rank to rate a private plane.* But now from Rechlin, the airbase in the same area, Himmler sent him a Junker–52, with pilot, for the journey back to Berlin. It was too dangerous to fly the slow, lumbering Junker–52** by daylight. Fegelein thus waited at Rechlin until around 9:00 P.M. He was then flown to Berlin, landing at Gatow. The pilot took off back to Rechlin, his home station.

Here a common-sense point arises. If, by Wednesday, April 25, Fegelein's simple and only motive had been to escape from the Fuehrerbunker and thus avoid the doom awaiting the other members of the Hitler court, the man, on this busy day, most obviously had it made. And he could still have escaped the clutches of the Red Army avengers as they now closed so rapidly on Berlin. As an SS Obergruppenfuehrer, Fegelein knew what he had to expect from the Russians. Fegelein was no hero, and normally no fool.

The wrath of the Fuehrer? Geography had come to his aid. Fegelein, the former jockey, always calculated the odds. Instead of flying back to encircled Berlin, he could have motored in the opposite direction—back to Hohenlychen. Here he could have joined the well-armed entourage of his chief, Heinrich Himmler. Fegelein had been keeping Himmler informed of the "lunatic conditions" prevailing

---

* Private planes were reserved for senior ministers or military men of four-star rank.
** The Junker–52 was one of the great planes of all time, a workhorse similar to the American C–47 or Dakota. But it was slow.

in the bunker. Himmler had drawn his own personal and political conclusions. He would understand.

Himmler was longing for Hitler's demise any day, expecting it perhaps any moment. He thought this would secure for him the "succession," now that Goering was out of the running. Hitler and Bormann's murderous writ, in short, no longer extended west to Mecklenburg. Even a Fuehrerbefehl from the bunker, ordering Fegelein's arrest, could—would—be ignored. Only forty-eight hours before, Bormann had been able to pull off the arrest of Goering. The sinister long arm of the Berlin bunker still reached as far as Bavarian Berchtesgaden. But not into rural Mecklenburg, Himmler's bailiwick.*

We now know, and Fegelein probably knew at the time, what his creepy boss, Heinrich Himmler, was already planning. Himmler had not been back in Berlin since the Fuehrer's birthday, April 20. On April 22 he had, cagily, come back *halfway* to Berlin. He had had a roadside rendezvous at noontime, near Nauen, with his liaison man, General Fegelein. Himmler had then disappeared into North Germany, up to the Baltic coast, to begin his secret peace-feeler negotiations with the British and Americans, through his intermediary, the Swedish Count Bernadotte. Himmler was now meeting with the Swedish Red Cross representative on the quiet in the Swedish consulate in Luebeck.

Hence something—or a rendezvous with someone—made Hermann Fegelein's flying return to Berlin most urgent. Flying into and out of Berlin, as we know from the flight of Albert Speer (April 23 and 24) and that of Hanna Reitsch and Ritter von Greim (April 26 and 28) was most hazardous—if not downright foolhardy. In his ever-calculating mind, his rendezvous in Berlin must have been stern necessity.

It was certainly no sense of devotion to the utterly lost cause of his Fuehrer that compelled this return. Around noontime, in the officers' mess at Fuerstenberg, nervous SS fellow officers had asked their VIP Berlin visitor just what was happening in the bunker. According to SS Obergruppenfuehrer Max Juettner, Fegelein replied with jaunty insouciance, *"Menschenskind!* I have no intention of join-

---

* Mecklenburg is Germany's Sleepy Hollow. Bismarck once said, "If I heard the end of the world was coming tomorrow morning, I would rush to Mecklenburg. Everything happens there fifty years later."

ing those bunker maniacs in any mass-suicide ceremonies. The Valhalla stuff is for the Bayreuth Festival, but not for me. Goebbels is even sounding off about an SS plan to blow the whole bunker complex sky-high, with TNT. The place has become a lunatic asylum."

General Juettner, who had once been Fegelein's division comander, knew Fegelein as a member of the Hitler court and also as the husband of Gretl Braun. He *may* have known about the relationship of Eva Braun and Adolf Hitler, but we cannot be sure.

This delicate family matter was very much part of Hermann Fegelein's present pressing problem. He was, in one sense, the only Hitler relative or near-relative on duty in the bunker. There already had been much talk of a funeral pyre, and lurid hints from Eva that it should be a family affair, a kind of Nazi suttee. This must have set brother-in-law Hermann's teeth on edge.

Fegelein was a lifelong climber. He had married plump Gretl Braun at Hitler's suggestion, if not insistence. Gretl was known in the FBK as the "nymphomaniac of the Obersalzberg." It was strictly a marriage of convenience, for Hitler as well as for Fegelein. Now, less than a year later, this connection so close to the toppling throne was a distinct embarrassment for Fegelein.

He was by no means the only outspoken "survivalist" in the Reich Chancellery Group. For all his blatant cowardice, the man was at least rational, and usually as shrewd as an outhouse rat. Unlike most other bunkerees, the special nature of his liaison job had give him a much clearer topside view of reality.

Fegelein knew that the chances for survival outside the bunker catacomb were far better than inside. A quick discarding of the uniform, a disappearance into the universal chaos of the collapse, a quiet rustication to await better days. Maybe in Switzerland. These must have been his thoughts as he flew in from Rechlin to Berlin, late in the evening of Wednesday, April 25. Fegelein arrived in time to make the midnight bunker conference, but he did not attend. This was not too unusual, nor was it even remarked by others. As liaison man, he had often of necessity missed the regular conferences in the past hectic fortnight, since he was en route between Himmler and Hitler. All day Thursday, April 26, Fegelein again did not show. Yet still no one missed him, officially. Eva Braun was aware of his prolonged absence and was worried, but she did not, of course, dare say anything to Hitler.

Hitler on this day was busy with sundry other matters. Hanna Reitsch and Ritter von Greim had flown in, dramatically. It was not until the next day, Friday, April 27, around noon, that Hitler finally missed Fegelein and noted that his SS liaison man had played truant from six briefings running. Here we get still another revealing picture of how much the old, accustomed FHQ-bunker routine was cranking down.

Guensche related, "The routine matter Hitler wanted to check out with Fegelein was some trifle, so minor that I forget just what it was. I believe it had something to do with the soldiers of Himmler's honor escort, of whom the Reichsfuehrer had now sent Hitler some three hundred and fifty. They had been thrown into the Berlin fighting on the rim of the Tiergarten. However, when Fegelein was not immediately available, Hitler's suspicion flared like a sudden flame. Hitler and I now recalled that we had not seen brother Fegelein around the bunker for two full days. Hitler, livid with anger, rang for General Rattenhuber."

Nobody present in the bunker at this moment had a clue as to where Fegelein could be located. He had not called in, had left no covering message, no Berlin address, no telephone number. Only Major Guensche, who was a tippling companion of Fegelein's, quietly nursed a vague hunch, but he said nothing. Several weeks back, after one of their wassailing evenings out on the town, Fegelein, with a wink, had given Guensche a phone number where he could be reached "in a real emergency." This emergency had now clearly arrived. But Guensche decided to remain silent. "I was not even sure that I still had the notebook with the jotted phone entry."

At this point in our narrative, sex rears its lovely head. For the past year, man-about-Berlin Fegelein had been keeping a very good-looking, tall, classy mistress in a modest furnished flat at Number 10–11 Bleibtreustrasse. This cosy dwelling was in a large, rambling apartment house. The Bleibtreustrasse is just off the fashionable Kurfuerstendamm, in the middle-class borough of Charlottenburg, only about four miles from the Reich Chancellery. By a freak, this was one of the few large downtown houses that had escaped serious bomb damage. Both Fegelein and his lady friend had been bombed out of an earlier luxury apartment. Their new flat was registered in the name of a friend of Fegelein's. To this convenient and inconspicuous hideaway, far from the madding bunker crowd, Fegelein had now retreated.

The sands in the Berlin hourglass were running out, rapidly. The Russians were already much closer to Fegelein than to Hitler and company. They were, in fact, only four blocks away—an immediate problem. General Fegelein had already changed into mufti. He was drinking regularly. It was obviously high time to take it on the lam. Equally obvious, something was delaying him.

The scene shifts back to the Fuehrerbunker, four miles to the east. The short briefing was over. It was now about 2:00 P.M. on Thursday, April 26. Hitler had had Rattenhuber on the mat and had been chewing him out unmercifully. No Fegelein for more than forty-eight hours, and Rattenhuber, fine security man, had not even noticed this defection. Nor had he the foggiest idea where Fegelein might be.

Rattenhuber emerged from Hitler's study wringing his hands. He appealed to Guensche for help. It was only now that Guensche mentioned the telephone number, located the notebook, and gave the number to Rattenhuber. The chief detective at once asked Sergeant Rochus Misch at the switchboard to trace the number to locate the exact street address. Misch promptly did. The Berlin telephone central was still functioning with its usual Prussian efficiency—tracer service as usual during altercations.

Around two-thirty, General Rattenhuber got through. Fegelein himself answered, blearily. He must have been *bouleversé*. His snug hideout had been discovered. But after the initial surprise, foxy Fegelein played it cool. He told Rattenhuber that he had been drinking and still had a terrible hangover. This was certainly true enough. He went on to say that he had not yet shaved but would report within two hours. Rattenhuber, quoting a Fuehrerbefehl, ordered Fegelein to shave and leave immediately. If he did not have transport, Rattenhuber said, he would send a car. Fegelein again gave his "word of honor as a German officer" that he would appear "within two hours."

At first sight, in reconstruction, it seems that the usually canny Fegelein had made the first of several appalling blunders. Why did the man answer the phone at all? A fair surmise is that he must have been waiting for an

urgent call. He could, for example, have been waiting for
a woman or a plane—or both. He needed a plane, for
there was now no other way to leave Berlin—except on
foot—and decamping was now his obvious intention. A
plane would not be able to land at the Brandenburg Gate
before nightfall. Fegelein clearly was playing for time.
Had his female companion been present, she most certainly
would have been the one to answer the phone. So we can
assume he was, in fact, alone.

Liquor, too, was playing its role. Fegelein must have
been reeling, for his astonishing next move was to call Eva
Braun. To her, he had already made his escape intentions
crystal clear. He simply wanted to disappear from world
history, and he now brazenly invited her to do the same.
Come fly with me! Fegelein apparently did not know very
well the deep death wish of his sister-in-law. She was
naturally indignant and tartly reminded Fegelein of the
Fuehrer's seething wrath, the obvious danger to his life,
and the fact that his wife, far away in Bavaria, was expecting a baby any week now. At this point—the source here
is Sergeant Misch—Fegelein, that good Bavarian family
man, got off one of his deathless lines: "The proper place
for an expectant father is at the bedside of his spouse."

There is no evidence that Eva Braun, caught up in a
deep conflict of loyalties, reported this highly indiscreet
conversation to Hitler. She did not know it, nor did
Sergeant Misch at the switchboard—but Hitler most probably heard every word. There was a concealed microphone
in the switchboard piping directly into Hitler's study.*

Five o'clock came and went. No Fegelein; no phone
call. It was still late afternoon, spring sunlight. Rattenhuber sent out a posse of four men in a German jeep, or
Kuebelwagen, to contact Fegelein. This detail was commanded by SS Captain Helmut Frick. Frick was not
normally one of Rattenhuber's men; he was a member of
the rival FBK. A decorated soldier with battle experience,
he was chosen because this was clearly a military situation,
a risky trip to the front, which had now reached the streets
of Berlin.

Usually, in peacetime, a drive from the Reich Chancellery on the Voss Strasse to Bleibtreustrasse would have

---

* My source is Cheftechniker Johannes Hentschel. He had installed the
microphone, on Hitler's orders, in 1944. There were two others in the
bunker, known only to Hitler and Hentschel.

taken ten to fifteen minutes, depending on traffic. Now, because of a long detour through the bedroom borough of Wilmersdorf, to loop around the street fighting, it took Frick more than an hour. Thrice, he and his men had to dismount to take cover. A brisk exchange of fire with Russian snipers near the Savigny Platz led to the severe wounding of one of the party, an SS second lieutenant. This did not increase SS fraternal feeling for the delinquent General Fegelein. Their wounded comrade lay moaning and groaning in the back of the jeep during the rest of the escapade; he had been shot in the groin.

Captain Frick did not have orders to arrest Fegelein. A captain does not arrest a general officer. He was simply to case the premises and try to use "friendly persuasion" to induce Fegelein to come along quietly for his rendezvous with the Fuehrer. When Frick arrived, he found Fegelein alone, still not in uniform, still unshaven, still drinking. There were three cognac bottles on the table. Fegelein brashly tried to induce this young captain to decamp while the decamping was good. Even had he been alone, Frick, a loyal soldier, would hardly have deserted. After a half hour of heated, fruitless parley, Frick and his party drove back to the Reich Chancellery. The street fighting was no longer quite so fierce, but the Red Army artillery barrage, now in full blast, made their re-entry hazardous. The jeep was hit in the Voss Strasse by shrapnel and limped in with two flat tires, a badly bleeding young officer, and no General Fegelein.

Martin Bormann had appeared on the scene. He ranked General Rattenhuber, of course, and proceeded to bawl him out for having sent such a low-ranking officer on so important a mission. Hitler was berating not only Rattenhuber but also Bormann. Another long lower bunker parley was held. Finally, it was decided to send a full colonel, SS Standartenfuehrer Hoegl, with a larger "commando of six." They took off in an armored weapons carrier. It was now dark in Berlin, around 10:00 P.M. Captain Frick, because he knew both the route and the Russian positions, was again in the reconnaissance party.

Hoegl's rank is important here. He was a full colonel in the SS, though not really a professional soldier. He was a detective by profession and held the civilian rank of Kriminalrat. This means that, had he not got the wartime call to serve with Dienststelle I, he might well have been a plainclothes detective in some German provincial town.

Was Colonel Hoegl now being sent to arrest Fegelein?
I ran into some quite hot debate on this prickly point.
General Mohnke, a stickler for just such nuances, insisted,
even in 1975, that this was not the case. A colonel does
not arrest a general. The Nazi world was madly rank-
conscious; the Reich Chancellery Group even more so.
However, the only two SS generals present were Mohnke
and Rattenhuber. Mohnke obviously could not leave his
battle command post, and Rattenhuber was not overeager
to risk his own skin in the dark streets of Berlin. Apparently Hoegl's orders were ambivalent. He was not to arrest
Fegelein. But he was also aware that it would be most
unwise to return without his man. Hoegl had been around
long enough to know the Fuehrer.

Once again, it took almost a full hour just to reach the
Bleibtreustrasse. In the ghostlike streets of Berlin, the party
had to weave its way through fresh, fuming rubble. They
were driving with dimmed blue headlights, under a clouded
three-quarter moon. Without any battle incidents, they
arrived at around 11:00 P.M.

It all reads like a movie scenario. The script now called
for a man of Hoegl's experience to approach his target
from the rear, to ring the building, to place at least two
guards outside. Anyone who goes to the movies knows
that. Instead, these dicks from the bunker now tramped
en masse up to the second story, like Nazi Keystone cops.
Hoegl and a husky adjutant rushed the door. It flew open.

The posse found Fegelein inside, now back in uniform,
his collar open, his face clean-shaven. He was standing at
a round mahogany table together with a young woman.
She was tall and blond, with a tint of red in her shoulder-
length hair. Both were busily engaged in packing a woman's
hand valise, much smaller than a normal suitcase. Standartenfuehrer Hoegl saluted snappily. He then politely but
firmly reminded Herr General Fegelein of the long-standing
Fuehrerbefehl that he return to the Reich Chancellery
immediately. Fegelein, still in his cups, first pulled his
rank, protesting the brusque manner of the breaking and
entering. But after some woozy palaver and the lighting of
two or three cigarettes, Fegelein did agree to come along.
To Hoegl's relief, the tacky problem of a formal arrest
thus never arose.

It seems a silly point, this arrest protocol, but it is what made Colonel Hoegl very nervous. Hoegl was well aware of Fegelein's high standing in the Nazi pecking order because of his family relationship to Eva Braun. This nervous hesitancy must account for a whole chain of blunders that not even a German provincial detective should ever make.

Not only had Hoegl forgotten to post guards around the house, but he paid scant attention to the young woman who quietly slipped out of the living room during the talk. Carrying a tray of empty glasses toward the kitchen, she seemed to be fetching water for the cognac that Fegelein had graciously offered his guests. Hoegl was concentrating his powers of persuasion on Fegelein. The others were simply listening. All were highly relieved when Fegelein agreed to go.

By this time, one of the other detectives did notice that the unknown woman had not returned, though he could hear water running in the kitchen. Thirsty, perhaps, he went to have a look. The lady had vanished; the window was open. He closed it—a delightfully German touch. On a night like this, anything could happen. It might rain. He also turned off the tap.

That the woman had walked out so impolitely on the SS party disconcerted Hoegl. So he confiscated the valise. He next went to the telephone to call Rattenhuber and set him at his ease. Hoegl reported that he was en route with Fegelein. He made no mention of the woman. He had not even asked Fegelein who she was.

The rocky ride back to the Chancellery was uneventful, if not particularly jolly. Fegelein, who does not always seem to have realized what a jam he was in, alternated between loud singing and profanity. The other six SS officers and men were still bitter about the wounding of the lieutenant in the first sortie.

Hoegl felt he had a good night's job behind him. He had carried out the precise orders of his mission; he was bringing back his man and that valise. The thought of opening it to examine and list the contents did not cross the serene mind of the veteran Herr Kriminalrat. Hoegl, one feels, had not read many thrillers, though at the moment he was right in the middle of one. It was, indeed, about to blow up in his face. In fairness, one must record that Hoegl had now been on continuous duty, under-

ground, for all of the last long fortnight. This experience
was not conducive to clear thinking, not even in the bracing
fresh air of nighttime Berlin.

The trip back to the Chancellery was made in half the
time it had taken the group to reach Fegelein's flat; the
Berlin street fiighting had died down, a familiar nighttime
phenomenon even in these last days. The Russians were
bivouacking. Around midnight on Friday, April 27, Hoegl
and his group, with Fegelein, reached the Chancellery.

Hoegl's nighttime mission seemed all but completed,
though he had to report in to his boss, Rattenhuber, before
turning in. Still clutching the valise, the colonel walked
through the long tunnel from the Reich Chancellery to
the Fuehrerbunker. He had announced his coming by
phone. Now, in the lower bunker, he was startled to be
confronted by a group that included not only General
Rattenhuber and Major Guensche, as expected, but also
Martin Bormann and Gestapo Chief Heinrich Mueller. A
powerful reception committee.*

Colonel Hoegl saluted, reporting successful completion
of mission. Neither Bormann nor Rattenhuber was at this
moment in the mood for official congratulations. Obviously,
they had talked with at least one other member of the
Hoegl party and thus already knew what had taken place
in the Bleibtreustrasse apartment. When Hoegl, giving his
account, came to the seizure of the valise, Bormann
quickly grabbed it and tumbled the contents on the old
map-room conference table.

The valise contained a chamois bag that, when opened,
spilled out several diamonds, amethysts, rubies, an opal,
a diamond brooch, several rings, a pearl necklace, three
gold watches (including one Eva Braun had given Fegelein
to have repaired), 105,725 Reichsmarks (around $40,000),
3186 Swiss francs (around $800), two passports, both
made out to the same woman (that is, they bore the same
picture although they had different names) and some
road maps.

The least common denominator of these sundry items
was glaringly obvious. It was just what any well-fixed
Berlin couple would scrape together before trekking west

---

* Goebbels was also almost certainly present, but he seems to have
kept silent. He played no major role.

as the capital was about to fall. There was easily enough money and precious stones for barter in a time of *Zusammenbruch*, total collapse. In the anarchy of 1945, for example, those humble Swiss francs were about to acquire more real value than the Reichsmarks, whose nominal value was collapsing with the Reich. (Swiss money did not necessarily mean that the couple was heading for Switzerland. Swiss money is crisis money—always good anywhere.)

Martin Bormann, who had an instinct for the jugular, spotted something else. One of those two passports was British. It implied that Fegelein, a lieutenant general in the Waffen SS, was scheming to skip off with a woman who was not even a German. She was probably an enemy national. Not only in the feverish mind of Bormann, but also on the material evidence before the eyes of all Germans present, the case of desertion at this moment became something more: treason.

Bormann, roaring like a wounded bull, pounding the table with both fists, now exploded in Hoegl's face. "Hoegl, you flatfooted idiot! *Das Weib! das Weib!* The woman! Why did you not grab her and escort *her* back here, instead of this damned valise? Fegelein is a traitor; this woman is British, an enemy agent. Fegelein went to bed with this spy and blabbered everything. *She* was *das Leck.*"

Bormann spoke fast, perhaps too fast. Someone born in Ireland, for example, could have had a legitimate United Kingdom passport (on request) and still have been a neutral resident in wartime Berlin. There are Irish and Irish, a metaphysical British nuance one can be reasonably sure was beyond the ken of either a Bormann or a Fegelein. (One would really like to know what kind that second passport was. Probably Hungarian.)

The great clichés of life often have a way of coming true. Bormann had just invoked one—*cherchez la femme!* Further recrimination could wait. Bormann now took charge and mounted two more motor cavalcades to roar through the night. Hoegl was sent back posthaste over the same rubbly streets he had traversed just one hour before. Bormann also dispatched Heinrich Mueller by a different route.

Hoegl was the first to arrive on the scene. Mueller and his Gestapo squad, in a bulletproof gray Mercedes, pulled up five minutes later. The flat was empty. What had they expected to find on this double wild-goose chase? The real wild goose had flown the coop.

Keystone comedy, as it might have been rewritten by Kafka. The spectacle of the chief of the Gestapo careening through the back streets of battlefield Berlin is grotesque, but it underscores how important this affair had become in the myopic eyes of those in the Fuehrerbunker.

Mueller did not return with the others to the bunker. He went directly to his own cellar to begin the intensive interrogation of Hermann Fegelein. One can assume that his first and leading question was precisely the one that most concerns us here: Just who was this woman, and what was her real mission in Berlin?

*   *

I have talked to four witnesses—Guensche, Baur, Mohnke, and Misch—all of whom had met the lady in question at least once. There is, alas, an all-pervading vagueness in the descriptions they give. This is not too odd when one remembers they were recalling times long ago, chance meetings, a woman who was by no means the only female they had seen in Fegelein's company. A woman of no importance—or so all thought.

Major Otto Guensche—one remembers here the little matter of the telephone number—recalled her best. While by no means a close friend of Fegelein's, and of far lower rank, Guensche had joined him on several occasions at a popular Berlin nightspot, the Groschenkeller. This was on the Kantstrasse, at the corner of Weimarer Strasse, only four short blocks from the Bleibtreustrasse. In 1943, Goebbels had closed all Berlin nightclubs. But the Groschenkeller was more of a beer cellar. It had been allowed to remain open because it also served as a convenient air-raid shelter, and it became a favorite haunt of the SS, both officers and men, a place for meeting lonely women.

Guensche's description was this. "Fegelein's mistress was classier than most of his other women. I can remember only that she was good-looking, tall, well groomed. Her hair was blond with a reddish tint. She was thirtyish. She spoke German, with an accent, and at least two or three other languages. I heard that she had a husband, some foreign diplomat, conveniently out of town. I met her two, maybe three, times, but always briefly. She and Fegelein came for a quick drink and then left. One talk was about horses. Fegelein was a cavalryman."

Not much, but something. As Guensche spoke, I thought I was at least about to clinch the nationality point. An Irishwoman, out with an SS Obergruppenfuehrer, might quite likely chat about horses. Sergeant Misch, however, who had also met the woman, said he thought she was Scots and "married to a Hungarian." Mohnke, too, was aware that the woman was of another tribe, but he said Danish. All three agreed that she was working in broadcasting.

Where had Fegelein met this woman, his *femme fatale?* Hans Baur, who let drop the information perhaps without realizing its significance, said the meeting had taken place at a 1944 summer party in the swank Goebbels villa in Schwanenwerder. And just what was the Irish lady doing there? A fair guess, I believe, was that her first affair— affair in the sense of her penetration of high Nazi circles —was not with Hermann Fegelein. It was, I now suspect, with Goebbels, the most notorious wolf in town and the man who had just become her boss.

This was the connection. Mata O'Hara—and on this Baur, Mohnke, and Guensche are all agreed—was the wife of a fairly senior Hungarian career diplomat. The couple had arrived in Berlin some time in 1943, that is, at precisely the time when German-Hungarian relations, never really warm, were getting cooler. Events were building up to a major showdown between the Nazi regime and the government of the Hungarian regent, Admiral Miklós Horthy. Neither Horthy, who had read Admiral Mahan's *Influence of Sea Power Upon History,* nor his prime minister, Miklós Kállay, had ever really believed in an Axis victory. Kállay was both courageous and often outspoken in his anti-German sentiments. He hated Hitler; the feeling was mutual. By 1944 the desperate Hungarian statesmen were pro-West, but trapped by geography. Their Hungarian game was, by hook or by crook, to extricate their nation from the war and pull their east-front army back to Hungary.

Hence arose a peculiar drama in the Hungarian legation in Berlin, which was in the heart of the diplomatic quarter on the edge of the Tiergarten. It reflected the grim behind-the-scenes political struggle unfolding in Budapest. By the spring of 1944, with the Red Army already flanking the Carpathians and rolling toward the Hungarian-Rumanian border, the Hungarian diplomats in Berlin were mainly interested in what was happening in their capital on the Danube.

The situation in the legation itself was tense, and as complicated as Hungarian politics usually are. The minister, General Dome Sztojay, was a staunch Horthy man, as were the career diplomats on his staff. But the Hungarian legation also housed a special pro-Nazi political section, manned by members of the Arrow and Cross, the native Hungarian Fascist movement. This was headed by Ferenc Scalasi, a Hitler admirer and protégé. Thus, a real Balkan situation existed right in the heart of Berlin. Hitler, who both hated and mistrusted most Hungarians—this was his Austrian inheritance—had ordered Himmler, Kaltenbrunner, and Walter Schellenberg (a high-ranking SS intelligence officer) to watch the Hungarians like hawks, in Budapest as well as in Berlin. (The Berlin legation was bugged, according to Schellenberg.)

When the long-simmering crisis finally broke, in the spring of 1944, Hitler, after a stormy session in Salzburg with Admiral Horthy, had forced the Hungarian acting chief-of-state to sack Premier Kállay. Horthy then named his own Berlin man, Sztojay, to the post. Hitler had agreed, with the proviso that Scalasi also return to Budapest. (To groom himself for a Quisling role.) The crisis mounted all summer. In the autumn, with the Red Army already approaching Budapest, the military situation was truly desperate. Admiral Horthy, sensibly, wanted to sue for peace. Hitler countered by ordering Horthy's arrest, which took the form of kidnapping by SS commandos. First interned in the Salzburg area, Horthy was later thrown into Dachau. Some dozen of his followers in the Berlin embassy were also arrested by Himmler and sent to keep Horthy company.

This bizarre situation explains why Mata O'Hara was so suddenly stranded in Berlin, unable to get to Ireland, Hungary, or even Switzerland. It also suggests that she was an amateur rather than a professional agent. Whatever funds she might normally have had access to were outside Germany. With her husband interned, the woman needed a job, some source of income.

Goebbels, who always had a keen eye for a good-looking woman, had found work for her in the logical place, his own shop. The Berlin-based Deutschlandsender* broadcast round the clock in several of the languages in which we know Mata O'Hara was fluent—she knew English and French and possibly Hungarian. Her routine job was not voice broadcasting; it was simply translating. In addition, as everyone in Berlin social circles knew, when Goebbels lined up a job for a woman, she was expected to go to bed with him.

Her later switch to Hermann Fegelein is easy to explain: she had found a better source of information. Goebbels was not so stupid as to babble military secrets in the boudoir, and he was no drinker. Fegelein, a true *miles gloriosus*, was both.

Her chance came in late 1944, when Hitler pulled his elite Sixth SS Panzer Army out of action on the eastern front to spearhead the Ardennes offensive. This was Fegelein's old outfit, and when General Sepp Dietrich and most of his staff officers passed through Berlin in November, nothing was more natural than a get-together between Fegelein—with his elegant new mistress—and his old comrades of the staff. The lady soon flashed the news of the coming attack to London. And there, some clod in Intelligence refused to believe it.

That story is as old as the tale of Cassandra in the *Iliad*. Just as the most successful spies of World War II were often doubted at the home office—as Stalin had distrusted Richard Sorge in Tokyo, as Ribbentrop and Hitler had distrusted "Cicero" in Ankara, as British and Americans had distrusted the Abwehr (German Army Intelligence) tip on the July 20 plot against Hitler's life—so did some nameless British functionary ignore the news from Mata O'Hara.

An emerging picture, but a faint one, a tantalizing phantom. For a few weeks, and with these random clues, I had hoped that it might not be too difficult to locate this mystery woman if she was alive, or to identify her if she was dead. On both counts, I was too sanguine. The leads trailed off to Budapest, London, Dublin, Galway, Salzburg, well out of the framework of this book. But I

---

* The foreign-language program "Germany Calling."

still hope to find her. At least we know enough about her
to realize why she could well have been what cost Hermann Fegelein his neck.

*   *

I felt it only fair to readers to place at the beginning of
this chapter earlier knowledge I already had that was not
available to such men as Guensche, Baur, and Mohnke.
Back in 1955, in Paris, my friend the late Richard Crossman had spoken to me about the mystery women he
whimsically called Mata O'Hara. What I can recall today,
from that casual chat, are six specific things Crossman had
mentioned: (1) the woman was in wartime Berlin; (2)
she was a British agent, at least in the sense that she was
reporting to London; (3) her material was used on Soldatensender Calais; (4) the milieu she was working was SS,
the Hitler entourage; (5) she was Irish; and (6) she was
never located after the war. No Victoria Cross. A few
weeks after my talk with Crossman I spent first a fortnight in Berlin, then another two weeks in London, drawing blanks, smiles, long faces. In London I was reminded,
a bit pointedly, of the Official Secrets Act.

Was the legendary Mata O'Hara the same lady who
went out the window that midnight on the Bleibtreustrasse?
It is a fascinating angle to an otherwise sordid story—
"How I slept with Hermann Fegelein and screwed the
Fuehrer." Worthy indeed of a Victoria Cross. Except—
another odd angle—I have often wondered how this Irishwoman would have broken the news to that Hungarian
husband. That could explain the long post–1945 silence.

The Official Secrets Act has a thirty-year clause about
just such matters and binds all those who have had official
knowledge. The thirty years ran out in May 1975, and I
have been watching the British press with some interest
since. The memoirs of Mata O'Hara—if she is alive—
clearly would fall under the thirty-year-silence clause.*

Let us therefore re-examine the evidence in terms of
what we know was happening in Berlin—in the Bleibtreustrasse, in the Fuehrerbunker, and in the Gestapo cellar in
the Dreifaltigkeit chapel on Mauerstrasse.

---

* In London recently (1977) I discovered that there is also a fifty-year
clause when living people are involved. The story of the mutiny in the
British Army in France in 1917 was first revealed last year.

I have always found it odd that in all standard biographies of either Hitler or Bormann, Bormann's explosion in his confrontation scene with Hoegl, the man with the lady's valise, is either ignored completely or dismissed as one more example of "the delirium of treason" that had now descended on the bunker. (This is Goebbels' phrase, uttered the same night. He meant it literally, not ironically.)

It is also true that Martin Bormann's blanket definition of treason by now embraced every major Nazi leader not present with Adolf Hitler in the Fuehrerbunker. This was, indeed, his self-serving obsession. Missing were all Nazi big wheels—Goering, Himmler, Speer, Ribbentrop, Admiral Doenitz, Field Marshal Keitel, and General Jodl—except Bormann himself and Dr. Goebbels. We have seen how Bormann, just four days previously, manipulated an indiscreet Goering telegram into a treason charge when in fact no real treason was involved.

May not Bormann, so the argument runs, have been playing the same insidious knife game in the case of Hermann Fegelein? Not so much to destroy Fegelein, who was no serious rival of Bormann's, but as a master stroke against Fegelein's boss, Heinrich Himmler? Those who ask this question, I believe, anticipate matters. True, Bormann already did suspect Himmler of double-dealing—the man was absent from the bunker—but concrete news of Himmler's desertion of the Hitler cause did not reach the bunker for another twenty hours, which is to say, at the very end of *l'affaire* Fegelein.

Bormann's veracity or sincerity, however, is not the matter at issue here. The moment General Mohnke told me there had been no Fegelein court-martial verdict, that his prisoner had been handed over to the security people, elementary logic dictated that I discover when the desertion case was transformed into the far more sinister treason charge. Clearly, this was the moment: when Bormann confronted Hoegl. Bormann had destroyed Goering simply by waving a telegram. Now he had a whole valise with which to convince Hitler of Himmler's treachery.

The gravamen of the new charge against Fegelein, to my mind, deserves careful examination. Too often since 1945 it has been airily dismissed as a figment of Bormann's pathological imagination, as a Bormann exercise in perfidy, or, at the very most, a hasty jumping to conclusions. A natural human bias against Bormann, in short, clouds the fact that a lady did go out that window, which is not the normal way of freshening drinks.

The debunkers of Bormann—often the very same worthies who believe he is alive or that he was a Soviet agent—plead as follows: Fegelein was obviously a deserter, caught *in flagrante*. He was also an adulterer and a lush. But only in the overheated imagination of Bormann was he a traitor, about to flee to Switzerland with an enemy agent. Poor Fegelein was simply too drunk to explain away his own follies.

Here one must check back to what Bormann really did say, making fair allowance for the fact that those who actually heard him (Guensche and Misch) are quoting from memory. Bormann did not accuse Fegelein, flat out, of conscious treason. Bormann and others, including Hitler, knew of Fegelein's weak character and his lechery. Bormann's stated case against Fegelein was simply that the man had been foolhardy enough to bed down with a foreign woman and had whispered indiscretions on the pillow, had betrayed military secrets. Bormann was thinking very clearly when he said to Hoegl that it was the woman who was important; that she was the leak.

Sergeant Rochus Misch later overheard another bawdy remark that sums up what Bormann really thought of Fegelein: "The man's brains were in his scrotum." Under the circumstances, an apt description. Coming from Bormann, doubly apt. He himself was the bunker authority on drinking and fornication. On the morning of May 2, only four days later, Bormann was in pretty much the same shape Fegelein was in on April 28.

At this point I leave it to reader—since this matter may never be completely clarified—to judge whether Bormann, in the moment just after he had seen the contents of the phantom lady's valise, jumped to false conclusions.

We know the reason why Bormann's reaction was so *blitzschnell*, why he tumbled to the real situation before all others. Bormann simply knew more. Investigation of the leak had been in his domain weeks before Gestapo chief Mueller had been called in. Bormann, who ran Hitler's shop, was responsible for, among other things, checking out most of the personnel in the Fuehrer's headquarters. Even so late in the game, superbureaucrat Bormann could now vindicate himself by solving the problem that Hitler, in sheer despair, had handed over to the Gestapo.

We know quite a bit about this persistent leak. It concerned Soldatensender Calais. As its name was meant to imply, this was a secret, or "black," radio station supposedly run by an SS opposition group but in fact operated by the British. Beginning in 1943, the shortwave broadcasts were beamed from England. The name "Calais" was chosen to confuse German Army listeners with access to direction-finding devices. In 1943 the Germans were still in Calais, just across the Channel from Dover. A direction-finding radio "cut" would, therefore, pass through Calais. The transmitter, if I remember correctly, was located on the southern coast of England, between Dover and Dungeness.*

Soldatensender Calais had a phenomenal success with its German Army audience. So clever was the dissimulation, so German the voices, so attractive the programs, that only the most sophisticated of listeners recognized this new art of black propaganda in the British bag of dirty tricks. Goebbels had been gone one better. As he noted in his diary, the propaganda minister himself was too clever to expose the station. He knew that even in wartime, indeed especially in wartime, the prestige of the BBC was so high in Germany that to unmask the operation as British would only enhance its appeal.

The British psychological-warfare stratagem was ingeniously simple. The station's programs captured a mass audience of German soldiers in the first weeks on the air simply by the playing of traditional German military tunes and the reading of Wehrmacht bulletins. Only slowly did experts begin to put in the propaganda needle, many weeks later, and only in the evening programs, which came in prime listening time. A man called "Der Chef," pretending to be a loyal but disgruntled SS man, began to expose the goings-on in the Fuehrerhauptquartier. Adolf Hitler was never criticized directly—that would have scared off Nazi listeners—but everybody around him was. Rather good, sharp jokes directed at American, Russian, and British soldiers convinced most continental listeners that they were listening to a German program.

* After the 1944 Normandy invasion, the name was changed to Soldatensender West.

In fact, and in retrospect, the British psy-warriors were successful beyond their wildest dreams. Some of their solid information, of course, came from prisoners of war or genuine anti-Nazi sources; some from a careful perusal of captured German Army newspapers and magazines; some from the usual agent, underground, or intelligence sources. The special SS angle was always played up. News from the Fuehrer's HQ—most Germans were news-starved on that score—was always stressed, in terms of promotions, decorations earned and otherwise, anecdotes, and randy tidbits about who was sleeping with whom. Goebbels' mistresses, and those of Himmler and Bormann, got steady coverage. The soldier audience slowly got the sly message: "These, comrades, are the rogues who are leading you while you fight and bleed for your fatherland. If the Fuehrer only knew."

I can personally attest to the stunning success of Soldatensender Calais. As a U.S. Army signals officer, I knew the name of the British game and spent many an evening hour monitoring it with some glee. Then came the Battle of the Bulge and hotter problems. While I was interrogating a particularly arrogant SS major in the Ardennes, he tried to educate me about the Soldatensender. I found this piquant, and let him talk on. The major was also a signals officer. He suddenly claimed to be one of the disgruntled SS group that was running the black radio station. He had helped set it up, wrote the scripts, knew Der Chef personally, et cetera, et cetera. *Besserwisserei*, pretending to know everything better, is perhaps the most annoying of German traits.

Finally, to knock him down a peg and prove that I knew he was lying, I escorted him to our company D/F (direction-finder) and showed him where the Soldatensender transmitter was. This simple trick worked. Deflated, the major began to eat humble pie. He let slip the little bits of signal information I badly wanted from him, that cold late 1944 winter evening near Houffalize, in Belgium.

More than a quarter of a century later, as I talked to members of the Reich Chancellery Group, several told me something the British could not have known at the time. They, too, right in the FHQ, were steady, if discreet, fans of the Soldatensender. In fact, they were not only fans, but now and then appeared as actors. Some of the stories that I have referred to in this report as "bunker gossip" came up, night after night, over the air waves. It was gossip, but very accurate gossip; it always checked out. I cite a few choice items to give the flavor. After Gerda Daranovsky jilted Erich Kempka, to marry Luftwaffe General Christian, Kempka married a local tart in Berchtesgaden. But now Die Daran had a new lover, Lieutenant Colonel Richard Schulze-Kossens of the FBK. Albert Speer's favorite après-ski partner was Leni Riefenstahl. Three members of the FBK had been sent to the special SS VD clinic in Vienna. When Captain Fritz Darges of the FBK refused to marry the pregnant Gretl Braun, Hitler packed him off to the eastern front. Martin Bormann, with his wife's approval, was keeping an actress in his chalet on the Obersalzberg.

None of this leering chatter, with its high porn content, was world-shattering news. But that is precisely the point. To Hitler and Bormann, if the perfidious British had a source that close to the FHQ and the FBK, obviously they must also be getting more important information that they were *not* broadcasting. Hence the loaded sarcasm of such Hitler remarks as the one he often threw at Keitel and Jodl: "I wonder if we can get this order to the troops at the front before we hear all about it over the BBC."

Many pieces of the puzzle begin to fall into place. Here, I believe, is the explanation of why this pesky matter of the leak, which had been going on for more than a year, concerned Hitler more than ever in these last days in the bunker. His security barrier had been penetrated, and he knew it; this was no imaginary obsession. The Fuehrer was terrified that his body might fall into enemy hands, a prospect that worried him far more than the thought of death itself. It was thus imperative for him to locate the leak before his suicide could safely take place. Time was running out.

*   *

At this point in my researches I took the rough draft of this espionage chapter to one of the best, most balanced American Intelligence officers I know. He, too, had once worked, long ago, on the vexing Fegelein affair. He was, in fact, the first to tell me that all hitherto published versions are either inadequate or, somehow, fishy. His reaction was this. "About Mata O'Hara, or the woman on the Bleibtreustrasse, if you prefer; here I give not an Irish but a Scottish verdict. The evidence is strong, it could explain a lot, but the case is not proven. You have overlooked one major factor, and it disconcerts me."

A bit crestfallen, I asked for details.

He continued, "British Intelligence is by no means infallible, but in those days it was pretty good. It violates a very basic rule of the spook game to waste such a prime plant. On the one hand, the British had penetrated the Fuehrerbunker, a magnificent coup—"

I interrupted. "Careful! *Not* the Fuehrerbunker, only the Hitler entourage. None of my sources ever saw this woman in the bunker or even in the Reich Chancellery or the nearby SS barracks. She was much too shrewd for that. My argument is that had she been nothing more than a mistress, the Reich Chancellery is just where she might have headed. Most mistresses did."

His response was, "Yes, that figures. She did not need to enter the lion's den to get the kind of information she wanted. Fegelein would have been more talkative in the boudoir. And she wouldn't have gone to the Chancellery at the end either, because she had compelling reasons for wanting to get out of Berlin, and by that time so did lover-boy Fegelein. She did not want to fall into the hands of the Russians, and she surely was eager to turn her SS Obergruppenfuehrer over to the British. A great Noel Coward scene on the Elbe.

"My main point is, I believe, still valid. Do you really think the British would have wasted this agent's reports on a mere propaganda radio program? That was just a side show. Above all, in the last months of the war it was not more than fun and games for London's psychological warriors."

This professional skepticism seemed valid. It put me in the embarrassing position of seeming to have jumped to the same rash conclusions as Bormann might have. I therefore next went to Sefton Delmer,* the British news-paperman who had been the boss, or Der Chef, of Soldatensender Calais.

---

* Sefton "Tom" Delmer, who is as English as Yorkshire pudding, was able to broadcast to Germany because he had been born and brought up in Berlin, where his British father taught English. He spoke fluent colloquial German with a colorful Berlin accent. However, he only wrote the script for Der Chef. A German voice was used. Delmer had another program going under his own name.

Delmer observed:

All was grist that came to our mill. The material we had from Berlin and the Fuehrer's HQ was well filtered or "laundered" long before it ever reached me. My colleague Dick Crossman may have known about Mata O'Hara, and after the war I heard something similar. But I never could run the story down. Naturally, I would never have knowingly blown an agent. But how could we know, in London, whether what agents kept sending us was true? Women in particular all claimed to be sleeping with someone in high place. Don't forget, Der Chef was pretending to be the leader of a browned-off, disgruntled SS group. So I just picked the items that seemed most plausible, that would register with our German soldier audience and help undermine their fighting morale.

For skeptics who may feel that I was pushing Delmer toward my own approved solution, I point out that I had to be circumspect with him. I did not let him know what I already knew, for obvious reasons. I am grateful to Thomas Agoston, another British friend from wartime days, for pointing to me the following passage in Sefton Delmer's memoirs, *Black Boomerang*, published in 1960 —more than 15 years before I talked to Delmer. Here he describes exactly how he was directing Soldatensender Calais:

We told of the adventures of the popsies brought in to amuse a tired Fuehrer. For example, the boisterous highjinks of the blonde, Elizabeth Blanda, the young wife of Dr. Walter Hewel, who represented the Foreign Office at the Fuehrer's headquarters. How, for instance, in a gay party at the *Berchtesgadener Hof* hotel on the Obersalzberg she had shown off her prowess as a barber by soaping up and shaving Hermann Fegelein, the SS general who had become the Fuehrer's unofficial brother-in-law by marrying the sister of his mistress, Eva Braun.

I knew this story from several members of the Reich Chancellery Group. It did so happen. Elizabeth Blanda, or "Blondie," was one of the wealthy highsteppers among the mountain people. She had been Fegelein's close friend before he married Gretl Braun. Whereupon, a few weeks later, she married Hewel. *La Ronde.*

As so often happens in intelligence work, there is a boomerang factor at work here. I am now sure that the British in London really did have no way of knowing how accurate the gossip reports coming in from Berlin actually were, whereas the Germans, at least those in the Reich Chancellery Group, *did*. One of these was Adolf Hitler.

A few loose strings in Fegelein matter remain to be tied together:

Did Mata O'Hara succeed in making her getaway?

Given the hazardous situation then prevailing in and around Berlin, one can only calculate the odds. We do know that, two days later, seven couriers left the bunker and made their way up the East-West Axis, passed the Olympic Stadium, worked their way down the Havel River, and then got off safely to the west. All were men, but all were also in uniform, which was more dangerous. Four days later, four women we know would leave the bunker in the breakout. Fräulein Manzialy, the cook, disappeared. Gerda Christian, Else Krueger, and Gertrud Junge all were robustly raped. The three secretaries later made it to the west. The timing, the situation, and the point of departure were not quite the same, but our woman's chances of heading west and making it seem to have been better than even, 4 to 1.

For a woman of any nationality in Berlin, rape was then the clear and ever-present danger, more terrifying than all the artillery, bombs, and street fighting. Wise women headed for whatever shelter they could find. When she went out that window, Mata O'Hara was alone. Agents, however, seldom are operating alone. It is most unlikely, for example, that she was radioing her reports; German counterintelligence in Berlin was far too expert in locating clandestine transmitters. She almost surely had been using what is called in the espionage trade a "dead-letter drop." Most probably, in this case, a neutral embassy. The compelling logic would have been for her to head there. But most embassies, including the Irish and the Hungarian, were located in the blasted Tiergarten area, where the fighting had become fiercest. She may well have been cut off from this possible avenue of escape, although it is only a mile from the Bleibtreustrasse to the Tiergarten.

As resourceful and cool-headed as this woman clearly was—Hitchock would have loved the ruse with brandy glasses and the trip to the window—her luck may simply have run out on her. Our shamrock lady now had no passport, no valise, no handbag, no money, no transport—nothing but the clothes on her back. She may, after all, have fallen into the hands of the Gestapo at the last moment.* Since she was in movement, in the heart of falling Berlin, the possibility that she fell in the street fighting is not negligible.

What was Hermann Fegelein's fate? The report of his execution brought out by Hanna Reitsch was one of the first stories to emerge from the Fuehrerbunker back in 1945. Reitsch had left the bunker with Robert Ritter von Greim late on Saturday, April 28. She reported that Fegelein had been executed just before she departed. Thirty years later the matter is by no means so clear. All agree with Reitsch that Fegelein was executed on the same evening. Bunker witnesses can peg the event well, since it came just before the Hitler–Eva Braun nuptials (an event about which Hanna Reitsch at the time knew nothing). In fact, the ceremony was delayed at least twenty minutes, according to Sergeant Misch, while Hitler consulted with Mueller and Rattenhuber "to make sure Fegelein was dead."

However, I could find no concrete evidence to support the story Hanna Reitsch then told, and which she today admits she had only on hearsay evidence. The hot rumor flying around the bunker as she prepared to depart was that "Fegelein had just been shot, by a firing squad, in the Ehrenhof of the Reich Chancellery." This was 11:00 P.M. on Saturday, April 28.

There would almost surely have been eyewitnesses of any execution in the Ehrenhof. Eyewitnesses and ear witnesses, as well as participants in the firing squad. I found none, at least none who was willing to talk. All today deny the old rumor that lots were drawn for the firing squad. I have come to the conclusion that the execution did take place, at the generally agreed time, but in quite another place—the Gestapo cellar. Bunker witnesses—the sole exception was Baur—did not, after all, know about this secret Gestapo cellar. This could explain some of the confusion.

---

* Gestapo General Mueller, although himself busy interrogating Fegelein, would not have slipped up here. He was not, like Hoegl, a stupid man. Several people who were interrogated by him—and survived—rate his intelligence and counterespionage experience as high.

The most important nugget of evidence Hanna Reitsch did come up with relates to something she saw not inside the bunker but shortly after she had left. Reviewing what she told her American interrogation officers in May 1945, I found Miss Reitsch dropping a casual remark that, although she and her interrogators did not realize it at the time, is a most important clue in the solution of the Fegelein matter. She said, "As I took off around midnight with Ritter von Greim, just as we were airborne we both saw, near the runway, a Junker–Fifty-two transport plane. A lone pilot was standing by in the shadows. He was obviously waiting for somebody."

Indeed. Her 1945 American interrogation officers, pricking up their ears, instantly jumped to the conclusion that this mystery plane must have been waiting for Adolf Hitler. But as we know from Baur, the plane that might have taken the Fuehrer out of Berlin and halfway around the planet was not in Berlin; it was on standby at Rechlin. And it was not the old-fashioned, conventional short-hop Junker–52. It was the Junker–390, an ultramodern, fast, long-range, four-engine transport. This hot prototype plane could never have landed at the Brandenburg Gate, or even at Berlin-Gatow.

That Junker–52 waiting in the shadows was, I strongly suspect, the plane Fegelein had been so eagerly expecting when he answered that fateful Friday telephone call in his flat. Probably the same plane, and the same pilot, that had brought him to Berlin on April 25 and then returned to home base at Rechlin. Fegelein, I surmise, had ordered it up again as his getaway plane. Like most planes trying to get into Berlin, it had been delayed and did not make the April 27 rendezvous. On April 28, it had arrived, but this time Fegelein could not keep the rendezvous. I asked Hans Baur about my speculation and he agreed. "Fegelein always flew in a Junker–Fifty-two, and that must have been the plane he was waiting for, in from Rechlin. Himmler had put this plane and pilot at his disposal."

I had asked Baur because I knew he had gone out at midnight to the Brandenburg Gate, to see off Reitsch and Ritter von Greim, old flying friends. Baur did not, however, see any Junker–52. Nor had its landing ever been reported to him. If Baur had known about any plane coming to fetch Fegelein, he would, of course, instantly have told Hitler. Otherwise, Baur himself would have been summoned on the mat. That would explain this unannounced nighttime landing; because of the fighting, now so close to the gate, Baur's control tower had already closed down.

Fegelein's fate was sealed, that Saturday evening, by another freakish bunker event. Far away in San Francisco, where the United Nations Organization was being born an alert Reuters man had just broken the news that Heinrich Himmler had made a peace-feeler to the western powers. Up on the Baltic, Himmler was still holding secret parleys with Count Bernadotte. The scoop had been broadcast in German by Radio Stockholm. It was picked up, by chance, in the Fuehrerbunker around 9:00 P.M. Heinz Lorenz of the Propaganda Ministry, who had a cubbyhole office in the tunnel leading from Goebbels' ministry into the bunker, delivered the bulletin to Martin Bormann. Such was the ludicrous state of FHQ intelligence. An event taking place in Germany only 200 miles from Berlin became known through a wire-service flash filed from 8000 miles away.

Himmler a traitor! Heinrich the True! When Hitler got this shattering news, pandemonium broke loose. According to Hanna Reitsch "He paced about in the corridor, showing the bulletin to all he could buttonhole." Keening rang out through the shelter. It had taken finesse for Bormann to knife Goering. None was now needed to make the treason case against Himmler. The Reuters dispatch had done the job for him. It was at this point—and not in his encounter with Colonel Hoegl almost twenty-four hours before—that Bormann stoked already overheated emotions. The delirium of treason now engulfed the bunker.

Colonel von Below, the Luftwaffe attaché, reported how Bormann managed this. Von Below himself, who regarded the bunker as a *Klapsmuehle* (nuthouse), was already making plans to leave as quickly as he could. He was able to do so the next day, as a volunteer courier.

He spoke of the sheer hysteria of the bunker atmosphere that Saturday night. "General Burgdorf, drunk as a goat, ran up and down the corridor, claiming that Himmler had a plan to deliver the cadaver of Hitler to General Eisenhower, as a pledge of his serious intent. The document, he said, had been discovered. It was Himmler's liaison man, Fegelein, who was to secure and deliver the body from the Fuehrerbunker, after the Fuehrer's death." General Burgdorf was the one man in the bunker known as a "good friend" of Hermann Fegelein.*

In the infectious frenzy of suspicion, not even cooler heads like von Below paused to ask why a man with a body-snatching mission would have absented himself from the Fuehrerbunker in the first place. Pure logic, circumstantial evidence, even plain common sense, could no longer save Fegelein. He was a gone gosling. After a lifetime of vaulting ambition, the gentleman jockey had been thrown at the very last jump. A telephone call, a delayed plane, a radio bulletin from San Francisco—the playboy SS general's luck had really run out.

To summarize: Fegelein seems to have escaped the original desertion charge; the Fuehrer might have even forgiven this womanizer the affair on the Bleibtreustrasse. After all, from Hitler's point of view, it had cleared up the vexing leak. But a plot against the Fuehrer's person—worse still, a ghoulish plot against his remains, the sacred ashes—that did it. Hermann Fegelein had first entered the Hitler inner circle as Heinrich Himmler's man. Himmler was now unreachable. Bormann soon saw to it that General Burgdorf got in to report the body-snatching plan to Hitler. Hitler ordered Fegelein's instant execution.

Inasmuch as we know Fegelein had been in the Gestapo cellar all day—no one had seen him in the Reich Chancellery since that last postmidnight meeting with Baur—my assumption is that his execution took place there, not in the Ehrenhof. For it was, after all, only the Gestapo who had the special technical instruments tyrant Hitler always ordered up for those who had conspired against his person. Slow strangulation, with piano wire, while hanging from a butcher's bloody meathook cemented into the wall. This had been the horrible fate of several hundred officers of the abortive July 20, 1944, revolt.

One hour later—the timing here is blood-curdling— Adolf Hitler married Eva Braun. Another deed of black midnight, murder, followed by marriage. The bridegroom clearly saw to it that Fegelein did not live to become his brother-in-law, a traitor in the bosom of the family. The bride knew this. She did not hesitate or balk or even bat

---

* Asked to comment on this chapter for accuracy, Else Krueger, Martin Bormann's secretary, said, "Fegelein, until these very last days, had a second friend in the bunker. It was my boss." This only doubles the irony.

an eyelash. As Gerda Christian reported, "There were tears in her blue eyes, but they were tears of radiant joy."

Up to this point in the bunker narrative, including Hans Baur's account of his talk with Eva Braun this same morning, the picture we have always had of Hitler's mistress, although sentimental and dripping with treacle, has been rather positive. I have dutifully recorded it. But this marriage scene is what really gave the bride away. Her character, too, was suddenly "isolated by a single deed."

•

CHAPTER VIII

The Shot Nobody Heard

That civilization may not sink,
Its great battle lost,
Quiet the dog, tether the pony
To a distant post;
Our master Caesar is in his tent
Where the maps are spread,
His eyes fixed upon nothing,
A hand under his head.
Like a long-legged fly upon the stream
His mind moves upon silence.
—WILLIAM BUTLER YEATS, 1939

HITLER'S LAST DAY began in total quiet. He had retired just before sunrise. He was up and about one hour later. It was Monday morning, April 30, 1945, *dies irae*. Sunrise was at four-thirty. The artillery barrage had again fallen off. All hands still on duty in the Fuehrerbunker had welcomed this chance to snatch at least a few hours sleep.

Except for the lonely Fuehrer himself. Reversing his usual bunker behavior pattern, Hitler was up betimes and was pacing about the bunker, alone. He had probably slept no more than an hour. This after a long evening filled with desultory dialogue on the hopeless military situation, suicide and cremation, and death as the great deliverer, *der Erloeser*. At 6:00 A.M. the Fuehrer, as related, had suddenly summoned General Mohnke to report to the lower bunker.

After the Mohnke interview, until 8:15 A.M., Sergeant Rochus Misch and one lonely guard were the only souls on

> **"Adolf Hitler must have put the muzzle on his black Walther directly to his graying right temple. He then squeezed the trigger and simultaneously bit into his capsule. Given his physical condition, this called for one last, vehement act of concentrated will power."**

early morning duty as Hitler wandered listlessly about the lower bunker. He shuffled hither and yon in the cramped quarters, his eyes usually cast to the floor, his hands clasped behind his back. He paced from his quarters to the corridor, from the corridor to the staircase, like a frustrated zoo animal new to the cage. Two other staffers were present, but both were fast asleep in bed rolls spread on the concrete floor—Gerda Christian, now Hitler's senior secretary, and General Hans Krebs, the Acting Chief of the General Staff. Several times Hitler brushed past Sergeant Misch without even nodding.

Misch noted, "I knew this was the end, or very close to it. To me and most of the other old hands it had long been clear, at least since the stormy Hitler explosion of April twenty-second, that our Fuehrer had no realistic choice except suicide. We were all nervously waiting for just that to happen, the sooner the better. At the same time, we were trying to conceal our nervousness with frantic little flurries and shows of activity. So I just crouched over my switchboard, fiddling about with the plugs, though few calls were now still coming in."

The old FHQ, once really the Supreme Headquarters, had by now all but ceased to exist. Even the last land-line field telephone to the city commandant, General Weidling, who was less than a mile away in the OKW bunker on the Bendlerstrasse, was not always functioning. It was twice knocked out of action during this same morning, though it was quickly repaired by signal troops. The military routine, such as it now was, spluttered, yet droned on.

"The Fuehrer is still alive and is conducting the defense

of Berlin . . ." So ran the telegram Martin Bormann had
dispatched to Admiral Doenitz earlier the same morning,
around three-thirty. Admiral Doenitz was already installed
in his new command post on the Ploener See, a remote lake
in Schleswig-Holstein, 270 miles away. In this same telegram, Bormann also relayed a Fuehrerbefehl that the admiral "must move quickly and strictly against all traitors."
The special traitor Bormann here had in mind was Reichsfuehrer Heinrich Himmler, who at this same moment was
holed up in a red-brick police barracks in Luebeck. Physically, Himmler was only about thirty miles southeast of
Admiral Doenitz. In between his "momentous, historical
sessions" with Count Bernadotte, Himmler was now blithely
working on his own "governmental and cabinet list."

He told his staff, "Gentlemen, you will soon see that the
western powers have a real need for just such an experienced man as I. Europe cannot possibly be held in any state
of law and order without some stable figure of recognized
authority. Surely General Eisenhower will soon come to
see this and will negotiate with me."

Himmler's serene belief that he could play the role of a
modern Fouché or *grand gendarme* for liberated Europe
was preposterous, and everyone present except Himmler
knew it.

Around 8:30 A.M. in the bunker, as Hitler was still at
breakfast, the several hours' respite from artillery fire ended
abruptly. The guns of Major General Pereviorkin's 69th
Elite Storm Troops from the Russian Third Assault Army
opened up with a mighty morning cannonade. Their pri-
mary target was not, however, the Fuehrerbunker. This
ninety-minute barrage was to prepare for the upcoming
final assault on the Reichstag. The Red Army infantry attack kicked off at 10:00 A.M.

General Krebs now came up with a situation report even
more alarming than that given the Fuehrer by General
Mohnke only three hours before. Krebs reported how—
slowly, remorselessly—the Red Army generals were closing
the iron ring. Their troops had taken both sides of the
Leipziger Strasse, which was Berlin's main commercial
thoroughfare. It runs parallel to the Unter den Linden and
is one block closer to the Reich Chancellery. The Anhalter
railroad station had also, by now, been stormed. Krebs had
one fillip of idiotic optimism: "The German resistance, because of shortened, interior lines, has also stiffened."

Russian General Vassily Chuikov, the highest-ranking Red Army officer actually inside the city of Berlin, was at his advance field headquarters on the Schulenburgring, near Tempelhof. He was thus only about five miles from the center of the city. His superior, Marshal Georgi Zhukov, was at his headquarters, which was still outside Berlin, some twenty miles due east in the town of Strausberg.

It was Zhukov, not Chuikov, who had the only direct red-line telephone to the Kremlin. Almost every hour, apparently under pressure from Stalin, Zhukov was impatiently calling Chuikov to ask whether Berlin could be taken. General Chuikov replied, "Marshal Zhukov, I doubt it. Some German SS units are still fighting like tigers."

According to those present, Hitler listened "in apathetic silence" as Krebs droned on. He did not even pose any questions. At the end of this briefing, the last, he turned to one of his military aides and dictated a Fuehrerbefehl, the last written order Hitler was to give.

> To: The Commanding Officer of the Berlin Defense Area, General of Artillery Weidling:
>
> In case there is a shortage of either ammunition or provisions in the Reichshauptstadt, I herewith give my permission for our troops to make a breakout attempt. This operation should be organized in battle units as small as possible. Every effort must be made to link up with German troops still carrying on the fight outside the city of Berlin. If such cannot be located, then the Berlin force must take to the woods and continue resistance there.

A document, in short, expressly forbidding even the thought of capitulation. No surrender. This was typed up by Frau Christian on the large block-letter typewriter. For some reason, it was on Hitler's letterhead. An SS captain was sent as officer-courier to hand this order to General Weidling in person. It took the courier almost two hours, along the Landwehr Canal, to traverse the distance of less than one mile, 1200 meters. He returned wounded, mission completed.

This order did not, however, come out of the blue. The evening before (Sunday, April 29) General Weidling, during his final visit to the Fuehrerbunker, had shown Hitler a breakout plan that had been worked up by several of his staff officers. Hitler had haughtily refused to discuss it or even to accept a copy for later perusal. According to Gen-

eral Mohnke, these were the salient points, as he recalled
them thirty years later.

Troops still actively defending Berlin were to march, in
three battle groups, along both sides of the Heerstrasse.
The Heerstrasse is an extension of the East-West Axis, leading out of the city to the northwest.

The twin bridges over the Havel River just south of
Spandau were to be held—by armed Hitlerjugend, at whatever cost—until all three battle groups had crossed over
and left Berlin behind them.

All clear enough. The number of combat troops involved in General Weidling's plan was not more than 30,-
000, if that. Weidling's staff men had also put in a bit of
General Staff eyewash for optical purposes. Weidling himself certainly knew by now that Hitler had no intention
whatever of quitting Berlin. But it did make the plan seem
more impressive (for the history books as well) to include
the Fuehrer and his court in the middle of this German
Thermopylae operation. Neither Weidling nor his staff
wanted to create the impression that they were abandoning
Hitler to his fate in the Fuehrerbunker. This was another
German cosmetic touch, for it was, in cold fact, precisely
their intention.

According to those who were still present with General
Weidling in the Bendlerstrasse, the general, during midmorning of this Monday, April 30, had called together his
five or six division commanders and told them he intended
to order this breakout attempt on his own authority. The
H-Hour he then gave was ten o'clock that same evening.*

Even on this last day, it is still easy enough to reconstruct, pretty much, just what Hitler was doing. General
Mohnke has covered us well for the period of 6:00 A.M. to
7:00 A.M.; Sergeant Misch, for 7:00 A.M. to 8:15 A.M. As
a hungry Misch then left for the canteen, Gerda Christian
was again at Hitler's side, ready for work, such as it might
be. Major Otto Guensche was on deck by 9:00 A.M. Martin
Bormann, badly hung over, managed to show up around
10:00.

Frau Gerda Christian spoke of this last morning.

I soon gathered, from the general, glum mood, that this was
to be our last bunker day. But nobody yet dared say or even

---

* Somehow, one senses that Weidling had heard of Hitler's decision to
commit suicide on this day. He could have had it from Krebs or Burgdorf.

hint as much. And yet, all things considered, it was routine enough, taken up with the usual rounds of conferences, parleys, dictation. Hitler also had a fairly long session with Hans Baur, followed by talks with such old cronies as Ambassador Walter Hewel and Professor Haase. Bormann, having slept things off, was around, as were fellow tipplers General Krebs and Burgdorf. Goebbels was also closeted with Hitler, although only for a short while, perhaps twenty minutes. This was around noontime.

Frau Christian, the best source on this particular morning, continued her recollection.

I suppose it was around twelve-thirty when my relief, Trudl Junge, arrived. This was the usual time—we were still working in shifts—and it was also, again as usual, the familiar signal for lunch. Hitler, "for old times' sake," now invited both of us secretaries, along with Fräulein Manzialy, to join him for lunch at one o'clock. He came out into the corridor to announce this—it was some time after his talk with Goebbels—and soon Fräulein Manzialy, a mousy but pleasant little Innsbruckerin, arrived with the victuals.

We ate at the small table in Hitler's study, the so-called map room. The only other male present was an SS orderly, Corporal Schwiebel, as I recall. It was a melancholy and rather tasteless repast, spaghetti and a tossed salad. Very little was said, certainly nothing new, or I would surely remember.* We had often eaten alone with Hitler before, of course, but this was the very last lunch, and everybody knew it. It was a peculiar honor, qualified by our depressing knowledge that, with Hitler soon to be gone, the breakout would be our only hope. This was a harrowing thought for all three of us women. The Berlin rape stories had given us the shudders, so the topic was avoided.

It seems strange that Eva Braun Hitler was not at her husband's side in this cozy little luncheon group. It was the group in which she had been a familiar figure since 1933.

Frau Christian observed, "Perhaps a simple explanation is that the Fuehrer really felt, now that E.B. was legally Frau Hitler, that she was no longer on the same quite humble social level she had been as his mistress. He was rather persnickity, in his Austrian way, about just such

---

* Gertrud Junge recalled that the one topic was the proper mating of dogs; another, that French lipstick was made from grease gathered in the Paris sewers.

minor table formalities. Or perhaps poor Eva just wasn't hungry. I did not see her again until ten minutes before the end."

Just after that last lunch, Trudl Junge had taken it upon herself to seek out Eva Braun Hitler in her private quarters. This was around two-thirty. The secretary found Frau Hitler sitting before her dresser, sorting out and preparing to give away her more valuable belongings as last presents. She gave two large bundles to her faithful maid, Liesl Ostertag. As Trudl Junge entered, Eva greeted her in a friendly, almost exuberant way. She made her a present of her one fairly valuable fur, a silver-fox wrap, saying, "Trudl, sweetheart, here's a present for next winter and your life after the war. I wish you all the luck in the world. And when you put it on, always remember me and give my very best to our native Bavaria—*das schoene Bayern*."

Das schoene Bayern, Bavaria the beautiful. Other than the formal farewells in the corridor at the very end, these are the last known words of Eva Braun Hitler. As an exit line, the girl from Simbach could have done worse.*

Those final goodbyes came shortly after three o'clock, when the newlywed Hitlers, so seldom together since the bleak midnight wedding some forty hours before, now made their last appearance in the main corridor of the lower bunker. It was *ave atque vale* to what was left of the bedraggled Reich Chancellery Group. Present were Goebbels, alone; Bormann; Generals Krebs and Burgdorf; Ambassador Walter Hewel; Vice Admiral Voss; Professor Werner Haase; Major General Rattenhuber; Colonel Hoegl; the senior valet, Heinz Linge; Major Otto Guensche; the three secretaries, Frau Christian, Frau Junge, and Fräulein Krueger (Bormann's secretary). This is close to the complete final cast. Missing were only Chefpilot Hans Baur, Reichsjugendfuehrer Artur Axmann, the chauffeur Erich Kempka—and Magda Goebbels.

This formal bunker leave-taking was brief; it lasted less than three minutes. No one later recalled any last, immortal words. In the awkward silence, it was finally Linge, who, after a cue from the Fuehrer, opened the door leading to

---

* Baedeker, 1925: Simbach, small Bavarian town with 4000 inhabitants. *Gasthaus Alte Post.*

Hitler's private apartment. Hitler, with a courtly gesture, directed his doomed spouse to precede him.

Then, just before disappearing forever, Adolf Hitler turned to Heinz Linge, shook hands with him, and said, "Linge, old friend, I want you now to join the breakout group."

Linge, taken aback, asked, "Why, my Fuehrer?"

Hitler said, "To serve the man who will come after me."

Whatever that may have meant. These were Hitler's last words in the presence of the court. The silence was almost tangible.

Now Hitler, moving slowly but steadily, passed through and closed the door. At this point Linge, according to others present, lost his composure completely. For no apparent reason, like a startled raccoon, he ran up all forty-four steep steps of the four-flight emergency-exit staircase. Soon he came running back, speechless, wild-eyed. Yet Linge still had one more important assigned role to play. All the others, stupefied, simply watched Linge's antic activity.

Major Otto Guensche was the next to make a move. He left to round up several young officers of the FBK and post them in the upper bunker. Their imminent chore was to lug the two Hitler corpses out of the lower bunker. Guensche soon returned and stationed himself directly before the door to the Hitler apartment. His legs were spread, and he was clasping his machine pistol at port arms, before his breast. All present expected the end at any minute. All ears were cocked for the sound of a revolver shot, possibly two. As a soldier, Guensche himself began to wonder, as the minutes ticked by, whether anyone would really be able to hear a shot through the heavy, vaultlike steel door. Two doors, in fact, because there was also the small vestibule before the Hitler living room.

Action outside the door, however, was not quite over. Two important latecomers who had missed the corridor farewell ceremony now suddenly appeared. The first was Magda Goebbels, who bolted toward Guensche. Surprised and perplexed, Guensche, flourishing his weapon, tried to wave her back. But the frantic Magda persisted. She was determined to see Adolf Hitler, and Guensche relented. He entered the room to relay Magda's request to the Fuehrer. At this unguarded moment, Frau Goebbels burst past him and lunged into the Fuehrer's study. This unplanned interlude lasted perhaps three minutes. Hitler gruffly refused to talk to Magda Goebbels or even listen to her plea that "there is still a chance to take off for Berchtesgaden."

The second VIP late arrival—he appeared on the scene while Frau Goebbels was still closeted with Hitler—was Artur Axmann. He had been delayed because he had had to come from his battle post across the street, crossing the Wilhelmplatz under fire. Axmann had arrived with his senior aide, Major Guenther Weltzin. Both wore wet handkerchiefs, tied bandit-style over their faces, to protect their eyes from hot ash and phosphorous fumes. Axmann had also stopped in the conference room to chat with his old friend and sponsor, Dr. Goebbels. When he approached Guensche, who was again at his post before the door, this time the irritated major was adamant. He told Axmann bluntly, "Too late; too late for anyone."

It was one, possibly two, minutes later that "a single shot was heard." So ran the version as the world first heard it in 1945. It has since been recorded in most historical accounts of Hitler's last moment. That version was based on the original testimony of Erich Kempka (and that of Linge as well), one of the few key witnesses destined to evade the Red Army dragnet and to surface in the west. However, as he sheepishly admitted in 1974 to this reporter, Kempka was not even among those present in the corridor at this critical moment. He was en route to the Fuehrerbunker from the Chancellery—aboveground—and he had thus obviously not as yet entered it.

Back in 1945 the contrary evidence of Artur Axmann—his testimony became available late in December 1945—was dismissed or ignored. Axmann then said simply, "I was standing right there, as close to the door as possible, but I certainly heard no shot." This was the truth. The Fuehrer was exchanging his last blunt words with Magda Goebbels. Guensche was the one man who was really center-stage at this critical moment. Wherever I could check him out, I found Guensche to have, like Axmann, a very high veracity-ratio.

Nobody, among those who were really present, did hear any shot. This, as they later reported, is what increased the tension. Guensche corroborated, saying,

Nobody was standing closer to that door than I, that is for sure. I have very good ears, and I was listening intently. The nineteen forty-five testimony of both Linge and Kempka just does not stand up; they must have been confused or were under interrogation pressure. Linge, for example, was really beside himself, running up and down those stairs like the King of Spain, and Kempka, a real stumblebum, was not present, as he damned well should have been. Kempka, as I recall, was not even present when we first entered the death chamber. I first met him at the bottom of the stairs, when we were carrying the bodies away. That was ten or even fifteen minutes after Hitler's suicide.

This testimony of Major Guensche is the clincher. Guensche did not return from Russia, where he had been a prisoner, to East Germany until 1955 and did not arrive in West Germany until late in 1956. The Russians had grilled Guensche,* for literally hundreds of hours, on this very point: the moment of truth in the bunker. In 1974 I asked him why.

Guensche replied:

In retrospect, and much as I hate even to recall those long Stalinist interrogation sessions, I believe the Soviets had two things in the backs of their minds. First, the Russian suspicion that either I or someone else very close to Hitler had in fact shot him. Shot him in the sense of having given him the coup de grâce with his own pistol; either they really believed that, or they *wanted* to believe it.

Second, the so-called carrot-and-stick method. The Russians offered me "instant freedom" if I would "confess." All I had to do was to sign a document to the effect that Hitler did *not* shoot himself, and I would be a free man. I didn't bite that carrot because I was afraid of the stick. Nothing is more dangerous than to lie to the Soviets, above all in a written protocol. You will notice that even today they use my testimony wherever and whenever it contradicts such historians as Professor Trevor-Roper, but seldom when what I have said corroborates western sources.

Otto Guensche then returned to his narrative of what really did happen that mid-Monday afternoon in Berlin, April 30, 1945.

---

* One point on which I agree with Soviet Intelligence. After initial skepticism, they have tended, in recent years, to accept Otto Guensche as a most accurate witness.

There were, as I now recall, at least six people almost as near that door as I was. These were Goebbels, Bormann, Linge, Generals Krebs and Burgdorf, Axmann, maybe one or two others. None of us heard a shot. I believe this was because of the sealed double doors. Both these doors were fireproof, gasproof, hence soundproof. The last instruction both Linge and I had—directly from the Fuehrer—was to wait ten minutes and then, and only then, to enter the room. This is just what we did. I kept glancing at my watch. I thought it must have stopped; they were the longest ten minutes in my life.

To make triply sure, I went back once again to Kempka, whom I had first talked to in 1973. I sent him a copy of Guensche's testimony and pointed out the obvious conflict. Kempka told me in 1974,

Yes, Major Guensche is right. He had sent me off to round up at least two hundred liters of gasoline, ten jerry cans, but I was able to find only six or seven in my Reich Chancellery garage. I "pumped" [that is, borrowed] two more from Cheftechniker Hentschel. I was thus on my way back to the Fuehrerbunker when I met up with the funeral cortège. That lout Bormann was carrying the body of Eva Braun, clutching her breast with his apelike paw. Somehow this maddened me. He was carrying her as if she were a sack of potatoes. Just as they all started to ascend the staircase, I reached the bottom. So I grabbed the body of Eva Braun Hitler from Bormann and began to carry her up the stairs myself. I think if Bormann had resisted my effort, I would have hauled off and clobbered him, but he made no protest.

I asked "Herr Kempka, why did you tell your nineteen forty-five interrogators a quite different story? As you now admit, you were still aboveground, only just approaching the bunker entrance, at the moment Hitler shot himself."

Kempka responded, "That was nineteen forty-five. It is now nineteen seventy-four. So let me level with you. Back in forty-five, to save my own skin, I told American and British interrogators just about anything or everything I thought they wanted to hear. Since they kept grilling me about 'that shot' I finally told them that I had heard it. It seemed to make things easier."

Why did Kempka invent this shot story? The real reason his story was more than slightly fishy was that he was then trying to cover up his own major goof-off. As boss of the Reich Chancellery garage, he was responsible for an adequate supply of gasoline. In the earlier stages of the siege of Berlin, Kempka did have an ample cache of gasoline, some 40,000 liters. It was hidden in subterranean plastic tanks in the Tiergarten, only 400 meters away. There was also an underground pipe from this secret reservoir direct into the Chancellery garage. But this rubber pipe apparently had been too close to the surface, for it was knocked out when the first artillery shells reached the Tiergarten. Kempka had forgotten to build up a reservoir of filled jerry cans in the garage itself. The man was not really minding his shop.

There were reasons for this, too. Kempka, who died in 1975, was a primitive, vulgar, thoroughly unpleasant man. He was one of the more notorious bunker boozers, along with Bormann, Stumpfegger, Baur, General Burgdorf. A vainglorious blackguard, he also prided himself on his reputation as a *Hecht*. *Hecht* means pike. It also means machismo. In terms of seniority—Kempka had been with Hitler since 1932—he was one of the oldest members of the chummy Reich Chancellery Group. Hitler was usually, though by no means always, amused and bemused by Kempka's Casanova conquests and the rooster boasting sessions these produced. "A good sex life relaxes chauffeurs." So the omniscient Fuehrer said. (Source: Speer and Guensche.)

For security reasons, Hitler was also not unhappy when such lowbrow intimates as Kempka kept their sex escapades within the group of mountain people. He smiled benignly at Kempka's affair with Gerda Daranovsky before she jilted the chauffeur to marry her Luftwaffe pilot, General Eckard Christian. It was after this that Kempka cranked up an affair with Gretl Braun but was jilted once again when she married Hermann Fegelein. In mid-1944, Kempka married a local tart in Berchtesgaden. Frau Kempka had a long police record as a registered prostitute. This information was gleefully dug up and broadcast by Bormann.* When Hitler heard of this he banned the wife—not Kempka —from the Berghof.

Hitler had a thing about chauffeurs. This came in part, no doubt, from his basic security problem. Security was always in the back of Hitler's mind, but it was also a re-

---

* Which probably explains the body-snatching incident Kempka described.

flection of his own uncouth leanings. He liked his chauffeurs
to be rough, tough, and Bavarian, which is what led Albert
Speer to refer to Hitler's cronies as the "Chauffeureska."

This, too, goes deep back into Hitler's past. Even during
these last days in the bunker—according to valet Linge—
there were only two framed photographs on Hitler's small
bedroom dresser. One was of his mother, Klara, whose
death in 1907 had been a traumatic experience for Hitler.
He was then seventeen. The other framed photo was of
his first and long-time chauffeur, Emil Maurice. Maurice,
who had also served as Hitler's secretary in the mid-twenties
(until he was squeezed out of that job by Rudolf Hess),
was one of the half-dozen cronies with whom Hitler exchanged the familiar *du* (thee).* This warmth had persisted
despite a 1928 brawl in which Hitler, the jealous uncle,
found old *Duzfreund* and chauffeur Emil in bed with Hitler's niece, Geli Raubal. Hitler on that occasion (the source
is Dr. "Putzi" Hanfstaengl) "chased his errant chauffeur
three times around the Berghof cracking his hippopotamus
riding-whip." According to Hanfstaengl and others, Emil
Maurice was not the only one Hitler went after with a whip
on that wild Bavarian evening. Geli Raubal committed
suicide in September 1931.**

After her death, Hitler and Maurice were reconciled, but
the favorite chauffeur-bodyguard died young—some time
in the mid-thirties. He had already been replaced as chief
chauffeur by Julius Schreck. When Schreck was killed in
an auto accident in 1936, Kempka took over. Kempka,
though an important Fuehrer crony, was never really as
close to Hitler as either Emil Maurice or Julius Schreck
had been. For one thing, according to Hitler, "He could
not drive as well."

The Hitler biographers and historians have never cleared
up this messy triangle: Hitler–Geli–Maurice. All the old
mountain people I have talked to insist that Hitler at that
time, from 1928 to 1931, was much more passionately in

---

* Maurice, originally a watchmaker and, according to some reports, an
ex-convict, helped Hitler set up the first "storm troopers" as early as
1921.
** In her recent memoirs, the wife of Rudolf Hess, Ilse, who was very
close to Hitler in those pre-1933 Bavarian years, has an astonishing footnote. She insists that Hitler's vegetarianism, which most biographers have
maintained traces back to his pre-1914 Vienna days, dates only from
1931 and emerged from the deep mental depression caused by the death
of his niece. Frau Hess says she often had served Hitler Munich *Weiss-
wurst* (white sausage) and *Leber Knoedel* (liver dumpling) before 1931.

love with Geli Raubal than he ever was, later, with Eva Braun. The 1945 presence of that picture of his old chauffeur on his dresser, next to that of dear old Mom, is one fascinating clue.

To return to Erich Kempka—another matter he held back from his 1945 interrogators was a proper explanation of just how he had managed to become one of the very few of the bunker inner circle to hide out successfully in Berlin—and also to escape to the west early in May 1945. In the running account of the breakout we will note that Erich Kempka suddenly vanishes from the scene, shortly after a brisk tank battle at the Weidendamm Bridge. It was at this moment that Kempka claimed, also quite erroneously, to have seen Martin Bormann "cold stone dead, killed by a tank explosion." From this moment in the narrative of the breakout, Kempka, according to all other eyewitnesses (Baur, Axmann, Naumann, Guensche), did a quick disappearing act. He left the group and sallied off on his own. In 1945, in western captivity, Kempka blandly told his interrogators that he had the good fortune (it was 3:00 A.M.) to stumble into a Berlin cellar, "where I found two friendly Yugoslav women who fed me and gave me civilian clothes."

This, as Kempka rather sheepishly admitted to me in 1974, was no chance encounter. The two Yugoslav women were mother and daughter. They were running what Kempka called "a kind of walkup pension" in the Friedrichstrasse. This end of the Friedrichstrasse* was (and still is) Berlin's Forty-second Street, and it is almost certain that the "pension" was a brothel. One must thus give Kempka some credit for cuteness under fire. A brothel was indeed one of the very best places in town for Hitler's now ex-chauffeur to go to cover. He knew the surroundings.

Still according to Kempka—who told the story with some glee—when Russian soldiers broke in, as they did, a rousing good time was had by all. Kempka spoke neither Yugoslavian nor Russian. But he probably did not have too much trouble convincing the boisterous Russians that he was the resident pimp, the friend of the madame and quite possibly of her daughter, too.

Given the hairy circumstances, it is a rather funny story. The Russians never knew that this one male resident of

---

* Today, it is in East Berlin.

the pension was both Hitler's chauffeur and a full colonel in the SS. If Hitler in the bunker had known about Kempka's bordello liaison with the Yugoslav females, which had existed for weeks at least, the Fuehrer would have had words, and probably more than words, with old friend Erich Kempka.

That diversion into Kempka's past was necessary at this point to underscore why most of his earlier testimony can, indeed must, be dismissed. He himself has shown us why this is so. To reconstruct what really did happen behind those closed doors—for there can be no question of any direct eyewitness, any third person in the room—is not difficult. It is not as mysterious as the ominous door in Bluebeard's palace—"And now, my darlings, any room but that."

Despite the Bluebeard atmosphere surrounding the event, we do have the testimony of at least three of the five bunker witnesses who were the first to enter that room, around 3:40 P.M.: Kempka and the much more reliable Axmann and Guensche.

For the hour of Hitler's death, we also have, albeit secondhand, the very important contemporary account of Professor Haase, as recalled by Dr. Schenck.

Shortly after 4:00 P.M., less than one half hour after Hitler's death, the now breathless Professor Haase gave Schenck a quite precise account of his last, long consultation with Adolf Hitler. This had taken place, Haase said, in the lower bunker at around 3:00 or maybe 4:00 A.M.,* Monday, the same day. Hitler had once again queried Haase on the foolproof or pistol-and-poison method recommended by the latter. If Hitler followed Haase's clinical instructions to the letter—and all later circumstantial evidence indicates that he most certainly did—then what follows is a fair reconstruction of what probably happened.

Hitler had in his possession two pistols. The larger and far more potent was a standard Walther 7.65 caliber. The Fuehrer had been carrying this gun in his tunic pocket since April 22, possibly earlier.** The smaller pistol was another Walther, a 6.35. This was the weapon Hitler had been carrying for many years, concealed in the leather holster sewn inside his trousers near the right pocket. This

---

* The consultation Dr. Schenck had seen on his way to the latrine.
** When senior adjutant Julius Schaub saw him remove it from the bedroom safe.

smaller gun he now placed on the table before him in front of the sofa. One assumes this was simply a precaution in case the heavier pistol, with which Hitler was far less familiar, should jam.

Then Hitler sat down on the left-hand corner of the narrow sofa (left, as viewed from the door). Next, he took out of his tunic pocket two poison vials. One he placed on the table between the pistol and a vase. This was a reserve. The other he put into his mouth.

His bride, Eva, was seated in the other corner of the blue-and-white sofa. They were only about two feet apart. Eva had kicked off her buckskin spectator pumps and pulled her feet up snugly under her lithe body. She had two similar capsules. One of these she placed on the same round table. Beside it she put her own small pistol, also a Walther 6.35. Next to it was a raspberry-colored silk scarf. She put the second capsule into her mouth. Eva was not holding any pistol in her hand.

Hitler was. She must have been watching him. On the matter of timing, Hitler had told Haase that it was his last wish that the double deaths be simultaneous—"We both want to go together when we go." (Haase told this later to Schenck.) After his last conference with Hitler, to make doubly sure, Professor Haase had visited Eva Braun Hitler in her chambers and told her, "Simply bite quickly into your capsule the moment you hear a shot." The girl apparently did just that; she had some reason to fear that the sight of her dead lover might shatter her resolution. Eva Braun Hitler was thus almost surely the only person to hear the single shot many millions in this world would have been most delighted to hear.

Professor Haase, in his talks with Schenck just after the event, was not quite clear as to whether Eva was programmed to use her own pistol. The choice may have been left to her. But the tenor of his advice seems definitely to have been *not* to use it. And, in any case, she did not. Eva's pistol was later found by Linge; it was still on the table, the chamber fully loaded. This was the same pistol with which Eva Braun had been practicing, some ten days before, under the blasted springtime leaves of the nearby Tiergarten. Eva was familiar enough with firearms to have used her pistol had she so chosen.

Adolf Hitler—again assuming he had followed the last advice not only of Professor Haase but also of his senior

military men, Krebs and Burgdorf—must have put the
muzzle of his black Walther directly to his graying right
temple, right-angled at eyebrow level. He then squeezed
the trigger and simultaneously bit into his capsule. Given
his physical condition, this called for one last, vehement act
of concentrated will power. We know Hitler had that quality right to the end. Bang! So one records the most important shot fired in all of World War II. The pistol
slipped from the tyrant's right hand. It fell to the carpet
at his feet. This is a sign that the poison, potassium cyanide,
had done its job quickly. Most pistol-only suicides are
usually found clutching the weapon with clawlike tenacity.

For Eva Hitler, too, death must have come quickly, if
not painlessly. Her frail body was found in the same position she had assumed when she kicked off her pumps. The
double odor from the pistol shot and the cyanide, a mixture of acrid cordite and bitter almond, now filled the
small, stuffy death room. But it did not seep into the vestibule or into the corridor outside from the room proofed
against poison gas.*

Heinz Linge's going around the bend during these
emotion-charged moments put a hitch into the smooth running of this much-rehearsed Hitler last performance, for
Hitler had commissioned Linge, rather than the younger
but more stable Major Guensche, to be master of the immediate post-mortem ceremonies. Linge had been ordered
to give the word when to enter the death room. He later
said, "I was told we were to wait at least ten minutes, and
then to enter if we had heard no sound."

Instead of waiting, Linge, on that sudden wild impulse,
had dashed up the steps of the emergency exit.

Bormann and Guensche were standing together near the
door to the vestibule. Four others were present: Goebbels,
General Krebs, General Burgdorf, and Artur Axmann.
All hands had been told by Hitler just how he wanted
them to go about the disposal of his body and that of his
wife. He had made each of them swear to see to it that his
instructions were carried out meticulously, for all in the

---

* Some readers may wonder if this fact would have frustrated Albert
Speer's February 1945 assassination plan, which called for poison gas.
Speer today says no. He had chosen an hour 7:00 to 8:00 P.M., when
Hitler would not have been in these private quarters, but in the map or
small conference room. Moreover, Speer's gas would have penetrated into
Hitler's private quarters through the ventilation system.

bunker had heard by this time some of the sordid details of what had just happened down in Italy to the corpses of Benito Mussolini and his mistress, Clara Petacci.*

Somebody had to be first to enter that sinister room. In the end it was poor Linge, who was the second lowest-ranking member in this small group (like Kempka, he was a colonel in the SS). As he slowly opened the door, he was taken aback. The strong fumes from the pistol shot and the poison made his eyes smart. Choking, Linge closed and locked the door. He then turned back to summon Bormann. "Frankly, I was trembling," Linge says, "and I simply did not have the gumption to go in there by myself. It was too eerie."

With Bormann leading, the small group (Linge, Guensche, Goebbels, and Axmann) finally entered, gasping from the toxic fumes.

Three of the witnesses to this grim yet fascinating moment—Linge, Guensche, Axmann—are still alive, and I have talked with them. All three agree pretty much on the horrible historical tableau.

Eva Braun Hitler was in the snug schoolgirl position. Her small pistol was next to her brightly colored scarf. Hitler was more slumped-over, but was still on the blue-and-white velvet sofa. Blood was oozing in steady drips from his right temple. A small Dresden vase, which had been filled only that morning with greenhouse tulips and white narcissi, had tipped over. It had spilled water on Eva's blue chiffon spring dress, near the thigh, and had fallen to the carpet, unbroken. Linge, ever the valet with a sense of order, picked up the white vase, examined it for cracks, filled it with the fallen flowers, set it back upon the table.

"At least two minutes—two very long minutes—passed before any of us said or did anything, except watch what Linge did with the white vase," Guensche related. Guensche finally snapped out of the trance and directed Linge to move aside the two chairs and the table, in order to spread two woolen military blankets onto the floor. He then left

---

* As Trevor-Roper was the first to point out, they most definitely had *not* seen the disgraceful pictures of Il Duce and his paramour hanging by their heels from a Milan filling-station marquee. These pictures were first published in May, and thus would not have been available in Berlin, certainly not in the bunker, on April 30.

the room to summon three young officers of the FBK who were waiting nearby in the guards' room. At this moment a sixth witness arrived. It was Colonel Ludwig Stumpfegger, the surgeon. He examined both bodies and pronounced Adolf and Eva Hitler dead. Goebbels, Bormann, and Axmann were wordless spectators.

Now General Rattenhuber appeared. The general in charge of internal security was so shaken that he did not venture into the Hitler apartment but sat on a bench in the main conference room, "moaning and groaning," according to Guensche. Rattenhuber knew, of course—for he had it from Stumpfegger—that the latter had supplied both Hitlers with cyanide vials. He also now heard from Linge, who had come out of the study to place both of Hitler's pistols and Eva Braun's unused weapon on the small dresser-shelf in the vestibule, that the chief valet had noticed a pool of blood on the rug near Hitler's end of the sofa. The pool of blood, rather obviously, must have come from the gaping wound in Hitler's shattered temple. But the news somehow puzzled Rattenhuber. Although by profession a detective, he did not have the courage to enter the death room to see things for himself.

At this moment Rattenhuber, who was obviously quite drunk, jumped to a false conclusion. For some reason, he apparently had not been informed by Haase or Hitler about the pistol-and-poison suicide method, so he managed to convince himself that Hitler, distrusting the poison that had come from Himmler, had ordered someone to give him a coup de grâce with his own pistol in case the poison did not do the job. The addled chief detective further reasoned that the someone could have been only Linge or, just possibly, Guensche.

Nor was this a merely momentary mental aberration under the stress of Hitler's death and alcohol. General Rattenhuber, after he reached confinement in Russia several weeks later, persisted in his stubborn suspicion. During his decade in Soviet captivity, he got Linge and Guensche into a peck of trouble. High-ranking Soviet interrogation officers—secret service creeps of much the same caliber as Rattenhuber—tended to believe his story. It fitted snugly into the official Soviet line, which persists to this day, that Adolf Hitler chose "the coward's death" in the sense that he did not shoot himself.

Thirty-three years later, this point is hardly worth caviling about. My own conclusion is that Linge and Guensche are probably telling the truth.

It is true, of course, that Linge and Guensche might have been lying. Both hearties, even today, remain staunch admirers of their former chief. Both men are today fairly prosperous businessmen in West Germany, Linge in the Hamburg area and Guensche just across the river from the federal capital in Bonn. Today neither would want to be known, down at the local *Kneipe* (pub) as "the man who shot the Fuehrer." This theory of a cover-up story could also apply to Axmann. Kempka was a crude and unreliable braggart, but Axmann is more intelligent and more believable.*

To my mind what really clinches the circumstantial evidence about Hitler's death is what I heard from Dr. Schenck. He told me about the long conversation he had had with Haase within less than an hour after Hitler's death. Haase, as Schenck described him, was not the type of man to be part of an elaborate cover-up story, nor is Dr. Schenck.

Schenck added a final, psychological sidebar. "After all, many people tend to forget that Adolf Hitler was not alone when he shot himself. He was in the presence of a brave woman who was very much in love with him. Why, therefore, should he arrange a coup de grâce for himself but not for her? One can despise Hitler, believe only the worst of him, if one will, but we should not diabolize him. He was not a coward. Morever, as we now know him, he was a great actor and a born show-off, above all before women. For him to have flinched at this last moment, before Eva Braun, *that* would have been quite out of character."

One can only agree. Among those present, none was more shaken than Dr. Paul Joseph Goebbels. The otherwise cynical little doctor really worshiped Hitler this side of

---

* Axmann's biography, if he ever gets around to writing it, might turn out to be worth reading. As a young man he was a red-hot National Socialist, one of the few who really came from the working class. After 1945, he seemed to undergo a genuine political conversion. When I first met him, at his denazification trial in Berlin in 1947, Axmann told the story of his life in a way that was both convincing and believable, not so much the contrition as his explanation of how Hitler ever happened. He also took a fair share of the blame upon himself, a refreshingly rare standpoint in the denazification courts of those days. Artur Axmann is today a businessman in the Canary Islands.

idolatry. He had just become Hitler's successor as chancellor. But now rank meant nothing to him. Goebbels turned to his old disciple Axmann and said, "I intend to go out now onto the Wilhelmplatz, reach for a rifle, and keep running about until a Russian bullet finishes me off."

It all sounds like a quote from that forgotten novel *Michael, A German Destiny*, written in 1922 by the then unknown and unemployed young Ph.D from the Rhineland, before he had ever met Adolf Hitler.* In fact, however, both stayed below, watching from the conference room as the cortège headed slowly up the spiral staircase. Then they brought up the rear, Goebbels limping.

Three of the tallest young SS bucks from the FBK were lugging Hitler's corpse. They had no stretcher or portable bier, not even a plank. Hitler's blood-stained cranium was hidden from the view of pallbearers and mourners. Visible were only the familiar black trousers of the simple uniform Hitler had donned back in September 1939. Hitler weighed about 180 pounds, so it was a somewhat awkward task to get him up those steep, narrow stairs. They hauled him up head first, two stalwarts clutching the still-warm corpse near the shoulders, the third pushing from below with a firm grip on both ankles.

Carrying the smaller, lighter body of Eva Braun was an easier task. Her head, face, and shoulders were quite visible. "She looked serene in death," says Linge.

Kempka, after grabbing her body from Bormann, found that he could make it only halfway up the stairs. Here he was relieved of his burden by Major Guensche. Guensche in turn handed the body over to SS officers as he reached the top of the stairs. This curious mummery on the staircase—no word was spoken—was a reflection of old bunker tensions. Both Kempka and Guensche well knew how much Bormann and Hitler's mistress had loathed each other for years; both men resented Bormann's mock solicitude at this solemn moment. More important, this otherwise trivial pantomime underscores the almost instant collapse of Bormann as a figure of any real authority, pushed aside by a chauffeur and a mere major.

---

* "God, how I want to be a hero." Michael died underground in a coal-mining disaster "with a laugh on his lips." On his body was found a copy of Nietzsche's *Thus Spake Zarathustra*. Underlined twice was the quotation "Many men die too late, and a few too soon. Few learn the lesson: manage to die at the right time."

Once the group was out in the Berlin fresh air, the stage was set for a kind of instant state funeral, probably the shortest such requiem in world history. As they emerged from the bunker, there were now but nine of the major Nazi spear-holders still present for the obsequies. These were Goebbels, Bormann, Hewel, Axmann, Rattenhuber, Stumpfegger, Schaedle,* Linge, and Guensche.

During the last days in the Fuehrerbunker, all nine had been briefed by the Fuehrer personally on how to render him their last service. Yet, in the general confusion, they were unable to carry out two of his express orders. Hitler wanted no spectators from among the some 700 Reich Chancellery and bunker supernumeraries. Second, and far more important, Hitler wanted to make sure that both his body and that of his wife be destroyed *spurlos*, without trace.

But there were, in the event, three quite minor interlopers, *Zaungaeste*, or peeping Toms, who managed to see most of the macabre show in the rubble-filled Chancellery garden. All uniformed personnel normally on duty in or near the Fuehrerbunker on this Monday had been issued their daily rations around noontime. They were then told to disappear to their quarters or the canteen. The Fuehrerbunker was placed off limits, as was that part of the New Reich Chancellery within 150 meters of the scene of the upcoming funeral ceremony.

But some of the lads were curious, with, one strongly suspects, at least some of the *Schadenfreude* with which enlisted men in every army in the world would enjoy catching the big brass in uncomfortable moments, awkward poses. The death of Hitler was, after all, something to write home about.

The first interloper was SS Sergeant Erich Mengershausen, of General Rattenhuber's RSD. Mengershausen was stationed in a camouflaged cement watchtower in the Chancellery garden. When he saw the parade of crestfallen pseudo-Norsemen emerging from the emergency exit of the bunker, against orders he left his hidden post and hustled over to have a look. As Mengershausen came close to the procession, Major Guensche, with drawn pistol, shouted at him to "vanish on the double."

---

* Schaedle, in these last days, received a painful foot wound. He was hobbling about on a crutch, like Philoctetes. Thus he missed much of the action.

FBK Sergeant Erich Mansfeld was on patrol near the old Mosaic Room of the New Reich Chancellery, about 135 meters away from the bunker. Looking from one of the rear windows, he also saw the procession. The bodies of the two Hitlers, he reports, were still wrapped in blankets. With his binoculars, he could just make out the face of Eva Braun; he had no idea, of course, who the lady was. He saw the three SS officers lower the corpses into a long, rather shallow, makeshift ditch. It was less than ten meters from the bunker exit. Two of the FBK officers, Helmut Beermann and Hans Horbeck, emptied several jerry cans over the corpses, probably something less than fifty gallons of gasoline. They then stepped back and tried to ignite the two splashed cadavers in the soggy blankets by tossing lighted matches toward the trench. Nothing happened; there was too much wind.

Too much wind and also, now, a good deal of metal flying about in the form of shrapnel. This accounts for much of this hectic, anarchic, if sometimes intrepid dramaturgy. The Soviets, although at the time they could not know this, were supplying the non-Wagnerian funeral music—Stalin organs.

Thus it was that the action was interrupted, three or four times, as the agitated principals waited for those few pauses which meant that the Red Army artillery men were reloading. They would move out on the double from the bunker entrance for a few seconds only; then duck back to take cover in a kind of vestibule to the bunker exit, which had a cement canopy.

Heinz Linge had a bright idea to get the show moving. To light the emergency butane lamp in the bunker, Linge had been in the habit of carrying slips of paper tucked into the broad lapels of his fancy butler's uniform. These, when needed, he would twist into a fidibus, a kind of pipe-smoker's paper spill. Linge now twisted one of these to make a flare, lighted it with his pocket lighter, and then handed it ceremoniously to Bormann. Reichsleiter Bormann, cosy as ever, did not move out from the shelter. Instead, he tossed the fidibus, which sailed through the air like a schoolboy's paper dart. His first attempt fell short. On the next try, a lighted flare landed directly in the trench, close to the two bodies. A second later, both cadavers burst into sudden blue flame.

Without anybody having been given an order, the participants, as one man, stood at rigid attention at the graveside to give the stiff-arm Hitler salute. The salute was returned from the other side of the burial trench by SS Colonel Schaedle and two fellow FBK officers. There was no music, no flag, no swastika banner, no funeral oration by Dr. Goebbels.

* *

Later that afternoon, when everybody had returned to the bunker, Frau Christian recalled,

> the mood was détente. The bunker tension, which had been all but unbearable for the last fortnight, relaxed, at least for a few hours. At the same time, we all knew that the Russians were still moving toward us. We knew that the breakout, when and if it ever came off, would be a rough experience.
>
> We still thought the breakout would come that day. Monday, any time after sundown, so we began to pack our clothes. I pulled on a good pair of army boots that one of the officers had kindly given me. I had to put on heavy wool socks to make them fit. I had grown up in Berlin, so the layout of the streets was familiar to me. Still, I had not seen much of Berlin for long weeks, and wondered what the big city would now be like.

It was around 7:00 P.M. when General Mohnke dropped by—he had not been present during the afternoon ceremonies—to announce that the breakout had been postponed for at least twenty-four hours. Since all old bunker hands were already packed and ready to go, some just hit the sack without unpacking. They wanted to catch up on much-needed sleep. Others took to drinking and reminiscing, above all the mountain people—Joseph and Magda Goebbels, Baur, Rattenhuber, Ambassador Hewel, Artur Axmann, Gerda Christian, Trudl Junge.

From the enlisted men's canteen, which was to the north, facing the Tiergarten, about 200 yards away, an SS disk jockey was having a ball. Apparently a fellow with a sense of black humor, he mounted a loudspeaker outside the canteen and give a special Monday concert to announce the new freedom. He had actually cranked up this curious program the night before, until an order had come over from Bormann in the Fuehrerbunker to pipe down.

Contrary to general belief, American jazz and swing bands were never officially banned in the Third Reich, despite Hitler's scornful remarks about "Jewish and jungle" music. Many American top tunes—it was the era of the big name bands—came blaring across the Reich Chancellery garden, along with such international evergreens as "Tipperary," "The Lambeth Walk," "J'attendrai," "Caprifischer," "Rosalinda." The last was the German version of the Czech popular song known to us as "The Beer Barrel Polka," the song to which Europe had marched off into war in September 1939. But Sergeant Misch observed, "The song I best remember from that blaring concert was *'Es geht alles vorueber, es geht alles vorbei . . .'*"*

Yet with Adolf Hitler gone, only one figure moving about the Hitlerless bunker can, by any stretch of the imagination, be called a major historical personality, a man of a certain character, formation, intellectual depth. This was Joseph Goebbels. Hitler was the messiah; Goebbels was his prophet. True, there could have been no Goebbels career without the phenomenon Hitler. But it is equally true that there probably never would have been a Reich Chancellor Hitler, never a Third Reich as the shuddering world came to know it, without the brilliant mouthpiece and impresario Goebbels. It is the Faust and Mephistopheles story once again. The comparison has often been made; few who make it, however, go on to point out that Goebbels in reality was the Faust, the seduced German professor; Hitler, the Mephistopheles. It was Goebbels who had really sold his soul to the devil.

Although Goebbels at this moment was Hitler's successor as Reich chancellor, only a few bunker insiders—and nobody outside—yet knew this. It was not known even to Grand Admiral Doenitz, now Reich President Doenitz, who was up north in Schleswig-Holstein. Bormann, still trying to manipulate the power that was flowing through his fingers like sand, had failed to inform the admiral—or anyone else—either of the death of Adolf Hitler or of the clauses of his testament. Goebbels, however, in no mood to take any nonsense from Bormann, sent a telegram to Doenitz that evening, telling him what had happened in Berlin and informing him, correctly, of the new power

---

* The irony here lies in the words: "Everything passes, everything has its day/After every December comes another May."

situation, such as it was. This was one of Goebbels' few official acts as German chancellor.

The new chancellor and his wife spent almost all of that long evening in the conference room of the lower bunker, reminiscing. He was called away two or three times by pressing business, but he always soon returned. Those who had gathered about him were either his few very close personal friends or some of the old mountain people.

What is astonishing is that no one in this elite Nazi group, not even Goebbels, showed the least interest in what had happened—or in what was still happening—to the Hitler remains. Artur Axmann gives one plausible explanation. "The subject was a kind of taboo that night. No one spoke of Hitler, not of Hitler as a dead man, a mortal corpse. It was perhaps beyond our ken. His death may have been on everybody's mind, but it was pushed into the subconscious. Goebbels, for example, talked on and on about his first meeting with Hitler, about the great triumph of nineteen thirty-three, about pleasant days in Berchtesgaden. He managed to transport us all out of the bunker and off to the magnificent Alps. *Es war einmal . . .*"

At about 10:00 P.M. Otto Guensche wrenched himself back to reality. He sent up one of the young FBK guards, a corporal, to inspect the corpses. This guard soon returned to report that the body of Adolf Hitler was "no longer recognizable." The face and head, he said, had been "consumed by fire beyond all human recognition." Eva Braun, he reported, "had burned away to fine ash." This double-cremation report was grossly exaggerated. One rather doubts that the frightened young soldier ever examined the cadavers.

Shortly before midnight—the source here is Hans Baur —General Rattenhuber, by this time well into his cups, also sent a soldier topside to report. This envoy came back and reported to Goebbels, "Both bodies have now been so burned that only very small remnants still remain. These are unrecognizable."

Close to midnight, Rattenhuber gave an order to remove the remains from the incineration trench and to bury them nearby; he did not specify where. Why both these soldiers gave reports so basically false no one today knows. Probably because they were too moved, or too reluctant, to make the kind of businesslike inspection they had both been ordered to do. It is even more puzzling that none of the weary paladins, all of whom had sworn a solemn oath to Hitler that they would see to it that total cremation did take place, made any move to make sure for himself that such had, in fact, happened.

Cremation is not a process to be carried out by novices. Novices, moreover, acting under shock and quasi-battle conditions. In order for any human body to be burned to ash, both intense heat and proper fuel, on a prepared site, are necessary. Otherwise, as in this case, the product is bound to be a charred torso. The casual trench into which the two Hitler bodies had been thrown did not allow for any real combustion; there was no draft of air from below. Moreover, it is probable that most of the gasoline, splashed onto the bodies in such a wild hurry, sank quickly into the sandy Berlin soil. Hitler's bones, teeth, and skull were only charred. Identification was thus easily possible.

There was one last, gruesome touch, which indeed may have been what frightened the two soldiers away. According to Linge (who said he did finally go up),* "Eva Braun's once-trim figure had jackknifed, under rigor mortis, into what the morticians called an 'equestrian posture.' That is, she was now sitting upright as if riding in a saddle. Both arms were outstretched and her hands seemed to be holding imaginary reins." It was grotesque.

Still stranger, considering the possible political implications, was that no real effort was made to collect and conceal Hitler's remains. (This is what aroused intense Russian suspicion.) Except for General Rattenhuber's casual burial order, there seems to have been no effort toward preserving possible "relics." On Rattenhuber's orders, some time after midnight—it was already May Day—three of his soldiers placed the two charred bodies on a tent shelter-half and dragged the load to a second nearby trench. This trench was deeper, six feet. It had been dug out of a pot-hole made earlier by artillery and was about the same distance from the bunker emergency exit as the cremation trench, but in the opposite direction.

One of these soldiers, with a certain sense of awe and even dignity, came back into the lower bunker and politely asked for a flag. A short frantic search ensued. But there was no flag, not even a last swastika banner. So the dis-

---

* More likely, I suspect, he had later talked to one of the soldiers, several of whom were milling about above.

consolate soldier returned to his grave-digging detail and helped toss the bodies into the second trench. The three soldiers filled it with earth and rubble, pounded the grave firm with a wooden pestle, and that was that. It was almost dawn.

Tyrants propose; the gods dispose. In Berchtesgaden, in the Reich Chancellery, in all the clutter of wartime bunker FHQs, including this last cement rathole in Berlin, Adolf Hitler had spent scores of evening hours spieling to the mountain people just how and where he desired to be buried.* In a legally valid will, drafted in 1938 (before he saw Les Invalides), and deposited with the Berlin Kammergericht (superior court), Reich Chancellor Adolf Hitler had been quite specific.

> Upon my death, my remains shall be transported to Munich ... They shall be properly displayed on a catafalque before the Feldherrnhalle [The Hall of the Field Marshals, site of the 1923 beer hall *Putsch*] before the interment. After the state funeral, which is to be solemn yet simple, my body is to be removed to the Temple of National Socialism on the Koenigsplatz. There I shall rest—under the eternal flame.

Isaiah, an earlier and better prophet than Dr. Joseph Goebbels, had written the fitting text for this funeral day in Berlin, Monday, April 30, 1945.

> Yet thou shalt be brought down to hell,
> To the sides of the pit.
> They that see thee shall narrowly look upon thee,
> And consider thee, saying,
> Is this the man that made the earth to tremble,
> That did shake kingdoms,
> That made the world as a wilderness,
>   and destroyed the cities thereof;
> That opened not the house of his prisoners?
> All the kings of the nations, even all of them,
>   lie in glory,
> Every one in his own house.
> But thou art cast out of thy grave
> Like an abominable branch,
> And as the raiment of those that are slain,
> Thrust through with a sword,
> That go down to the stones of the pit;
> As a carcase trodden under feet.

---

* At various times, he had favored either Bayreuth or Linz as a last resting place.

CHAPTER IX

•

Death of the Mythmaker

What we are here experiencing is a historical drama
of such dimensions that there is nothing in this
century to compare with it, nor in any earlier century—unless one thinks back to Golgotha.

> —GOEBBELS to Werner Naumann,
> in the bunker, 1945

After all, the Cross had been the final curtain of
a lost cause.

> —VICAR COLIN CUTTELL,
> All Hallows by the Tower,
> London, 1975

SOME TIME BEFORE his twenty-first birthday, Paul Joseph
Goebbels had abandoned the faith of his fathers. But what
survived Goebbels' loss of traditional Roman Catholicism
was his yearning to be a believer. And now, at the bleak
end, he still saw one last despairing chance for a certain
kind of scrawny immortality. He could "scratch his name in
history" by pulling off two last propaganda coups.

The first was apotheosis: the Hitler death arranged like
the departure of a later Roman emperor, to become a god
in some post-Christian pantheon of the next millennium.

And to shake the conscience of what remained of
Christendom for a long time to come, the prophet con-
cocted a dreadful human sacrifice. Goebbels prepared to
offer up his children on the altar of his own savage god.
Not because he did not love them, but precisely because
he did.

"Magda Goebbels was not insane in the legal or clinical sense of the word, but she was Hitler-crazed. She was to commit the act that all bunker witnesses agreed was the most perverse in this cave of horrors."

In my interviews with bunker survivors, even the most hard-boiled, I found no theme quite so hushed, so wrapped in elegiac sighs, as the fate of the six Goebbels children. The oldest was Helga, twelve, her father's favorite—intelligent, tall, mature for her age; she had her father's walnut eyes and dark hair. Then came Hilde, eleven, the prettiest, also a brunette; Helmut, ten, the only boy, a dreamy youngster with bad grades in school; Holde, eight, blond, the *Familiendepp*, the one the others always teased; Hedde, six, blond; Heidi, not yet five, the family pet.

Many men and women came to know these children well in those eight long days the youngsters were scampering blithely about the upper bunker. For adults it had become a chamber of horror. For these innocents, bunker life was an exciting diversion, a sport, fun and games with the grownups in an upside-down, night-is-day world.

Several plans were afoot to whisk the children away. Albert Speer had worked out a scheme, and Werner Naumann, Goebbels' state secretary, had another. General Mohnke, on one late occasion, offered to put a tank at the disposal of Goebbels to evacuate the children. Goebbels' younger sister, Maria Kimmich, who was in Berlin, wanted to flee west with the brood. Even Liesl Ostertag, the simple country girl from Berchtesgaden who was Eva Braun's maid, wanted to grab Heide and carry her away in the breakout. But any scheme to save the children would have involved direct action against both parents—such as putting them into straitjackets.

Those in the bunker who most detested Goebbels are guilty of sentimentality when they place sole blame on him as father. Magda Goebbels dazzled men with her charm and beauty, women with her eternal maternal histrionics. She was able, at the end, to evoke a good deal more sympathy than the hard facts in her case warrant. Frustrated Magda was a natural actress, as theater-minded as her huband. And she knew how to forge for herself a bogus martyr's crown.

What many people in the bunker did not know was that there had been several occasions when Goebbels had shied from the idea of slaughtering his own offspring. "Children," he had once written, "are the bright ideas of God." For all his black malignity of mind, Goebbels had moments of sanity. It was precisely on these occasions that the female of the Goebbels kind proved deadlier than the male.

Magda Goebbels' death wish had lurid sexual overtones. For her, it was just not dramatic enough to die with Adolf Hitler. Her cerebral propagandist-husband might have been interested in the death of Hitler as a historical, mystical event. Magda's hopelessly warped emotions were far more personal, visceral. She was determined to pile up the corpses of her own children on the underground cement altar. Those offspring, as she had said so many times, she had borne "for the Third Reich"—though she would have preferred to have had them by "Him." Eva Braun may have become Frau Hitler, but too late to offer him children. Only by her children could this woman achieve a morbid, Medea-like triumph over her childless, younger blond rival. Magda's was a spiritual history that really belonged in the casebook of Dr. Freud. The same can be said of all the women close to Hitler.[*]

By the time Adolf Hitler came back to Berlin, in the third week of January 1945, Goebbels had moved his children out of town to escape the bombings. They were now on his country estate (a different place from his summer house), about one hour's drive northeast of Berlin, near the village of Lanke. This retreat was called the Haus am Bogensee. It was on a pleasant lake in a pine forest, the rolling heath district of the Mark of Brandenburg. A long, one-story, slate-roofed building, with gables, it did not rival Herman Goering's Karin Hall, which was farther out of town on the same road. Still, it had cost three million

---

[*] Although all four of Hitler's private secretaries, Johanna Wolf, Christa Schroeder, Gerda Christian, and Gertrud Junge, survived the bunker, none ever married or remarried after 1945. Frau Christian divorced her husband in 1946. When I asked why neither she nor any of her colleagues had ever married or remarried, she was quite forthright. "How could any of us have remarried after having known a man like Adolf Hitler?"

Reichsmarks (more than $1 million), "a contribution of the German film industry." For the children there were ponies and riding horses, a tennis court, a swimming pool. Here, too, Goebbels could lead the life of a country gentleman, if only on weekends. He had lackeys dressed in livery of black, white, and red.

On Saturday, January 21, 1945, Goebbels, after welcoming Hitler back to town,* left Berlin with his personal press aide, Lieutenant Wilfred von Oven. Goebbels always encouraged his aides to keep diaries, so it is seldom difficult to follow his daily movements in the last months and weeks of the war. Von Oven has described how, late that wintry weekend around a crackling beechwood fire, Magda calmly broke the news to the small gathering that when the end came, she and her husband planned suicide with the Fuehrer. There was a long, solemn silence. It was broken by Goebbels' quoting, with his one-volume copy of Thomas Carlyle's *History of Frederick the Great* in his hand, the passage wherein the Prussian king, writing to the Marquis d'Argens, scoffed at "the events of our little planet which, as important as they seem to us, are of no significance."

To which Magda replied, "You may be right. Still, Frederick the Great had no children."

The woman was an actress, and this was one of her better, more lucid lines. She left the fate of her children unclear.

Three weeks later, with the children still in the Haus am Bogensee, von Oven recorded another conversation that did concern their fate. This talk took place in Berlin, in the well-furnished Goebbels luxury bunker under his official residence, near the Brandenburg Gate. It was during a thunderous midnight RAF raid. Magda now said that she had obtained enough poison capsules from Dr. Morell for herself and all the children. Goebbels had long since been carrying his own. As Albert Speer noted in Berlin on July 20, 1944, Goebbels carried his poison capsules in a vest-pocket pillbox.

At this point, the father and husband interceded to make a completely rational suggestion. "*Suesschen*, my sweet one, please take the children with you and head for somewhere in West Germany. I know the British will not harm you."

---

* Hitler sent Magda a large bouquet of out-of-season lilies of the valley, "all I could find in the market." About which Magda said, "You just can't imagine him being as friendly as all that with the Goerings!"

The nuance here is revealing. Goebbels had often said that if the Russians ever captured his brood, the commissars would give them the usual Bolshevik brainwash and would raise them to hate their own father. And the Americans, according to Goebbels, would make democrats of them "in a Germany being fed by Quakers."* Goebbels, like Hitler, had a hidden Anglophile streak in him. It was the silent tribute of two thorough cads to a nation they knew little about and had often publicly mocked and derided. Privately, they both were convinced the British would "always act like gentlemen."

But later that same evening—the source is still Lieutenant von Oven—Goebbels became more bloodyminded, perhaps because he had been drinking brandy.

"Neither my wife nor a single one of my offspring," he said, "will be among the survivors of the coming debacle." This time Magda was silent; it was the silence of consent.

By early March, when the Red Army offensive across the Oder seemed about to begin, Lanke became unsafe. It was less than twenty-five miles from the front. Now the whole family, including Goebbels' seventy-six-year-old mother, Maria Katherina, and his sister Maria Kimmich, were together again at Number 20 Hermann Goering Strasse, in the heart of the city. No sooner were they established than a U.S. Air Force daytime raid dealt the heaviest blow yet to the downtown government area. Knobelsdorff's eighteenth-century Staatsoper, the Royal Palace or Schloss, and a score of buildings on Unter den Linden were blasted. The New Reich Chancellery was struck directly. Goebbels' official residence was not hit, but the blast effect shattered all windows. Most of the upstairs, soaked by the hoses of the firefighters, were no longer habitable. Goebbels therefore decided to open up his summer house, and he moved the family out to Schwanenwerder. He himself, however, remained downtown.

Goebbels' proud office on the Wilhelmplatz was in the Ordenspalais, architecturally one of the finer buildings in Berlin. Built in the eighteenth century, it had been remodeled by Schinkel, the best of the Berlin classical masters of the early nineteenth century. Unscathed through many air raids, it stood until the night of March 13, 1945, when

---

* A really vicious crack. As a student in 1919, he himself had been fed by food furnished by a prominent American Quaker, Herbert Hoover.

it was completely destroyed by a random hit. One lone RAF Mosquito dropped a parachute mine that demolished the whole structure. Goebbels then moved his office into his official private residence.

It was in mid-April, after the family had been settled in at Schwanenwerder, that the two plans already mentioned were afoot to save Magda Goebbels and her brood. Speer's plan, as we know, was to whisk Magda and the children aboard a barge and float the craft down the Havel to the Elbe, where the Americans had arrived on April 11. A similar plan, involving a stationary barge, was worked out by Werner Naumann. Unlike Speer's scheme, Naumann's plan had been revealed to, and approved by, Goebbels. This barge, hidden in the reeds, was to serve as a hideout for mother and children until the worst was over. But the distraught mother was in no state to be approached with any plan. She said, nobly enough, that she now must refuse to abandon her husband. She also stated that she was determined to die with the Fuehrer and take her children with her "because my darlings are simply too good for this bad world." But the problem still nagging Goebbels was to make sure that the Fuehrer stuck to his decision to end his life in the German capital. For several long weeks, the minister's had been the sole voice resolutely holding out for this last stand in Berlin. The vast majority in the bunker favored the Alpine Redoubt alternative and yearned to decamp to Berchtesgaden.

An earlier crisis had come just after Easter weekend, on March 29. The strong Berchtesgaden clique in the bunker, led by Bormann, had caught the Fuehrer in a moment when he seemed to be suddenly overcome by a yen for the air of the Obersalzberg. Goebbels got wind of this and came bustling over. SS Major Otto Guensche described this tense scene. "Goebbels, clutching his Fuehrer by both lapels, implored him to remember the solemn oath that he had once sworn, with Goebbels, toward midnight on January thirtieth, nineteen thirty-three, the day Hitler had become chancellor and entered the Old Reich Chancellery: 'We shall never abandon this building voluntarily. No power in this world can ever drive us out.' "

Goebbels had a good memory for historic moments, and he knew his man. The mystique of January 30, 1933, *die Machtergriefung* (seizure of power), was much on Adolf Hitler's mind as the end approached. And so was the haunting *genius loci*, the spirit of the present surroundings, which reminded him of former triumphs—the Chancellery itself, the Kaiserhof Hotel, the Wilhelmplatz, the Brandenburg Gate, the scenes and symbols of that torchlight parade celebrating the political victory, now so long ago, that was supposed to have inaugurated a German Reich lasting one thousand years.

There was at least one side of Goebbels' sophisticated mind that was always coldly rational. He did not, for a single instant, doubt the validity of the Hitler myth. The messiah must die. This was the whole purpose of the exercise. To be meaningful, death must be in Berlin, in the historic governmental area, at the last possible moment.

Goebbels appeared often enough in the bunker, but he never tarried long. As Gauleiter of Berlin he was visible every day aboveground. He was the German Churchill. As propaganda minister, he kept his mill turning over at full turn. It was still the most active ministry in Berlin, and—after April 16—the only one.

While Hitler lost himself in deploying ghost armies, Goebbels scraped the Berlin manpower barrel and mustered 80,000 Volkssturm soldiers, armed with Berlin-made bazookas. He shipped these off to the Oder front in double-decker, cream-colored Berlin buses. He often visited that front. His conferences with the harassed generals were a good deal more realistic than Hitler's. There was method in his madness. He was setting the Berlin stage for the grand, fighting finale. He did not want it to be fouled up by any premature Russian tank breakthrough.

The weekend of the Fuehrer's birthday, Friday, April 20, saw the last parade of the familiar VIPs of the Third Reich, limping in from the provinces to say farewell to their Fuehrer. All were most anxious to leave quickly—Goering, Himmler, Ribbentrop, Ley. Goebbels saw these crestfallen peacocks strut in and out. He watched with haughty disdain. He had often predicted they would all leave before the end, as they were now doing. This, too, fitted the script just as the prophet wanted it. It strengthened his own bond with the Fuehrer. Although Goebbels showed up briefly at the bleak birthday festivities, he soon left. He turned to tidying up several of his personal affairs.

With Lieutenant von Oven, Goebbels stood before an old-fashioned tile stove in his office, consigning mementos to the flames: a picture of himself at the age of seven, clad in a sailor suit; his grammar school report cards; a packet of letters from his father; a confirmation picture; a group picture of his high school graduating class.

Last to go into the flames was a glossy photo of a young woman. This picture was a gift to her German lover from Lida Baarova, the Czech beauty who had left Berlin forever, back in 1938, and driven off into the Bohemian mountains.

Next day, this time with his secretary, Richard Otte, and Werner Naumann, Goebbels meticulously supervised the burning of his diaries. These were by now a monumental collection, dating back to 1924. By 1945 the diaries filled a cabinet room "the size of four telephone booths," Naumann noted. Since January 1945, Otte had been microfilming the lot. Werner Naumann and SS Captain Guenther Schwaegermann, another aide, were entrusted with hiding them.

This method was designed to keep the diaries out of the hands of the oncoming Russians. Somehow, someone slipped up. One of the hidden microfilm sets did land, eventually, in either Russian or East German Communist hands. Finally, in 1974, they reached the west, and parts of them have been published. Goebbels, even after this burning ceremony, kept making diary jottings in a black notebook up to Hitler's death and during his own last hours on the next day.*

This same weekend, the third in April, after he had taken care of the diary matter, Goebbels sat down at his office desk to record what he knew would be his last speech to the German nation. During the recording, Russian shell bursts brought down plaster from the ceiling, and General Reimann, who was present, slid under a desk. But Goebbels flicked the plaster from his manuscript and kept on rolling with the speech. (It was put into cans, to be broadcast as close as possible to the end, but was actually broadcast nationwide five days later.)

Some time between the recording of the radio speech, on Friday afternoon, and his appearance next morning at his last staff conference, Goebbels' nerves momentarily gave out. The strain was now telling on his frail body and his

* The notes were published as *The Final Entries: The Diaries of Joseph Goebbels* (New York: G. P. Putnam), 1978. The book is not, alas, the final entries, for the notes end abruptly in mid-March, 1945. Compared with Goebbels' usual writing, they are astonishingly dull dishwater.

badly overloaded emotional system. The twenty-two senior ministry officials who had been seeing Goebbels every day were shocked to see him haggard, his eyes bloodshot, his temples twitching. His complexion, normally tawny, seemed to have turned to chalk overnight, a ghostly effect in the candlelight, for all windows had been boarded up against the danger of flying glass. Goebbels launched into a vitriolic monologue, the theme of which was that the Fuehrer was surrounded on all sides by traitors.

This thesis, familiar enough in the bunker, was new to the mandarins of the Propaganda Ministry. Goebbels unloaded scathing scorn on German generals, the soldiers, the civilian population. At this point one of the star propagandists, radio commentator Hans Fritsche, had had enough and dared talk back to Goebbels. "Herr Minister, what you say is not true. While there may have been a few traitors here and there, the record reveals that the German people have shown this regime more good will than any people in history."

The unprecedented contradiction infuriated Goebbels. He dropped the mask. "The German people? What can you do with a people whose men are no longer willing to fight when their wives are being raped? All the plans of National Socialism, all its dreams and goals, were too great and too noble for this people. The German people are just too cowardly to realize these goals. In the east, they are running away. In the west, they set up hindrances for their own soldiers and welcome the enemy with white flags. The German people deserve the destiny that now awaits them."

Sunday, April 22, was a momentous day in the bunker. Shortly after noontime, Hitler cracked up, dismissed his generals, and ordered Julius Schaub to burn his private papers. He confided to Eva Braun that he intended to commit suicide. In the afternoon, Goebbels dissuaded him and wrung from Hitler permission to announce that "the Fuehrer was in Berlin and would die fighting with his troops." And 6:00 P.M. the whole Goebbels family moved into the bunker.

Goebbels, in the following days, was left with much time on his hands. Bunker inmates reported that he spent long hours, in his office next to Hitler's, simply reading and writing. He was still making diary entries. He was also working over his last testament, to be appended to Hitler's.

It seems probable that he worked on the rough draft of Hitler's political testament. Much of the phrasing has the Goebbels touch. And he attended the military briefings.

Goebbels, as father, found he now had abundant time for his children, time he had never quite found before. He read to them, told stories, played games, sang songs. This was not just an act—Goebbels was most fond of his children—but it added to the stupefying unreality, as Liesl Ostertag reported. "You simply could not watch those touching family scenes and still believe this doting father had multiple murder in his heart."

Sergeant Rochus Misch recalled a family scene.

I remember how on Sunday, April twenty-ninth, the day before the Fuehrer died, Dr. Goebbels gave a small party over in the cellar of the New Reich Chancellery. It was, he said, to be his last farewell, and that of his family, to the Berliners among whom they had lived through all the war years. The room was right next door to Professor Schenck's casualty station. There were about forty guests, women—nurses—some twenty other young Berlin boys and girls, and a few of the ambulatory wounded soldier-patients. A fifteen-year-old Hitler Youth, still in uniform, sang while accompanying himself on his accordion:

> *"Die blauen Dragoner, sie reiten*
> *mit klingendem Spiel durch das Tor.*
> *Fanfaren sie begleiten*
> *hell zu den Huegeln empor . . ."**

Goebbels, with his wife and all six children, was seated at a long oak table. All joined in and lustily repeated the chorus. It was eerie, this soprano choir of young, unbroken voices trying to drown out the louder, more ominous noise of bursting artillery shells.

Though there was now a distinct cooling-off of the old friendship between Goebbels and Hitler, they met for at least an hour every day during the last week when Goebbels apparently was drafting notes for Hitler's last testament. Goebbels knew, as most educated Germans did, that both Frederick the Great and Bismarck had left behind

---

* "The blue dragoons, they are riding
Through the gate as music thrills.
Fanfares are their companions
As proudly they ride to the hills . . ."

such loaded testaments. These were designed to guide their
successors—and also to embarrass them in case things went
wrong.

Goebbels certainly did not want his idol to miss this last
historical opportunity to have a voice in history from beyond the grave. *Exoriare aliquis nostris ex ossibus ultor*
("Arise, avenger, from our bones"). Goebbels knew his
Virgil, and knew how to twist his lines.

Here again many historians have missed what I believe
to be a vital point, the real clue to what was going on.
Gertrud Junge was alone with Hitler when the Fuehrer dictated his will. Both had left the wedding reception abruptly,
around 2:00 A.M., and retired into the smaller study across
the gangway of the lower bunker. Frau Junge says she
took shorthand dictation. But she also adds that Hitler was
"speaking from notes." Who wrote these notes? The general assumption that they must have been Hitler's own
does not stand up to a critical text analysis. Moreover, as
we know, there was a real question, by April 29, as to
whether the doomed dictator's right hand was steady
enough for him to write legibly. I suspect it is much more
likely that these notes came from Goebbels.

As can be shown by a look at the written record, Adolf
Hitler's political testament begins:

> It is not true that I or anyone else in Germany wanted war
> back in 1939. It was desired and provoked solely by those
> international politicians who either come from Jewish stock
> or are agents of Jewish interests. After all my many offers
> of disarmament, posterity simply cannot pin any blame for
> this war on me . . .
> After a struggle of six long years, which in spite of many
> setbacks will one day be recorded in our history books as the
> most glorious and valiant manifestation of the nation's will
> to live, I cannot abandon this city which is the German cap-
> ital. Since we no longer have sufficient military forces to
> withstand enemy attacks on this city, and since our own re-
> sistance will be gradually exhausted fighting an army of
> blind automata, it is my desire to share the same fate that
> millions of other Germans have accepted and to remain here
> in this city . . .

I submit that to any critical reader reasonably familiar
with the distinct literary styles of both men, this diatribe
reads much more like the writing of Goebbels than that

of Adolf Hitler. Nobody, not even Hitler, could prevaricate with such suave if preposterous grandeur on the origins of the world war just then ending. There are several other little revealing tricks of style. *Automata*, for example, is a Latin neuter plural, just the kind of word Goebbels knew how to use correctly. It is not in the vocabulary that came naturally to Hitler. For him the Red Army was "the Bolshevik horde." The very thought pattern, too—the symbolism of Berlin—has much more of the Goebbels ring. Goebbels had been resident in Berlin since 1926, and he regarded himself as a Berliner by adoption; hence the tribute.* Hitler had never before praised either the city of Berlin or its inhabitants. He hated the metropolis and despised the Berliners as German Cockneys.

Another argument for Goebbels' hand in the Hitler testament is a comparison with the propaganda minister's own political testament, composed on the same day, and simply "added" modestly to the Hitler document as an appendix.

> The Fuehrer has ordered me, should our defense of the Reich collapse, to leave Berlin and to participate as a leading figure in the new government he has appointed . . . For the first time in my life I am forced, categorically, to disobey an order coming from the Fuehrer. My wife and my offspring join me in this refusal . . .
>
> In the frenzy of betrayal that has now enguifed the Fuehrer, in these last most decisive days of the long war, there must be someone at least who will stick with him unconditionally, loyal even unto death. Even if this clashes with the formal and—in a material sense—quite justifiable order that the Fuehrer has given in his own political testament . . . There will always be men who can be found to lead the nation forward again into freedom, but a true revival of our life as a nation will not be possible unless built upon the firm foundation of clear, shining examples.

And there we have the Goebbels martyr line, rhetorical, bombastic, vainglorious. Yet Goebbels the prophet is evoking a certain grand manner, an appeal to the dignity that many another lost cause has managed to acquire. This man

---

* When Rudolf and Ilse Hess had their first child, Hess wrote to all fifty Gauleiters and asked for a handful of their "good German earth" to bless the cradle. The Goebbelses considered sending them a Berlin paving brick.

was thinking not of the year 1946, or even of 1976, but of the millennial year 2000.*

Yet while he was busy with the hollow eloquence of these two curtain speeches, Goebbels was being undermined. And as he lost influence with Hitler, he was replaced as chief adviser and intimate by Martin Bormann. How did this come about? The fact seemed to puzzle most of my bunker witnesses as they recollected the scene.

Thus, I asked myself what had been the major new development in the bunker during the forty-eight hours preceding the drafting of the testaments and Hitler's last will?

As we now know, it was the Fegelein affair. And where had Fegelein first met his *femme fatale*, Mata O'Hara? At a summer party given by Goebbels at Schwanenwerder. Casual and natural though the meeting was at the time, in 1945 "delirium of treason" Hitler was now suffering, everything and everyone was suspect.

Bormann, we know, kept a blackmail notebook and Goebbels was in it. On Blue Monday (April 23), Bormann had convinced Hitler of the preposterous notion that Goering was a traitor. He had then destroyed Himmler and his liaison man, Fegelein, by means of the Reuters dispatch from San Francisco. Now, as for Goebbels, all Bormann had to do was mention *das Leck* and to point out slyly that Goebbels had given Mata O'Hara a job and an introduction.

Is there any circumstantial evidence to support my surmise that such a Bormann-Hitler conversation took place? I believe so. First, in his private will (a document most historians have given only cursory notice), Hitler calls Bormann "my most loyal party comrade." This is astonishing because Goebbels had always outranked everyone in the Nazi pecking order except, perhaps, Goering. Bormann, the faceless bureaucrat, had achieved real influence only after the descent into the many bunkers.

Another interesting bit of evidence comes from Sergeant Misch.

For years, in all thirteen of the wartime FHQs, my standing orders [at the switchboard] were to put Dr. Goebbels through directly to Der Chef when he called. But, around

---

* In one of his last staff meetings he told his underdogs, "Act now so that you will look good on color TV in the year nineteen ninety-nine." Goebbels never saw TV in color, but he knew it was coming.

April twenty-seventh, Reichsleiter Bormann came to me and insisted that all calls be routed through him. He told me that this had the weight of a Fuehrerbefehl. I, of course, had to obey.

I sensed that Bormann was now out to slit Goebbels' throat by interrupting his line to the Fuehrer. It was a ridiculous situation, in view of our cramped geography. Although Hitler and Goebbels were in adjoining rooms and I was seated just outside in the corridor, I now had to reroute Goebbels' calls to Hitler through Bormann's phone.

After the first or second rerouted call, Goebbels came to me and asked in a friendly, almost plaintive, way if I was having trouble with the switchboard. When I told him about the new order, he asked if it had come "directly from Der Chef or from someone else?"

Bormann had stressed that "he would have my ass" if I told anyone the answer to this and so I said, "Dr. Goebbels, it is a Fuehrerbefehl but I did not get it directly from Der Chef."

Goebbels was thunderstruck, but he simply said to me in a soft and unruffled tone, "Thank you, Sergeant, for telling me the truth."

This is a historical footnote of some importance. As late as April 20, Hitler's birthday, there were still seven Nazi VIPs who could get through directly on what we would now call the "hot line." In order of precedence, they were Goering, Goebbels, Himmler, Speer, Doenitz, Keitel, and Bormann. Now, near the end, Bormann had overleaped every rival, and the only direct line of power left in the crumbling Third Reich was Hitler-Bormann.*

*   *

How does a mother go about killing her six children? Magda Goebbels was not insane in the legal or clinical sense of the word, but she was Hitler-crazed—a madness of a different order. (About her, Kempka made one of his typically crude—but pertinent—observations: "Whenever she was in the presence of the Fuehrer, I could hear her ovaries rattling.")

---

* Some who have read this book in manuscript point out that Hitler's political testament left Doenitz as president, Goebbels as chancellor (an odd revival of Weimar Republic offices), and Bormann, third on the list, as senior minister for Nazi Party affairs. But the levers of power (imaginary as they were by now) were in the party.

In the grip of this obsession, she was to commit the act that all bunker witnesses agreed was the most perverse in this cave of horrors.

Those witnesses—and the number of reliable ones was fewer than ten—were not unanimous about the deed. Some suspected Dr. Ludwig Stumpfegger, Frau Goebbels' attending physician, and others mentioned Dr. Ludwig Kunz, an SS major who ran a small dental laboratory in the new Reich Chancellery, because he was present at about 5:00 P.M. on Wednesday, May 1, in the upper bunker.

Dr. Kunz is still alive, but he refused to talk about the event. Involved in a mid-1960s libel and slander suit, Kunz denied under oath that he had given the Goebbels children lethal injections. Those who were fellow SS prisoners in the Soviet Union still say, however, that he has changed his earlier story. It does seem most probable, in any case, that one of the doctors supplied the mother with sleeping potion and poison. But the fact is that it was Magda Goebbels who killed her own children, and the evidence is damning. It rests on three points:

1. In a letter to Harald Quandt, her son by an earlier marriage (a letter carried out of the bunker by Hanna Reitsch), she wrote, "God will forgive me as a mother provided I have courage to carry out this deed myself and do not leave it to others. When the time comes, I shall give my darlings sleeping potions and then poison, a soft and painless death."

2. Werner Naumann testified, "I could not talk this willful woman out of her deed. Her husband was not present nor was I. We absented ourselves from the hour of five to six P.M. When I returned, around six-fifteen, I found Dr. Goebbels with his wife. She then told us what she had done. There were no eyewitnesses, though Drs. Stumpfegger and Kunz had been standing by in an adjoining room."

As Naumann got the story, partly from Magda Goebbels and partly from her husband's reiteration of what she had told him, this is how she had proceeded. First, she had gathered her brood together in one room. She told them the whole family would soon be leaving for Berchtesgaden with "Uncle Fuehrer." She then prepared all for bed. She fed each child chocolates, "to prevent air sickness." These bonbons had been doped with a soporific drug called

Finodin. These preliminaries over, she next led them back to their beds. They soon fell asleep.

The mother had in her possession six of the familiar cyanide capsules, the blue plastic vials with the brass rings. They were the kind Dr. Stumpfegger had been distributing all week in the Fuehrerbunker. It may be, however, that Frau Goebbels had got these capsules earlier and had brought them with her into the bunker.

3. Sergeant Misch, not an eyewitness but very close to the scene of action, reported, "I had come on duty at the switchboard that day at two o'clock. The three younger Goebbels children were romping about in the lower bunker, playing with a ball. I gave them some soda. With the Fuehrer dead, most of the lower bunker was now empty, and the youngsters were using it as a playground. After a while, they left."

Then, around five o'clock, the three rompers reappeared. Five minutes later Frau Goebbels arrived, bringing with her the three older children. She was wearing a long-skirted navy blue dress with white collar, cuffs, and piping. Her face was ashen. She took all the children into the room just opposite Misch. This usually served as an off-duty room for the guards, the same room in which Frau Junge had typed out Hitler's last will and testament.*

Misch went on:

All of the children were now clad in white nightgowns; this was their usual bedtime hour. Five were sitting in chairs, Heidi had scrambled up onto the table. She was still suffering from tonsilitis and had a band around her neck. Helga, the tallest, oldest, and brightest, was sobbing softly. I think she dimly suspected the mayhem about to come. She was most definitely Daddy's girl, with no great fondness for her mother.

Frau Goebbels, as usual, was playing her attentive-mother role to the very hilt. Carefully, she combed the long hair of the five girls; she then brushed down Helmut's cowlick. Next, she kissed each of them, very affectionately, as she had done every evening during the last week.

I watched all of this with apprehension; I was appalled. I still have on my conscience that I did nothing but sit there on my duff, because I sensed what was about to happen. At the same time, watching the mother, I just could not believe it. I suppose I did not *want* to believe it.

---

* It was sometimes called the "Dog Bunker," in SS jargon. (Not to be confused with the real kennel, which was next to one of the lavatories.) The word in German is *Hundebunker*.

Now, without saying goodbye, Frau Goebbels, like a mother duck with six ducklings, headed for the door, up the spiral staircase into the upper bunker. Heidi, the youngest and a little flirt, turned back to the sergeant and said, *"Misch, Misch, du bist ein Fisch."* She was giggling. But her sister Helga was morosely dragging her feet. The mother had to push her oldest daughter on her way.

Misch continued, "I sat alone, paralyzed, not so much by fear as by frustrated compassion. I was ashamed of myself even then. I began saying my rosary, praying for all six little souls. I prayed for the mother, too. I guess I was praying she would relent."

Sergeant Misch also reported that about a half hour later, Werner Naumann appeared in the lower bunker. Naumann told Misch, "Colonel Stumpfegger has supplied some doped candy for the Goebbels children. Both the mother and the father insist their children must die now, because we are running out of time."

"At this news," Misch said, "I got a cramp in my heart. I recalled how, just the day before, I had seen the father playing with them and joining in as the youngsters sang 'The Blue Dragoons.'"

Naumann left after a few minutes. Then, according to Misch:

At least an hour must have passed. It was now as quiet as a tomb in the lower bunker. Only one or two calls came in. Finally, Frau Goebbels reappeared. This time she was alone. There was no expression on her face. Her blue eyes were ringed with red. At first she stood there, just wringing her hands. Then she pulled herself together and lit a cigarette. She did not speak or even nod to me, though she was only a few feet away as she passed by.

There was a small champagne bottle, a *piccolo*, which someone had left on the long table in the main corridor. She took it and proceeded into the room next to the watchroom, the one Dr. Goebbels had been using all week as his study. She had left his door open. I got up, walked past, and could see that she had taken out a pack of small cards and had begun to lay down a solitaire hand. Instinctively, I knew that her children were no more of this world. Another ten minutes or so passed. Then she arose, stalked out. Again we did not speak to each other. What was there to say?

Misch, during this long hour, remained on duty in the lower bunker. From time to time, apparently after each separate child murder, Magda Goebbels had emerged into the corridor of the upper bunker for a break. She was seen there, between five and six o'clock, by at least three people —Professor Schenck, Gerda Christian, and Captain Helmut Beermann of the FBK.

Nor did this coldly calculated, multiple infanticide go off quite as smoothly as planned. There is evidence that the oldest daughter, Helga, apparently awoke in fright as her mother approached her bedside. It seems possible that this eldest child, the brightest of the brood, had not believed the lie about the airplane and therefore had not swallowed the chocolate. Or, more likely, the dose was insufficient. The autopsy report signed by several Soviet doctors one week later records, laconically, that Helga Goebbels had "several black-and-blue bruises." These were almost surely sustained as the terrified girl struggled for her life. The report for some reason does not specify whether these bruises were on the neck, head, shoulders, or body. But the inference is clear enough.

I never did discover where Goebbels betook himself during the awful hour of five to six on Tuesday, May 1, 1945. Nobody seems to know. (Naumann, I believe, almost certainly knows, but has been tongue-tied on the matter.) Apparently, Goebbels was either walking about in the garden outside the bunker or had gone into one of the many empty rooms in the New Reich Chancellery. Quite possibly he was writing in his diary, on the meaning of sacrifice. Naumann has hinted as much.

Wherever Goebbels had been, he reappeared shortly afterward, in the glimpse we get through the eyes of Artur Axmann. He said:

I came over from my command post in the Wilhelmstrasse and into the lower bunker around six-thirty, Tuesday, May first. I wanted to say goodbye to both the Goebbelses. I found the couple sitting at the long conference table with Werner Naumann, Hans Baur, Walter Hewel, General Krebs, three or four others. Goebbels stood up to greet me. He soon launched into lively memories of our old street-fighting days in Berlin-Wedding, from nineteen twenty-eight to thirty-three. He recalled how we had clobbered the Berlin Communists and the Socialists into submission, to the tune of the "Horst Wessel" marching song, on their old home ground. He said one of the great accomplishments of the Hitler regime had been to win the German workers over almost totally to the national cause. We had made patriots of the workers, he said, as the kaiser had dismally failed to do. This, he kept repeating, had been one of the real triumphs of the movement. We Nazis were a non-Marxist yet revolutionary party, anticapitalist, antibourgeois, antireactionary.

It was on the streets of Berlin that we had won over the workers, the young, the unemployed. This, one day, would be the true verdict of history, if Germans were ever to be allowed to write their own history again. Starch-collared men like Chancellor Heinrich Bruening had called us the "Brown Bolsheviks," and their bourgeois instincts were not wrong. Red Bolshevism is Asian, as we are now seeing and witnessing in the streets of Berlin. "Well," he said, "let us leave that to the money-changers and their screaming brokers on the rotten bourse of world capitalism. It is their problem now." But there was not a word about his family. Magda Goebbels just sat there, saying little, head high. She was chain-smoking and sipping champagne. I did not ask about the children because someone, either Baur or Hewel, had whispered to me that they were already dead.

Axmann says the reminiscence session ended around 7:00 P.M. This was about the time Sergeant Misch left his switchboard to go out of the bunker for air and a cigarette break. Except for Johannes Hentschel, in the machine room, and one FBK guard, the lower and upper bunkers were both empty.

Misch again picked up the account:

I know it must have been around seven o'clock because the sun was still up, but was now deep behind the tall wall of the Reich Chancellery. The evening shadows were already long in the garden. It was a strange sunset, the sun's rays trying to shine on a dense, overhanging cloud of choking yellow dust and black smoke that was blanketing the city. I was beginning to wonder how long I was supposed to remain at the switchboard. The Fuehrer was dead; all day there had been but three or four calls.

I heard over the grapevine that the breakout was being planned for later this same evening. But I wasn't sure even of that, because I had heard the same rumor the night before.

When I got up to the Chancellery garden, the only person I saw was Dr. Goebbels. He was now Reich chancellor and in this sense, I suppose, my new Chef. He was alone, without his usual aides, just strolling about. He was smoking a cigarette. I decided to tell him about my small problem and seek his advice. He told me he did not see sense in my manning the switchboard any longer. He suggested that I join the breakout: "General Rauch's troops are still holding out in Charlottenburg."* He advised me to try to join up with them and he wished me "all the luck in the world." He was calm, matter-of-fact. He spoke without any show of nerves. As I was talking with him, I guessed that his children were already dead, but he spoke no word about this. Hentschel, horrified, confirmed the deaths after I was back in the bunker. He said the cadavers had been left sprawled in a single room, covered with winding sheets. We first thought of burying them, but to tell the truth, neither of us had the gumption to enter the death room.

The Goebbels whom Misch had bumped into so casually must have been prospecting for the spot where he intended to commit suicide. The absence of the one aide who had stayed with him to the end—Guenther Schwaegermann— is explained; Schwaegermann, with the chauffeur Rach, was off searching frantically for jerry cans. After the double immolation of the Hitlers on the previous day, full jerry cans were now in short supply. The two aides finally located six and brought them to the foot of the bunker emergency-exit stairway. It was too dangerous to leave them at the top, exposed to shell bursts.

This was the time of year when Berlin nightingales, winging in from the south to end their long spring migration, seek out familiar nesting spots amid the bramble of the islands in the boating lakes of the Tiergarten. They had returned this year on schedule, baffled to find no green Tiergarten. They burst into song, perhaps out of astonishment. Perhaps because, in ancient legend, Philomela, the nightingale, is always singing of the murderous heart of mankind.

Blackout time in Berlin, Tuesday, May 1, 1945, was 8:29 P.M. At eight-fifteen Joseph Goebbels, who had re-entered the upper bunker, went to his wife's chamber. To-gether, they descended into the lower bunker. Only three people were still present—General Mohnke, SS Captain Schwaegermann, and Olds, Goebbels' junior aide. All had been told the precise details of the ceremony about to come. Goebbels gave Schwaegermann his autographed pic-ture of the Fuehrer, an unconscious touch of black humor. His last words were rather thoughtful, or perhaps a lame

---

* In fact, they had retreated across town that morning and were by then in Potsdam.

attempt at irony. "At least you good people will not have to lug our bodies up that long flight of stairs."

General Mohnke gave us the last, crisp, eyewitness account we have of the living Goebbels. "Going over to the coatrack in the small room that had served as his study, he donned his hat, his scarf, his long uniform overcoat. Slowly, he drew on his kid gloves, making each finger snug. Then, like a cavalier, he offered his right arm to his wife. They were wordless now. So were we three spectators. Slowly but steadily, leaning a bit toward each other, they headed up the stairs to the courtyard."

Night had fallen in Berlin; it was eight-thirty. The waning lemon moon was riding high. At the bottom of the cement stairs the couple passed, in silence, the six jerry cans standing ready. Forty-four long steps. At the head of the stairs husband and wife met one FBK officer, an SS captain. Briefed to give the coup-de-grâce, this officer was standing by, just in case. He remained in the shadows, in the door frame of the emergency exit. He was the only eyewitness. His special service was not needed.

For both Joseph and Magda Goebbels had carefully rehearsed Professor Haase's approved bunker method, pistol and poison. The wife went first. She bit into her capsule, sank slowly to the ground, lay prone on the soft spring earth. She was wearing, for a brooch, Adolf Hitler's golden party badge, which the Fuehrer had given her as a parting present the day before his own death. Her husband fired a bullet into the back of her blond head. Goebbels then bit into his own capsule, squeezed off the trigger of his Walther P-38 pistol, and put a bullet through his right temple.

Thus, there was some lingering trace of classical style in the death of this failed prophet. He chose to separate himself from his master by dying outside the squalid Fuehrerbunker. And the most loquacious man of his times—a type Cicero described as *ignobilis verborum opifex*, a concoctor of unworthy phrases—now discovered the eloquence of silence. At journey's end, he took *la mort sans phrase*.

At this moment, one hears again the morose, Austrian, know-it-all voice from the Obersalzberg, in the summer of 1927, long ago and far away: "Hanfstaengel, there are two ways in this world to judge a man—the kind of woman he marries, and the way he dies." Hitler had uttered a fitting epitaph for his own prophet—and for himself.

•

CHAPTER X

The Breakout

But night again is rising; time is now
That we depart from here. We have seen all.
          —Inferno, Canto XXXIV

WITH ADOLF HITLER DEAD, a change in atmosphere pervaded the bunker. The mood of the *Inferno* yielded to that of the *Purgatorio*. The situation was still grim, but at least it was no longer heroic-hopeless. The breakout offered hope, however perilous.

The breakout was indeed the only military operation that had been fairly well planned in the bunker, and, at least in its initial stages, it was rather shrewdly executed. Yet it was to fall apart in the middle of a long, twelve-hour operation. Only a lucky handful of this Reich Chancellery Group was destined to get out and away from Berlin forever.

The breakout had originally been planned to begin in the late hours of Monday, April 30, when the bodies of Adolf Hitler and Eva Braun Hitler had not even been buried. It was postponed, less out of respect for the Fuehrer and his consort than because of the rapidly disintegrating military situation in Berlin. By now, the Soviets had closed off the familiar and only major escape route: Tiergarten–Kantstrasse–Heerstrasse–Havel River. This was the route used but two days before by the seven couriers who had

> **"In some of the upper rooms, drinking parties were already in progress. Several hysterical women were fleeing the invading Russians. Group sex took over on the top floor."**

left the Fuehrerbunker over the weekend.* A second reason for the delay was the utterly exhausted state of most of the Reich Chancellery Group. All hands were advised to spend Tuesday, May 1, sleeping; most did so.

On Tuesday, toward sundown, General Mohnke summoned a staff conference in his cellar command post. In his double capacity as bunker military commandant and also commander of all troops still defending the Zitadelle, Mohnke was the logical man to take charge, since he was also the most experienced front-line soldier.

Field-grade officers had been ordered to show at 7:00 P.M. sharp. All did. But General Mohnke—and this was rare—did not himself arrive until 8:45 P.M. He was accompanied by Colonel Klingemeier, his senior aide, Reichsjugendfuehrer Artur Axmann, and several SS officers from other commands. The Mohnke party had come directly from the Fuehrerbunker; what had delayed them was the ceremony connected with the deaths of Joseph and Magda Goebbels.

General Mohnke now launched into a matter-of-fact account of the major bunker events of the thirty-six hours just past, events still unknown to most of these troop officers, who had been fighting outside the bunker. Mohnke

---

* The seven couriers were carrying documents. There were, in the order of departure: Around noontime, Sunday, April, 29, Major Baron Freytag von Loringhoven (aide to Krebs), Lieutenant Colonel Weiss (aide to Burgdorf), and Cavalry Captain Gerhard Boldt (aide to Freytag von Loringhoven). Midafternoon, same day, Major Willi Johannmeier (Hitler's army adjutant), SS Colonel Wilhelm Zander (a Bormann aide), and Heinz Lorenz from the Propaganda Ministry. The seventh and last official courier to leave the Fuehrerbunker was Luftwaffe Colonel Nikolaus von Below, liaison man for both Goering and Speer. Von Below took off around midnight. He was thus the last officer to leave the bunker before Hitler's death, fifteen hours later.

Both Major Johannmeier and Colonel von Below were accompanied by enlisted batmen, Corporals Hummerich and Heinz Matthiesing. The sum total of Sunday departures was therefore nine.

Schultheiss-Patzenhofer
Brewery

Flaktower

Humboldthain

Museum of
Natural
History

Stettiner
R. Y. Station

Lehrter
S. Bahn
Station

Bridge

Humboldt
Hafen

Charité
Hospital

Lehrter
R. Y. Station

Weidendamm Bridge

Friedrichstrasse Subway
and S. Bahn Stations

Spree River

Reichstag

Brandenburg Gate

Unter den Linden

East-West Axis

Französische
Subway Sta.

Gendarmen-Markt

Reich Chancellery
and Hitler Bunker

Stadtmitte
Subway Sta.

Voss Str.

Kaiserhof
Subway Sta.

Central Berlin

Group I route
Group III route

Belle-Alliance
Place

told of the Hitler wedding, the execution of General
Fegelein, the Hitler suicides, the death of the Goebbels
family. He then noted the breakoff in the desultory negotiations between General Chuikov and General Krebs. Next,
he spoke of the now painfully obvious nonarrival of General Wenck's Twelfth Army. All rumor of a falling-out
between the British and Americans and the Russians, he
said, was premature at best.

Most of this news came as some shock to these medium-
rank officers. The fourth and last issue of the *Panzerbaer*
troop paper (April 29) had informed them, "Our troops
on the Elbe have now turned their backs on the Americans
and are marching rapidly east to relieve their hard-pressed
comrades in the German capital."

This widespread belief that the beleagured Berlin garrison was about to be relieved by one, possibly two, German armies (General Wenck's Twelfth and General Busse's
Ninth Army, last reported southeast of Berlin) is what
had kept many troops fighting so doggedly. Now they
would have to be told that there was no hope.

Mohnke continued his report to the officers.

The news that the Fuehrer is dead, and the other events I
have just described, must be kept from the troops until at
least ten o'clock. Panic and chaos must be avoided at all
cost. General Weidling [the commandant of Berlin] has
ordered that active position fighting shall cease at eleven
o'clock, whereupon all German troops must be prepared to
try to break through the Red Army iron ring now closing
around Berlin. We must attempt this in small battle groups,
probing for weak links wherever we can find them. Our first
goal inside the city will be Gesundbrunnen in Wedding, near
the *Flak* tower. Once outside Berlin, our general compass
direction will be northwest, toward Neuruppin [which lies
forty miles north-northwest of the capital]. If you get that
far, keep moving. This is a general order; there are no more
specific details. I regret that I have no better information
than some of you do about the battle situation in several of
the outer boroughs of Berlin. Battle groups will simply have
to play by ear, probing to find their best march route. No
provision can be made for any rear guard. We *are* the rear
guard.

This briefing was over in twenty minutes. In consternation, these battle-wearied officers departed and returned to
their troop sectors. Some were quite nearby, in the Wilhelmstrasse, the Voss Strasse, and on the Potsdamer Platz.

Others were farther away, near the Brandenburg Gate or along Unter den Linden. Like gray ghosts, the parade of officers vanished into the night.

The most elderly of them, sixty-year-old General Krukenberg, later reported:

> If General Mohnke did not have a clue about Russian troop dispositions, I did, for I had been operating out of my command post in the Stadtmitte subway station, having retreated there from my earlier CP in the Staatsoper on Unter den Linden. At least half of my troops were non-Germans, either Scandinavians and Dutchmen from the Nordland Division, or Frenchmen from my own Battle Group Charlemagne, the small remnant of my old Charlemagne Division, which I had marched down from Pomerania. I had also inherited a battalion of Latvian riflemen. I by now had the definite feeling that these Europeans had been doing more of the fighting than Mohnke's own LAH [Leibstandarte Adolf Hitler] troops in and about the Potsdamer Platz. There was much heavier fighting on Unter den Linden than ever took place near the Reich Chancellery.

This is quite true. Most of the severely wounded in Professor Schenck's casualty station, though the doctor did not realize this at the time, were Krukenberg's, not Mohnke's men.

Mohnke's lack of specific order-of-battle information is explained in part by the maddening distractions of the Fuéhrerbunker itself. He did not know with any certainty just where Krukenberg's troops were and how many combat-ready tanks he still had left. (The answer was five.)

In this first account of the breakout, which now follows, there was no dearth of informed witnesses. I relied therefore on the major surviving marchers with whom readers will already be familiar—Generals Mohnke and Krukenberg, Chefpilot Baur, Colonel Schenck, Artur Axmann, Erich Kempka, Heinz Linge, Gerda Christian, Gertrud Junge, Else Krueger—as well as some dozen others. As was perhaps inevitable, given the chaotic circumstances of this night, even three decades later there remained conflicts of testimony, some minor, some major. Some serious clashes of testimony between otherwise reliable witnesses I managed to straighten out.

Another rule I followed was to trust the more reliable witnesses over those who, on other, earlier matters, had shown themselves to be something less than trustworthy;

for example, Baur over Kempka, and Axmann over Linge. Finally, I left certain conflicts standing, for conflict or utter confusion was the very atmosphere in which these events took place. To have smoothed out the whole account would have definitely falsified it.

The number of unwounded Germans still left in the Reich Chancellery was fewer than 800. About 700 of these were SS soldiers of the LAH guards who had been fighting outside the Chancellery. About eighty were men of the FBK or General Rattenhuber's RSD, the security people. The members of the Hitler court proper had by now dwindled to fewer than twenty. All were scheduled to take part in the breakout, except for three who had opted for suicide (Generals Krebs and Burgdorf, Colonel Schaedle). A majority of the people still in the Chancellery were destined to survive. My estimate is that somewhat fewer than 100 were killed in action during this long evening, though no exact figure exists.

Of most interest to our story is the utterly new psychology of the Fuehrerbunker denizens. They were exhausted, demoralized, and desperate. Most knew less of the geography of Berlin than of Berchtesgaden, except perhaps for the handful of native Berliners (Axmann, Gerda Christian, Johannes Hentschel). Until the very end, the rigid National Socialist hierarchical principle had shaped and dominated their daily lives. Now Hitler was dead, Goebbels had followed him, and Bormann, though still alive, was at loose ends.

Reichsleiter Martin Bormann should have taken charge at this critical juncture. Formally, such men as General Weidling and General Mohnke should have been taking orders from Bormann as the new Number One. But, de facto, Bormann had already been reduced to Number Zero. His high-sounding title, Reichsleiter, soon became one of the grimmer jokes of a Berlin evening not brimming over with humor. Nor did Bormann ever even make much of an attempt to assert himself. Only once, around noon on May 1, did he try to countermand a Mohnke military order. Mohnke, quite brusquely, told him to vanish.*

---

* This is not only according to Mohnke, but as recalled by several others present, who all noted it with glee. Goebbels showed up at this moment and in a soft voice cautioned Bormann not to interfere in purely military matters: "We National Socialists must not now have a falling-out among ourselves." Goebbels had many moments of some dignity in these last days.

Mohnke told me:

I spent the whole long afternoon working out the details of
the breakout with Colonel Klingemeier and my staff. We established the march route, organized the separate groups, calculated and synchronized the timing. Then we went over to
consult with Generals Krebs and Burgdorf, who approved
our plan. On this occasion both of these senior military men,
normally my superiors,* confided to me that they were
resolved not to leave the Fuehrerbunker but would commit
suicide after the last soldiers had departed. Finally, I informed my one remaining acting superior, General Weidling,
who was a mile away in the Bendlerstrasse. My agreement
with General Weidling was that he would not sign any capitulation document before daybreak on Wednesday, May
second. This would give us more than five nighttime hours
to make our getaway. General Weidling kept this gentlemen's agreement.

Our plan called for ten breakout groups, some large, some
small. I took command of Group One. General Rattenhuber,
I named to lead Group Two. Group Three, I put under the
command of a responsible civilian, Werner Naumann. Bormann was in this Group Three at his own request. Each
group was to vacate the Reich Chancellery in twenty-minute
intervals, so that the initial takeoff itself was to last a bit
more than three hours.

As long as the coast remained clear, each group was to
bolt as quickly as possible across the Wilhelmplatz and head
for the protective shelter of the Kaiserhof subway station.
The march was then to head due east to the next subway
station, Stadtmitte. The planned route then turned north,
still through the subway tube where it runs right under the
Friedrichstrasse, until we were to come to the central Friedrichstrasse subway station.

From there, we intended to head under the Spree River
to the Stettiner Bahnhof subway station, which is in the
borough of Wedding, in north Berlin. Our hope was to surface outside the Russian ring. From this point, general direction northwest, each gorup was to be on its own.

---

* Mohnke is still very rank-conscious. He was then, at thirty-four, one
of the youngest generals in the German Army. As long as the Commander-
in-Chief Hitler was alive and in the bunker, Mohnke of course reported
to him and to nobody else. But now the situation had changed, and Mohnke
was aware of this. To give the man credit, what he was asserting was his
own personal prestige, ever careful not to offend higher rank. And it took
real courage to stand up to Bormann, even though Bormann was a civilian.

If everything went according to plan, General Mohnke had some slim hopes of a rendezvous of all ten groups in a wooded area near Schwerin.* He explained:

> If we had ever got that far, we would have kept on the move until we got to Admiral Doenitz's HQ in Schleswig-Holstein, on the Ploener See. I stress this simply because, in several versions of our flight I have since read, the quite false information is conveyed that we were actually on our way to join up with General Steiner's army, or what was left of it, just north of Berlin. I had no mission to General Steiner, nor was I even sure he was still there. [He wasn't.] Admiral Doenitz was now the new Reich president, and I was supposed to deliver into his hands several documents of state that had been drawn up in the bunker during the last two days. These were a protocol drawn up by Reich Chancellor Goebbels on May first and a copy of both Hitler testaments of April thirtieth.

> Late in the afternoon of Tuesday, May first, I went into the Reich Chancellery casualty station to look for some kind of waterproof container for these documents, and also for a leather sack for some diamonds I was carrying. These jewels I had, in a sense, "inherited" from Hitler. At any rate, he had given me custody of them. There were several hundred, the kind that were normally attached to the Knight's Cross when it was awarded with diamonds and oakleaf cluster. Hitler, in those last days, had a whole carton filled with these medals. The diamonds were separate, in a chamois pouch.** I knew we might have to swim the Spree and other rivers beyond. Finally, I located some wax paper. I fashioned a kind of long packet, which I was able to sling about my neck so that it rested on my breast, under my uniform.†

As for equipment, I wanted to travel lightly. I had, as always, my service pistol and one machine pistol, with clips. Also, of course, my steel helmet. That was all. We were not

---

* Schwerin is in Mecklenburg. It lies north of the Elbe River, about eighty miles northwest of Berlin, sixty miles due east of Hamburg. It is only twenty-five miles from the Baltic Sea.
** Some readers may be puzzled by this seemingly odd way of awarding what was the highest German decoration for valor, roughly the equivalent of our Congressional Medal of Honor. Because it was almost always awarded to men about to return to the thick of battle, the real diamonds were wisely put in the chamois pouch, glass or paste diamonds in the medal itself. The latter were known as "Gablonz diamonds." Gablonz, in the Sudetenland, specialized in costume and junk jewelry. At least one German World War II hero, Luftwaffe fighter-pilot ace Major General Adolf Galland, gaily defied this practice. He always flew wearing his real diamonds, boasting he would never be shot down. He wasn't.
† According to the version of another member of the party, Mohnke was carrying the diamonds attached to the belt of his athletic supporter, in the small of his back.

planning to fight unless cornered. "Keep moving" was the order.

It was hard to calculate our chances. We were quite ignorant of the real military situation from borough to borough, nor did we know for sure whether Red Army riflemen would already be in those dark subway tubes. Our chances were always much less than fifty-fifty. I was just hoping, somehow, to survive the upcoming twenty-four hours, after which the opportunity to fade away would naturally have become much greater.

General Mohnke had about thirty experienced field officers still under his command. At that staff briefing on May 1, he had told them that Adolf Hitler's last order to him had been to deliver copies of the two Hitler testaments to Admiral Doenitz. Then, Mohnke had sonorously read both documents aloud, asking all officers to memorize as many of the details as they possibly could. He had also given the order that if he should fall, the documents were to go to his aide, Colonel Klingemeier. And if Klingemeier should be hit, the third in line was to be Colonel Schenck. It was the theater of the absurd again. Yet somehow solemn, at least in the memory of Mohnke and many others who were listening to him at that moment.

The breakout rendezvous point General Mohnke had specified in his briefing was in one of the underground garages, beneath the Ehrenhof, facing the Wilhelmstrasse. This was the place where the fire-brigade engines had previously been stationed. The action was scheduled to begin at 11:00 P.M.

This garage, as described by others, had a very low ceiling. Here the electric-light system, for some reason, was no longer functioning. Fuming pitch torches cast a flickering, ghostly light on several bullet-proof, brightly lacquered, black government limousines. According to chauffeur Kempka, he had moved them here from his larger, main garage on the Hermann Goering Strasse. (Twenty-four hours later, these would be requisitioned by the Soviet city command.) On this night, the vehicles had already been pushed aside to make a passageway for the gathering escapees.

Dr. Schenck described the scene:

Now, from the dark gangways, there kept arriving, in small groups, both the fighting troops being pulled in from the

outside, then the officers and men of the Reich Chancellery
Group. The troops, many of them very young, were already
street-fighting veterans. Other soldiers had stubble beards,
blackened faces; they wore sweaty, torn, field-gray uniforms,
which most had worn and slept in, without change, for almost a fortnight. The situation was heroic; the mood was
not. The official announcement of Hitler's suicide had not
yet reached the lower ranks. But they guessed as much—
from the silence of their officers. There was little talk now
of "Fuehrer, Folk, and Fatherland." To a man, each German soldier was silently calculating his own chance of survival. For all the discipline, what was building up was less a
military operation in the classic sense than what I imagine
happens at sea when the cry goes out to man the lifeboats.

Punctually, ten minutes before eleven, General Mohnke
and Colonel Klingemeier arrived in the garage. They began
to chat in whispered tones with the special group that had
been in the Fuehrerbunker. Most of these would leave
with General Mohnke's Group I. They were Major
Guensche; Ambassador Hewel; Vice Admiral Voss; Hitler's
last two secretaries, Gerda Christian and Gertrud Junge;
the cook Constanze Manzialy; and Bormann's secretary,
Else Krueger.

General Mohnke began to give last instructions. He
turned to the doctor, Colonel Schenck, and formally placed
the four women in his special care. They were all clad in
masculine uniform—jackets, trousers, heavy marching
boots, coal-scuttle helmets. At eleven o'clock sharp,
Mohnke gave the order to his lead group to line up and
prepare for departure. It numbered twenty men, four
women. Mohnke next ordered that the bricked-up cellar
window be broken through with crowbars. Then he himself quickly clambered up and out, cocked pistol in hand.

At this breakout moment, Mohnke was just under the
special balcony of the Old Reich Chancellery, the one
Albert Speer had built at Hitler's request in 1934. He had
come up and onto the sidewalk of the Wilhelmstrasse,
which was here cluttered with large chunks of fresh rubble.
The general paused under the balcony, peered about like
an Indian scout, then hand-signaled to Colonel Klingemeier
to follow. The breakout into the unknown had begun.

The first obstacle course to be traversed, from the Chancellery cellar to the subway entrance, was only 120 meters,
down the Wilhelmstrasse and across the Wilhelmplatz. But

it might have been the most dangerous stretch of all, a shooting gallery, had anything alerted the Russians. Although it was long after dark, the darkness was broken by a crimson glow from several raging fires. Even breathing was a problem, above all for frightened people now about to run for their lives. For a full two minutes or so, Mohnke and Klingemeier warily cased the lay of the land. They heard sporadic smallarms fire. But it did not seem to be aimed at them, so they signaled a go-ahead to the others. The dash was made, without incident, in groups of four to six. This mean that the Russians had as yet not discovered the operation.

In these last days, Red Army artillery, mainly the multi-barreled Katyushas, had blasted away most of the granite steps that led down into the Kaiserhof subway station. It was now less a staircase than a rough granite chute. Most simply slid and bumped down. They dared not use flashlights, for they could not know just who might be inside this station. Undercover now, it was dark, deathly still. The soldiers in the lead crawled cautiously on hands and knees until they came close to the station platform. Here they sensed, in the total darkness, the presence of other humans, for they heard low murmurs. A raspy cough. A long minute passed before Mohnke dared shine his flashlight. To everyone's relief, the whole station platform was crowded with Berlin civilians, men, women, and children. They, of course, had feared that those approaching were Russian soldiers. This was only the first of several such surprise encounters. A short scrap of dialogue ensued:

A BERLINER TO MOHNKE: "We kept as quiet as mice, putting out all our candles and hushing the babies. We thought you were all Ivans. Have you see any Russians yet?"

GENERAL MOHNKE: "No. And you?"

THE BERLINER: "No, none has been down here."

MOHNKE: "Well, you good people must move aside. We soldiers have to push on."

This station platform, 100 meters long, pitch dark and crowded, also housed several stretchers and cots. Some of the civilians had been here as long as a week; most had arrived in the last two days. Now the Mohnke group, with sharp elbows, had to force their way through to get down onto the rocky railroad-track bed and head east.

This first stage of the long operation was eminently successful; it gave all marchers a flutter of hope, like a soft sea breeze in the nostrils of a pack of lemmings. In the briefing, General Mohnke had been queried as to whether the third rail was still electrified. He had to reply that he had been told it wasn't; did not know for sure. He now sent a signal officer ahead to check out this important matter. The officer came back to report the good news, "No current in the third rail." He had established this simply by trying to produce a short, by stringing telephone field wire across two rails. Unfortunately, there was no way of relaying this information back to the others in the nine follow-up groups. As one of them (Baur) put it, "I was never quite sure but that one false or awkward side-step might lead to electrocution. And even if the current was off, as I supposed it was, I had another dread. It was that, with the Russians now in charge of the Klingenberg power plant, one of my superefficient, damned-fool fellow countrymen would start showing off and get the damned current flowing again!"

Group communication, even with the immediate follow-up Group II, under General Rattenhuber, was already non-existent. There was no provision for radio contact. Those bringing up the rear of Mohnke's group were too far ahead of Group II for voice or courier contact, or even for simple Morse signals with a flashlight. As it happened, on this 1500–meter march through the subway system, Group II, having taken off after a twenty-minute interval, was now following Group I on the agreed route. Naumann's Group III, as we shall learn, missed the critical turn north, at the Stadtmitte station, and emerged into the street.

This raises the question as to whether General Mohnke's earlier decision to go all the way underground was correct. In retrospect, it obviously was. Both Group III and a later group, under Artur Axmann, ran into the street fighting and took several casualties. The only worry that had made Mohnke hesitate was the persistence of rumors, throughout the last week, that special Russian rifle units were already operating in the subways.*

---

* According to my own researches this was very seldom the case. The Russians, operating in small units in a very large and strange city, were, quite rightly, even more leery of the underground tubes than were the German troops. The Germans could count on the friendliness or at least the docility of the civilian population, some 20,000 of whom were now living in these subways. The Russians could not be so sure. The Russians also feared that the Germans had a plan to flood the whole system, for key parts of it ran under both the Spree River and the Landwehr Canal.

Most of the military were equipped with flashlights, and some now started to use them, but Mohnke gave a sharp order to extinguish them, pronto. They made a too-obvious target. Stumbling along, again in total darkness, on the crossties, the group slowly began to lose cohesion. Mohnke was still in the lead, with Klingemeier and Guensche. They were followed, at an interval, by Schenck, with his four female charges. The others followed, in groups of three or four, strung out over perhaps 100 meters. They had no visual and little voice contact. Mohnke made frequent pauses to stop, look, listen; above all, when there was any strange noise. This allowed stragglers to do some catching up.

Dr. Schenck recounted:

At any moment, I expected to hear some Russian voice shouting "*Stoi*." We all knew the meaning of that word [Stop]. Shots would then surely have rung out, ours or theirs. The women in my charge were carrying on bravely—wordless, marching in single file. We tried for a time holding hands, but this proved both awkward and tiring. So we began to communicate in whispers. Sometimes I would let the four girls pass me, just to make sure they were all still there, giving each a friendly pat on the rump. Then I would overtake them again. I reckon we were usually at least twenty meters behind Mohnke, so I seldom could see or even hear him.

It must have been at least midnight as we plodded into the next station. This was Stadtmitte, the familiar transfer station. I remembered it from my student days in the bustling Berlin of the nineteen twenties. Here, on upper and lower levels, the tracks cross at right angles. This was our first and very welcome break in the long march. A breather for some, a cigarette break for smokers. We all clambered up like squirrels onto the station platform.

We had come out of the total dark again and were blinking. The scene was similar to what we had found back at the Kaiserhof station. It was, however, a bit more orderly; there was more glimmering light. I soon spotted an emergency hospital, operating by candle- and gaslight in an abandoned, side-tracked, yellow subway car (U-Bahn). Several surgeons were operating, under the direction of Oberarzt [head doctor] Zimmermann. This reminded me of my own station, back in the Chancellery cellar, which now seemed so far away in time and space. The four or five surgeons here appeared as exhausted as Professor Haase and I had been.

The scene described by Colonel Schenck is the same that came into the account of Major General Krukenberg. Until early this same evening, the Stadtmitte station had been Krukenberg's divisional command post, the one he had set up after taking over command of the SS Nordland Division. General Krukenberg later explained, "On April twenty-seventh, a Russian artillery shell had exploded right in our midst in this station, killing four and wounding fifteen. The roof over our heads was much too close to the street surface for real safety."

Most probably, then, some of the patients Dr. Schenck now saw were survivors of this mishap. Both Krukenberg and Schenck recalled that there were three or four other such shell penetrations along the route, either in places where the subway tunnel ran too close to the surface of the street, or perhaps where random hits had penetrated into the ventilator shafts.

The next lap was a very short one, only 250 meters, on to the Franzoesische Strasse station. General Mohnke's group now had a chance to re-form and count heads. Although they were by now much more accustomed to the dark, contact remained difficult, and the number still marching in Group I had dwindled to fifteen. Instead of holding up for the others, Mohnke impatiently opted to push on.

The new worry was caused by the sudden loud sound of renewed artillery action. The tunnel and even the tracks began to tremble, as if in an earthquake. Mohnke concluded that the Red Army, at long last alerted to the breakout, was counterattacking. He calculated that the loudest explosions were less than a mile away, in the general direction of the Chancellery. This led him, in turn, to fear that the last four or five groups might now be interdicted and unable to depart. In fact, however, at least six groups had taken off by this time, which was around 3:00 A.M. on Wednesday, May 2. The other four were to push off later, for, despite Mohnke's fear, the Russians were not yet aware that the breakout was in progress.

Now came a truly farcical touch that, somehow, could happen only in Germany. Indeed, only in Berlin, the city that once produced the Captain of Koepenick.* General

* On October 16, 1906, Friedrich Wilhelm Voigt, a whimsical shoe-maker from Tilsit, marched into the local city hall of Koepenick, a township then in the southern suburbs of Berlin. Announcing himself as "Cap-

Mohnke is something less than droll, but he did manage a smile as he told me of this incident.

It was by now around one o'clock, and we were again down on the tracks leading out of the Friedrichstrasse station. We were dog-weary but still tensed up, for we feared that we might meet up with Russians at any turn in the winding track. We were coming ever closer to where I assumed their lines must be. The one organization we were not braced for was the BVG. That's the Berlin Municipal Transport Company.

Less than a hundred meters after we had passed the Friedrichstrasse station platform, we can on a huge steel bulkhead. Waterproof, it was designed to seal this tunnel at the point where the subway tube starts to run under the Spree River.

Here—and I could not believe my own eyes and ears—we spotted two stalwart, uniformed BVG guards. Both, like night watchmen, were carrying lanterns. They were surrounded by angry civilians imploring them to swing open the bulkhead. They kept refusing. One clutched a giant key. When I saw this ridiculous situation, I ordered them to open the bulkhead forthwith, both for my group and for the civilians. The guards categorically refused. They cited regulation this and paragraph that of their "BVG Standing Orders."

Not only were these stubborn fellows going by the book; each had a copy of the book and began reading from it. The regulation, dating from nineteen twenty-three, *did* clearly state that the bulkhead was to be closed every evening after the passage of the last train. It had been their job for years to see that just this happened. I was flabbergasted. No trains had been running here for at least a full week, but these two dutiful characters had their orders, and that was that.

We were armed, of course, and they weren't, and I feel that we just might have made our escape had we been able to follow my original plan to the letter. I sat for long years in Soviet captivity, quietly cursing myself for my strange hesitancy at this critical moment. Perhaps there is no rational explanation. As German soldiers, we had been raised in the strictest of Prussian tradition. Orders are there to be obeyed, even if, as in this case, the order was no more than

tain von Malzen of the Kaiser's Royal First Infantry Guard Regiment," Voigt arrested the Koepenick mayor and the city clerk, requisitioned the cashbox (4000 Reichsmarks and seventy *Pfennigs*) and then vanished in his stolen uniform. To pull off this coup, he had used some ten soldiers he had picked up along the way. Voigt wanted the money to emigrate. He was arrested a fortnight later and served two years in prison. The late playwright Carl Zuckmayer later used this incident to produce a sparkling satire on Prussian militarism. Koepenick today is one of the eight boroughs of East Berlin.

a BVG regulation, not even a military command. Even to-day, though I admit the situation was ludicrous on a night of such galloping chaos, I harbor a lingering respect for this eccentric devotion to duty of those two stubborn, Cerberus-like guardians of the bulkhead. I suppose it was my own ingrained sense of duty that led me to respect theirs.*

This seemed to be the proper moment to question Mohnke about the rumored and, in 1945, disputed Hitler plan to flood the downtown Berlin subway system.

Yes [he replied], I have since heard and even read several such lurid accounts. It all belongs to the wilder Berlin myth-ology of May nineteen forty-five. To my certain knowledge, there never was any such Fuehrerbefehl. I believe the rumor got launched because on April twenty-fourth Martin Bor-mann—possibly on Hitler's orders but more likely on his own—did telephone the BVG people to inquire whether it might be feasible to flood the tunnels as a military measure.

The experts told him that such a flooding, easy enough to execute, could serve no useful military purpose. The waters in most places would not rise more than a meter above track level. This could not seriously impede troops, but it could panic the several thousand refugees sheltering there. Bormann therefore dropped the plan. When I was being interrogated by the Russians, they too raised this matter. But they soon dropped it, and I gathered that they must have been convinced by the technical argument.

There may have been places where water had got in, but the stretch we traversed was as dry and sandy as a desert all the way, even there where we were close to, and below, the Spree level—at that point where we came across those ada-mant BVG guards. It was here that we turned back, retracing our steps to the Friedrichstrasse station. I decided now to go aboveground, up into the S-Bahn [elevated station]. I wanted to reconnoiter the overall situation. This station platform was all but destroyed. Klingemeier and I had to climb up through twisted girders and crawl crablike over wobbly planking.

For the first time since fleeing the Reich Chancellery, I now had a panoramic view of the Berlin nighttime battlefield. It was unlike any previous one I had ever seen. It looked more like a painting, something by Hieronymus Bosch. Even to a hardened soldier, it was most unreal, phantasmagoric.

---

* Somebody with less Prussian sentiment than Mohnke seems to have overpowered these two BVG characters within the next few hours. When Sergeant Misch arrived at this same spot, three or four hours later, the bulkhead was slightly open. The guards themselves had vanished. Misch, alone, made the passage under the river. He reported that the bulkhead must have been forced, because he could only just squeeze through.

Most of the great city was pitch dark; the moon was hiding; but flares, shell bursts, the burning downtown buildings, all these reflected on a low-lying, blackish-yellow cloud of sulphurlike smoke. I could make out nothing remotely resembling a clear battle line. But I spotted the launching sites of the Katyushas, and I knew that these were theirs, not ours. I calculated that they were only about a mile away from us, in the direction of the Tiergarten.

Soon my attention was directed down to the dark Spree, just before and below us. We had to pass over the river. From my perch, I could see dimly that Russians already controlled the upper Friedrichstrasse, three or four blocks away. I could just make out a tank trap in the middle of the Weidendamm Bridge. It had been erected by German defenders, and it marked the perimeter of the Zitadelle. This much I knew; it fitted the logic of what was left of the military situation. I could see that we would now have to move in another direction.

Luckily, after some reconnoitering we located, just north of us and to our left, a narrow catwalk or swinging bridge. It was less than two meters wide. Passage was blocked by concertina barbed wire, and it we quickly cut that away with our field pliers. My group—which had now dwindled to twelve—all scampered across on the double, for our silhouettes were casting long dancing shadows on the water below. We made most excellent moving targets, like dummies in a shooting gallery. But we all got across. No shots rang out.

This is one of the moments I still remember most clearly, for the dark was now light enough, and reflections of the burning ruins were mirrored back from the water of the river, itself rippled by a steady nighttime breeze. The Spree was now black, now red, very eerie. Again it was deathly quiet. Only the ghosts of shadows, sometimes real, sometimes imagined, lurked in the streets leading to the stone quays on both sides of the river.

Once safely across the Spree, the fugitives clambered down an iron staircase and made for the nearest rubbled cellar. They were now on the Schiffbauerdamm, where Berlin shipwrights had once worked and lived in the days of the Great Elector and Frederick the Great. The time was around 2:00 A.M. It was cold and damp. Now and then the waning, slowly setting May moon floated into view between the clouds.

After a pause of ten to fifteen minutes, Group I spent almost an hour following an unmapped, winding, narrow path. This fresh path had been beaten through whole alps of rubble in a northerly direction from the Spree River to the Invalidenstrasse. It led through old cellars, through walls or tenement courts, through ruined buildings where combat engineers had blasted away walls and partitions in the recent fighting. Again and again Mohnke's group stumbled on clusters of terrified civilians, huddled around lighted candles, in cellars or impromptu air-raid shelters. These civilians seldom knew whether the people coming toward them in the night were the last of the Germans or the first of the Russians. Apparently a few Russian patrols had already been through the area earlier this evening, but they had not occupied it.

There was one exception. This was the great Charité Hospital, which here covered several blocks. It is Berlin's largest, most famous hospital. It lies between the Spree and the Invalidenstrasse, which is to say, only a block away from the Mohnke march route. Professor Ferdinand Sauerbruch, then the most eminent surgeon in Europe, was still in charge here. He was actually at the operating table, assisted by his physician-wife, Dr. Margot Sauerbruch, when Red Army storm troops burst in and pandemonium broke loose. A wild chase of the nurses and even of women patients began.

In 1946, Professor Sauerbruch described this scene to me. "It was pretty awful. Still, please do not forget to record that most Russian officers, brandishing pistols, tried to control those berserk troops. The disaster was that the troops had, most unfortunately, got hold of our supplies of ether alcohol and guzzled it as if it were vodka. One of these Russian medical officers was Professor Visnievski, from Moscow. He had been one of my star students, right here in the Charité, in the mid-nineteen twenties."

General Mohnke, aware that the Russians had already stormed the Charité, decided to give it a wide berth. The group could hear wild Sabine screams piercing the Berlin night. As one of the soldiers put it, "I had been in Russia, so I knew there were two sides to this ugly story, atrocity followed by counteratrocity. Still, it is just not a pretty sight to see a terrified, naked woman running along a roof top, pursued by a half-dozen soldiers brandishing bayonets, then leaping five or six stories to certain death."

The Charité behind them, the Mohnke group next emerged near another recognizable Berlin landmark, the ruins of the monumental Museum of Natural History. This meant that they were now across the Invalidenstrasse. On their way, they had been joined by at least a score of military stragglers. As one of these derelicts remarked to Major Guensche, who suspected he might be a deserter, "When you are lost in the desert, the best thing to do is follow any caravan that moves."

For a long hour, from one-thirty to two-thirty, there had been no sound of nearby artillery. Now it flared up again, suddenly and violently. It seemed to be mounted in the Tiergarten, centering fire on the Friedrichstrasse, which lay about one mile back. The target was, in fact, the Weidendamm Bridge and the streets leading to the west bank of the Spree. Now the Berlin battlefield was lit up with giant searchlights,* in addition to the familiar rockets and flares.

The group again took cover, this time on a low garage roof. From here, with night glasses, they could look back and observe the brisk skirmish that was building up on and near the Weidendamm Bridge. Both Russian and German tanks were finally in action.

Although General Mohnke had no way of knowing it at the time, the Germans who had triggered this brisk Russian reaction were those of Group III, which included Martin Bormann, Chefpilot Baur, Werner Naumann, Kempka, and Artur Axmann. Axmann had originally taken off with another group, under his lead. This group had come all the way overland, suffering very heavy casualties, so Axmann had attached his remnant to Group III, which had also been joined by General Krukenberg. Krukenberg still had five Tiger tanks. He lost all of them here at the bridge.

While this battle was still in progress, General Mohnke wisely decided to head north again and finally entered the Chausseestrasse, an extension of the Friedrichstrasse and the main artery leading northwest toward Wedding. Moving now in Indian file along a wall, Mohnke's people soon came to the familiar Maikaefer (May beetle) barracks, once the home of the kaiser's elite Royal Fusilier Guards. Before the late-Victorian main gate of this brick barracks, the Volkssturm had erected a cumbersome but somehow formidable barricade of rubble and brick, but the Volkssturm soldiers themselves, mostly middle-aged World War

---

* The Russians had captured German antiaircraft searchlights, which fleeing ack-ack crews had failed to destroy.

I veterans, had long since vanished from the scene. Now
Mohnke and company suddenly spotted a Red Army T-34
tank, looming above and behind this barricade. Its muzzle
was slowly swiveling, targeting in on the advancing
Germans.

The general himself, along with Colonel Klingemeier,
Major Guensche, and three Panzergrenadiers at his side—
wily old east-front veterans all—quickly took silent cover.
Then, instinctively, they began moving along the wall in
order to get as close as possible to the tank before engaging
it. However, they had few grenades, no bazookas, no bullets that could pierce armor. Luckily for them, the tank
did not move or fire. The Germans were able to retreat
discreetly. Four terrified women were still of the company.

What one notes here—and the phenomenon keeps popping up in all other accounts—is how wary, on this event-
ful evening, both the German and the Russian soldiers
were. Nobody was particularly eager to fight; soldiers seldom fired unless fired on. The Germans simply wanted to
fade away with a minimum of fuss. Moscow epic films to
the contrary, the Russian soldiers, sensing that Berlin had
all but fallen, were not looking for any extra medals. Again
and again, small German battle groups moved through or
around larger Russian units like ships passing in the night,
under total blackout conditions.

The members of the Mohnke group, their progress
blocked by the formidable tank, now had to double back
to seek another main artery leading northwest. But the
direction they finally had to choose was south. This soon
brought them back again close to the Spree, hence within
earshot of the fighting still in progress at the Weidendamm
Bridge. Russian artillery and Katyusha shells, most of
them coming from the Tiergarten, whistled over their heads.
Suddenly, one shell fell several hundred meters short of the
bridge. It exploded in the middle of Group I. Major General Juergen Ziegler, whom General Weidling five days
before had relieved of his SS Nordland Division command,
was hit and killed instantly.

The time of this incident was close to 3:30 A.M. True to
the old saying, this was indeed that darkness that comes
just before dawn. It was also the coldest, windiest, most
desolate hour. Dew was falling on chapped lips, a dew
mixed with the bitter taste of ash. At this point, shaken by
the explosion so near them, the women announced that

they were utterly exhausted and could no longer keep up with the group.

Fatigue, in fact, was overcoming everybody. The group was just about to reach the Stettiner Bahnhof, the trunkline terminal for trains coming from the north. General Mohnke realized that it had taken more than four hours to move less than four miles. There were still two miles to go before Gesundbrunnen, the second major goal of this night march, could possibly be reached, so he called for a halt. Dawn might bring a bit more warmth and cheer. It would also bring heightened danger.

The halt was supposed to last one hour. The location chosen was a freight yard near the Stettiner station, on a lot that was overgrown with forsythia and lilac bushes and hence offered some concealment. Here the roof of an old wooden locomotive-shed was still burning; the men gathered a few of the charred beams and used them as a fire for warming their hands. Sentries were posted. The famished marchers opened their rations of tinned meat and hard bread, but they found the food difficult to eat; all canteens had long been empty and there was no water. Some soldiers did stretch out on the ground to try to get some sleep, but cold, exhaustion, and fear made this impossible.

Some, to their regret, were already wearing summer uniforms. Most uniforms were now torn, grimy with sweat, clammy from the night air. All faces were covered with dust, foreheads smeared with ash, hands chapped, eyelids a feverish red. Major Guensche later said, "Most of us old soldiers sat dumbly around that fireside. We watched how the silhouettes of night began to fade, and the smoldering ruins slowly began to take on their real shape."

The moon, sometimes silver but often strangely orange or even red, emerged from time to time through holes in the lowering clouds. As the dawn slowly broke, it revealed a huge cloud of yellowish dust floating over the ruins "like mist over a mountain lake," as Captain Beermann described it.

It struck me as curious, in interviewing these survivors, how often they mentioned not so much the noise of war as its sudden still moments. Many told me how silently this slow dawn came on Wednesday, May 2, 1945. I suspect that they remember and describe it so vividly because this was the last dawn they were destined to enjoy before a captivity that lasted, for most of them, ten years. Around the impromptu campfire, though there was not much to talk about, the one-hour break Mohnke had originally announced finally lasted three hours.

It was now almost 7:00 A.M. In the broad daylight, General Mohnke's small group of a dozen discovered they were not the only derelicts to have sought shelter in this immediate area. At least a half-dozen other motley units, with no particular goal other than to keep out of the hands of Russians for as long as possible, had joined them. As General Mohnke gave the signal to break camp and take off once again, the column behind him had become much longer, 150 to 200 people.

Elsewhere, the sound trucks were getting ready to move out to announce General Weidling's official capitulation of Berlin and a general cease-fire. But none of these marchers heard this news en route.

As the long Mohnke column entered the Bernauer Strasse, it arrived in the borough of Wedding. The course was still north, into the Brunnenstrasse. Here, the marchers noticed that the damage to the tenement houses was considerably less than it had been in downtown Berlin and that there seemed to have been little fighting in the vicinity. Several curious civilians had crawled out of their cellars and shelters —family groups, grandfathers, children. They stood in proletarian awe as the Waffen SS marched by. I asked General Mohnke, as I had already asked Colonel Schenck, about his memory of this moment. Both men were quite aware of the psychology—and sociology—of "Red" Wedding.

"You mean class-feeling, or revolutionary spirit?" Mohnke began. "Some of us SS men really feared that, but it was anything but the case. These Berlin workers were too beaten, too groggy, perhaps just too afraid, afraid both of us and of the Red Army about to arrive. I assure you, we were not marching through any sea of red flags. I saw three or four clenched Communist fists from the windows. That was all."

No other chapter of this report required interviews over such a long period as did this story of the breakout. I heard my first account from Dr. Schenck in Aachen in the spring of 1970, and my last interview came six years later, when I located Gerda Christian in the Ruhr and she finally consented to tell her story.

In the intervening years, as I moved from one major witness to another, most matters of dispute or confusion were ironed out. There were some exceptions, however, and here I cite one as an example of how seemingly solid testimony can still prove to be quite wrong.

Dr. Schenck, when he told me about the artillery burst that had killed General Ziegler, had then gone on to say, "It was at this time that I lost sight of and contact with Fräulein Manzialy. Hitler's cook had gone along without a murmur up to this point. When we pulled ourselves together in the dark [it was around three o'clock] she was among those missing. Somebody came up and told me that she had been hit and killed."

Others agreed with this version, so I came to accept it. Yet in one of my last interviews, Gerda Christian said to me:

Oh no, that can't be true. Some time after the General Ziegler incident, I caught up with Constanze Manzialy. We were plodding along the same side of the street, I believe it was the Invalidenstrasse, just before we reached the Stettiner Bahnhof. Suddenly we heard strafing fire ahead. As usual on such occasions, we quickly broke for available cover. I remember hiding under a low balcony. I saw Fräulein Manzialy, who was just in front of me on the same side of the street, disappear through a gaping hole in a brick wall. A few minutes later, I went up to look for her and I called out, not too loudly, perhaps. No answer. She had vanished. We never saw her again. But I heard no nearby shot, no scream, saw no one else about. I had the hunch she might just have taken off on her own.

And why not? The only valid reason for assuming today that Constanze Manzialy was killed in the breakout is that she has not since surfaced. As a simple cook and quite harmless soul, the lady had no reason to fear criminal charges. As an Austrian citizen, moreover, she would have enjoyed "liberated" status, one of the quainter juridical twists of the year 1945. Why, after all, keep trudging on with soldiers, SS soldiers in the bargain, when she could quietly fade into the anonymous mass of civilians?

This slight mystery about a minor character deserves mention here because it helps throw some light on a major mystery woman still missing—Mata O'Hara. On a simple calculation of the odds then prevailing in Berlin, a woman's chance of physical survival was far better than fifty-fifty, for even if we number Fräulein Manzialy as among those probably killed, she was the only one of some twenty women who died on this march. On the other hand, almost all of the women who did escape from the Fuehrerbunker were raped within the next twenty-four hours—usually after they had reached the outskirts of the city. The innocent-looking pine woods around the lakes turned out to be the most dangerous hideaways of all. Woods furnished ideal cover for multiple rape in an area stricter Red Army officers could not control. They were themselves afraid to enter the forest after dark; indeed, they had orders not to do so.

With the Berlin spring sun now high and the morning warming up, the long march ended, around nine o'clock. The exhausted Mohnke group had finally come to the Humboldthain, a heathlike, spacious municipal park in the heart of Wedding. It was also the site of a fourteen-story *Flak* tower, one of the largest and tallest in Berlin. This was right next to Gesundbrunnen, the old spa site that had been mentioned in the briefing in the Reich Chancellery cellar ten very long hours back. All hope of any further progress, to Neuruppin, Schwerin, or on to Schleswig-Holstein, had now been quietly forgotten.

Moments of sheer astonishment were not quite over. As the utterly bushed Reich Chancellery Group staggered out of the night, it came to the Humboldthain in bright, streaming spring sunshine, and the marchers rubbed their eyes in disbelief. Before them stood what looked like a new German Army host, banners still flapping in the breeze, as if it had come out of nowhere. The *Flak* tower and huge bunker was ringed with some twenty German Tiger tanks, all stripped for action. Heavy field artillery, with crews, was drawn up into position. There were weapons carriers and armored personnel wagons, bristling with soldiers behind mounted heavy machine guns. Several companies of tank and infantry troops, in fairly fresh battle dress, were being briefed by their officers.

General Mohnke related, "It was a fantastic apparition, like a Fata Morgana. I had to rub my eyes. This otherwise unreal scene reminded me of prewar maneuvers in my days as a young troop officer, somewhere off on the Lueneburger or the Romintern Heath. The sunshine, the shining weapons, the distribution of field rations. No sign of serious battle fatigue. We who had been trudging all through the Berlin night were astounded. A crazy new hope rose briefly."

At the very center of this unlikely apparition of fresh troops with fresh arms (directly out of Berlin factories) stood twenty-seven-year-old Major General Erich Baerenfaenger, one of the half-legendary figures of the Battle for Berlin. Only nine days back, Baerenfaenger had been but a lieutenant colonel. Suddenly, on an absurd whim, Hitler had named him commandant of Berlin, a post he held for only about eleven hours on April 23.* Although a highly decorated infantryman, Baerenfaenger, by his haughty refusal to obey any orders save those coming from Hitler, had only added to the general confusion of the already chaotic German command structure.

Seated grandly in the turret of his own Tiger tank, this Nazi bitter-ender was out to enjoy every minute of his brief but meteoric general officer's career. Baerenfaenger (the name means "bear catcher") now ordered all other troop commanders to report directly to him, including Generals Mohnke and Krukenberg. They found him with maps of Berlin and environs spread out beside his tank. A heated discussion was in progress about a massive breakout north and west. Finally, cooler heads among the senior officers prevailed, for somebody who had a functioning radio had now picked up General Weidling's capitulation order. It was midmorning, between ten and ten-thirty. Here, too, we have one obvious reason why the Russians had not long since stormed this last brazen German citadel.

The order went out to destroy or dismantle quickly all weapons. The tanks were immobilized, the larger guns spiked, machine-gun casings removed, rifle bolts thrown away. Hand grenades were detonated against the thick wall of the *Flak* tower. Most officers, however, still kept their pistols, a quaint caste touch that was to have odd consequences.

Unarmed as they now were, the veteran German soldiers were none too keen to remain under the looming and con-

---

* General Mohnke disputed the story, which I had heard from others, that Baerenfaenger ever did take over this high command. "It was a Hitler whim only, forgotten in a few hours. He did name Baerenfaenger as commander of two of the seven sectors of the so-called Inner Ring, Sectors A and B. And he did promote him to major general. After this day, I never saw or heard of this young general again." A few others say they saw him briefly in captivity in Russia. He never returned.

spicuous tower, yet to disappear inside it could be even more dangerous. They therefore left these gray concrete premises to the cowed, exhausted civilians.

No one can recall just who came up with the eminently sensible idea of moving on a bit to still another fairly well-known, popular Berlin institution, the Schultheiss-Patzenhofer brewery, only a few blocks away. By this time, according to General Mohnke, practically all the survivors from the ten Chancellery groups had managed to get this far.

It was already high noon before the short trek to the brewery began. It led from the Humboldthain along the Brunnenstrasse to the Gesundbrunnen S-Bahn. From there the troops took off over the Badstraase to the brewery, which was on the Prinzenallee. All in all, four fairly long Berlin blocks, a march of perhaps twenty minutes.

The brewery was in good physical shape. Although it housed large air-raid shelters, it had hardly been hit in the long air war and had come through the battle unscathed. There was a large courtyard, forming the center of the main building, with the usual spreading chestnut tree, now bursting into early bloom. The simple soldiers and lower ranks decided this was as good a time as any to take a spring sunbath.

Where were the Russians? None of the Germans knew for sure. But they were nearby, invisible, simply biding their time. All Red Army troops on this sunny afternoon of Wednesday, May 2, had by this time heard the joyous news of the capitulation. They therefore simply seem to have continued the celebrations of the day before, a kind of prolonged May Day. True, some time before noon several NKVD search teams had already entered the Fuehrerbunker. They, at least, were thus aware that the bulk of the Reich Chancellery Group had decamped during the night. But as yet the Russians did not know where the group was.

Most of the SS officers had discreetly retreated into the deeper cellar caverns of the brewery. Here they were destined to spend a surprisingly tranquil, long afternoon.

There were, of course, several hundred other Germans, military and civilian, who had also taken refuge in this convenient Berlin hideaway on the last day of the dwindling battle, and morale and discipline began rapidly to disintegrate. In some of the upper rooms, drinking parties were already in progress. Somebody had located the reserve of kegs. Several hysterical women who were fleeing the invading Russians, the "Bolshevik horde" Hitler had been so eloquent about, now threw themselves into the arms of impromptu—and startled—German lovers. Group sex, what the French sometimes naughtily call *"un parti allemand"* took over on the top floor. "It might have been a lot more fun if we were not so utterly exhausted," one of those men told me.

All this was a bit sordid, since there were still many wounded here, in a makeshift ward on the third floor. Apparently there were no doctors, and one paratrooper on crutches hobbled through the corridors shouting, "My comrades are dying like dogs, but we cannot find a single medic or nurse." Dr. Schenck, as exhausted as he now was, might still have volunteered. But, as he told me, he was quite unaware of the situation on the upper levels. (Nor did he ever go to look.) He was deep in the lowest cellar, with General Mohnke's group, listening to Walter Hewel telling the long story of his life and times with Adolf Hitler.

Some time around 2:30 P.M., General Mohnke went with Colonel Clausen to seek out the Russian general commanding in the Wedding sector. He soon returned, leaving Clausen (who was a non-SS officer) to parley. He then convoked his senior officers for a last staff meeting. They discussed how, when, and if they should surrender. Most were of the opinion that the Red Army would simply storm the brewery after nightfall. There was no way as yet to know. Clausen had not returned, was indeed gone for several hours; many assumed he was gone forever. But he was to return under dramatic circumstances.

General Mohnke finally told the soldiers what the officers already knew—that Adolf Hitler was dead. But he did not report the death as suicide. He told me:

I decided it was wiser to report that "the Fuehrer had fallen in battle." Many of the women, when they heard this, broke out sobbing. Others, still as fanatic as Valkyries, roundly cursed us soldiers as quitters and cowards, delivering German womanhood up to wholesale rape. They insisted it was our duty to keep fighting to the last man, the last bullet. However, I took upon myself the responsibility of telling all officers and men that their old oath to the Fuehrer was binding only up to his death. I advised them, now, to try to escape capture when and if the chance should ever come, even by changing into civilian clothes.

Many eagerly took the chance, this same afternoon, of slipping out of the brewery and heading north and west. It was still about ten miles to the outskirts of Berlin. Some Luftwaffe sergeant who was a Berliner, and thus knew the way, volunteered to escort the three secretaries—Gerda Christian, Gertrud Junge, Else Krueger. As I was later to hear, the small group did reach the outskirts of Berlin that evening and hid overnight in the forest. They eventually all made it to the west.

This is all true enough, as far as it goes, and echoes what I had earlier heard from Professor Schenck, who had seen the party off. It concerns us here only because some of the more vivid details are relevant to clear up the minor mystery of just what had happened to General Mohnke's nest-egg of diamonds. For the three women were now joined by a fourth, Elisabeth D. She was a German Signal-Corps telegraphist from the Chancellery. Because she came from the Luebeck area, General Mohnke rather naïvely entrusted the diamonds to her.*

General Mohnke, one remembers, had been carrying the precious stones in a wax-paper packet hung around his neck. Now in the Schultheiss-Patzenhofer brewery, a quiet shift was made. With adhesive tape, Mohnke strapped this fairly heavy packet between Elisabeth D.'s shoulder blades, under her bra strap. The general wished her bon voyage and all the luck in the world. It was agreed—or so Mohnke has said—that if she ever got through to the west, she would dutifully deliver the diamonds to—of all people—Frau Mohnke! The general's wife was then living in Luebeck.

The escorting Luftwaffe sergeant did get the four young women out of Berlin, again resorting to the subway tun-

---

* In the first version I heard of this story, from other bunker people, General Mohnke entrusted the rocks to Else Krueger, with whom he was on friendly terms. Moreover, she came from Altona near Hamburg, which is not too far from Luebeck. This may have been Mohnke's original intention, but he apparently had second thoughts. With the help of Else Krueger, I finally located Elizabeth D. She indignantly denied the general's story. I talked to her at some length and had the feeling that she denied it under pressure from her present husband, a man of some prominence. However, since I have no interest in embarrassing her or her husband—and also no interest in a possible slander suit—I leave it at this: diamonds, as always, are a girl's best friend. Their worth, at best, was only a few thousand dollars. Moreover, the present Frau Mohnke is not the Frau Mohnke of 1945. There was a divorce.

nels, avoiding main highways, and taking a rowboat across
the Havel River at sundown. Once safely outside the big
city, the small party then took to a Scots pine forest on the
familiar road to Nauen. This was most unwise. A roving
party of Russian soldiers, on the nighttime prowl, captured
and dispatched the sergeant and then lined the women up
for the usual. From the account I finally got, indirectly, it
was a boisterous and unchivalrous performance, hectic while
it lasted—and it lasted two long hours. Rape is not a funny
topic, but at least one angle had a touch of black humor. As
Elisabeth D., many years later, told a woman friend, "Those
lusty peasant characters were all in such a hurry that I
managed to keep my bra on."

The girl from Luebeck saved the precious rocks at the
expense of what was left of her virtue. On this same wild
night out under the pines in the Mark of Brandenburg,
Gertrud Junge, Hitler's youngest secretary, resisted like a
tigress and was cruelly beaten up, her skull fractured. She
was finally rescued and taken to a doctor by a Russian
major, who then kept her for a year in Berlin as war
booty.

Gerda Christian and Else Krueger, however, traipsing
through Mecklenburg, at last made it to the west, not without other adventures. With the friendly help of two British
soldiers, they managed to board a refugee train disguised as
"French repatriates." Russian and French officers, discover-
ing the ruse, threw them out of the train, but the British
train commander smuggled them back aboard. So both
arrived in the British Zone of Germany, under the Union
Jack. Gerda Christian said, "In retrospect, you just *have*
to admit Hitler was right on one point: in a time of total
chaos, only the British will still act like gentlemen."

As for the diamonds, what became of them is still a
mystery.

This story of the secretaries has a sequel, a subplot that
goes beyond the limits of this bunker report. The post—
1945 fate of the many people who fled the Hitler bunker
had many surprising twists, none more *rocambolesque* than
what life still had in store for Fräulein Else Krueger. Some
time late in May 1945 she made it home to Altona. Because she had been secretary to Martin Bormann—then
still listed as missing and presumed not dead—Else was
soon picked up by British Intelligence and underwent intensive interrogation.

One year later—it all reads like a Fielding novel—Else Krueger fell in love with one of these interrogation officers, a Captain Leslie James. The couple were married in Wollashey, near Liverpool, on December 23, 1947. She thus became British and a subject of the queen. The captain of those days is today a professor of international relations at Cambridge University.

•

CHAPTER XI

The Flight That Never Was

> I have rarely met with two-o'clock-in-the-morning courage.
>
> —NAPOLEON

THIS CHAPTER concerns an event that has become a matter of major—and sometimes ridiculous—controversy: the question of Martin Bormann's death.

Having followed General Mohnke's group, we now return to the Reich Chancellery at the hour of 11:40 P.M., when Group III was about to depart on the prearranged route. The four escapees we shall be shadowing in this group are Artur Axmann, Werner Naumann, Hans Baur and, most important, Martin Bormann. The events compel careful examination because nothing in this story—not even the death of Hitler—has received such vivid attention as the fate of Bormann. And as we shall see, his fate was closely linked with that of Hans Baur, Hitler's pilot. Their relationship is the key to the whole puzzle, and it explains every move the rattled, drunken Bormann made during that wild Berlin night.

Martin Bormann became famous only in death. Before that, he had been virtually unknown in Germany, a colorless, faceless, toadlike bureaucrat who had been Hitler's secretary. He loved both anonymity and power. Juvenal describes his type well: "He could cut a throat with a thin whisper."

Bormann's corridors of power were the thirteen wartime bunkers (whose cement gangways he ordered covered with

> "Martin Bormann became famous only in death. Before that, he had been virtually unknown in Germany, a colorless, faceless, toadlike bureaucrat who had been Hitler's secretary. He loved both anonymity and power."

red carpeting). He had moved into the New Reich Chancellery in 1938 as Rudolf Hess's deputy, but, because he handled the paperwork far more efficiently than the erratic Hess, Bormann won Hitler's confidence. One of Bormann's first moves was to take over the handling of Hitler's mail—a job that seems routine but is, in fact, one of the keys to power under any dictator. In the easy life of the Chancellery, while Hitler carried on with his two daily receptions, luncheons and suppers, double-feature movies and midnight fireside sessions, all with the Nazi elite, Bormann watched and waited.

A case can be made that Hitler's first descent into the bunkers of wartime was the beginning of his decline and fall. As Goebbels, Speer, and others have observed, the isolation of the Fuehrer was the making of Bormann. The cramped geography of bunkers was ideal for his slow takeover operation, and by 1943 Bormann controlled all access to Hitler except that of the high military. During the last years of the war, Hitler was locked in a two-front battle, against the enemy on one hand and against his own generals on the other. In addition, his health was failing. "I know Bormann is ruthless, but I need him," he once said.

For different reasons, Bormann and Eva Braun were two of the best-kept secrets of the Third Reich, which probably explains the morbid public interest in them after 1945. At the Nuremberg trials, Bormann was sentenced to death *in absentia*. Could the truth about his fate have been even then established and the furor over this mystery laid to rest? I believe so. That, however, would have involved bringing together four key witnesses: Artur Axmann; his aide, Major Weltzin; Goebbels' aide, Werner Naumann; and Hans Baur.

Axmann and Naumann escaped to the west; Weltzin and Baur were captured by the Soviets. The missing piece of the puzzle was in Baur's hands. But in 1945, when Hugh Trevor-Roper, investigating on behalf of the British Military Government, requested transcripts of the Baur and Weltzin interrogations, the Soviets churlishly refused to furnish them. Thus, Trevor-Roper was finally reduced to the testimony of Axmann and was forced to return a verdict of "not proven." There seemed a possibility that Bormann was still alive.

With the respectable name of Trevor-Roper giving some substantiation, every journalistic chalatan now had a chance to float a Bormann rumor in the form of a news story. The story that he had escaped and was living high on the hog in South America made many headlines. And, in the emotional postwar era, millions of readers had visceral reasons for wanting Bormann to be captured alive. Hitler, Goebbels, and Himmler had cheated the hangman, and Goering and Robert Ley were to do the same. Also, it seemed somehow credible that the mystery man in the bunker power structure should escape to become a mystery man elsewhere. (It is hard to imagine Hitler and Goebbels, with their familiar faces, living incognito anywhere, but Bormann's face could have been lost in a crowd. On a visit to his native town of Halberstadt a few years ago, I saw a dozen Harz Mountain peasant types who looked very much like him.)

But to return to Bormann and his situation before the breakout: He already had inherited the shadowy eminence of Reichsleiter and was now the highest Nazi Party official in the new government Hitler had so pedantically spelled out before dying. In the bunker after April 30, however, with General Mohnke in clear command, Bormann had no influence. His only hope for a role in the future came from the curious legacy Adolf Hitler had left him. And that legacy involved much more than the nomination to high rank.

Those details were not to be revealed until Hans Baur finally returned from Soviet imprisonment ten years after the fall of Berlin. They came out partly in my long talks with him, partly in interviews he gave to the press and to *Life* magazine in 1955, and partly in a bouncy book of flying memoirs (*Between Heaven and Earth with the Mighty*, Oldendorf: K. W. Schuetz, 1971) he later wrote.

In October 1955, he related this account to *Life*.

On the morning of Saturday, April 25, Hitler sent for me and told me that there was still a chance for me to get out. I replied, "My Fuehrer, I have already once asked you to let me remain. I would like to repeat that request."

On the evening of Sunday, April, 29—it was perhaps six or seven o'clock—a messenger came over from the bunker to fetch me and my copilot and aide-de-camp, Colonel Beetz. Hitler said, "Baur, I would like to bid you farewell. It is drawing to an end."

I tried to plead with him. "My Fuehrer you can still get out. You can take a tank—we still have one in the Chancellery garage—and go westward. The bridge on the Heerstrasse over the Havel River is still free. My planes are still in Rechlin, ready to fly. I can fly you wherever you want to go."*

Hitler shook his head. "Baur, it is out of the question for me to leave Germany. I could possibly go to Flensburg, where Doenitz will have his headquarters, or to the Obersalzberg. But I would have to face, within two weeks or so, what I face here right now. Some of my generals and my officers have betrayed me. My soldiers do not want to go on any longer. And I can go on no longer. We would perhaps hold the bunker for a few more days, but I am afraid that the Russians will shoot gas at us here. We have gas traps built into our bunker, but I do not trust them.** I cannot imagine what would happen if the Russians should catch me alive."

He then thanked me several times for my services and said that he had two final orders: "You must take the responsibility," he said, "that the bodies of my wife and myself are burned so that my enemies do not do the same mischief with me as was done with Mussolini.

"My second order: Doenitz will be my natural successor. *I have given Bormann several messages for Doenitz. See to it that you get Bormann out of Berlin and to Doenitz by means of your planes at Rechlin.*" (Author's italics.)

Nothing could be more explicit.

We can assume that Bormann was present at this last interview to hear the words that seemingly spelled out his salvation. Bormann, as secretary, was invariably present

---

* Baur must have abandoned his earlier proposal to fly directly from Berlin to Rechlin.
** This is a reference to the metal chimney Hitler had had Johannes Hentschel install in March, the chimney that had frustrated Speer's assassination plan.

at such interviews, sometimes standing just behind Hitler and looking over his shoulder. In earlier, more routine, days, he would have written a memo of these two Fuehrer-befehle immediately after the talks.

Then came a last handshake with both hands, a characteristic gesture of Hitler when saying goodbye to a close friend. And his last, biting words: "Baur, one must write on my tombstone: He was the victim of his generals."

Hitler was to commit suicide a little less than six hours afterward, but Baur, never informed of the timing, failed to carry out the first order. ("Never mind," Goebbels said, excusing him, "he gave the same order to five or six of us.") Instead, Baur went about the business of preparation for the breakout, which was then planned for the night of Monday, April 30. He rolled up the oil painting of Frederick the Great—Hitler's last gift to him—and strapped it to a knapsack so that it would rest against the small of his back.* He changed into a *Tárnjacke* (camouflage suit); he gave away his clothes to Dr. Haase for use by the wounded who would be left behind; he reported to his superior—"When I was *marschbereit* [ready to leave], I went to Reichsleiter Martin Bormann and placed myself at his disposal." When he finally did hear about the Hitler suicides, he later said, he did not have "the urge or gumption" to climb up to the Chancellery garden to see if the cremation had been properly carried out.

The next day, Baur reported, he had a last conversation with Goebbels, who wished him luck and, echoing Hitler, said, "See to it that you make it. Bormann has been given important matters to take up with Doenitz."

When the postponed breakout was finally ready late on May 1, Baur was assigned to the fifteen-man Group III. This is significant. The only men of rank in it were Bormann, Baur, Dr. Stumpfegger, and State Secretary Werner Naumann. Thus, Bormann had gathered around him a pilot, a surgeon, a high bureaucrat, and a small body of battle-trained soldiers. I submit that this is strong circumstantial evidence of "an operation within an operation."

General Mohnke, in his briefing just after sundown, warned all escapees to keep close to the wall of the Chancellery and to make a fast break across the Voss Strasse.

---

* A gesture not entirely sentimental—the painting was worth approximately $25,000.

The troops of his Kampfgruppe were now pulling out of the line, and scouts had reported Red Army sharpshooters on nearby roof tops. But, as luck would have it, the Russians were less alert than they should have been. Officers and men were still celebrating the most triumphant May Day in their lives. Outside, the scene was Tolstoyan. It was bitterly cold, and groups of soldiers huddled around campfires in courtyards. On the horizon, a score of large buildings were aflame. There were no firefighters because the entire Berlin fire department had left in its red trucks more than ten days earlier.

Baur recalled:

> Around eleven P.M. we were lined up for the breakout. I stuck close to Reichsleiter Bormann, as I had been ordered to do. I watched the first group take off, five or six at a time, through a window and shellhole in the Chancellery cellar wall. They drew only occasional fire, as did the second group.
>
> Our group decided to chance it together. We all ran pell-mell out of the huge main portal where, for years, the tall, white-gloved, black-uniformed SS guards had stood their silent watch. Less than two minutes later, I was sliding down into the Kaiserhof subway station on my royal Bavarian ass, like a kid on a playground chute. Now it was pitch dark—stupidly, few of us had brought pocket flashlights—and, like blind mice, we began to probe our way along the tracks.

Halfway along the prescribed route to the Friedrichstrasse subway station, Group III lost contact with the group ahead and so missed a critical left turn to the north. As a result, this third group decided to surface from the Stadtmitte station. They emerged into the Gendarmenmarkt, once a lovely Baroque square in the center of the old city, where the Max Reinhardt Theater faced two cathedrals. Now it was a blazing chaos.

They raced back into the station, regrouped, and began to make their way, Indian file, northward up the Friedrichstrasse. They crossed Unter den Linden and approached the Weidendamn Bridge; in the flickering firelight, they saw that it was blocked by a "Spanish rider" tank barrier in the middle. There was no artillery at the moment, but Russian mortars were beginning to zero in just south of the bridge—a sign that the Soviet troops had finally been alerted to the German movement. Bodies were scattered everywhere, a mélange of Germans, Russians, French and Scandinavian volunteers, and corpses of Berlin civilians.

As we have seen, General Mohnke and at least some of his group had already crossed the Spree on the catwalk bridge. Others—Kempka, for one—had failed to cross. Now all three groups had arrived at roughly the same point, but in the general confusion and lack of communication few were aware of it.

Some time within the hour, the five Tiger tanks of the SS Nordland Division arrived at the bridge, blasted the barrier, and rumbled across. The escapees followed, amid the sulphurous clouds that now and again blotted out the moon.

Baur had been separated from Bormann for the past twenty minutes, but, once across the bridge, he caught sight of him again. "I found Martin Bormann sitting on the stone steps of a bombed-out house. It was the corner house where the Schiffbauerdamm meets the Friedrichstrasse. A dead Russian soldier was sprawled in front of him."

A question of topography becomes relevant here. The Bavarian Baur had lived in Berlin since 1933, and he knew the center of the city fairly well. Bormann, a Saxon, had never really learned his way around. That explains, I believe, why Bormann stuck to the one route familiar to him. It also happened to be the most dangerous route.

Still, even for those who knew Berlin very well, the going was difficult. During their last weeks in the bunker, the city had been transformed and whole blocks had become unrecognizable. "We moved along once-familiar walls using a Braille system of memory," Kempka observed.

The heart of the problem was that most fleeing Berliners had as their goal the tall *Flak* tower on the Humboldthain in Wedding. The most direct route was along the Friedrichstrasse, which, after crossing Unter den Linden, bends slightly northwest and becomes the Chausseestrasse. This street was now blocked by the Russians north of the river.

The Russians were unaware that the bunker breakout was taking place, but they did sense a German movement within the closing ring, so they blocked all radial streets and strafed them sporadically. Yet the Russians were always leery of the masses of ruins; the Germans who did escape managed to do so by moving across the rubble, between streets.

The Zieglerstrasse begins at the Weidendamm Bridge

and runs east. Here, Group III stumbled around for about
an hour but made no progress. The Schiffbauerdamm (later
famous for Bertolt Brecht's theater) runs along the north
bank of the Spree in a generally westerly direction. From
the Weidendamm Bridge to the Reichstag and then to the
Lehrter railway station is roughly a mile. This was the
course Group III ultimately took. It was a very bad
decision.

It was now around 2:30 A.M. Group III was no longer
a cohesive body of fifteen, but Bormann, Baur, Stumpf-
fegger, and Naumann were still with it. Moving out of their
Zieglerstrasse cellar along a still-standing yellow-brick
wall, they suddenly blundered into a fierce tank battle. Tank
battles—as anyone who has ever been near one knows—
are a horrendous eruption. This one, confusing as it must
have been on the spot, was to become even more confusing in postwar legend.

Erich Kempka told me that he suddenly saw Martin
Bormann "blown up" (though he also confessed that he
himself was blinded by the flash). Others told of seeing
Bormann in one of the tanks—by which they must have
meant that he was riding aboard one. Baur said, "I was
standing directly in front of a German tank as it began to
fire. The blast blew me to the ground and left powder
burns that remained in my pores for many months afterward."

Here, part of the bogus postwar Martin Bormann legend
was born. This, according to the story, could have been
that last tank left in the Reich Chancellery garage, now
coming at a prearranged time to pick up Martin Bormann
and vanish into the smoke.

All that is absurd. As we know from General Krukenberg's account, these were *his* Nordland tanks that had
begun to leave the Zitadelle and move north as soon as
the word was passed that Mohnke had decamped. If Bormann had had any such deus ex machina available, he
surely would not have exposed himself to that perilous
march from the bunker to the Schiffbauerdamm.

After this episode, Baur was able to rejoin Bormann
and the two others in the entrance hall of a ruined tenement. In the courtyard to the rear, they could hear staccato
smallarms fire and so, like an Indian scout in the fiction
of Karl May (which Baur had read in boyhood, as had
Hitler), he crawled cautiously up the stairs to a window.

He counted twenty Russian soldiers in the courtyard and reported to Bormann, "They have only to come in the back door to grab us. In an hour it will be daylight; we must get a move on."

Here ensued an odd conversation about the *Kellerkinder* (cellar urchins), those working-class boys and girls who, in the late war years, had made the ruins their playground. They knew the maze of rat-haunted tunnels in the sewer and subway systems and every passage through the honeycombed tenement district. In the last days, they bravely led thousands of German soldiers under the Russian lines and off to the west. The irony, of course, is that these Nazi brass did not know a single *Kellerkind*, nor was there one around at the moment.

At last they moved out again, single file and about twenty meters apart, following the course of the Spree. There was now a lull in the fighting, and they moved quickly along to a spot opposite the Reichstag, where Russian snipers were on the lookout. Coming under fire, the Germans took separate cover in the shelter of the railroad embankment—and this was the last Baur ever saw of the other three.

He looked up and saw the first streaks of dawn.* Soon he moved out alone for the agreed-on rendezvous point, the Lehrter Bahnhof S-Bahn station. He came to a wide bridge over the Humboldt Harbor, crawled across it, jumped into the street, and ran for the station entrance. And here the pilot's luck ran out.

He was gunned down by machine-pistol fire. Severely wounded in both legs, his chest, and one arm, Baur managed to crawl to a burning house. But he still had the rolled portrait of Frederick the Great strapped to his back. As the flames licked closer, he prepared to kill himself with his service pistol. Then the flames receded, and he changed his mind. After four more hours of anguish, he was picked up by German stretcher bearers who, under Russian orders, had begun to clear the battlefield of wounded.

---

* The meteorology is important. There was a waning, three-quarter moon, four phases after the second full moon after Easter, April 18. It was 15 degrees above the horizon, setting in the west. Baur was seeing the *Morgengrauen*, the first streaks of dawn in the east, at 3:45. Comparing this with Axmann's account, we find that Bormann had already met his fate.

We now must pick up the story of Artur Axmann and return to his Wilhelmstrasse starting point on this night.

That story was well known to the judges sitting at Nuremberg in 1945–1946. After more than thirty years of critical examination, it still stands up. But in the emotional climate of 1945, it was received skeptically for several reasons. Axmann had escaped from Berlin to Mecklenburg in the Soviet Zone and then had been arrested by the U.S. Army CIC (Counter-Intelligence Corps) when he had ventured into Upper Bavaria in December 1945. As Reichsjugendfuehrer, leader of the younger Nazi generation, he was suspected of being a "keeper of the flame," perhaps even the custodian of Hitler's ashes. All this sounds absurd today, but 1945 was a different time.

Axmann's testimony about Bormann's eventual fate might have been corroborated by Hitlerjugend Oberbannfuehrer (Hitler Youth Major) Guenther Weltzin, who accompanied him in the escape. But Weltzin later died in Russian imprisonment—not, one must assume, before the Soviets had interrogated him thoroughly. Still, no testimony of Weltzin's was ever introduced by General Rudenko, the Russian prosecutor at Nuremberg.

Curiously, Axmann's British and American interrogators never asked him a certain important question. The fact was that Axmann hated Martin Bormann with a passion. From mid-1944, Bormann had managed to exclude him from direct contact with Hitler, and it was not until April 1945 that Axmann persuaded Hitler to overrule the secretary.* Axmann, in the last bunker days, ranked high among the Reich Chancellery Group, and he was one of the five chosen to do honors at the Viking funeral of Hitler and Eva Braun on that somber last Monday in April.

An hour before jump-off time, Axmann had consulted with General Mohnke, but the briefing must have been sketchy. Axmann told me that he never knew of Mohnke's *Flak* tower destination and was aware only of the immediate downtown goal, the Weidendamm Bridge. Axmann, who had lost his right forearm in his first action on the Russian front, in 1941, was no real soldier; he chose to take his group into the city aboveground. This blunder was to cost him seven of the ranking members of

---

* He did this persuading when he was finally invited to the April 20 Hitler birthday party.

his group—including two women from his staff—in the next two hours.

Here is his story, as he told it to me thirty years later.

I tried my best to time our breakout with that of General Mohnke's group. We set out some time between ten and eleven o'clock. Our compass reading was north, straight up the Wilhelmstrasse toward the Brandenburg Gate. At this stage, we did not run into any fighting. Nor did we even see any Russians until we reached Unter den Linden [about four blocks from the point of departure]. We were moving silently along what was left of the walls, like shadows, single file.

Just before we turned right and east, into Unter den Linden, we suddenly saw the giant hulk of the old Reichstag, which was still smoldering. Even closer, we could now spot Russian infantrymen and tankers in bivouac, directly around —and under—the Brandenburg Gate. Other Russians were roasting an ox on a spit set up in the middle of the Pariser Platz, halfway between the ruined mansions of the American and the French embassies. The Russians seemed rather keen about minding their own business, which suited us desperate Germans perfectly. It was all like a dream, the kind one has after falling asleep while reading one of those epic Russian novels. We mosied silently past the Adlon Hotel and the Russian embassy, under cover of dark. The Russians simply did not see us. Many of them were singing. We were not . . .

There was still no fighting as we moved now, as fast as possible, down the once-fashionable Unter den Linden. It was only after we turned north again, entering the Friedrichstrasse, that we landed plumb in the middle of a very brisk skirmish. What we saw before our astonished eyes was a kind of SS international brigade—very few Germans but a lot of Danes, Swedes, Norwegians, Dutch, Belgians, Latvians and that French group called Kampfgruppe Charlemagne. (These were the remnants, of course, of General Krukenberg's SS Nordland Division and other cat-and-dog SS outfits.)

Axmann estimated that an hour had passed since he had started out, but actually two hours had gone by. He said that four tanks of the Nordland Division had burst through the tank barriers on the Weidendamm Bridge.

Thus, at this point, the Axmann group had now nearly caught up with the lead element of Kampfgruppe Mohnke because, as we know, Mohnke and his men and women were already across the Spree, lying in the rubble and watching the progress of the follow-up groups. The groups that now had to cross were Axmann's and, nearby, Group III with Martin Bormann.

Axmann continued, "What happened now was that suddenly, in the pitch dark, one of our Tiger tanks exploded. I was blown through the air. I was not knocked unconscious and was only slightly wounded by a sliver of shrapnel in the calf of my leg. Five minutes later, when I recovered my bearings, I crawled into the nearest shellhole. It was here that I first met up with Bormann, Naumann, Baur, Schwaegermann, Guenther Dietrich (another Goebbels aide), and Stumpfegger. This was between two and three A.M."

Thus, Bormann had come out of the skirmish alive—and he was definitely *not* riding in a tank. General Krukenberg attests that the existence of these Tiger tanks was unknown to Bormann—until, of course, they began to blast away in his immediate vicinity.

Axmann went on to describe how this augmented party chose to proceed along the raised railway embankment from the Friedrichstrasse station to the Lehrter Bahnhof—the Spree River route already described by Baur.

Axmann also related another bizarre, theatrical incident —one in which his artificial right arm was the central prop.

We reached the bridge over the Friedrich-List-Ufer just west of the Humboldt Harbor. This bridge leads to the Lehrter Bahnhof S-Bahn station. Several of us jumped down from the bridge and found, to our chagrin, that there was a whole Russian infantry platoon in bivouac under it. They promptly surrounded us. But to our amazement and joy they simply kept announcing in a boisterous chorus, "*Hitler kaputt, Krieg aus!*"

Next, they engaged us in a very pleasant chat in broken German. All seemed to be fascinated by my artificial arm, and I kept showing it to them as if it were the latest product of some Nuremberg toy factory. Then they graciously offered us *papirosi*, cigarettes with paper mouthpieces. Apparently they thought we were simple Volkssturm men returning from a long, hard evening at the front.

What spoiled this bit of fraternization was a psychologically false move by the tipsy Bormann and Dr. Stumpfegger. They began to edge away and finally broke out running. This made the Russians suddenly suspicious, but Weltzin and

I were now able to shuffle off as casually as possible without being noticed.

Axmann and Weltzin proceeded west along the Invalidenstrasse. After about four or five city blocks, they ran into a sudden explosion of Russian tank fire and had to hide in the rubble until the tanks lumbered past. They decided to retrace their steps along the street. About 150 meters from the spot where they had talked with the Russians, they reached the bridge that passes over the great trunk lines into the Lehrter Bahnhof, the lines from Hamburg and the north.

Axmann recalled, "We now came across the bodies of Martin Bormann and Dr. Stumpfegger, lying very close together. I leaned over and could see the moonlight playing on their faces. There was no visible sign that they had been shot or struck by shellfire. At first, they looked like men who were unconscious or asleep. But they were not breathing. I assumed then, and I am sure today, that both had taken poison. Weltzin and I did not linger to take pulses. We were in danger and hardly interested in historical moments. We continued eastward. The dawn did not break until about a half hour later, after we had arrived in Berlin-Wedding."

Axmann then went to the house of a former sweetheart and there found a hiding place. Weltzin continued on and was captured that morning.

There are two points in this straightforward Axmann narrative that call for comment and clarification.

First, the timing. Axmann was a Berliner and always had a good sense of his location at any time. But in clocking events, he tends to be off a bit, timing many things at least an hour before they could have happened. The moon, it is true, was still visible at dawn that morning—but it would have been first light rather than moonlight that lit up the faces of the two dead men on the bridge. Axmann put this at "before three o'clock," but it must have been three-thirty by then. I would estimate this time as perhaps fifteen minutes before the pilot Baur (by profession, more conscious of weather and light conditions) noticed *Morgengrauen*, the first rays of actual sunrise.

In short, Axmann and Weltzin saw the bodies some fifteen minutes before Baur was shot. It seems quite likely

that the Russians under the bridge had been alerted by
Bormann and Stumpfegger's sudden dash. And thus Baur
was the victim of their fire. Another irony: if all had gone
smoothly, Bormann might have rejoined his pilot in the
S-Bahn station a little later. With a bit of luck, they might
have reached Rechlin and a plane.

Second, two minor but revealing details of topography.
Too many authors have written about the alleged escape
of Bormann without having retraced his steps on that
fatal journey. On May 2, 1973, I did.

As was the case with most of the great Berlin railroad
terminals—those cathedrals of the industrial nineteenth century—there were *two* Lehrter railroad stations. The major
one was for the long-distance trains. A separate one, nearby
and to the north, was the S-Bahn station. Indeed, the purpose of the S-Bahn elevated railway, built 100 years ago,
was to link the great terminals in "the Ring." When he
was shot, Hans Baur was heading for the entrance to the
S-Bahn station.

Just as there are two Lehrter stations in this part of the
story, there are two different bridges—a fact that has led
to further confusion in the Bormann escape myth.

One of the persistent Bormann legend-makers once asked
me this: "If Baur crossed the railroad bridge to the
Lehrter station around daybreak, as he asserts, how could
he have missed seeing the bodies of the husky Bormann
and the giant Stumpfegger?" (The latter was six foot six.)

The answer is simple. It's clear from Baur's account that
he was speaking of the bridge that crosses the waters of
the Humboldt Harbor, then over the street called
Friedrich-List-Ufer to the S-Bahn station.

Axmann had been at this bridge; it was where he had
had the odd palaver with the Red Army men. But Axmann
then moved on. The second bridge, where he came across
the bodies, is some 150 meters farther westward. This
bridge is at street level; it is the Invalidenstrasse, and, as
described, it crosses the north-south trunk lines that enter
the major Lehrter station. This is not a "railroad bridge,"
but a span for automobile and pedestrian traffic over the
railroad tracks.

To readers who do not belong to the Martin Bormann
Myth Club, I apologize for my plodding pedantism. While
following the footsteps of that 1945 May night, I have
often paused at some lonely Berlin street corner to under-

score the obvious. But whole tomes have been hung on imaginary clues.

All that is now missing from the story are two bodies. But Berlin was filled with dead bodies on the morning of May 2, 1945. Thousands were shoved into unmarked graves, and others were cremated as a health measure. It is true that some search was made for identity cards, but Bormann and Stumpfegger, on the run, would have destroyed theirs. No trace was turned up for twenty-seven years.

Then, on a snowy morning in 1972, workers constructing an exhibition park just opposite the site of the vanished Lehrter railway station—that is, within fifty feet of the street-level bridge—uncovered two skeletons, side by side. One was an extremely tall man and the other was that of a short man. Splinters of plastic cyanide capsules were lodged in the jawbones of both. The hardhats called for the police, and subsequently the police were able to make a positive identification from dental records.

There is a coda to this account. It is a coda directed to those who enjoy the variorum possibilities of history: If only some small incident had taken an opposite twist, would the course have been changed? If only some Russian lieutenant had not decided to bivouac his men under the bridge to the Lehrter S-Bahn station on the night of May 1, 1945. If only Bormann and Stumpfegger had not panicked in the presence of these momentarily amiable soldiers. If only . . . Could Bormann have then escaped not in myth but in reality? The possibility did, indeed, exist.

Admiral Doenitz, as we know, then had his headquarters on the Ploener See in Schleswig-Holstein, 200 miles to the northwest of Berlin. Between Berlin and the headquarters lay the great Luftwaffe base at Rechlin, only ninety miles away. The Red Army had not yet reached Rechlin, and there were still planes there (as the flights of Speer and Ritter von Greim had recently demonstrated).

In a telephone conversation with Albert Speer at his home in Heidelberg, I brought up the speculation about this means of escape. Speer replied:

In the last days of the war, there was much loose talk in Berlin, among higher ranking Nazi officials, about the prospect of fleeing Berlin and Germany by air. I, too, in moments of aberration, talked to some of my Luftwaffe friends, like

General Galland, about the prospects of an escape flight to Greenland. I even had extra fuel tanks built into my own Condor. But in April I came to feel that it was the stern duty of a Reichsminister not to desert the sinking ship.

Baur was a very good pilot; I'll say that for him. That he had seriously proposed to fly Hitler out of the bunker on April twenty-third and again on April twenty-eighth and twenty-ninth, I can believe. The fact that Baur seriously spoke of Manchukuo as the ultimate Hitler destination, however, shows how desperate the bunker scheming was. Aeronautically, such a trans-hemispheric flight might well have been feasible; politically, it would not have been Hitler's style.

The plane in which the Fuehrer normally flew with Baur was a Condor, a high-quality Focke-Wulf product. It was only a medium-range plane, however. According to Baur, at the time of his last talk with Hitler he had moved his three Condors [the Fuehrer's plane and two standbys] from Berlin's besieged Gatow airport to Rechlin, and at Rechlin he had four other planes—at least one of them a Junker–Three-ninety. Now, if Baur was preparing for a long flight, I am quite sure that the Junker–Three-ninety was the plane he had in the back of his mind. It was still in the tricky prototype stage, but it could, in a pinch, fly to Manchukuo. Late in the war, a Luftwaffe test pilot had flown a Junker–Three-ninety nonstop from Germany to Japan over the polar route. Baur would have known of this secret flight—and I suspect that is where the fantastic Manchukuo idea came from.

Baur had talked to me about the Junker–Three-ninety. He used to drive over from Rastenburg to the Luftwaffe base at Insterburg in East Prussia to watch test flights of this and other "hot" planes. He described the latest prototype as a six-engine job that could carry thirty thousand liters of fuel and had a cruising range of eighteen thousand kilometers.*

Now, we know that Baur had a late plan to fly Hitler nonstop out of Europe. We also know that Hitler attached tremendous importance to the matter of preserving his last will and testament for future generations—and this is why he had spent several hours on April 29 planning the overland escape of couriers who would carry copies. In the bunker, their chances were rated about fifty-fifty (though, in the event, all did reach the west). But Hitler

---

* Baur has read this comment by the former minister and, although he loathes Speer, he agrees in substance about the theoretical possibility of an escape by plane. Still, he adds, "Both Bormann and Stumpfegger were drunk as billygoats" during the breakout. And so, I suspect, was Baur.

gave the originals to Martin Bormann. It must be stressed again that Hitler could not imagine that the Reich would cease to exist as a historical entity.

Thus, Martin Bormann was to be his emissary to the future. I feel that there is good reason to believe (and Baur agrees) that Bormann was simply substituted for Hitler in Baur's already-completed flight plan. As we have seen, that escape ended abruptly in the cold May dawn on the bridge. It is one of the story's final ironies that so much of the world has for so long believed that Hitler's last fantasy actually came to pass.

One more irony. On December 9, 1972, I visited the site of the exhumation of the two skeletons. The opened grave was empty, and snowflakes swirled in the air above it. About twenty feet away were the windows of Police Precinct 71 in Berlin-Moabit. This is the office of the West Berlin homicide squad. One wonders how many of the detectives enjoyed the sensational accounts of Martin Bormann's hidden life far away in Paraguay while, a few steps from their windows, two cadavers slowly decomposed in the yellow sand.

•

CHAPTER XII

The Double Symposium

Death of the Loyal Liegeman

Seduction with power overwhelms a man,
For it is the offspring of encompassing ruin,
And now no medicine can avail him,
His crime no longer smolders,
But burns with felonious beauty.
As shoddy bronze, when rubbed,
Disintegrates, black, grimy, dull at the wheel,
This man, put to the proof, falls apart.
Vain as a boy striving to snare a flying bird,
He wins only shame, and brings down his city.
— AESCHYLUS, *Agamemnon*

IN THIS STORY of the disintegration of the Hitler court, readers have surely been aware of the presence of a silent self-effacing figure about whom little has been said—Ambassador Walter Hewel. He is an interesting paradox. A fairly sympathetic, shy, and rather droll man (in comparison with some of the poltroons and cutthroats we have been watching), he was usually a moderating, common-sensical influence on Hitler. Still, he was almost the first and almost the last true liegeman of Adolf Hitler. And the manner of his death has a kind of symbolism in it.

It was at the Schultheiss-Patzenhofer brewery, in which Mohnke's group had sought refuge on May 2, that Dr. Schenck met Walter Hewel again; the two had known each other casually back in the Fuehrerbunker. Schenck came

> "Dr. Schenck could not help recalling a final vision. 'The ruined hulk of a man I saw standing near the spiral stairs struck me as a patient suffering from morphine-withdrawal symptoms.'"

upon him in the brewery cellar, sitting on the lower tier of a wooden double bunk. He was wearing the tailored but tattered blue ambassador's uniform. With the toe of his boot, Hewel was idly nudging some spilled coffee beans into neat, pyramidal piles. The two fell into conversation—there was not much else to do—and Hewel showed Schenck his special diplomat's pass ("Ambassador of the Greater German Reich"), gold-embossed, in a blue leather case, and some snapshots of his young bride, Elizabeth Blanda, whom he had married in 1944 at Berchtesgaden. Walter Hewel's last conversation on earth went on for a full five hours, and Dr. Schenck was able to recall much of it.

Hewel had never given a speech, never kept a diary, and he wrote few letters. This is a pity, for he had a rather special story to tell, full of vignettes of Hitler in his more relaxed moments. The long talk with Dr. Schenck will have to stand as his memoir.

On November 8, 1923, the eighteen-year-old student, Walter Hewel, and the twenty-three-year-old chicken farmer, Heinrich Himmler, carried a swastika banner under which Adolf Hitler marched into his first world headline. This was the raucous beer hall *Putsch* in front of the Feldhernhalle in Munich. Throughout the rest of his life, Hitler would return to the memory of that trial and triumph—not so much for the sixteen Nazi martyrs (whose Hitler-composed epitaph was "*Und Ihr habt doch gesiegt!*" or "In defeat, you have won a victory!")—but for the way he had so effectively prosecuted the Weimar Republic during his trial. Hewel was closely associated with those days and he held a very low number (in the 200s) in the Nazi Party.

Hewel and Hitler were jailed together in the Landsberg prison, and there, for a few months, Hewel served as

Hitler's volunteer valet. Released because of his youth, Hewel took off to spend many years in Southeast Asia. He became a salesman for a British firm and later a coffee-planter. On his return to Germany, he entered the diplomatic service and was stationed in Spain.* In 1938, he was recalled to become Ribbentrop's representative in the Chancellery—and it was then that he resumed his close relationship with Hitler.

Walter Hewel was an agreeable man, more traveled and worldly wise than the provincial Nazi types around him. He was a Rhinelander who had grown up in Bavaria, and, according to General Guderian, he was "a good raconteur and a good listener." It was this that appealed to a special side of Hitler's South German nature. "Surabaya Wally" was tall and corpulent in a Rhenish way, not especially intelligent, but good company and a bon vivant.

A Berlin waiter from the old Horcher's restaurant told me, "Well, he was the kind of fellow who always knew how to get a good table by tipping the headwaiter in advance. I remember that he would insist on artichoke hearts with his venison. He specialized in that kind of *Gemuetlichkeit* that's never quite genuine unless it's a bit artificial." In short, the kind of man-about-town whom headwaiters respect—but not too much.

Bormann encouraged his propinquity with Hitler; Hewel was obviously no rival, and his good nature helped to calm the Fuehrer. Hewel described a proper diplomat as one "who could serve seven long years as liaison between a chancellor like Adolf Hitler and a foreign minister like Joachim von Ribbentrop. That, I say in all humility, often called for the tact of a mandarin and the footwork of an egg-dancer." Indeed it did. The power center of the Third Reich was not in any modern sense a government; it was a royal court. And Hewel became a polished courtier.

The haughty, humorless foreign minister never succeeded in wriggling his way into the Nazi group around the throne. He never got invitations to those light suppers, double-feature movies, or the Hitler fireside chats that droned on until dawn. This irked him, so he planted Hewel inside the magic circle to be his eyes and ears. It could have been a dangerous move—Bormann had displaced his

---

* Where he was almost certainly an agent of Admiral Canaris' Abwehr.

boss, Rudolf Hess, with just such a chance—but Hewel was no Bormann.

Hewel, with his natural bonhomie, was an ideal straight man for Hitler. In the years of triumph—in the Berghof on the Obersalzberg, in Rastenburg in East Prussia, or in the Berlin Chancellery, Hitler and Hewel worked out a brisk vaudeville act. Like two Minsky comedians, they sprang into action as soon as some underling announced, "The foreign minister is on the line."

Nervous Nellie Ribbentrop always avoided calling Hitler directly, because he knew the switchboard operators had orders not to put him through to Der Chef. He would ask for "my man Hewel."

Once Hewel was on the phone, Hitler would stand shoulder to shoulder with him and whisper any kind of absurdity that popped into his head. Hewel would parrot all this into the mouthpiece as his master fed him malicious lines. Ribbentrop would mount into a towering tizzy. As he sputtered in the distance, Hewel would cover the phone and repeat the Donald Duck sounds for the benefit of the company. Since everyone present—except, possibly, Hewel —loathed Ribbentrop, the act was always a hit. All this at the expense of the man Hitler had, in 1938, publicly eulogized as "our greatest foreign minister since Bismarck."

Hewel had one dining-out anecdote that Hitler loved to hear him recount again and again. This was his tale of the farce that had taken place at the Foreign Ministry across the way on the occasion of Ribbentrop's fiftieth birthday, in 1943. The senior officials there had decided to give their chief a showy mahogany dispatch box inlaid with semiprecious stones. This birthday coffer was supposed to contain parchment copies of all treaties and international agreements negotiated under Ribbentrop since he had taken office in 1938.

Then came Hewel's punch line: "The trouble was that we had a devil of a time rustling up any treaties that hadn't since been violated or denounced by Germany." Gales of laughter from the guests. Albert Speer, a bit shocked at the cynicism, noted, "Hitler was doubled up, laughing till his eyes were filled with tears."

Those night-long fireside sessions with Hitler were not always so diverting. Hewel confided to Schenck, "Once, in East Prussia, in nineteen forty-three, these evenings got so soporific that we devised a scheme to share the burden. Half of us would stay up one night with the Fuehrer and the other half the next night. That way, some work could get done." Hitler had owl blood. Often, he did not fall out until noon.

In his capacity as autocrat at the supper table, Hitler was a crashing bore. All sane observers who ever sat there agree on this. Some of his remarkable rhinestones of wisdom were set down in the "Table Talks." Because this stenographic record was edited "for history" by Martin Bormann, some historians have questioned its authenticity. I asked Albert Speer about this, and he replied:

> Except where Bormann doctored the text to make himself look good, this rambling nonsense is on the whole authentic. Hitler was not a stupid man, and from time to t'me he had shrewd insights, along with a truly remarkable memory for detail. But he was also a born dilettante, with a smattering of knowledge. He was that classic German type known as the *Besserwisser*, the know-it-all. His mind was cluttered with minor information and misinformation about everything. I believe that one of the reasons he gathered so many flunkies around him was that his instinct told him that first-rate people couldn't possibly stomach the outpourings.

Here are some of the pithier *aperçus* from the "Table Talks." They date from the 1942–1943 period, when Hitler was still master of Europe from the Pyrenees to the Black Sea.

> Only the classical Greeks knew how to build a perfect roof . . . Napoleon should never have abandoned the title of First Consul. That's what led Beethoven to tear up his *Eroica* dedication . . . Deep red is the best color for political posters . . . Hunting is green Freemasonry . . . It might not be wise to name a battleship *The Adolf Hitler* . . . The father of Jesus was not Joseph but an Aryan, a Roman legionary . . . If we double the ration in Czechoslovakia, the whole nation will go Nazi . . . Birth control killed the Roman Empire . . . It might be a good idea to transplant the Germans of the South Tyrol to the Crimea . . . Eleanor Roosevelt is a mulatto . . . All great American inventors were immigrants from Swabia . . . The Jews are perverting the culture of Lapland . . . The future belongs to us vegetarians . . .

And so the marathon conversation between Schenck and Hewel continued on that melancholy afternoon. Both were educated men with some measure of objective judgment, but both lingered under the spell of the late tyrant. Even now, they would have described themselves as "convinced National Socialists." But there was some process of rethinking going on, some subconscious denazification. All in all, it was like a *Waiting for Godot* dialogue, this macabre interview in the brewery cellar.

The talk turned to bunker days. There, Hewel was the only resident diplomat, an ambassador to nowhere. It was his job—as it had been for the past seven years—to give Hitler a nine-thirty breakfast briefing from the reports of the German Foreign Office. His subject was the world picture, but, as the clock of history moved around—in Hewel's words to Hitler—to five minutes before midnight, the world picture narrowed to the space between the Brandenburg Gate and the Potsdamer Platz. Hewel finally gave up the farce.

He could have left the bunker, as Ribbentrop did on April 23. But his old friend the Fuehrer asked him to stay, and like a loyal liegeman he remained to the end.

Inevitably, the brewery conversation came round to the subject of Adolf Hitler's health. Schenck began pumping Hewel on what he knew about Hitler's personal physician, the sinister Dr. Morell. Hewel, as Schenck later recalled, said, "With mounting frequency as the years went by, Morell gave him what must have been more than a thousand injections. In fact, Goering dubbed Morell 'Der Reichsspritzenmeister' [Master of the Imperial Needle]. Hitler's trust in this notorious Kufuerstendamm VD specialist was boundless. Every time bad news came in from the front, Hitler would summon Morell to give him another shot. He would then be lively for hours, bounding back with new energy. In the last weeks in the bunker, Morell's visitations became a daily affair."

Back in September 1944, an attack af jaundice, stomach pains, and headache had knocked Hitler out completely, and two really competent Berlin medical men—Dr. Erwin Giesing and Professor Carl von Eicken—were finally called to the sickroom. When they induced Hitler to show them the pills Morell had been giving him, Giesing discovered to his horror that the "harmless charcoal tablets" for gas on the stomach contained both strychnine and atropine. Dr. Giesing took some of them away with him and experimented on himself. He was severely affected within a week.

Morell had also been feeding his patient a new sulfa drug called Ultraseptyl, which, because of its unknown side effects, had never been released for the German market. It just happened to be produced by a Budapest firm in which Dr. Morell had a substantial financial interest. (The same firm also produced a fake penicillin.)

In that 1944 September, Hitler was in such bad health that he left his bunker in East Prussia for Berchtesgaden. There, he was in bed for three weeks, and it was during those weeks that he dreamed up the Ardennes offensive.

Thanks to the care of Von Eicken, Giesing, and a third man, Dr. Hans Karl Hasselback—who had been called in by Dr. Karl Brandt—Hitler recovered. Soon after, however, Martin Bormann saw to it that Morell was restored to favor.

This episode had an ironic twist. Hitler had also been afflicted by persistent sinusitis ever since the July 20 attempt to blow him up, and it was the reputable Dr. Giesing who prescribed moderate doses of a 10 percent solution of cocaine. Linge administered these with an eyedropper, one a day at first. But during the last two weeks in April, Hitler was demanding a dose ten times a day. This was the one drug for which Morell was not responsible.

Schenck, in his comments over thirty years afterward, voiced his suspicion that Morell's early shots contained a less harmful mixture of caffeine and the new drug Pervitin (which was similar to Benzedrine) but that later injections included such bizarre stuff as concoctions of pulverized bulls' testicles and "hormones from healthy Bulgarian stock." But there may have been even worse.

Schenck could not help recalling a final vision. "The ruined hulk of a man I saw standing near the spiral stairs struck me—as it would have struck any experienced doctor—as a patient suffering from morphine-withdrawal symptoms."

Hewel, when speaking to Schenck, would only go so far as to say, "Yes, I think that Dr. Haase may have taken over where Morell left off. The Hitler of the last days had many calm, almost placid periods. At the very least, he had been given strong tranquilizing shots."

This led on to the unavoidable query, which Schenck put this way: "Do you think that Adolf Hitler, in those last weeks, was of sound mind?"

This had been an unspoken question in the minds of many Germans in a position to observe him at close range. In prewar days, Hitler had wallowed in the acclaim of crowds; during his early war triumphs, he had been ebullient. But when the Russian campaign bogged down in late 1941, he disappeared underground like a troglodyte. Trips to the Chancellery became rare; long Obersalzberg weekends, rarer still. He avoided the sight of bombed cities, speeding to the airport in a limousine with curtains drawn. The salon car of his special train had its windows painted black.*

So Schenck asked the heretical question: Had the Fuehrer indeed become *geisteskrank*, sick in mind and spirit?

Geisteskrank? Never to my knowledge [replied Hewel], and I was with him every day and almost every night to the very end. Long fits of sullen silence, yes. Volcanic explosions, yes —although the lava was usually controlled. Hitler was a consummate actor, not a rug-chewer. He produced vicious diatribes against all and sundry in his presence—except for the women. Toward women, he was touchingly gentle.

Hitler became more morbidly suspicious than ever, more erratic, more murderously vindictive—as he was with Fegelein. Toward the end, he was less the leader, Der Fuehrer, than a man flinching from reality as it advanced on him. He blithely ignored the chaotic destruction, may even have reveled in it, as I now suspect. Or at times he would dismiss it as a trifling episode in his great mission.

In his last years, he began more and more to invoke Providence, whatever he may have meant by that. During our final talks, he shrilly insisted that the war had been forced on him by Bolshevism, international Jewry, and Anglo-Saxon capitalist plutocracy.

Then, there was a maudlin touch as Hewel gave his *in memoriam.* "As I watched him, the sovereign conqueror of earlier years, he struck me, sadly, as one of those panting runners who realizes his rivals are gaining on him and

---

* It is only fair to record the dissenting comment of Lieutenant Colonel Richard Shulze-Kossens of the FBK: "Hitler often spoke of the ruined cities. But he said any city could be rebuilt within thirty years. Another of his predictions that has come true."

will soon snatch the wilting laurels from his perspiring brow." Whether these are Hewel's direct words or whether they were recollected with Dr. Schenck's literary collaboration, they are vintage 1933–1945 stuff. Nazis with some pretence to formal education were full of such rhetoric.

Hewel continued his discourse with Schenck.

Even in the last days, Adolf Hitler was convinced there would soon be a war between the advancing British and American troops and the Russians. He said they would be exchanging artillery fire over the roof of the Reich Chancellery. He had convinced himself that from this confrontation, he and National Socialism would emerge, newborn and purified.

At the end, he had lost all confidence in the old clique. He ranted and fumed at the earlier [1941] treachery of Hess and the last-act, deciduous loyalty of Goering, Himmler, Fegelein, and Speer. He had always hated Prussian generals—especially the landed-gentry types—and in the last days he wanted to hang them all. His only words of praise were for his secretaries and a handful of young front-line officers he had decorated for gallantry. He told me they reminded him of his own role as a simple soldier in the trenches in World War One.

As I look back at those long briefing sessions, it strikes me that Hitler was hopelessly engulfed in the grandeur of his mission, a sense that was now disintegrating into self-pity. When the goddess Nemesis began to avenge his hubris, he lost his nerve.

In all this, Walter Hewel never seemed to understand that what was true about Hitler in 1945 had been equally true in Munich in 1923. The man's character never changed. In the epilogue of the monodrama, he was repeating his old lines from the prologue.

In midmorning on April 30, some five or six hours before Hitler's death, Hewel had a last interview. First, they chatted for about half an hour about the old days. Then Hitler, coming to the point, told Hewel that if he, as a Hitler confidant, fell into Russian hands, he would be "squeezed until the pips squeak and then displayed in the Moscow zoo."

The sequence of those last-morning interviews is relevant. First, at seven o'clock, Hitler had had a long philosophic talk—with vintage passages from *Mein Kampf*—with General Mohnke. He was relaxed, viewing the big picture. Next, he spoke with Dr. Haase. Then came the morbid talk with Hewel. At ten o'clock, Hitler was calm again in his conversation with Hans Baur, giving Baur his departure orders and presenting him with the portrait of Frederick the Great.

What had happened in the Haase discussion that returned Hitler's mind to forebodings of mortality? As Haase later told Dr. Schenck, they had talked about the best way of disposing of a body. Haase had recommended cremation, and Hitler had nodded agreement. Undoubtedly, he was filled with the thought that he would soon be barbecuing in his own garden.

Thus, it was probably Hewel's bad luck to be next in line. And in his monologue Hitler displayed a characteristic spirit of malignity—but this time toward an old comrade, who had served him loyally and selflessly. "Hewel, they will torture and kill you and mount you in a waxworks," he said. As they talked, a Walther 7.65 pistol lay on the table. At this point, Hewel told Schenck, the diplomat raised his right hand and swore to take his own life rather than fall into Red Army hands.

His old friend now made him a present of the pistol and a cyanide capsule. These were the only parting gifts. A little later, Hewel got instructions from an officer about how to load and handle the pistol and from Haase how to bite into the capsule.

Walter Hewel was the only one of his retainers Hitler ever pressed to commit suicide.

Hewel and Schenck at last had come to the final moments in that afternoon's long story. Schenck, playing the role of priest, tried desperately to dissuade Hewel from suicide. He reminded Hewel of his bride. He stressed the hope (not completely forlorn) that Hewel could legitimately claim diplomatic status. As for the oath of loyalty to the Fuehrer? That had lost all meaning with the Fuehrer's death. Loyalty beyond the grave was something for the Nibelungs. It was all to no avail.

"With the world-weary, exhausted look of a man who had made up his mind, Hewel, in a friendly way, bade me cease. He was a tall, corpulent man, and he had trouble fitting into the lower berth of the double bunk. And so he sprawled there for another hour or two, silent now, his cocked pistol in his right hand and the left hand clutching his other farewell present, the cyanide capsule."

Dr. Schenck added, "On an upper bunk to the rear, we had another suicide candidate, SS Obersturmfuehrer [first lieutenant] Stehr. Stehr was not silent. He kept jeering at us for what he called running out on the Fuehrer—by being alive."

The time was now about 7:00 P.M. on May 2. General Mohnke, sitting nearby, was still in command but saying little. Around 2:00 P.M. he had left with Colonel Clausen to negotiate with the Russians and he returned at three o'clock, having left Clausen to continue the parley. From time to time he dispatched single scouts to snoop down the corridor, checking on Russian progress. These scouts reported back that Red Army soldiers were approaching warily, room by room, softly now, in no great hurry. Outside, an early May twilight was dropping on the fallen city. Artillery was silent. The thrush-nightingales had begun to sing.

There was compelling reason for this Russian super-caution. Red Army soldiers knew the SS, from long, bitter battle experience. This last cellar-retreat was half-concealed behind brewery boilers and coiling steam pipes. It could be defended. Finally, hearing approaching footsteps, Mohnke and the other twelve field-grade officers arose and came to attention as one man. They all cocked their weapons. The word had been passed around, "Empty pistols of all but the last bullet," a typical piece of SS braggadocio. Even Colonel Schenck, so he later said, was, for a brief moment, caught up in this feckless appeal to mass-suicide camaraderie by men who had eaten of bread baked in the dark.

The padding footsteps, however, in the best thriller tradition, proved to be those of Colonel Clausen. Clausen (who was to die a few months later in captivity) knew his SS, too. To identify himself, he first struck one arm, with its white brassard, into the room.

Colonel Clausen also brought the news that the Battle for Berlin was over. This was the first that Battle Group Mohnke had heard of the capitulation, which had, in fact, been signed by General Weidling that morning, some eight hours back. All German officers, Clausen reported, would be allowed to keep their sidearms—a symbol, to field officers, of honorable surrender. There was a silence of long seconds. Then, after a nod from General Mohnke, came the unanimous, metallic click of uncocking pistols. Battle Group Mohnke had surrendered.

Unanimous, that is, except for two staccato shots, almost simultaneous, which now sounded as the desolate group had begun to file out. A pistol shot fired in a closed room sounds as loud as a hand grenade. Startled, Schenck and the others spun around, to discover that both Ambassador Hewel and Lieutenant Stehr had blown their brains out. They had opted for the dark.

Schenck said, "I was, at this moment, less than three paces from Hewel. In the general tension, I had half-forgotten him. I now rushed over, but it was too late, even for a doctor. Death had come in a matter of four to five seconds. Aghast, I now saw precisely what he had done. He had first put the blue vial between his lips, clenched his jaw, then squeezed off the trigger."

The reader should, I believe, be convinced that this is the way Adolf Hitler did it. The odds are at least 10 to 1 —Haase to Hitler to Hewel. And here, too, we have a fair answer, I believe, to the version of the Russian author Lev Bezymenski. I quote the relevant passage.

Our Moscow investigations also examined the hypothesis of shooting. The theory that Hitler might have shot himself first, and then taken poison, was excluded from the start. The reverse order seemed unlikely. Cyanide acts instantly, and it is therefore hardly conceivable that a person who crushed an ampule of poison in his mouth would also be able to pull a trigger. I inquired of the foremost Soviet forensic scientist, Professor Dr. Vladimir Mikhailovitch Smolyanivov, whether he had knowledge of any such cases. In his entire working career he had not come across a single instance. This method would, in any case, require a strong will, lightning reaction, and a steady hand. But we know how severely Hitler's hands shook.

With all due respect to Professor Smolyaninov, he was neither in the bunker nor the Schultheiss-Patzenhofer brewery, rather special situations involving rather special human beings. Second, if he is indeed the foremost Soviet forensic scientist, he could have told Bezymenski that few if any poisons act instantly, certainly not cyanide. And while it is true that Hitler's left hand shook, the man was not left-handed. Finally, Adolf Hitler lacked many human qualities; but, really, did he lack a strong will? There must be some Russian proverb for giving the devil his due.

Twenty-four-year-old Lieutenant Stehr also earns his place in the story. American veterans who fought against him and similar young zealots, products of the Hitler-jugend, can never forget the type, "tough as leather, fast as greyhounds, hard as Krupp steel." Stehr had fought in the Ardennes, in December 1944; then, switched with his unit (LAH) to the Danube front, he had been severely wounded in the hip and invalided back to Berlin in February. But on the day of Operation Clausewitz, this young veteran deserted his sickbed and volunteered to fight in the Reich Chancellery.

Now the "battle for the world," of which the Hitler-jugend had sung so lustily back in the old peacetime youth hostels, was ending in a dank brewery, and the reality broke this young fanatic's heart. Stehr could have been the subject of that bitter lyric, written around this time, by the disillusioned Berlin bard Gottfried Benn: "The myth had lied." From his perch in an upper bunk, Stehr had been shouting for hours for mass *Heldentode*. Schenck, as he had with Hewel, had again tried to play chaplain (an office that did not exist in the SS). Stehr had a young wife and two children in Berlin, and Schenck had worked that angle. To no avail.

Schenck observed, "Stehr was the last to carry the swastika banner high, the waves now engulfing him, the loyal retainer on his way to Valhalla . . . It was all so long ago, but somehow, even today, I feel that this young man had a sense of loyalty and fidelity far greater than that of higher-ups to whom he had sworn eternal fealty. Albeit in a senseless way, he was true, in his fashion, to what he called his creed."

It is likely that the case was quite different for Walter Hewel. As a diplomat, he had had less to fear in the way of reprisal than had an SS officer. And, as his words to Schenck reveal, he was no bitter-end fanatic like Stehr. The simplest diagnosis was offered by Dr. Schenck: "The human emotional system can take just so much duress and then it snaps. As we say in German, '*es dreht durch*' [It flips]. This can happen to the psyche when the worst is over, in that curious moment our ancestors called the darkness before the dawn. I believe that Walter Hewel, emotionally and physically exhausted, simply blew a fuse, short-circuited. And we were not quick enough to save him."

Thus, the career of the loyal liegeman that began in the beer hall *Putsch* in 1923 and ended in a Berlin brewery in 1945 yields a kind of yeasty symbolism. Perhaps Walter Hewel's last true service to Adolf Hitler was to furnish a footnote by the manner of his death. As most historians should now agree, Hitler *did* shoot himself and *did* bite into the cyanide capsule, just as Professor Haase had clearly and repeatedly instructed both men to do. Pistol and poison, Q.E.D.

Rendezvous in the Belle Alliance Strasse

At 8:00 P.M., a half hour after the surrender, three olive green Red Army jeeps pulled into the dark courtyard of the brewery. As the twelve German SS officers walked out, however, garish searchlights played on them. A young, stocky, blond Red Army second lieutenant ordered his prisoners into the three waiting jeeps. He said only that they were being taken "to the Kommandatura."

The Germans at first were familiar with the route being followed. It was due south through the battered borough of Wedding along the same streets Kampfgruppe Mohnke had marched northward in the early morning hours of this same long day—Badstrasse, Brunnenstrasse, Chausseestrasse. When the small convoy reached the center of the city, it was dark, and most of the Germans no longer could make out exactly where they were, nor by just which bridge they had crossed the Spree.

The Russian drivers drove very fast. Skirting the rubble dexterously but not always missing the craters and potholes, they roared on through the rainy night over streets now quite empty of pedestrians or bystanders. To avoid falling out of the open jeeps, the Russian guards and the morose German prisoners clung to each other, strange partners in the Berlin dark.

The twelve officers of Kampfgruppe Mohnke, still bouncing about in the jeeps, gazed out now and then on the same city they had made their way through from midnight to dawn of this same tumultuous Wednesday. It still resembled a churned-up battlefield—abandoned artillery pieces, charred wrecks of tanks and armored vehicles, discarded bazookas, burned autos and jeeps, crashed

planes, spiked ack-ack guns, dead horses and dogs, soldier
and civilian corpses. Some of the bodies were already
piled neatly for hecatomb burning; most were still sprawled
where they had fallen.

The ride lasted some twenty minutes. The small convoy
had come to a section of the city much less bomb- and
battle-damaged than that they had just traversed. Half of
the apartment and tenement houses were still standing. At
this moment, most of the Germans were still not sure just
where they were. The jeeps had pulled to a halt before a
large, four-story, gray-stucco building. Military guards
posted at the entrance showed that it had become a Red
Army headquarters. The day had been warm and sunny
until noontime, but rainfall and the east wind had brought
another chill evening. Ordered out of the jeeps, hurry up
and wait, the Germans stood about, shivering.

During this ride, General Mohnke and Major Guensche
were seated next to each other in the same jeep, the
second.

Colonel Schenck, who had been riding in the third jeep,
always had a fairly good idea where he was because he
recognized the familiar route he had often taken to Tempelhof airport, only about four miles from the center of
the city. Near this airport, at Number 2 Schulenburgring,
Colonel General Vasili Chuikov, commander of the crack
Russian Eighth Guards Army, had established his forward
headquarters a week before, in the middle of the battle.
It had been in this building, that very morning, that General Chuikov had negotiated the official surrender of Berlin
with General Weidling. Three blocks away, Chuikov had
set up a senior officers' mess in a building in the Belle
Alliance Strasse.* The small jeep convoy had first drawn
up at the headquarters building, apparently to get instructions, and proceeded ten minutes later to this new Red
Army officers' mess.

These German SS officers, all at least of field grade,
had every reason to expect the worst. All were aware of
Adolf Hitler's order of March 1941, the briefing for the
attack on the Soviet Union: "German officers must free
themselves of all conservative and conventional inhibi-

---

* Belle Alliance was that part of the Waterloo battlefield where the
Prussian Marshal Bleucher was the victor.

tions. Such documents as the Geneva convention do not apply in the East."

General Mohnke remembered:

We did not talk at all as we raced along in those jeeps. Most of us were too exhausted, dispirited, suspicious that at least some of our Russian guards could understand German . . .

However, I thought of such things as Hitler's order of May thirteenth, nineteen forty-one, which called for the shooting of all captured political commissars, even in battle. Although, as a professional soldier, I believe most of us in the Waffen SS fought bravely against the Russians, and that they as good soldiers respected that fact, still, many cold-blooded crimes had been committed.

What happened next was this: we were led into this new officers' club, up four flights of stairs to the top floor. At the head of the stairs we were met and greeted by a German-speaking staff officer, a major in a formal, well-pressed uniform. He opened the door and cordially invited us to step into a kind of combination living-reception room. Several other Russians were there, smoking and reading, chatting in small groups.

As described by General Mohnke and other of the party, this room, not very large, was rather crowded. Several upholstered and leather chairs were available, supplemented by a large sofa that probably had been hauled in from another room. This, too, helped give the crowded effect. The dozen SS officers remained standing, nonplussed, embarrassed. The half-dozen Red Army officers present were soon joined by an equal number, all officers of field-grade rank. An atmosphere of military punctilio dominated the scene. The obvious difference between victors and vanquished was evident not only from the color, but also from the condition, of their uniforms. The Germans were in tattered, torn, dusty field gray. Most of the Russians had already changed into brand-new, olive tan dress uniforms, with battle medals and campaign ribbons.

Soon a Russian full colonel entered the room. He invited the still-astonished, still-apprehensive Germans to be seated. They complied, several on the sofa, the rest in chairs toward the center of the room. The Russians also took seats.

The colonel spoke. "We are all aware that it has been a long and active day, and now is a good time to relax.

Would the German officers and gentlemen like to remove their pistol belts? If so, here is a small table reserved for that purpose. It has been a long war."

General Mohnke and his fellows demurred, afraid of some trick. They had been promised, in the terms of their formal surrender in the brewery a short time back, that they would be allowed to keep their sidearms. In any case, the very polite colonel did not press the point. Only three Germans put their pistols and webbing belts on the small red mahogany table.

For the next fifteen minutes or so nothing happened, the Germans conversing with each other in German, the Russians in Russian. General Mohnke heard one of his comrades murmur something about a *Henkersmahlzeit*, the meal the hangman traditionally gives the condemned. An odor of cooking wafted over from the next room.

There was a reason for this awkward delay. Now a second Russian full colonel entered the room and came to the table in the center. The seated Germans promptly arose and stood at attention. At the colonel's side stood a young officer-interpreter. He gave a fluent rendition of what turned out to be a speech of welcome.

Good evening, gentlemen. I have the honor to extend to you a military welcome in the name of the chief of staff of our army and to greet you here in our club on your safe arrival. Unfortunately, the commanding general of our army has been delayed on urgent official military business and cannot be here personally to greet you on arrival, as was at first planned. His chief of staff is with him, but should be with us very shortly. In the meanwhile, the commanding general has asked me to bring you his personal respects and his high regard for your soldierly merits. So please be patient; your host will be here soon.

Once again the Germans sat still, baffled. Not knowing what else to do, they simply nodded their heads in silent recognition of the compliments uttered with no seeming trace of irony. They studied the colonel's face, found it open, bland, almost friendly.

This second colonel now left the room. He returned two or three minutes later, leading a general officer who had arrived with several colonels and majors. The general leading this group was a tall, erect man in his late forties, very correct in manner and bearing. On his epaulets were three stars, indicating that he was a lieutenant general. This was the slightly delayed host.

Although the Germans did not know this—nor were they ever told—he was Lieutenant General Vladimir Alexei Belyavski, chief of staff of Chuikov's elite Eighth Guards Army, the tank army that had defeated von Paulus at Stalingrad and spearheaded the long drive to Berlin.

Now the young interpreter moved forward to translate this second official welcome speech. Lieutenant General Belyavski began with a short bow in the general direction of his German guests.

> Gentlemen, we pride ourselves on having fought in the field against such valiant opponents. We congratulate you on the soldierly valor your troops often displayed. The Battle for Berlin was a bitter encounter while it lasted, and this has been a long and cruel war.
>
> We Soviet officers are sure that a lasting peace will follow this terrible war, and that there will be a real rebirth of that once-traditional friendship that, over generations, has allied the German and the Russian peoples.

Such a complimentary speech, delivered with no trace of sarcasm—General Lee, meet General Grant—might under other circumstances have called for a reply. The Germans, still nonplussed, again demurred. They bowed their heads in awkward and silent acknowledgment that they had at least heard and registered the flattering words.

The gracious host went on, "May I herewith invite you to be our guests for supper this evening, to enjoy what hospitality we can offer?"

Bon appetit! A Russian orderly now swung open the door to the adjoining room. It was a much larger room, a long dining room, in the middle of which was a banquet table groaning with plentiful supplies of bread, lashings of butter, hams, cold cuts, sausages, chicken and fish, red caviar. The table was set formally. Before each plate stood a full bottle of vodka with a tumbler. General Belyavski took the place of honor at the head of the table. The Waffen SS officers, now separated from each other with Red Army officers at each side, sat the length of both sides of the table.

Next came several young waitresses, Red Army enlisted women, clad for the occasion in freshly laundered white aprons. Two were wheeling a copper samovar. They poured tea, brought freshly buttered bread, moved up and down the table with serving dishes and sauces.

General Mohnke remarked later, "We Germans were all very hungry and thirsty. Since the breakout from the Reich Chancellery we had had nothing to eat except for a few iron field rations we had managed to lug along with us on the long march."

Anyone who has ever attended such a show of Russian hospitality knows how embarrassing it can be if one does not drink the vodka, usually proffered in successive toasts. Abstinence may be interpreted as weakness, even as an insult to the host and the traditions of his country. A guest is supposed to down the vodka, chug-a-lug and bottoms up, in one shot, along with the hosts. This can be a bracing experience. I asked General Mohnke just how General Belyavski and his fellow Russian officers reacted to the cautious, still quite wary Germans.

"Naturally, at first they tried to insist that we respond to all toasts, to drink along with them. However, we simply raised the glasses to our lips, wet them, but did not really imbibe. The Russians, of course, noticed this. We knew that sooner or later interrogation would begin. Moreover, from our point of view, it would have been quite unseemly for us to drink to the health of the Red Army. That meant toasting the collapse of our own fatherland. This was not our mood that night."

I asked General Mohnke, "Did the Russians on this highly unusual evening know exactly who you and your fellow officers *were*? That you, for example, were an SS Brigadefuehrer and major general of the Waffen SS, commandant of the Zitadelle and the Reich Chancellery. Or that, at the end, you came directly under the command of Adolf Hitler?"

He replied, "It is hard to assume otherwise. That same afternoon, as you will remember, while we were still in the Schultheiss-Patzenhofer brewery, I left for an hour to negotiate with a Red Army General. At that time I gave him my name, my rank, and I definitely told him about my last command post in the Reich Chancellery. There was no point in concealing this."

More than thirty years later, General Mohnke spoke with profound professional respect for his Red Army opposite numbers on this unusual Berlin evening. "These were very superior, self-confident military professionals.

They were now all wearing spanking new uniforms, were erect in posture, well mannered, 'topfit.' They made quite a point of traditional military courtesy. At the same time, I believe they honestly tried to show proper tact for their defeated enemy's feelings. They definitely were not out to humiliate us. Almost all of them spoke enough German so that we could converse with them, after a fashion. Three or four of us Germans knew some Russian, which also helped."

I asked, "Was there, on that evening, any talk about Russo-German friendship in nineteen thirty-nine to forty-one, the years of the Ribbentrop-Molotov pact? Did they talk about the fate of Adolf Hitler? Did they not mention this, out of sheer curiosity?"

General Mohnke answered:

Please don't misunderstand the curious atmosphere that reigned at the table that evening. A question such as the fate of Adolf Hitler would have sounded like the beginning of an interrogation. That was definitely not the purpose of this Russian show. I am sure that the Russians must have been curious about the fate of Hitler. They did not yet know he was dead, and we did. They suppressed this natural curiosity of victors.

However, one cannot say that there was normal table conversation in any convivial sense. The Russians never forgot for a single moment that we were their prisoners. We Germans, in turn, could not ignore that grim reality, either, which is why we were so stiff, so sober, so restrained. As the evening wore on, our hosts became more and more ebullient. You know how vodka works, even on a Russian. The banquet was becoming a kind of *Uralfest*, a real binge.

What did General Mohnke himself make of the significance of this banquet, then, or later? He said:

I believe there were several reasons for this *Gastmahl*, or banquet. First and foremost, these were proud, victorious officers, not without an innate Russian national patriotism plus a sense of military chivalry.

I think they also wanted to show us that Propaganda Minister Goebbels was lying when he had repeatedly warned that German officers captured by the Russians could expect nothing but the worst forms of torture. Let me here make a personal, private remark. I was in Soviet captivity for more than ten years. I spent seven long years in interrogation. But

I was never tortured or threatened. I am not a Communist in any sense of the word. Yet I certainly have no antipathy toward the Russians as a people. The racist part of the Nationalist Socialist creed never appealed to me. It was primitive, false.

But, back to your question about that Wednesday evening, May second, nineteen forty-five, in Berlin. Our hosts, however genial, most certainly also had the mission to get us to drink so that they could acquire information that might be helpful in later military interrogations. We did not do them this favor.

I queried further, "Would an American be justified in drawing the conclusion that, at least among the professional officers in the Red Army in nineteen forty-five, there were those who favored the quick re-establishment of friendly Russo-German relations? Of the kind, perhaps, that had existed between the then-young Red Army and the Reichswehr of the Weimar Republic? Many German and Russian officers knew each other from this period."

General Mohnke said, "Even if this was so, the idea had no real chance of success. Stalin and his Politburo were clearly running the show, not the Red Army officers."

The jolly mood of German-Russian military confraternity began to wane the same evening, as the second round of vodka bottles appeared. *Voina kaputt, Gitler kaputt* (The war is over and Hitler is dead).* The Russian toasts grew louder and louder, the German abstinence more painful. The cultivation of harmony and appeals to historical friendship with which this improvised gala had begun now slowly soured. Host General Belyavski, who had not quaffed as much vodka as his fellow officers, glanced at his watch and suddenly ended the festivities. It was ten-thirty.

Now another door was opened by one of the Red Army orderlies. The Germans, without further ado, were shoved vigorously through the door by their rollicking hosts. The door was slammed, the bolt slid loudly into place. A double watch was posted outside the door. The honored officers were again simple prisoners.

What happened for the rest of that evening is best described by Professor Schenck.

---

* The aspirate *h*, in the Russian larynx, becomes the more guttural *g*.

The twelve of us were now locked into a kind of garret or servants' quarters, just under the roof, on the top floor. This is a familiar attic room in such older Berlin houses. There was only one small window. It gave us a view toward the inner court. Except for an old-style iron stove, there was no other furniture. From the ceiling a single electric bulb hung down at eye level. The shade had been removed.

For the second time this evening we had been surprised by the turn of events. You see, none of us Germans yet knew, at least from personal experience, that such sudden change of mood is very much a part of the basic Russian temperament. Later, we were to learn that this kind of hot-cold treatment is nothing unusual.

The first thing we thought of was the possibility of escape. But one glance down from that fourth-story window was enough to dissuade us. The outside wall of the building was a sheer drop, with nothing to serve as a break or a ladder. No balconies. The courtyard below already resembled a prison yard. Russian enlisted personnel—most of them women—were moving about constantly. They were armed. They would have spotted any escape attempt. Most lights were still on in this large building, and the courtyard was brightly illuminated. From the rooms and apartments below us we could hear raucous sounds of revelry. Several radios were all tuned in to Russian military music. The scene was like a country fair or kermess. Garbage was now piling up in one corner of the courtyard. The stench was unpleasant. To try to pass what was left of this night, we weary and exhausted Germans just sat on the floor, with our backs to the wall, and tried to catch some sleep. Tired as we were, this was at first difficult. Gradually, the jarring symphony of noise and music died down, and we were able to doze off.

But not for long. At five o'clock, now bright dawn, most of the German prisoners of war were up and about—the call of nature but no toilet. After much fruitless pounding on the door by the Germans, one of the guards finally opened. Vigorous sign language brought home to him what was needed—a chamber pot. He disappeared, to return a few minutes later with the *Gastmahl* copper samovar. It served the purpose.

Another two hours passed. At 7:00 A.M., a Red Army sergeant opened the door. He had with him a hefty platoon of some thirty-six MPs, three guards for each prisoner. They led the Germans down the three flights of stairs. Before leaving this house, however, three of the SS officers, recalling that they had left their sidearms on the small table in the officers' lounge the evening before, requested return of these weapons. The Russian sergeant, with a certain logic, countered, "What do you fellows need pistols for? The war is over, and besides you don't have any clips!"

A trivial, absurd event, perhaps, except that it brought home to the Germans that they were now no longer prisoners of the Eighth Guards Army, but had, during the night, come under different control. The sergeant had heard nothing of the "honorable surrender" deal and probably cared less. Some time during the night, what was left of Kampfgruppe Mohnke had passed from the hands of the Red Army into the custody of the NKVD.

General Mohnke was one of those who had not laid aside their pistols the evening before. Moreover, he still had a concealed clip. It was in his jock strap. In other words, he had not given up on the idea of suicide.

Mohnke commented, "It was obvious to me, at this point, that we had passed out of the hands of the Red Army proper. In fact, even at the banquet, one of the friendlier senior staff officers had hinted to me that this would soon happen. Now that it had, I was more despondent than ever."

Once again, now by morning light and in a larger truck, Mohnke and company were driven across Berlin. They noted signs of life springing up, civilians stirring in the great sea of rubble. The Berliners, wherever they saw Russians in groups, gave them wide berth. The civilian population was mostly women, elderly men, or the young. They could be seen carting their belongings out of bombed dwellings, queueing at the water pumps, standing in line for bread and soup, or idly reading posted placards of the conquerors of Berlin. Only the children were openly fraternizing. The Russian soldiers reciprocated this spontaneous friendship with gifts—chocolate, bread, rides on liberated bicycles. White bed sheets of surrender hung from whatever houses still had façades or walls. Here and there were red flags.

What street traffic moved was entirely Russian. Snappy Red Army traffic policewomen directed military traffic with red-and-yellow semaphore flags. This was Thursday morning, May 3, 1945. The scene made an indelible impression, even on the usually silent-man–type General Mohnke.

It was clear to me that we were being driven out of Berlin in a northeasterly direction. There was very little traffic moving in the same direction we were. But coming toward us now, column after column, endlessly, the Red Army support units. I say columns, but they resembled more a horde, a cavalcade scene from a Russian film. Asia on this day was moving into the middle of Europe, a strange and exotic panorama. There were now countless *panya* wagons, drawn by horse or pony, with singing soldiery perched high on bales of straw. Many of them had clothed themselves in all kinds of unusual civilian dress, including costumes that must have come from ransacked theater and opera wardrobes . . . Those who noticed that we were Germans shook their brown fists and fired angry volleys into the air . . . There were Circassians, Kalmuks, Uzbeks, Azerbaijani, Mongols . . . I saw a mass of light field artillery, all horse-drawn . . . Then came whole units of women soldiers, much better disciplined, marching on foot . . . Finally came the *Tross*, or quartermaster elements. These resembled units right out of the Thirty Years' War. All of these various wagons and carts were loaded and overloaded with miscellaneous cumbersome booty—bureaus and poster-beds, sinks and toilets, barrels, umbrellas, quilts, rugs, bicycles, ladders. There were live chickens, ducks, and geese in cages. I even saw cows and goats tied to the wagons, trotting behind. There were Gypsy-like women, and camp-followers. What was here underway through the streets of Berlin was something out of the great vastness of Russia beyond the Urals. We Germans knew it was a historical moment. We were fascinated—and speechless.

During this ride, not all the passengers had the same destination. Around noontime, Colonel Schenck and six other officers found themselves dumped off at a building on the grounds of Schloss Niederschoenhausen, still inside the city limits. It was now the NKVD headquarters. General Mohnke, General Rattenhuber, and Major Guensche, the latter serving as Mohnke's adjutant, were taken some twenty miles farther east of Berlin, to Strausberg. This had been Marshal Zhukov's headquarters during the Battle for Berlin. The camp here was a kind of reception center for captured general officers and their aides. It was here, five days later, that Mohnke heard the news of the official German surrender on May 8, 1945.

Next day, May 9, General Mohnke and Major Guensche were hauled out of the camp and driven to the nearby airport. The destination was Moscow. This was a flight the general came close to never making. As he told me about his experience at this airport, a bit sheepishly and reluctantly, I was once again reminded of what Professor Schenck had had to say, paraphrasing, about the suicide of Ambassador Walter Hewel in the brewery: The human constitution can stand up to an enormous amount of stress. Yet, when a certain borderline is reached and passed, there comes what he called "nervous decompensation." The critical psychic crisis, or crackup, can set in well after the moment of highest stress, when the worst seems to have been surmounted. The patient, as Schenck said, "flips."

As for Hewel in the Schultheiss-Patzenhofer brewery, as for Bormann and Stumpfegger in the moonlight on the bridge near the Lehrter Bahnhof, so now for General Mohnke, seven days later, at the airport, the war over.

Mohnke recalled:

Yes, I too tried to commit suicide. As a soldier, I had never considered any other method of taking my life except with my service pistol. I had no poison vial, no capsule. This all happened on May ninth, a very warm day. I still had my weapon on my pistol belt, and the clip I had hidden under the belt of my athletic supporter. Suddenly I decided to make use of the pistol, before it was taken away from me forever. The situation seemed hopeless. What had I now to expect or to live for? At any moment I would surely be disarmed. I confided my intention to Otto Guensche. It was he who really saved me.* He said, "Look, General, we survived the Fuehrerbunker together; we lived through the breakout; perhaps we can pull through whatever now lies before us, too."

Forsan et haec olim meminisse iuvabit.

At least in my capacity as reporter and author of this book, I have to thank SS Sturmbannfuehrer Otto Guensche for having kept his composure on this occasion at the Strausberg airport when General Mohnke was about to crack up. One of the key witnesses of the story of the Reich Chancellery Group had thus saved another. Both lived to help complete the historical story. General Mohnke returned to West Germany in 1955; Guensche, a year later.

---

* In a similar incident, in another nearby prisoner-of-war camp, Sergeant Rochus Misch kept Hitler's senior valet, Heinz Linge, from shooting himself. Misch knocked the pistol out of his hand.

What, more than thirty years later, should one make of that 1945 Russo-German "symposium"? Two points, I believe.

The first is that the speech of friendship given by Lieutenant General Belyavski, though perhaps nothing more than a curious fossil today, was, in fact, one of the last serious echoes of what *might* have been Moscow's 1945 policy in Germany—had the Red Army General Staff had more to say. Or anything to say, after the war was over. The tempting idea of a postwar alliance with a nationalist, united, Soviet-oriented but not necessarily Communist or even Socialist Germany had a rather natural attraction to the Russian military mind. It was part of a long military and political tradition, in Russia as in Prussia, at least since the time of Bismarck.

Stalin, when he set up in Russia the League of German Officers in the middle of the war, was also considering, or at least toying with, this same Bismarckian idea. By 1945, however, the opposite political decision had already been taken in the Politburo. Stalin decided to opt for the communizing of his zone of defeated Germany. On May 2, 1945, Walter Ulbricht, the German Communist leader who had been in Russia throughout the war, landed at that same Strausberg airport and headed into Berlin.

A second point: readers with any experience in intelligence work, at least as it is practiced in the western world, have probably already spotted the egregious blunder perpetrated by Soviet Intelligence on this very day and evening in Berlin, Wednesday, May 2, 1945. In fact, one can even mark the hour. It was that moment, just before midnight, when Mohnke and his companions passed out of the hands of the Eighth Guards Army to come under the *Politruks* of the NKVD. This was the symbolic meaning of that brusque push through the door at the end of the *Gastmahl*. It was a handover at midnight.

With the fighting over on this day, the some nine Berlin "search groups" of Russian Intelligence, which had been attached to the fighting armies, now began operating independently, beyond military control. This led to the dispersal of the Reich Chancellery Group. For the next days and weeks, key witnesses were scattered in a whole series of camps strung out on the long route from Berlin to Poland to Moscow.

In retrospect, it is easy to fathom what happened. On May 2, the Red Army dragnet had captured almost all of the leading members of the Reich Chancellery Group. Of those few still present in the bunker on the day Adolf Hitler died, only six of this inner circle had successfully eluded Russian capture—Artur Axmann, Werner Naumann, Erich Kempka, Gerda Christian, Gertrud Junge, Else Krueger. A few FBK officers (Beermann was one) and enlisted men (Karnau, Mengershaussen, Mansfeld) also made it underground to the west. Otherwise, the whole bunker cast, minus suicides, was present, now prisoners, still in Berlin. All told, there were more than fifty officers and men.

Why were they ever moved away from the scene of the action? Most obviously, there could have been no better place to reconstruct their story than the Fuehrerbunker itself—while memories were fresh, the survivors exhausted yet most willing to talk, all the props and artifacts still in place. In other words, there should have been a re-enactment on the scene, the standard police procedure in the reconstruction of any crime.* The whole story could have been cleared up in a week, at most a fortnight. It was by scattering the witnesses that the NKVD vastly complicated its own sleuthing task.

---

* Such a re-enactment did take place fourteen months later. I witnessed it, a strange epilogue.

CHAPTER XIII

•

Last Man Out

We are born into this time. There is no other way.
Our duty is to hold on to the last position, without
hope, without rescue, like the Roman soldier whose
bones were found in front of a door in Pompeii,
who during the eruption of Vesuvius died at his
post because they forgot to relieve him. That is
greatness. The honorable end is the one thing that
can *not* be taken from a man.

—OSWALD SPENGLER,
Technics, and Ideas, 1931

THE LAST MAN on duty in the Berlin bunker was der
Cheftechniker who, through the whole long melodrama,
had had to mind the shop. This was Johannes Hentschel
in the machine room.

He had a job to do, and he stuck to it above and beyond the call of duty. In his cramped machine room, he
sat, most of the time, on a high stool, tending the Diesel
engine that powered the ventilation system. This Diesel,
which also supplied power to run the smaller generator,
kept the water pump functioning.

The pump, installed back in 1943, had originally been
no more than an emergency device for use during air
raids. At that time, Hitler had instructed Hentschel to
have an artesian well secretly dug under the cement floor
of the lower bunker. The idea had arisen from the
Fuehrer's anxiety about *Brunnenvergiftung*, bacteriologi-
cal warfare, and the mechanism incorporated a special

> ## " 'The garden [outside the Bunker] now looked like some cemetery where the gravediggers had gone on strike.' "

tester to show impurities. Daily, a sample of the water was sent over to the Technische Hochschule laboratory for further testing. Now, at the end, the pump was serving an unforeseen, vital function. Hentschel was maintaining a flow of pure water from the well through a makeshift pipeline of red rubber garden hoses through the long tunnel that led to the casualty station, where Dr. Haase and a few orderlies and nurses were struggling to tend the many wounded.

In several interviews, Johannes Hentschel kept insisting that he had been much too busy during the last stand to appreciate the irony of his position. Amid the collapsing physical monuments of the older Prussia that Hitler and his National Socialist Wagnerians had now destroyed forever, one Prussian virtue survived. Hentschel quietly embodied it. For Prussia, in its better moments, was more than a state. It was also an ideal—the Protestant idea of duty.

There was a note of personal regret in his story. Johannes Hentschel, from the day of his marriage in Berlin, in June of 1933, had always yearned to have a son. It was the one consuming ambition of this modest, thirty-eight-year-old skilled worker. He was destined never to have one. But Hentschel's quiet gallantry in action managed, through one harrowing Berlin night, to help keep alive more than 300 wounded young soldiers, Colonel Schenck's patients, who lay in anguish on their cots in the nearby Reich Chancellery cellar.

Professor Werner Haase was still on duty, but Hitler's personal physician was too ill and weak to operate. The pure drinking water was an absolute necessity to keep his soldier-charges alive until the Russians came. "Who knows?" Professor Haase told Colonel Schenck. "A forlorn hope, perhaps, but maybe among the Russian medical officers there will be some of my former students here in Berlin. I had many in the nineteen thirties."*

The precise historical time, for those who like to read the sands sifting so remorselessly in the hourglass of world history, was now 11:59 P.M., one minute before midnight, Central European Time, Tuesday, May 1, 1945. The place, the now all but deserted Fuehrerbunker.

Like Vladimir and Estragon in that bleak Irish theater fantasy, there were now only two characters still on stage, underground, two old lower bunker familiars: Sergeant Misch at his silent telephone switchboard and Hentschel in the machine room. It was truly a *Waiting for Godot* situation. The victorious Russians were coming and the only operative question was "When?" This was the metastasis-midnight to end the long chain of bunker midnight madness. Our narrative is reduced, at last, to one, single, yet reliable, witness who managed to see it all through to the surprising end. For Sergeant Misch was blissfully asleep.

The last week had been full of horrors and specters. Soldiers entering the bunker from the outside had brought tales of "flying field tribunals" of SS commandos, roaming the battlefield and hanging any soldiers suspected of desertion. No one seemed to know who commanded these squads or how they had come into being.** Then, there was *Der Henker*, seen by Dr. Schenck and others. He was a monstrous, one-eyed, Jack Ketch figure with a hangman's rope slung over his shoulder. He came and went mysteriously, once hauling off a Luftwaffe captain and other times taking away ordinary soldiers who seemed to have fled to the relative safety of the Chancellery.

Crouched at his lonely command post, Hentschel glanced up nervously now and then at the large brass marine clock. It hung before and just above him on the rear wall of the *Maschinenraum*. Tick, tick, tick . . . midnight. Tock.

---

* Apparently at least two were—with orders to bring Professor Haase directly to Moscow by plane. Haase died in Moscow in 1947, in the Butyrki, a Moscow-suburb prison similar to Lubyanka.
** Though the existence of these "flying courts" is hard to document today, they were no battlefield myth. Major General Hans Mummert, commanding the "Muencheberg" Panzer Division, on Friday, April 27, issued an order stating that any such terror squads in his sector were to be disarmed and court-martialed. His division, fighting north of the Tiergarten, was by this time reduced to a battle group of some 3500 men and was attached to the 56th Panzerkorps.

One minute after midnight. A new day was born in bleak silence. For that long minute, Hentschel waited for something ugly to happen. But nothing did.

Der Cheftechniker began to breathe a bit easier. He took a glass of cold pump-water for his parched, burning throat. He was dog-tired. He had been awake now for more than fifty-five hours. He knew that he could not afford to doze off without first waking Misch.

The clock moved on slowly to two-thirty. Still black outside. Black and silent. Hentschel, a technician, was a methodical man. He liked to make his round-the-bunker checkup tours exactly once an hour, on the half hour. He wore two wristwatches. One was luminous, a gift from Hitler who had got it from Baur who had got it from the Luftwaffe. Hentschel, like Baur, always knew what time it was when he did this or that chore.

Hentschel said:

I was scared, believe you me, and, curiously, it wasn't only the threat of the Red Army arrival that frightened me, though my thoughts in that direction were rather morose. I tended to push them into the back of my mind. Midnight, as I recall it, was when I was literally trembling, a real case of the shakes, frazzled nerves. Then I began to pull myself together.

But the ambience, what was left of the German presence, was something less than *gemeutlich*. It was, to put it bluntly, as spooky as a *Polterabend* in a charnel house. I knew that there were at least nine unburied corpses about—either inside the bunker or nearby. Earlier in the evening, I had seen the stiff bodies of the six Goebbels children, just once, quickly. Then I closed the door in horror. I vomited. I just couldn't comprehend a father—or a mother—like that. Unnatural. You see, like all others in the bunker, I had come to know and like those children. They were a bumptious, pleasant lot. They came to call me "Onkel Hannes." The children's corpses were now piled, two by two, on three old air-raid shelter cots, the kind that fold into the wall. Rigor mortis. White sheets covered their faces. I saw only their nightgowns, bare legs.

No, I never did see the bodies of General Krebs, General Burgdorf, or Colonel Schaedle. But I suspected that long before this hour, as promised, they had done themselves in. There were plenty of closed doors in both the lower and the upper bunkers. I kept them closed. There were technical reasons for this. If the Russians stormed the bunker with tanks, or trained point-blank artillery at the tower entrance, it would make one hell of a difference whether doors were open or closed. You had to calculate the blast and percussion effect. Also with hand grenades, if they came bouncing down the stone steps like loose pineapples.

Fine fellows, I must say. Burgdorf was a drunken swine; Krebs a more restrained type, but at the end a milktoast namby-pamby. Schaedle a decent fellow, as SS officers went. I didn't know him very well; he was new to the FBK. And he was suffering from a very ugly gangrenous wound on his foot. He went up and down those steps once too often. The eager-beaver type.

The three spent their last hours drinking together, singing away like dying black swans. Loudest was Burgdorf, who had a big chest and a barrel-organ baritone. He kept singing a song, "Johnny come down to Hilo, poor old man," something like that. It was a mixture of German and English. I had trouble following it. Rather catchy sailor's tune, if you like that sort of thing.

It took some little research on my part to discover, in this wild scenario with sound effects, how such a land animal as German General Burgdorf, from Hanover, came to know a sea chantey. In this case, an American one . . .

> Oh wake him
> Oh shake him,
> The big buck nigger with the seaboots on.
>
> Oh Johnny, come down to Hilo
> Poor old man.

Hilo, for students of comparative international folklore, is in Hawaii, at this moment just about as far away from the Berlin bunker as Burgdorf's sodden fancy could transport him. Old Boozy reeled off several more bawdy verses, including a new one, in German-English gibberish.

> *Ich liebe ein Maedchen,*
> *Ich weiss nicht, warum.*
> *Mein Maedchen kaut Tabak,*
> *Mein Maedchen trinkt Rum.**
> Oh wake her, oh shake her,
> Oh wake that girl with the blue dress on
> When Blackie comes down to Hilo
> Poor old man.

---

* I love a gal,
   And I don't know how come.
   My gal chews tobacco
   My gal drinks rum.

Other bunker sources say they believe Burgdorf got this song from a captured phonograph record. It had been brought into the Chancellery canteen by one of the young naval lieutenant commanders who had been flown down from Rostock, on the Baltic, with sea-cadet trainees who were to be thrown into infantry battle defending the Reichstag. This was Grand Admiral Doenitz's belated birthday gift to the embattled Fuehrer. Almost none of these midshipmen radar-technicians had ever seen a rifle range. Most were slaughtered.

General Krebs was as maudlin, more lost in his own pathos, but at least less raucous than the execrable Burgdorf. Hans Krebs was a tall man, his monocle screwed into his oval, florid face. His cranium was shaved Buddhist-priest style; his skull still showed livid slash wounds and ugly red scabs. Back in March 1945, just before he succeeded General Guderian, he had been cut up by flying glass from a U.S. Eighth Air Force low-level raid on German Army headquarters in Zossen. Hentschel described him as he appeared in the bunker on the last day of his life.

> We all had some sympathy for Krebs. But it was the kind of sympathy I managed easily enough to ration. He was no longer young* and was deeply depressed by the utter defeat of German arms, "the second in my lifetime as an officer," as he put it. Krebs was worn to a frazzle by lack of sleep and by the twelve-hour, fruitless negotiations with General Chuikov in the latter's headquarters.
>
> Yet at the same time this man was a professional officer. The art of war was supposed to be his business. He had been one of the big bunker boasters, always spieling about how he had first met Stalin while standing with him on Lenin's tomb on an earlier May Day. He spoke fluent Russian. He could have used some of that lingo to surrender the bunker. Instead, ramrod-back General Krebs simply buckled when the heat was on. He did say one thing that impressed us: "There are no desperate situations; there are only desperate men." He could say that again.

Hentschel is probably quoting Krebs accurately. In Moscow, Krebs was first the assistant military attaché, later the attaché, during 1939–1941, the period of the

---

* General Krebs was fifty-seven.

Molotov-Ribbentrop pact. On May Day 1940 or 1941, as a member of the diplomatic corps, he may very well have stood with Marshal Stalin under the Lenin mausoleum reviewing the troop march-past. However, much more familiar, to German newsreel audiences and newspaper readers, was a picture of a smiling Stalin giving General Krebs the fraternal Russian buss on both cheeks when the two had met, apparently by chance, at Moscow's Byelorussian railroad station. Krebs, one of the most loquacious bunker reminiscers, said that this scene had been completely spontaneous, that he even had been embarrassed by Stalin's excessive camaraderie.

Krebs was a naïve man, a rare, red-hot National Socialist among the generalty. He was also a Russophile, a type not so rare among Prussians as many presume. In their autopsy report, not made public until 1968, the Soviets claim Krebs did not shoot himself in the bunker, but simply took poison. Since this is the dubious batch of documents in which the same claim is made about Hitler, one is justified in surmising that Krebs, like Hitler, used the "Professor Haase method," that is, pistol and poison.

Johannes Hentschel wished that he could at least talk with the Russians in their own language when they came. He also began to speculate about how much ideological ice his genuine workingman's status might cut with the uniformed sons of the world proletarian revolution—the overalls, the monkey wrench, the grease gun.

With more realism, he began to play his own little wargame, contemplating just *how* the Red Army would arrive. Although a civilian born and bred, Hentschel had seen enough German *Wochenschau* (newsreel) battle reports to know how briskly combat troops approach a pillbox. From aboveground and outside, after all, the bunker did resemble a pillbox, nothing more. Storming infantry, with flame-throwers? Point-blank artillery? A brisk tank charge with T–34s? Grenades? Combat engineers with nasty sticks of dynamite, mines? Bombs from the air? And then there was gas, Hitler's old worry. Or simply smoke bombs or tear gas. A multiple-choice situation.

He neatly calculated the relative merits of being in the upper or the lower bunker when Zero-Hour came. The lower bunker was safer against explosives because of the triple bulkheads. But the upper bunker had certain ad-

vantages, too. It could not, for example, be fired on
directly. Hentschel, the technician, also knew what the
really critical problem was. It was air pressure. He knew
how his lungs could be torn apart in any nasty vacuum
created by the penetration of high-velocity explosives.

Still, the bunker had held up against scores of British
and American air raids, including parachuted mines. That
was some comfort. Just three days previously, Sunday,
April 29, there had been a direct bomb hit on the Fuehrerbunker.* It had simply mussed up some of the wiring and
pipes. It had not even dislodged Hentschel's delicate little
topside air-raid warning microphone.

I also took some comfort in the fact that the original, pri-
mary purpose of the Fuehrerbunker was an air-raid shelter,
not as an FHQ. That came later. My *Maschinenraum* was
fully equipped to take over all facilities from the Reich Chancellery as soon as I got the top alert, Alarmstufe 10 [Planes
over Hanover, Braunschweig, Magdeburg, target the Reichs-
hauptstadt]. That was the signal for me to man the Diesel.
The switchover took exactly seven seconds.

Moreover, I had a special secret lever or panic button—
we called it the "*Notbremse*" [emergency brake]—to pull in
an extreme emergency only, such as a fire, an explosion, or
an assassination attempt. It blacked out the bunker, sealed
all doors, and started up the sprinkler system. I had never
had to throw that switch, except in rehearsals. But time for
its real use might soon be approaching.

There was one other critical factor in the whole complex equation that Hentschel had going for him. Like a
fox in his own burrow, he knew his way around. He knew
which corridor led just where. As they approached, the
Russians would be bound to be wary. He was unarmed,
but they did not know that. The SS men had decamped
four long hours ago—but the oncoming Russians might
not know that, either. The place could be mined. Therefore, so reasoned der Cheftechniker, they would first
approach with sappers, carrying portable mine-detectors,
flayers, or other antimine techniques.

Finally, another factor on the plus side of Hentschel's
calculation: the Russians, unless they were to storm the

---

* Probably from a Red Air Force fighter-bomber. The Russian planes
began appearing in the Berlin sky in the last week of the war. The last
U.S. Eighth Air Force raid on Berlin was on April 21, 1945.

bunker from both approaches simultaneously, would have to make a choice of entry. This would allow Hentschel to choose his path for a quiet exit. He felt it was more likely the Russians would come through the Reich Chancellery garden emergency exit. This, after all, was the only visible approach. Or, somewhat less likely, the Russians might come the longer way, which was through the Reich Chancellery cellar and tunnel.

It was now 3:00 A.M., Wednesday, May 2. Sergeant Misch, still at his post, was dead to the world, which created a tricky problem. Misch was armed. He was also SS. Much as Johannes Hentschel liked Misch personally, he now decided that it would be more discreet to face the music alone. The last thing Hentschel needed, against the whole Red Army, was a one-man SS bodyguard. It was high time to wake Misch and send him on his way.

Hentschel later mentioned that Misch had been drinking. He added:

> But Rochus was not roaring drunk, as were most of his superior officers. Otherwise, I would not have let him depart. Misch, during most of the bunker ordeal, had been very duty-conscious, but he had had little if any sleep for two long days. He had gulped brandy and pep pills, trying to keep awake at his switchboard. Misch was a young, strapping fellow, but by now he was utterly bushed.
>
> Rochus was also worried about his wife, out there in Rudow, and his one-year-old daughter, who was victim of a raging fever, something like scarlet fever. That's why Rochus was praying so hard to Saint Roche, his patron saint. Saint Roche is just the right fellow to ward off epidemics, according to the devout—and Rochus was very devout. He was the only SS man I knew who carried rosary beads and really prayed with them.*

Hentschel also had another valid reason for not waking Rochus Misch. It was the so-called Schwaegermann incident, which had happened around nine o'clock on the evening before, Tuesday. Even today, it is a subject of hot dispute among the last occupants of the bunker. First, the Hentschel version.

---

* One Sunday morning, the local priest in Berchtesgaden told me that there were at least three members of the Hitler entourage, the mountain people, who showed up for Sunday mass fairly regularly. SS General Sepp Dietrich, Sergeant Rochus Misch, and—this was the real surprise—Fräulein Braun.

General Mohnke, or some other great military brain, sent
Captain Schwaegermann back to the bunker. He was lugging
that second jerry can I had given him to burn the bodies of
Dr. and Frau Goebbels. Rach, Goebbels' chauffeur, was with
him. Either Schwaegermann or Rach soaked Hitler's study
with gasoline and then blithely tossed in a torch or a burning
rag. They must have shut that steel door in one big hurry.
Luckily, too, I had cut off the ventilation into Hitler's old
quarters. Otherwise, we would all have been blown to eternity right then and there. Or roasted like chestnuts. It was
an idiot performance.

Next, General Mohnke's account.

Hentschel simply doesn't have all the facts. It is true that I
gave Schwaegermann a direct order to burn the Hitler study
room. But—and I was very busy at the time—I naturally
assumed that any officer would have enough sense to check
out whether there was anybody still in the lower bunker. I
had been told it was empty. Colonel Schaedle had ordered
Sergeant Misch to join my group in the breakout. And
Hentschel? I thought that his ventilation job had ceased by
now. That there was also a well *under* the bunker, and that
he was pumping water to wounded soldiers—*my* wounded
soldiers—is news to me. I hear it now for the first time.

Hentschel replied:

Well, that's General Mohnke's version, but it isn't the whole
story. I was upset not only by Schwaegermann's appalling
stupidity, but also by the quite peculiar reaction of Sergeant
Misch. Misch was furious when he came on those two amateur arsonists. He did not dare tangle with Schwaegermann,
who was an SS captain, his superior. But he chased Rach the
length of the bunker and gave him one tremendous boot in
the buttocks.* Misch and I [Hentschel continued], still this
side of eternity after such a narrow escape, carefully examined the door to Hitler's study. It was as hot as a gridiron.
The red-rubber casing, which served as insulation on the
door frame, was melting. It ran down like lava. The red
light above the door was burning brightly—fire alarm. Then
it extinguished itself. We must have stood there frozen, panic-
stricken, for more than ten minutes. We were listening

---

* It was a bad night for Rach all round. He was jobless, Goebbels
having committed suicide. He had this painful run-in with Misch. Nor
was the night over. The two met again, downtown near the Stettiner Bahnhof, in the dawn's early light. There Rach was shot and killed, so Misch
later heard. According to another version, Rach died in Soviet captivity.

intently and finally came to the conclusion that the fire had slowly suffocated itself from lack of oxygen. The rubber was no longer melting. It was fuming, and it sent a powerful sulphurous stench and yellow smoke through the bunker.

Sergeant Misch was still hard to calm down. He was usually a quite sensible, stolid fellow, but these last few days all sorts of crack-pated schemes about blowing up the bunker were rife in the SS canteen. That was the special watering hole over in the SS barracks where those fellows cried into their beer. This was where Rochus usually ate and drank with the boys. Now he was convinced we were sitting in some kind of time bomb "set to go off at midnight."

So you see, I was mighty glad when friend Misch, on his own, had volunteered to stay in the bunker with me.* This meant that, for all the wild canteen rumors and SS bragging, Misch really knew of nothing definite. To be on the safe side, I got out my old voltmeter and ammeter and made a very thorough check of the bunker wiring. I also looked around for dynamite or suspicious packages. I listened for anything ticking. But I did not enter Hitler's study. Some abiding inhibition I can't explain. It gave me the creeps.

* *

Nothing was more symbolic of the bunker's winching-down than the silence that had now descended on the once-overloaded switchboard. In a night of chaos, the orders Misch received were enough to confuse even a general. After Hitler's death, his new boss was Goebbels, and Misch recounted their last conversation just outside the bunker.

GOEBBELS: "Any important calls for me, Sergeant?"

MISCH: "Yes. One from the Gauleitung, one from General Weidling, and a third from Lieutenant Colonel Seibert [commanding Sektor Z, or Stadtmitte]."

GOEBBELS: "Not so important, now. The war is lost; the dice have fallen. I don't really need you anymore, Misch. It might not be a bad idea for you to join General Rauch's troops. They are putting up a good fight in Charlottenburg. Sergeant, I wish you all the luck in the world."

Then he shook hands with Misch, something he had never done before. From this little vignette we learn that

---

* A perfect if minor example of the psychological atmosphere generated in the bunker. No one completely trusted anyone.

even Goebbels had lost touch with the situation-map. General Rauch, with what was left of his division (less than a battalion), was already in Potsdam, fifteen miles southwest.

Misch, like Baur, General Mohnke, Gerda Christian, and others, had only praise for Goebbels' stoic comportment as his end approached. Hitler, who knew Misch far better, never said goodbye to him or shook hands or wished him well or gave him a set of cufflinks. Thanks for the memories.

Misch said:

That talk with Goebbels was about seven o'clock on Tuesday evening, up in the garden. I then went below to pack my gear. Then I got a second order, from Colonel Schaedle. I was to go over into the Chancellery cellar and report to the General Mohnke breakout group. Just as I was packed, a third order came, some messenger I did not know. He told me to remain at my switchboard post. So I did.

Shortly after the Schwaegermann incident, four of Schaedle's comrades from the FBK came down into the bunker with an empty stretcher. They wanted to carry Schaedle in the coming breakout. He turned them down, saying this would endanger five lives instead of one. Schaedle sacrificed himself rather than his men—one thing, finally, that must be said in his favor.

Misch had last seen Colonel Schaedle, the limping Philoctetes of the bunker, moving toward the Reich Chancellery, supporting himself with a crutch, dragging his game leg. He almost certainly committed suicide there, rather than in the bunker.* Misch had then gone back to his switchboard and was soon fast asleep.

He continued, "Previously, when I dozed off with the earphones on, I could count on the phone to wake me. Or Hentschel, just next door. But the phone never rang again. And when Hentschel did wake me up, I thought I had just napped for an hour or so, *ein Nickerchen*."

Now Hentschel began to help Misch put on full field kit for his departure.

For the first time in six long years, Rochus Misch looked like a real soldier again, and not a soldier-valet-telephonist.

---

* That is, in his quarters in the Chancellery cellar. But it could have been in the bunker, since he was drinking there with Krebs and Burgdorf.

With his coal-scuttle helmet and pack, his pistol belt and canteen, his bayonet and entrenching tool, his musette bag loaded with hand grenades, he was off to what was left of the war he had last seen in nineteen thirty-nine, before Warsaw. He really looked quite formidable—like one of those SS recruiting posters of former days. He was wearing his Iron Cross. He also had those ivory rosary beads in his pocket.

Just before Misch left, we exchanged letters we had composed earlier that evening. He had a letter for my wife, Greta, in case I did not survive, and I had a letter from him addressed to his wife, Maria, to serve the same purpose. My sister-in-law lived next door to the Misches, in Berlin-Rudow. My secret hope was that, by some miracle in the chaos, good old Rochus might be able to sneak home, hide out in his own attic or cellar, or something. You have to figure the angles.

(Neither of these letters was ever to be posted; this same day both men became prisoners of war. It was months before either wife knew that her husband had survived this evening.)

Then Misch left the bunker by the tunnel route into the New Reich Chancellery, turned left, and crossed the Ehrenhof to enter the Old Reich Chancellery. He crawled out warily, just under the old Fuehrer balcony facing the Wilhelmplatz. It was only about 200 meters to his first goal, the Kaiserhof subway station entrance. Despite his full field equipment, Sergeant Misch said, he made it "in something close to Olympic time." The hour was about 3:50 A.M.

Hentschel went on with the story. "No sooner had he left than a feeling of desperate isolation overwhelmed me. It was like being left alone in a crypt. So, almost in panic, I took a quick nip up out through the emergency exit, just to relieve the tomblike atmosphere and get a whiff of fresh air. The sun was not yet up, but it was daybreak. The eastern sky was already a kind of pastel, pea soup green, streaked with yellow and orange. Black smoke was rising from burning buildings. It didn't look real. It looked like a stage set."

Since the Fuehrer's last birthday, less than a fortnight back, Hentschel had seen two Reich chancellors, a Reichsfuehrer SS, a Reichsleiter, a Reichsmarschall, one grand admiral, three field marshals, some fifteen ministers, and a dozen generals depart. Then Kampfgruppe Mohnke. Now, the last sergeant.

At five o'clock, Hentschel cautiously ventured out of the bunker for a second time. The whole landscape was brighter but hardly more picturesque.

It was ghostly, an effect heightened by the hazy half-light. The garden now looked like some cemetery where the grave-diggers had gone on strike. There were eight or nine bodies sprawled about in awkward, ghoulish poses, heads off, bellies torn open, here and there stray arms and legs.

When I strolled over toward the pergola, I spotted both Goebbels corpses, side by side still. They were not burned, only roasted. Goebbels' face was deep purple, like a mummy's. Frau Goebbels' face had been horribly consumed by the fire. Her dress was only charred. Captain Schwaegermann had not done a very efficient job of cremation.

Next, I did something rather *daffke* [quixotic]. Despite the pungent morning air, full of ashes and cinders that irritated my eyelids, I got a faint sweet whiff of jasmine and hyacinth. This perfumed air was coming from Hitler's *Gewaechshaus* [greenhouse], where the glass was shattered. So I went over and picked myself a dozen red and yellow tulips, some lilacs. A pathetic little bouquet to freshen things up a bit down in the bunker.

Amid the sickly odor of death, a touch of spring.

I could hear the war far off in the distance. Rumbly, vague, spasmodic. Rifle fire, lazy mortars, now and then a rocket or a green flare from a Very pistol. But no heavy stuff. No Katyushas, no rumble of heavy tanks. No planes. There was a heavy, low-level layer of cloud over Berlin, shimmering, now orange, now lemon, like a cloud of amberlike dust in the Sahara when the sirocco is blowing up. My eyes soon began to smart from irritation; the grit even got into my teeth. Much of the dust was rubble dust. Even the heavy morning dew was full of sharp particles. Mallards kept flying by in tight formation, like Messerschmitts. Ducks and drakes, I guess. It was springtime in the Tiergarten.

My teeth were chattering by this time. It was still beastly cold. After about ten minutes, I was glad to go below. I felt much safer there.

Der Cheftechniker was thus back in time, at five-thirty, to make the next of his every-hour-on-the-half-hour rounds. Even tension, he now noted, can become routine and verge on monotony when one is dog-tired. Another long half hour came and went. At six o'clock, with the Berlin sun now up and trying to announce a glorious day,

Hentschel surfaced again, like a turtle coming up for air. In these discreet pop-ups, he always used the emergency exit into the garden.

Hentschel recalled, "It was much brighter now, and a good deal warmer. But it was still deathly quiet. Suddenly, a whole wing of Russian fighter-bombers dropped out of the sky from the east, flying close to the roof tops. I stood there, as if in a trance, watching them. Then I noticed that at least one plane was fiiring tracer bullets. What is more, this eager fellow was firing them at *me*. The bullets whipped across the garden, just missing the open bunker door. I went back into my hole like a weasel. Shaken up by this narrow escape, I now decided Old Hentschel would stay put down below. Something must be coming, soon."

But nothing did. Hentschel then went back to his familiar workroom. He began meticulously to re-examine his gear. During the long evening before, he had spent almost an hour packing all sorts of items he might need for the road. He now swung them idly over his shoulder and groaned at the load. The pack was much too heavy. So he ruthlessly discarded all but real necessities. He counted the money in his wallet—2000 Reichsmarks in fifty-mark notes. He pulled on a pair of heavy woolen socks and a new pair of heavy boots. Hentschel then shaved. He donned a fresh pair of brown overalls.

Hentschel remembered:

One of the items I hated to throw away was my old combination diary and photo album. You know, all of my treasured memories of that eight-month bicycle grand tour I made, with my younger brother Rudolf, back in September nineteen thirty-two to May nineteen thirty-three.

As I looked backward, and I was doing a lot of that all evening, it certainly seemed the happiest period of my life. As journeyman-handymen, and with only a hundred and fifty Reichsmarks each in our pockets when we set out from Berlin, Rudi and I bicycled all through the Rhineland, over into and across France. Then down on into Spain and Portugal, which we reached around Christmas. Then Gibraltar, Morocco, Algeria, Tunisia. Back through Sicily and Italy. We covered almost twenty thousand miles. I spent a while remembering those happy days.

Hentschel had shown that book to Hitler several times. He recalled Der Chef observing that some young men were luckier than others. He said that, as a young man in

Vienna, he had been so poor that he had never had the chance to travel—except to France, as a soldier. And this recollection made Hentschel wonder if the Fuehrer had, in his whole lifetime, ever permitted himself to enjoy the ordinary and personal pleasures of men.

It brought back another conversation the two of them had once carried on in the bunker. Hentschel always felt rather sorry for E.B., with her touching attempts to stay bright and pretty—with all her changes of costume, manicures, perfumes, and her array of *Gablonz* (junk) jewelry. Somehow, the conversation had come round to women and the Fuehrer had grown vehement.

Hentschel, old man, let me tell you all there really is to know about this copulation business—the alpha and omega of it. Follow my advice and you'll never go wrong: trust no man, and no woman either, below the navel. You know why, Hentschel? [And here the Fuehrer had made that sweeping gesture of his, bringing his forearm parallel to his belt.] Below the umbilicus all men are goats or centaurs, horny goats when they are young and randy centaurs when they get older. And the women? Below those dainty waists they are all as hot-blooded as *Trakehnen** mares in the springtime. Worse than mares. All women are in perpetual heat, Hentschel.

After this reverie, Hentschel snapped back into his frightful Berlin reality. It was now 7:45, his usual breakfast time. Hentschel betook himself to the butler's pantry, Kannenberg Alley.

A Berlin breakfast, for one. Hentschel wondered whether his wife had made it to Berchtesgaden. Not the safest place to be heading at a time like this. He slowly scrambled three eggs, with bacon. He found slices of liverwurst, marmalade, black bread, and powdered coffee, of which he drank four or five cups. He then washed the dishes, another delightful German touch. He was still terribly thirsty, so he drank a bottle of *Fachinger* spring water. The beer tempted him; he refrained.

Hannes now went back into the *Maschinenraum*, to check on the instruments and to snap on the radio. He listened to the eight o'clock news in a German-language

---

* An East Prussian district famous for its breed of horses. The German Kentucky.

broadcast from London. Dit-dit-dit-dah. Even Beethoven
had now become an Englishman. The hard news was bewildering. Admiral Doenitz's announcement of the Fuehrer's
death, "fighting valiantly in front of his troops." Ha! May
Day in Moscow, the march-past. The Americans beyond
Munich. Mussolini and his mistress, filling-station end,
Milan. The United Nations meeting in San Francisco,
Four Freedoms, et cetera. Hentschel thought he heard a
short item about the red flag flying from the Reichstag.
But he wasn't sure. The broadcast faded. Otherwise, not
much news from Berlin. Odd.

Nine o'clock came—and went. Then, just a few minutes
later, while he was in the upper bunker making his weary-
ing routine rounds, der Cheftechniker thought he heard
voices, and they certainly weren't German. They were not
masculine voices, either. Pleasant surprise. He quickly
turned up the lights.

He could dimly make out, coming through the tunnel
from the Chancellery, a group of twelve uniformed Russians moving toward him. To his astonishment, they were
all women. Whispering, giggling, laughing—until they
spotted Hentschel, who promptly raised both hands high
in the air to show convincingly that he was not armed.

He saw that most of these women were carrying large
satchels or duffel bags. They were Red Army Medical
Corps personnel. Not nurses, as Hentschel at first guessed,
rather young women doctors or internes. This he was soon
able to make out from the familiar caduceus symbol, staff
and snake. At least four were doctors; the younger ones
appeared to be assistants. The oldest Russian woman, perhaps thirty, obviously the leader of the group, came straight
up to Hentschel; she asked him who he was and what his
duties were. He noted that her German was not only
fluent but that she spoke with an educated, pronounced
Berlin accent.

He described her as "a bit buxom, flaxen blond, with
high Slavic cheekbones and round, open face. A very impressive woman. She spoke softly, but with a tone of quiet
authority. The *Frau Doktor* type, a bit clinical. Well, her
next question was very much to the point. 'Where is Adolf
Hitler?' I told her of his death, the circumstances, the
burning in the yard. She listened intently. Then a second
doctor, who also spoke German, but a kind of stilted

school-German, cut in. 'Where is Gitler's *Frau*, Gerr Cheftechniker Gentschel?' " This was Johannes Hentschel's first, impromptu Russian lesson.

At this point, I asked him, "Wasn't that Russian doctor jumping a bit ahead of the story? How could she know about Frau Hitler, née Eva Braun? This strikes me as premature. It was more than a month later—June sixth —that the first Russian spoke in public about E.B. Marshal Zhukov, at a press conference in his headquarters in Berlin-Karlshorst, referred in passing to 'Iva Braun, Hitler's secretary.' How could a Russian junior officer know more than a marshal of the Red Army?"

Hentschel replied:

I'm no historian. I can only report on what I distinctly heard. Remember, she was speaking rather broken German. She did not say "Frau Hitler," but "Hitler's *Frau*," in the sense of his woman, mistress. I feel sure she knew nothing about the existence of Eva Braun. She probably just assumed a dictator would have some kind of bedmate. Now that you press me, she may even have said "Hitler's *Weib*." I really forget.

Then, very soon, the first woman doctor came directly to the point. *"Herr Hentschel, wo sind die Klamotten?"**

Now it dawned on me what these Russian females were really up to. To the victor belongs the spoils. After a long, bitter war in the field, they were simply out to liberate some proper civilian clothes. No problem, really. With a sigh of relief that our meeting was passing off so well, I took the women down and escorted them into Eva Braun's—pardon me—Frau Hitler's boudoir. E.B. had a dresser there half the size of the room. The other German women had said it was loaded with all sorts of frilly stuff. Changing her wardrobe at least five times a day had been that woman's major bunker activity. There was also Frau Goebbels' room, but she had arrived with only one valise.

Shortly afterward, around nine-thirty, I suddenly saw two male officers with drawn pistols. They had come the same way the women had. At that time I was still up in the *Vorbunker*. Once again, I raised both hands. Then something unexpected happened, thank God, which really helped to relieve the tension. Six of the Russian women rushed past, anxious, I imagine, to avoid the major, who ranked them all. He and his fellow officer, more surprised than I, just glared at the troupe as they ran by us.

---

* *Klamotten* is a true Berliner's word for "duds, clothes, the glad rags." It is slangy but apt here.

The ladies had their sacks now overloaded with all sorts of souvenirs—lamps, helmets, photos, vases, bottles, SS dress daggers, carpets, crystal glass, Hitler's monogrammed silver, an accordion, a tablecloth, copies of *Mein Kampf*, gas masks, even a table telephone. They were chattering like women returning from a rummage sale. They managed now to vanish very quickly, taking the same route they had come.

The officers facing me wore soft black leather jackets. This made me think they were commissar types. As I now know, this black uniform really meant that they were officers of an elite tank unit, but probably staff officers of some kind. One was a major, the other a captain. Both, I would say, in their mid-forties. The senior officer, the major, wore glasses. He was the intellectual type. He was Jewish.

How could I tell? *Er hat geyiddelt.* That is to say, he spoke some rather broken German with a Yiddish accent.* The captain was much less fluent in German than the major, and he was the one who started to give me a hard time.

He put his revolver to my temple and squeezed the trigger, click-click. It was his special form of Russian roulette, for my benefit. A real wag. Then he put a knife to my throat and started laughing. By this time I was just too damned tired to flinch. I think both Russians respected that. The captain got more friendly later.

The major was more businesslike. He asked me where Hitler was. I told him, but I doubt that he believed me, particularly since I did not have a body to show him, or any idea where it was. The major shrugged his shoulders. *Nitchevo.*

As for me, I guessed I convinced him that I was the Cheftechniker. At least, after he looked at the calluses on my horny hands. He nodded. Then the captain interrupted again. "You, Gentschel, nix *Maschinenmeister. You komm nach Moscow.* Stalin needs *Maschinenmeisters.* You will have plenty of time in Moscow to repent of all the lies you try to tell us today."

All this time, we were in the upper bunker, next to the room with the Goebbels children. The major next asked me curtly to open that door. I did. Both Russians blanched, stepped back, slammed the door quickly. Then they got ready to leave. The captain, now almost jovial, patted me on the back. "*Voina kaputt, Gitler kaputt!* You get a new job, high pay, Moscow. German technician, good man." He said *dos vydania* and waved gaily as he left, followed by the quiet major.

---

* Hentschel, who grew up in Neukoelln, or "Rixdorf," would know Yiddish to about the same extent as a working-class Gentile in, say, Chicago.

Again, risking the impatience of the reader, I interrupt to point out that Hentschel here, without a shadow of a doubt, has identified the first two armed military men of the Red Army to enter the bunker. Hentschel now continued his narrative. The time he had reached was about ten-thirty.

I was just about to go back down into the lower bunker again, on my usual tour, and this time I wanted to put the UTA pump on automatic control. Suddenly, I heard loud shouts, boisterous singing, coming from Kannenberg Alley. The corridor had been invaded by a group of some twenty young officers, Red Army captains and lieutenants. They were all infantry, real combat types.*

At first they didn't even notice me when I walked in. They had just discovered what was left of Kannenberg's wine cellar. Then a tall captain spotted me, neatly knocked the neck off a champagne bottle with his bayonet, and amiably offered me the first drink from the foaming bottle.

After all that I had been through, I did not now want to succumb to glass particles in my intestines. So I first reached for a handy stone mug and then took the proffered drink of bubbly. It was quite stimulating. The captain, laughing, watched the look on my face. He then promptly poured me another drink. Then all his chums began to sing, in rollicking chorus, some Russian drinking song. They danced around me, the German Hentschel, as if I were King of the May.

I don't know whether it was the effect of the two mugs of champagne or the unexpected Russian joviality, but anyway I began to feel woozy, very dizzy. My poor head began to spin, and so did the bunker. So I just sat myself down on the floor. Then the Russians poured a whole bottle of champagne over my crew-cut head.

I stayed at that fraternal jamboree about fifteen minutes and then decided to leave discreetly, before the Russians' victor mood changed. I was much more relaxed, but also more exhausted than ever. I decided I needed to surface again for fresh air. As I passed down through the lower bunker, I could hear some of those lady doctors chatting in Eva Braun's old living room. I climbed up the four flights of stone stairs, puffing, and out into the sunlight. It was very warm now, a beautiful Berlin day. No noise of war, except for Red Air Force planes slowly circling overhead. They were no longer strafing, however; simply photographing.

---

* These hearties were most probably from Colonel Antonov's 301st Infantry Rifle Division, the veterans who had stormed the Reichstag.

Some Russian enlisted men were fooling with the old abandoned cement mixer.

As I was standing near the emergency exit, a second set of two Russian officers approached me, again with drawn pistols. This time a colonel, I believe, and a younger lieutenant. Both looked very *barsch*, unpleasant. The lieutenant spoke a few words of halting German. He asked me where Goebbels was. I showed them. They examined the brace on his leg. Then, in a distinctly unfriendly way, the colonel jabbed his pistol into my ribs. He indicated that I was to escort them down into the lower bunker. He asked me, through the lieutenant-interpreter, just where Hitler's quarters were. I thought for an instant of pulling the *Notbremse*, a wild idea. Then I simply pointed to the door. They both suddenly rushed ahead of me, pushing me aside to get to the door. At this point I finally panicked and made a disastrous psychological blunder.

I should have let them do anything they wanted to, of course. But I was still somehow haunted by the memory of my long night watch, and I recalled how both Misch and I had hesitated to open this door. I noted that it was now frozen into its frame by the melted rubber, which had hardened. So at this moment, quite jittery, I gestured and shouted, "*Kommissar, Nix, Achtung! Minen, Minen!*"

This was a real bonehead performance on my part; sheer panic. I had no idea whether they were commissars or not. I also did not know whether the Russian word for mines was *Minen*. [It was.] It was a dismal failure of communication. They mistook my warning for a threat, or perhaps for guilty knowledge of a booby trap. I tried to gesticulate and explain, but it was too late. That was my ticket to Siberia. They left the door closed, but they pushed me up the stone steps with a pistol in the nape of my neck. From that moment, I was under arrest. They turned me over to a group of Russian MPs. One of them, rather kindly, let me go back into the bunker to fetch my knapsack. Then a chum of his promptly relieved me of it and both my watches.

It was eleven o'clock. With Hentschel no longer in charge, the door to the bunker emergency exit was now swung open. Suddenly, up from the depths emerged the remaining six of the Russian women doctors who had been ransacking the apartment of Eva Braun. Hentschel described the scene. "Those Russian women now came out whooping, like Indian squaws in one of your Western movies. Above their heads, one in each hand, they were gaily waving at least a dozen brassières, all black satin trimmed with lace."*

One is tempted to end the bunker story on this piquant note of the sheer absurd—not with a bang but twelve brassières.

The end of the Fuehrerbunker story, for Johannes Hentschel and many other Germans of the Reich Chancellery Group, was more somber. Just before he was ordered out of the bunker, der Cheftechniker had put his Diesel and the pump on automatic control. He hoped for the best. With the arrival of the Russians, his mission was accomplished. The water was still pumping; most of the young soldiers were still alive; the Battle of Berlin was over.

Now, at long last, Johannes Hentschel had time to start feeling a bit sorry for himself. He was sitting on the ground in the familiar but almost unrecognizable Reich Chancellery garden, basking in the warm spring sunlight. The ghost of Adolf Hitler walked again at noontime. Der Chef. The man he had seen here so many times, feeding red squirrels. Walking Blondi. Long, long ago. The Russian guards were noncommittal, after the watch-frisking party. One or two, trying out their German, sought to convince Hentschel and the other disconsolate German soldier-prisoners that Hitler was still alive. Johannes Hentschel shook his head, wearily, very wearily. Then he fell asleep.

He was rudely awakened, some ten or fifteen minutes later, by loud shouts of *"Davai!"* (Get moving!). With a mixed bag of other German prisoners, Hentschel was now frog-marched through the still-imposing main gate of the New Reich Chancellery toward a Russian truck.

The spring sun was shining brightly on gathering cumulus clouds. Johannes Hentschel saw the Voss Strasse, and what was left of the great city of Berlin outside the Chancellery, for the first time in what had been for him a nearly interminable fortnight underground. Blinking like an owl in the unfamiliar glare, suddenly Hentschel and the other Germans saw the last, most horrendous, of midnight scenes —darkness at noon.

Hentschel related, "I had begun to console myself. I was alive. Now, as we were herded out of the Reich Chancellery into the Voss Strasse, where a truck was waiting to

---

* These were once Eva Braun's and had come directly from Paris. SS officers on leave, like brother-in-law General Fegelein, bought them in a little shop near the Place Vendôme, in the Rue Faubourg St. Honoré.

haul us away, destination unknown but suspected, we looked up and saw a very grim sight. Dangling bodies of some six or seven German soldiers were suspended from lampposts. They had been hanged. Each had a crude German placard pinned or tied to his limp body—TRAITOR, DESERTER, COWARD, ENEMY OF HIS PEOPLE.

Here were the last, savaged victims of homicidal SS "flying court-martials," the mad hangmen.* These hangings must have taken place that morning, between four and nine o'clock, after Misch passed by. Which is to say, almost forty hours after the suicide of Adolf Hitler.

Hentschel continued:

They were all so young. The oldest may have been twenty, the others in their mid-teens. Half of them wore Volkssturm armbands or Hitler-jugend uniforms.

As we were shoved aboard our truck, prodded in the buttocks by bayonets, I saw that I could almost reach out and touch one of those lifeless boys. He looked sixteen perhaps. His wild, bulging, porcelain blue eyeballs stared down at me blankly, blinkless. I shuddered, looked away. I was ashamed in the presence of these Russian soldiers, peasant boys; their stoic, stern, silence was reproof enough. This hanged German youngster was not much older than my own son might have been, that son I had always wanted—and had never had.

Johannes Hentschel's long, dutiful watch in the bunker had ended. It ended just where the haunting, melancholy story of Lili Marlene had begun—"*Vor der Kaserne, vor dem grossen Tor, stand eine Laterne . . .*" (Before the barracks, in front of the big gate, there once stood a lamppost . . .) Six or seven lampposts. High noon, Berlin, Wednesday, May 2, 1945.

---

* In World War I, the German Army executed 42 soldiers for battlefield desertion. In World War II, official records show more than 20,000 executed for this offense by November 1944. For the last, chaotic six months of the war, there is no official figure but a good estimate would be around 7000. Only one American soldier was executed for desertion during World War II—Private Eddie Slovik, who was convicted of running away during the Battle of the Bulge.

Epilogue——1945 and After

Many men die too late and some die too soon.
Few manage to depart at just the right time.
                                    —NIETZSCHE

THE WORLD is indeed fortunate that the stark facts of the bunker permit no myth to be born. It is a shuddering thought to imagine what a bogus, pseudo-tragic legend might have arisen had Hitler been assassinated either in his days of triumph or even as late as July 20, 1944, by that near-miss bomb in Rastenburg. Then, Colonel Stauffenberg might have set the scene for some future demagogue to play Marc Antony to the fallen Nazi Caesar.

We can even be thankful that Albert Speer's forlorn and half-hearted attempt to infiltrate poison gas into the Fuehrerbunker failed. Germany mythmakers, steeped in the Niebelungenlied, might easily have envisioned a Siegfried Hitler struck down by a Hagen Speer just as he was about to unleash his wonder-weapons and win the war.

What did, after all, remain alive in the desolate bunker was a subtle virus that came, I believe, to contribute to that historical affliction we have since somewhat loosely come to call the cold war. Its first effect was a strange mystification about the existence and whereabouts of Hitler's charred corpse.

In the last week of August 1939, Ribbentrop and Molotov had signed the malignant pact between Hitler and Stalin. The British cartoonist David Low, drawing in the white heat of that moment, captured the reality and the symbolism of this awful event perhaps better than anyone else has done. The two dictators are shown meeting in Hades. Stalin greets Hitler, "The ruthless oppressor of the German working classes, I presume?" Hitler bows to Stalin and replies, "The scum of humanity, no doubt?"

Both are smiling with grand unctuous malice—at each other and, most likely, at all the fools and dupes in our western world who still cannot believe in the Devil. And at well-meaning but futile humanists who so often mistake the evil of banality for the banality of evil.

Hitler and Stalin were destined never to meet in real life, but at that moment of the pact in 1939 the black and savage atrocity of their minds met. Both were convinced that they had dealt the western democracies—specifically, Great Britain and France—a mortal blow. Each saw himself as the true revolutionary; each regarded the other as his eventual grand antagonist in the battle for Europe and the world.

For Hitler, the September 1939 to June 1941 war was not much more than a brisk prelude to the real thing. His armies surged in a Blitzkrieg through Poland, Denmark, Norway, Holland, Belgium, Luxembourg, France, Yugoslavia, and Greece. Though technologically new, this was really a conventional war on the classic European pattern. At the end of the prelude, Britain had been reduced to a blockaded offshore island; the United States seemed no more than a remote threat.

The real war, the history-changing war for the two dictators, began with the 1941 invasion of Russia. Both thought of Churchill and Roosevelt as minor actors, aristocrats of the old—and despised—order who had somehow wandered onto the stage of history and now had been brushed aside. The battle for the Mediterranean, so important to men who understood sea power, meant little to land-animal Hitler. He fecklessly left Rommel stranded in North Africa. And that struggle meant nothing at all to land-animal Stalin.

The grand clash of the century was to be fought with a revolutionary ruthlessness on the plains of Russia. And, strangely, this shared contempt for the bourgeois world, this belief in the primacy of their own battle, made for a kind of mutual admiration between Hitler and Stalin. "He is a beast," Hitler once remarked, "but somehow a stout fellow." Stalin revealed his similar feelings less in words

than in actions—no better shown than in the weird postscript to the bunker story. This postscript contains one
solid clue to the origins of the cold war. It had already
begun before the hot war was officially ended. It began
with a Byzantine mystification over the circumstances of
Hitler's death.

How did the world first learn of the death of Adolf
Hitler? Nothing helps better to capture the atmosphere of
1945, and the anarchic breakdown of communications,
than a reconstruction of just how the momentous news was
handled and mishandled. That news came in a quite roundabout way.

True, there had been an official German announcement
under dramatic circumstances. On the evening of May 1,
1945, the German public was told, by radio, to stand by
for an important bulletin. The world was of course listening in. An hour or so later, with the same Brahmsian
requiem note and roll of sepulchral drums that had introduced news of the end at Stalingrad, the announcer sol-
emnly broadcast, "It is reported from the Fuehrer's headquarters that our Fuehrer, Adolf Hitler, fighting to the
last breath against Bolshevism, fell for Germany this afternoon in his operational command post in the Reich Chancellery. On April thirtieth, the Fuehrer appointed Grand
Admiral Doenitz as his successor. The grand admiral and
successor to the Fuehrer now speaks to the German
people . . ." Brahms faded into Bruckner.

Doenitz then added his statement. "German men and
women, soldiers of the Wehrmacht, our Fuehrer, Adolf
Hitler, has fallen. In the deepest sorrow and respect the
German people bow . . . At the end of his struggle, of his
unswerving line of life, stands his hero's death in the capital of the Reich."

In retrospect, there is only one statement of fact in this
broadcast that stands up. Adolf Hitler *was* dead. All the
rest is either a garble or downright prevarication. Doenitz,
who had left the Fuehrerbunker on April 21, was speaking from a remote hideout in North Germany; his voice
was relayed over the Hamburg, not the Berlin, radio. What
information he did have at hand he had got from Martin
Bormann and Joseph Goebbels. It had been delayed for
more than twenty-four hours.

The gravel-voiced admiral himself was very much at
sea. Yet such is the capacity of the human mind to believe

what it wants to believe that this electrifying bulletin went round the world like a sonic boom. The news meant that the end of the war in Europe was now imminent.

A few high-ranking Russians had already learned from a reliable source the news of Hitler's suicide. They had it from General Hans Krebs, the last Acting Chief of the General Staff. Unlike the admiral, Krebs was in the bunker. He had been present at the time of the suicide, had seen the body. While the body was still burning, Krebs crossed the nighttime battle line under a truce flag. Two soldiers carrying pitch torches helped make the bed-sheet flag visible. Sent by the new Reich chancellor, Goebbels, the general was to feel out the Russians on the idea of negotiating a last-minute separate peace.

As credentials, Krebs had with him copies of Hitler's last will and testament. He also carried a letter from Goebbels, addressed to "the leader of the Soviet people." Krebs, as noted before, spoke fluent Russian. He had been the assistant military attaché in Moscow at the time of the Ribbentrop-Molotov pact.

Krebs's mission, under the circumstances of the battle in Berlin, was perilous. He emerged from the bunker shortly after midnight on Tuesday, May 1. It took his small party almost three hours to work its way like sand crabs through the crimson-tinted darkness to the Tempelhof headquarters of General Vasily Chuikov, three miles away. The scene has since been described by Chuikov, in his well-written memoirs, with a mild compassion shown for the hapless enemy general.

Krebs finally arrived just before dawn. He was rattled and exhausted. The first chivalrous thing Chuikov did was to brace him with a double brandy. This revived Krebs. His opening ploy was rather shrewd. He launched into a detailed account of the recent grisly events in the bunker, saying that, as Goebbels' emissary, he wanted his old friends the Russians to be "the first to know."

General Vasily Sokolovsky, chief of staff to Marshal Zhukov, was also present at this parley. The two Red Army generals listened with fascination because the news had the ring of desperate truth. They were indeed the first Russians to hear it. But then Chuikov—and this is a marvelous Russian touch—replied to Krebs's gambit by saying, "General, we have already heard that. It is yesterday's news. Now tell me, what is your *real* mission?"

Krebs, crestfallen to hear his bunker "exclusive" dismissed so casually, went on to stress that he had come to negotiate but had no authority to surrender. Impasse. There was thus really nothing to parley about, yet this tense meeting lasted for more than eight hours, until after noon.

Things went so slowly because Chuikov was often out of the room, on the land line to Marshal Zhukov, who was still in his Strausberg headquarters some fifteen miles east of Berlin. The marshal, in turn, had a direct radio-telephone link to the Kremlin. For the first hours, he conferred with the Red Army Chief of Staff. Later—it was May Day and parade day in Moscow—Stalin came on the line.

Thus it was Marshal Zhukov who was able to give Stalin the first concrete news of Hitler's death. If Zhukov expected kudos, he got nothing of the kind. Stalin merely expressed chagrin that the German dictator had not been taken alive. "So. The beast has escaped us." The Soviet dictator's next businesslike question was "Have you found the body?" Stalin's morbid obsession with Hitler's body had begun.

Whether Stalin at this moment believed the Krebs account is a moot point. Krebs had no rational or even opportunistic motive for lying; the death of Hitler was the *raison d'être* for his perilous mission. Moreover, he knew enough of Russian psychology not to try to deceive them. Krebs's last hope, and that of his new master, Goebbels, was "to play the Russian card." But the Germans no longer held any cards.

It is the timing here that is crucial. It establishes that Stalin had the Hitler-suicide news by breakfast, or certainly before lunch, Moscow time. The exhausted Krebs had returned to the bunker just after midday; he himself was a suicide by nightfall. This strange interlude had thus taken place a good twelve hours before the Admiral Doenitz broadcast that went round the world. Stalin must have gone to bed that night chuckling, aware that his old acquaintance General Krebs was a far better inside source than Admiral Doenitz.

At midmorning of the next day—Wednesday, May 2—as we know, the first Russian combat troops entered the Hitler bunker unopposed. Around noontime, the first of at least five search teams arrived. The quest for the Hitler body had begun. During combat, these teams were called "Smersch" (Death to Spies) and they were the Red Army equivalent of CIC, or counterintelligence. But with Berlin combat over, they had now reverted to direct NKVD control. Red Army military commanders thus lost control over their spook activities. This helps explain much of the flatfooted absurdity that now followed.

The leader of one of these search teams was Lieutenant Colonel Ivan Klimenko, a detective-interrogator who was not very bright.* His first official trip to the bunker was at midafternoon on May 2. He mosied around and located the body of Goebbels, which he rushed back to his new headquarters in Berlin's Ploetzensee prison. Klimenko returned later that evening. This time, another search team had pulled a body out of the old oak water tank, which had been found to be chockful of bodies. This particular one resembled Hitler—and was so identified on the dubious testimony of Admiral Voss—although the dead man was wearing darned socks, as even Klimenko noted. The body was actually that of a Hitler double.

This raises a minor, but interesting, question. Hentschel and Mohnke both mentioned to me something about the existence of a Hitler double, but it was Hans Baur who was more informative. When the Soviets interrogated him during his imprisonment, they showed intense interest in the matter, and Baur recalled that Rattenhuber had once told him that in 1934, Karl Hanke, Gauleiter of Silesia, had located a man in Breslau who bore a remarkable likeness to the Fuehrer, toothbrush mustache and all. Baur had even once suggested to Hitler that the double be employed to appear on the Chancellery balcony to greet the crowds waiting for a sight of their leader. But Hitler had replied, "That's not my style. It's better for a flat-footed fellow like Stalin, who has to stand for hours on Lenin's tomb." After hearing this story, the Russians actually traced and located this man from Breslau.

Baur, in his talk with me, said that he had never seen such a double in or around the bunker—but he believed that the agencies responsible for Hitler's security "may have had one or more doubles on tap, just in case. Had Hitler decided to take part in a breakout, a double could

---

* Klimenko will remind many readers of SS Standartenfuehrer Peter Hoegl, the detective who was sent to fetch General Fegelein in the Bleibtreustrasse. A type.

have been used to camouflage or facilitate his escape."
But, after Hitler's death, any double would have become
an embarrassment—and therefore would have had to be
done in.

In any case, the Russians were at first confused. When
Klimenko returned to the bunker the next day, Thursday,
May 3, he found the body of the Hitler double on prominent display in the Reich Chancellery main hall. So, completely forgetting the matter of the darned socks, he assumed the basic problem had been solved. Poking about
further, he found other bodies inside the bunker, those of
General Krebs and the six Goebbels children.* Then another full day passed. There is creepy black humor in his
official account of the next discovery. He himself related:

> Private Ivan Churakov climbed into a nearby crater that was
> strewn with burned paper. I noticed a bazooka in there and
> called out to Churakov, "Climb out quick or you may be
> blown to bits!" Churakov answered, "Comrade Lieutenant
> Colonel, there are legs here!"
> We started to dig and pulled from the crater the bodies
> of a man and a woman and two dogs. Of course, at first I
> didn't even think that these might be the corpses of Adolf
> Hitler and Eva Braun, since I believed that Hitler's corpse
> was already in the Chancellery and only needed to be posi-
> tively identified. I therefore ordered the new corpses to be
> wrapped in blankets and reburied.

Sheer police mentality was at work. It was a full two
days later, on Saturday, May 5, that Comrade Lieutenant
Colonel finally tumbled to the possible significance of his
crater find. He now rushed back—this time without
Churakov—and exhumed the two bodies. Thus the dull-
witted colonel, not the alert and curious private, was to
be awarded a Hero of the Soviet Union medal.

Klimenko took both bodies to Plòetzensee, but he was
soon ordered to send them on to the 496th Field Hospital
in Berlin-Buch. On May 8, V-E day, both bodies were
dissected and the first preliminary forensic autopsy performed.

Postive identification took place in a very simple yet
quite foolproof way. The man who deserves credit for this
is General, later Marshal, Sokolovsky. Sokolovsky had

---

* The bodies of General Burgdorf and Colonel Shaedle were apparently
never found.

already set out to locate the surviving members of the Reich Chancellery Group. He knew they were still in Berlin, because his own troops had captured them. But he soon discovered that they were being held incommunicado, in Berlin's Schloss Niederschoenhausen, the old Hohenzollern palace now converted into an NKVD prison. One, Professor Werner Haase, had already been flown off to Moscow. In Berlin, the matter was now rapidly passing out of the hands of the Red Army.

But not completely. General Sokolovsky, acting on a tip from a nineteen-year-old Bulgarian medical student, located two Berlin dental technicians, Fritz Echtmann and Kaethe Heusemann. It was Echtmann who had designed a special "crown bridge" for Hitler's molars, and Fräulein Heusemann had helped Hitler's dentist, Dr. Hugo Blaschke,* to fit it in November 1944. Both technicians were taken, separately, to the eastern outskirts of Berlin and were asked to sketch from memory the topography of Hitler's mouth. Each did so, with German attention to detail. A simple doublecheck was to have each of them pick out the crown bridge, which was now mingled with others in an old cigar box. Both passed this test, as well.** The Russians now knew they had the right bodies, beyond any doubt.

This resort to molar identification was a necessary substitution for the usual fingerprint method, because the Hitler cadaver no longer had any fingerprints. The hands were burned and flaked like crisp bacon. After this secret show, the two Germans were thanked and driven back to their homes. This, according to Echtmann, was on or about May 10. Two days later, NKVD spooks caught up with them. Having played their little role in history, they were now destined to join members of the Reich Chancellery Group in the long march through the Gulag archipelago.

Still, they had convinced General Sokolovsky, and hence Marshal Zhukov, that Hitler had died in Berlin and in the manner narrated by General Krebs. After more chemical lab tests, the final autopsy was made, the body burned, and the medical report sent through channels to Moscow. This

---

* Blaschke had, wisely, gone to Bavaria.
** And identified Eva Braun Hitler's molars in the bargain, though the Russians had little interest in her—for the Soviets, wives and mistresses are virtually nonpersons.

was on or about May 15.* The possibility that Hitler's ashes were sent to Moscow does exist, but more likely they were scattered in Buch, where the autopsy took place. By the dark of the moon, no doubt.

This molar playlet has its sinister overtones. In a Persian proverb it is written that when the king says it is midnight at noontime, the wise underling murmurs, "Behold the stars." By May 15, obviously, the high Russian military in Berlin had established to their own satisfaction that Hitler was dead. But not to Moscow's satisfaction. Stalin, from paranoid suspicion or cynical malignity or both, ignored all solid evidence coming in from Berlin. He soon began floating the rumor that Adolf Hitler was still alive.

In Berlin, Zhukov and Sokolovsky were flabbergasted when they learned this.** They had already told the "molar identification" story to several western military men and diplomats visiting Berlin for quadripartite preliminaries. (Specifically, Sokolovsky had told it to his opposite number, American General Lucius D. Clay, and to the American top diplomat, Robert Murphy.) Then, suddenly, both the marshal and the general began to "behold the stars."

On June 9th, in Berlin, Marshal Zhukov held a press conference in which he started to backtrack. He spoke of "Hitler's death or disappearance." A few days later, when the marshal paid a courtesy visit to General Eisenhower's headquarters in Frankfurt on the Main, Zhukov backed down completely. There was, he told Ike privately, "no solid evidence" of Hitler's death. Eisenhower, whose prestige throughout the world was then at its pinnacle, re-echoed these doubts in a press conference a few days later in the Hôtel Raphael in Paris. His was the first public western voice to do so.

This was the sticky atmosphere in which the Four Power occupation of Berlin began in early July 1945. Skeptics began to ask themselves, if the victorious powers could not lay the ghost of Adolf Hitler, what prospect was there of agreement on other, now far more weighty, matters?

---

* My narrative here is based on what my old friend and colleague, the late Cornelius Ryan, told me as he returned to Berlin after his interview in Moscow with Marshal Sokolovsky. I had helped Ryan locate Fräulein Heusemann. This was in 1964.

** Both military men knew the Soviet system. They knew, that is, that Stalin was out to cut the popular Zhukov—and the Red Army—down to size.

Stalin continued his duplicity at the Potsdam Conference. The conference convened in the Berlin suburb in mid-July 1945, and there Stalin repeated to President Truman, Secretary of State James Byrnes, and Admiral Leahy, what he had been whispering to Harry Hopkins earlier in Moscow. Hitler was alive, he stoutly insisted, and was residing in Spain or maybe Argentina.

By the sultry August of 1945, in the journalistic silly-season, Hitler *redivivus* stories, inspired by such new uncertainty on high, began popping up almost daily in the world press. Hitler had been seen living as a hermit in a cave near Lake Garda, as a herdsman high in the Swiss Alps. He was a croupier at the casino in Evian, a monk in the monastery of St. Gallen, a headwaiter in Grenoble. The one I liked best was his new job as a fisherman on the Aran Islands, far out. *Isvestia* finally ran a story that was not only false but invidious: Adolf Hitler and Eva Braun were "alive and well, and living in a moated castle in Westphalia." Westphalia lay in the British Occupation Zone of Germany.

In throwing around the names of such countries as Spain and Argentina, Stalin was probably just paying off old political grievances against Franco and other Latin neutrals. But in having a go at the British, he was blackguarding an ally that had been fighting Hitler from the very first day of the war. The Soviet leader was now accusing it of harboring a living Hitler.

In September 1945, the British Military Government in Germany, astonished and irked, turned to Whitehall for help. London sent out a gentleman-detective, a young Oxford don, whose mission was to discover just what had happened in the Hitler bunker, where the witnesses now were, the circumstances of Hitler's death, and the where-abouts of the body—no easy assignment. Sand had been flowing in the Berlin hourglass. The bunker, in the Soviet sector, was now off limits.* Most cardinal witnesses had been moved from Berlin to Moscow, Vorkuta, or Sverdlovsk. A few members of the Reich Chancellery Group had been skillful enough or lucky enough to evade the remorseless Red Army dragnet and make it to the west.**

---

* To the best of my memory, this off-limits was posted in September, but possibly it was in August 1945.
** See the list of names on page 342.

It is not for nothing that the British are known as the finest practitioners of the modern detective novel. They have a natural passion to discover who done it. Using the tried and true methods familiar to Arthur Conan Doyle and Agatha Christie, academic detective Hugh Trevor-Roper (today Regius Professor of History at Oxford) went to work. He did a masterful job in locating available witnesses, flushing them from their cover, and piecing together their bizarre stories. He reconstructed the world's first basically accurate, if condensed, account of the last days of Adolf Hitler.

A November ground fog shrouded Berlin's Kurfuerstendamm on a memorable 1945 evening as we all crowded into the Hotel-am-Zoo, the British press headquarters in one of the few buildings still standing on that once brightly lit avenue. Dapper in his wartime RAF squadron leader's uniform, Trevor-Roper, a droll man and a master of tart understatement, managed to disperse the propaganda miasma that had been rolling in from the east for weeks. As of that evening—November 1, 1945—most of the international press stationed in Berlin was finally convinced Hitler was indeed dead.

There was a documented press release. I quote here the salient points, since this was the first such official statement on the death of Hitler since Admiral Doenitz's dubious broadcast back on May 1, 1945.

Available evidence sifted by British Intelligence and based largely on eyewitness accounts shows—as conclusively as possible without bodies—that Hitler and Eva Braun died shortly after 2:30 A.M. on April 30, 1945, in the bunker of the Reich Chancellery, their bodies being buried just outside the bunker.

On the evening of April 29 Hitler married Eva Braun, the ceremony being performed by an official from the Propaganda Ministry in a small conference room in the bunker . . .

At about 2:30 A.M. on April 30 Hitler said goodbye to about twenty people, about ten of them women, whom he had summoned from the other bunkers in the Old and New Reich Chancelleries.* He shook hands with the women and spoke to most of them.

On the same day, at about 2:30 P.M., though the time is uncertain, orders were sent to the transport office requiring

---

* The scene described by Professor Schenck.

the immediate dispatch to the bunker of 200 liters of petrol. Between 160 and 180 liters of petrol were collected and deposited in the garden just outside the emergency exit to the bunker. At about the same time Hitler and Eva Braun made their last appearance alive. They went round the bunker and shook hands with their immediate entourage and retired to their own apartments, where they both committed suicide, Hitler by shooting himself, apparently through the mouth, Eva Braun, apparently, by taking poison, though she was supplied with a revolver.

After the suicide the bodies were taken into the garden just outside the bunker by Goebbels, Bormann, perhaps Colonel Stumpfegger, and one or two others. Hitler was wrapped in a blanket, presumably because he was bloody.

The bodies were placed side by side in the garden about three yards from the emergency exit of the bunker and drenched with petrol. Because of the shelling, the party withdrew under the shelter of the emergency exit and a petrol-soaked and lighted rag was thrown on the bodies, which at once caught fire. The burial party then stood to attention, gave the Hitler salute, and retired.

From then on, the evidence is more circumstantial. How often the bodies were resoaked or how long they burned is not known. One witness was informed that they burned until nothing was left; more probably they were charred until they were unrecognizable, and the bones broken up and probably buried.

The above evidence is not complete; but it is positive, circumstantial, consistent, and independent. There is no evidence whatever to support any of the theories that have been circulated and which presuppose that Hitler is still alive. All such stories which have been reported have been investigated and have been found to be quite baseless; most of them have dissolved at the first touch of fact, and some of them have been admitted by their authors to have been pure fabrication.

This was one way of calling Stalin a barefaced liar without actually naming him. Experts in Hitlerology may note several minor flaws in this version, but basically it is quite close to the reality. Russian historians, even post-Stalinist historians, have never quite forgiven the Oxford don for scooping them so grandly on their own story. He got the timing of the marriage wrong. Hitler shot himself in the right temple, not the mouth. Eva Braun Hitler had a pistol, not a revolver. Hitler also took poison. Save perhaps for the last point, these exceptions are nit-picking. The fact remains that it was a Briton, not a Russian, who gave the world the first authentic no-nonsense version of what happened in Berlin on Monday, April 30, 1945. It was fog-dispersal in November.

In retrospect, what was most remarkable about this detective-story coup was that, as of November 1, 1945, Trevor-Roper was fishing for trout in rather shallow waters. He had located but two major witnesses who had been present in the bunker on the last day—Erich Kempka and Else Krueger. He also had located three members of Rattenhuber's police squad who were on duty just outside the bunker and saw parts of the funeral ceremony—Hermann Karnau, Erich Mansfeld, and Hilco Popper. In 1946, while Trevor-Roper was expanding his report into a book, American authorities gave him access to two more major witnesses, Gerda Christian and Artur Axmann. These were about the only ones available who had not been captured by the Russians.

Altogether, there appeared to have been about forty survivors. But where were they? The Red Army, on May 6, had announced the capture of two of them, Hitler's pilot, Hans Baur, and the chief bunker detective, Major General Johann Rattenhuber. Then silence. Since many of these witnesses have lived to become the major sources of this present report, it is time to turn that Berlin sand clock to the summer of 1946, to pick up the thread of the strange story there.

*   *

More than a year had now passed. Because I had been kept preoccupied by other journalism, my first trip to the Hitler bunker in July 1945 had moved to the back of my mind. But I had not forgotten it; I had been paying a tipster in East Berlin to keep me informed on just such matters.

Early one evening, I received an urgent call. In guarded language, I was told that there was a bustle of camera activity at the old Hitler bunker site. By the time I arrived it was *Daemmerung*, the slowly fading light of a long midsummer evening. Moving about in the shadows, I spotted my friend and enterprising colleague, the late Marguerite Higgins of the New York *Herald Tribune*, on the scene. As we discovered later that evening, to our chagrin, we both had the same alert German tipster on the payroll.

When competing for something, Maggie, the blond bombshell, seemed to have three elbows, but that had not helped her to gain access to the bunker. She had already been twice turned away. Both of us were now learning Russian the hard way. We quickly joined forces and approached the bunker entrance.* This time, we were chased clear out into the Wilhelmstrasse by four sullen sentries flourishing submachine guns, and there we met a Russian officer who told us to vanish. He made his point with a drawn pistol.

We vanished, but only around the corner into the rubble-cluttered Voss Strasse. Sneaking into the New Reich Chancellery, we climbed our way to the roof of that now-ghostly edifice. Two owls flitted by on noiseless wings. Our shaky roof-top perch was about 100 yards above and away from the bunker, and our view of the entrance was partly blocked. Dusk had now fallen. In the quiet we could hear voices and could make out the shadowy forms of some twenty people milling about the entrance. But the action, to our disappointment, all seemed to be inside the bunker. Those figures who did emerge outside were simply taking a cigarette break; we could see the orange glimmer. A half hour passed. There was no moon. As our eyes adjusted to the dark, we could see Russian uniforms, with the now-familiar soup-plate hats and baggy-rump trousers.

Suddenly, Klieg lights illuminated the bunker and the Old Chancellery garden. Now we could see cameramen and hear the whirr of their cameras, in what looked like a movie stage set. Some four or five Russian officers were giving directions to a group of about twelve actors, silent performers who were clad in what seemed to be deep purple fatigue uniforms. A mélange of German words, Russian words, indistinct, floated across the chilly evening air. A scene was shot; we could hear the clapper. The group of mimes filed back into the bunker. Lights out.

But twenty minutes later, the same group emerged again to shoot a second scene. We guessed—correctly, as it turned out—that these two scenes must be the burial of the Hitlers and the suicide and burial of Joseph and Magda Goebbels. These, as we already knew, were the only two events that had taken place outside the bunker. Marguerite and I came to the conclusion that a Russian movie com-

---

* By this time, the old emergency exit had become the only entrance to the bunker.

pany was making a film documentary with Red Army help. Soon the whole mysterious troupe departed in trucks. A spooky feature, we thought; another Berlin midnight rendezvous and nothing more.

Higgins and I had missed a big story. Those shadowy figures in deep purple fatigues were indeed Germans. They were the some dozen missing major witnesses from the Reich Chancellery Group who had vanished from Berlin in the first week of May 1945. Now, some fourteen months later, they had been reassembled in Russia, flown back to Berlin, and made to reconstruct the bunker melodrama, step by step, on the original location. The next morning at dawn, they were flow back to Moscow. They had been in Berlin for less than twenty-four hours. They were destined to remain scattered in Soviet prison camps for another decade.

Readers familiar with normal police-detective practice will see what had gone awry here, the major intelligence disaster. Such a reconstruction scene, a good idea in itself, could and should have been performed in those first days of May 1945, when the key witnesses were still in Berlin. They had been through a harsh experience, but their memories were fresh. The bunker, though looted, was pretty much as they had left it on the night of the breakout.

Although it is usually a mistake to seek rational answers to events anything but rational, one major piece in the puzzle here fell into place. It was clear that the Red Army had surrendered its bunker prisoners to the NKVD, whose job was less to reconstruct the truth than to monopolize and manipulate the evidence.

Put another way, no reconstruction scene could have taken place in May 1945 because the witnesses had been put into an interrogation mill that ground slowly. Separate grillings went on every night for more than a year. Only then was it decided to return the cast to the scene of the crime.

Nothing captures better the *Darkness at Noon* aspect of those first long months of captivity than the later testimony of Hans Baur. As a flyer and a lieutenant general, Baur might normally have expected treatment milder than that given the SS. Moreover, he was now an amputee, having lost his left leg after being wounded in the Berlin street fighting near the Lehrter S-Bahn station. Instead, in the Lubyanka prison in Moscow, Baur was beaten, flogged, and kicked about until he could no longer stand. In protest, the pilot went on a hunger strike. He was then force-fed.

Although Baur could not know it at the time, Stalin had singled him out for this special, barbaric treatment. If Hitler had escaped, to Spain, for example, then he had been flown there. And he would have been flown by his best pilot.

Before I talked to Hans Baur, at his present home on the Amersee in Bavaria, I was fairly convinced, as I have indicated earlier, that Stalin's mischief-making was a propaganda ploy and perhaps a way of cutting war-hero Zhukov down to size. I felt that the Russian dictator was too much of a peasant realist to believe his own propaganda. But his moment of victory, as Nikita Khrushchev was later to testify, was precisely the point at which paranoia set in. Baur's harrowing experience would seem to offer confirming evidence of this.

Baur told me:

> When my midnight interrogators first accused me of having flown Hitler to Spain, I asked them just what I was doing there in Moscow? Why would I fly the Fuehrer to sunny Spain, and then desert him to fly back to besieged Berlin, and get my leg shot off in the bargain? I tapped my wooden leg. I thought I had made a convincing point.
>
> But the very next midnight they came back with the approved solution to my riddle. "Ah Baur, you are the clever one. On Hitler's orders you flew back to Berlin to murder your copilot, Colonel Beetz. He was the only other witness of your secret flight."

It was thus that Baur first learned that Beetz was probably dead.*

Baur is not the type to read George Orwell, but he was going through a real-life Orwellian experience. The process he described is known as "doublethink," a word Orwell got from Dostoievsky. No NKVD interrogator ever once admitted that Hitler might be dead. At the same time, like beavers, they went on piling up tons of documented testimony that only could prove he was.

---

* Beetz had been badly wounded in the breakout, his skull split open. He managed to crawl to the flat of Kaethe Heusemann, the dental assistant, and died there the next day. Captain Helmut Beermann also found refuge with Fräulein Heusemann. He saw Beetz die.

It was not until 1973, in a casual conversation with Sergeant Rochus Misch, that I got the explanation of that garish bunker filming scene Marguerite Higgins and I had witnessed on a long-ago summer evening in 1946.

After our first interview—Misch is one of the few bunker veterans still living in Berlin—we went for a midnight stroll around the town. We came to the Potsdamer Platz, which is today just inside West Berlin in the American sector. We gazed over at the old bunker site in the Soviet sector.

It is a melancholy place, haunted by a malignant *genius loci*. In the very heart of the big city, a yawning void. The Romans had plowed and strewn salt on Carthage. The Russians had used bulldozers here. The bunker has become a non-place, engulfed in vast emptiness. A flare goes off like a rocket; a shot rings out. Berlin *son et lumière*.

Sergeant Misch, back in 1946, had been one of those German performers in the Klieg lights of the re-enactment I had watched. Now, twenty-seven years later, we were meeting for the first time.

I asked Misch about the details of the 1946 replay, and he told me. He also gave me names of other members of the cast that night. They were General Mohnke, Hans Baur, Lieutenant Colonel Klingemeier, Heinz Linge, Major General Johann Rattenhuber, Colonel Hoegl (Rattenhuber's senior aide), Major Otto Guensche, Colonel Schenck, Johannes Hentschel, and two other young SS officers from the bodyguard, whom Misch could no longer remember by name. For a re-enactment of Hitler's last day, these represented the bulk of the original cast who were still alive.

We may recall that back on May 6, 1945, the Red Army victory communiqué had disclosed only the capture of Baur and Rattenhuber. About the rest, silence. Through Four Power channels, Trevor-Roper had politely approached the Russians to inquire about the Reich Chancellery Group, almost all of whose names he knew. No dice. Would they at least show him the protocol of the Baur and Rattenhuber interrogations? No answer. He was baffled.

He later wrote, "I now see how tiresome it must have been for the Russians in Berlin, when, in response to that silence, their western allies officiously offered to help them by producing what of all things they least wanted—more evidence."

*   *

Thirty-three years after the Berlin happening, the men and women of the bunker, the surviving old mountain people, break down into curious cliques. Some nurse ancient grievances; others, a fresher hostility. Some old friendships have endured, but many have long been broken. If an intruder into this odd circle wishes to strike sparks, all he need do is to mention casually such memoirs as those of General Guderian, Hanna Reitsch, Hans Baur, or Albert Speer. Above all, the two books by Speer. Major Otto Guensche was definitely speaking for most of the bunker people when he told me, "No, I did *not* read the Speer books. But I have been told how he tried to convert the bunker into a gas chamber with all of us inside. A friendly fellow."

Even on the main topic, Der Chef, there is something less than unanimity of opinion if one listens closely. There are overtones and undertones, and a general feeling that somehow the whole mad show was anticlimactic. There is no such thing as an annual bunker reunion, and there never will be. The bunker is still there, at least the underground chambers are, but these cannot be entered.* Nor can the grassed-over old Chancellery sites be approached by the curious. In East Berlin it is off limits because of its proximity to the Berlin Wall.

The old Leibstandarte, the Adolf Hitler elite guard division, does meet annually. It is a kind of veterans' jamboree, as boring and probably as harmless as such meetings usually are. I attended two such clambakes, one in Essen and one in Marburg on the Lahn River. The next day in Marburg in the *Aula*, or auditorium, of the university, I ran into a good many wild-eyed student political radicals, this time

---

* In 1963, Wolfgang Fuchs, twenty-five, the most successful of the Berlin tunnel-diggers, managed to work his way into the old Fuehrerbunker and planned to use it as part of a daring refugee escape-plan. Fuchs and his tunnelers were quietly put out of operation by the then Berlin mayor, Willy Brandt, and his police senator, Heinrich Albertz. Today's German politicians are totally lacking in imagination.

from the left. In a metaphorical sense, perhaps, they are
Hitler's children. But that is another story, for the coming
turbulent years.

*   *

Two of the major witnesses of great help to this book are
Hans Baur and Albert Speer. As we have seen in earlier
chapters, this pair were also the major antithetical personalities in the old Hitler court. Both were close friends of
Adolf Hitler, but otherwise they were men from two
different German worlds.

Baur and Speer have never met again since a last, shouting confrontation in front of the Brandenburg Gate in the
red-tinted, smoky dawn of Tuesday, April 24, 1945. This
surrealist scene is worth recalling since it still reflects two
opposite points of view among the people who survived the
bunker debacle. Seventy-nine-year-old Hans Baur narrated
it this way:

> There I was, with the whole mass of the Red Army steam-
> roller charging in on me. Artillery shells were bursting over-
> head. I was sweating to get a few planes safely down or
> others up into the air. One of those planes was Minister
> Speer's small Fieseler Stork. Although I suspected that Speer
> was taking a powder, I was happy enough to launch him,
> and good riddance. But what did the lofty Herr Reichs-
> minister do? Why, he spent one hour trying to countermand
> the order Hitler had given me to cut down a few hundred
> trees to clear our emergency runway. There was Speer, fran-
> tically running up and down the runway, grabbing axes out
> of the hands of my hard-working ground crews. Just picture
> it! The whole world was now collapsing around us Germans,
> and this born boy scout from the Palatinate promoted him-
> self to chief forester. Speer kept screaming at me, "I am,
> after all, the chief city-planner for Berlin, responsible for
> postwar reconstruction."

As he said this, the bumptious Baur was really wound
up, angrily acting out the whole scene while hobbling on
his wooden leg. And as he continued in his bow-wow Bavarian bark and growl, the pilot's weatherbeaten, aquiline
face lit up with sarcasm. "Well, as soon as I managed to get
Speer's ass into the turbulent air, which was the name of
my exercise, I went out personally and cut down ten to

twelve trees just to spite him. Speer was a real twister, one of the many traitors who betrayed Hitler and then ran—like Colonel Stauffenberg. I also would have cut down his three miles of bronze lampposts. Unfortunately, they were made of good German bronze. We just couldn't hack them."

Albert Speer's response, after he had read my notes on this choleric outburst, was low-key.

Well, I see that Baur has not changed. His description of the gate scene, from his own point of view, is accurate enough. I *was* distraught. Like a few others of the bunker people, Baur is so pig-headed and stupid that he has learned nothing and forgotten nothing from the Hitler experience and the German national catastrophe. He is an unteachable, a "keeper of the flame." Baur reflects, precisely, the nihilist bunker mentality at the end. Only Hitler, only that one bunker, only the mountain people really counted. Not Berlin, not the future of three million Berliners, not even the German fatherland they sang about so lustily when our army was winning its Blitz victories. Certainly not the trees.

But it was precisely Berlin trees, those lindens, sycamores, plane trees, and elders, that were, somehow and suddenly, of importance to me. A tree, even a blasted tree, is mankind's green symbol. It has roots in the past and spells a hope for the future. It has taken the new city of Berlin thirty years to replace the growth that Baur's men cut down in one feckless hour.* Perhaps we Germans, a forest people, have an ancestral thing about trees, what you Americans call a hang-up. If so, it is certainly not our worst national quality. A young man sits with a young woman under a chestnut tree planted by his great-grandfather—or maybe hers—Hermann and Dorothea. An old man plants trees, although he knows he will never live to enjoy the full shade or to pick any fruit. Martin Luther, a better German than either Hans Baur or Adolf Hitler, once said that if God told him the end of the world was coming in eight days, he would still go out into his garden and plant an *Apfelbaeumchen*, a little apple tree . . .

I am ashamed today of many things I did as a minister of the Third Reich. But not of my forlorn, perhaps sentimental, attempt to spare those trees. For the future of Berlin, even several hundred trees had become, to me, more important than the whole tawdry show in the Fuehrerbunker.

---

* Many of Berlin's Tiergarten trees today date from 1948-1949. They were a gift from Queen Elizabeth of England. The nursery trees were flown in by the RAF during the blockade.

As for those bronze lampposts Baur mentioned, they did survive—and are now all that is left standing of Speer's life work as an architect. A bit too Spartan perhaps, even for Berlin, the capital of the old Prussia. But at least they are functional; they shed light.

Albert Speer and I were walking under the replanted trees as we carried on that long outdoor interview in Berlin in the bright, blue autumn of 1976. Few Berliners passing by even recognized the tall, bushy-browed man who had once been this city's planner and who, for three critical war years as armaments minister, had bossed the economy of most of continental Europe. Technocrat Speer, in his days of power, could pick up his Berlin red-line phone and move a train or a factory from the Pyrenees to the Crimea, from Italy to the North Cape. Hitler's Europe, however perverse and rapacious the way, had elements in it that foreshadowed today's Common Market.

Had he won his war, Speer recalled, Hitler planned to rebuild Berlin completely, even changing the name to Germania. The city was to become Europe's Nazi supermetropolis of more than ten million, in a Greater German Reich of 140 million, the master of a helotized Europe of 350 million. This was to be the most compact military and industrial concentration on the planet.

The north-south axis of the planned Germania would have been the Prachtstrasse, the Street of Splendor. It was to be five miles long, as straight as an arrow, and almost twice as broad as the Champs Elysées. Along its borders would stand all major German ministries, a new General Staff building, a great memorial hall of the field marshals, a new Reichstag, and all important foreign embassies.

In the center at a round point, there was to be a new German Triumphbogen, or triumphal arch, four times as high as the Arc de Triomphe. In 1940, conquered Paris had fascinated conqueror Hitler; he fell in love with it. It was probably the Place de la Concorde that inspired his new plan for an Adolf Hitler Platz in the middle of the Prachtstrasse, where there was to be standing space for more than a million spectators. Plans were also made for a third Reich Chancellery, the Fuehrerpalast. This one residence would have occupied seven times the ground space of Philip II's somber Escorial, north of Madrid; it was to be at least twice the size of Nero's legendary Golden House.

To dominate this nightmare of a colossal brown Byzantium, Hitler and Speer dreamed up a fantastic superstructure to surpass all the others. This was to be the Kupferhalle, the great copper dome. Modeled on the Roman Pantheon, it would have been 1000 feet high, 850 feet in diameter, that is, seven times as large as St. Peter's in Rome and thirty-two times more spacious than our Capitol dome in Washington. With standing space for 160,000, this structure would have been the world's largest and most expensive edifice. The plans called for a ten-year crash-building program at a cost of more than $400 million (in terms of the 1940 purchasing power of the Reichsmark). Groundbreaking actually began in July 1940; Speer said the dome was scheduled to be completed by April 19, 1950, one day before the Fuehrer's sixty-first birthday.

In the real year 1950, in the Berlin sand glass, Adolf Hitler had been more than five years dead. Albert Speer, forty-five, was now Prisoner Number 5, serving his fourth year of a twenty-year term in Berlin's somber, red-brick Spandau prison. In 1976, Albert Speer and I were approaching the banks of the meandering Spree River. He remarked that the natural course of this green black river would have been diverted. As he spoke, I was idly watching a barge from Bordeaux, headed eastward through the locks to Warsaw, Leningrad, or maybe even to Moscow. Under the Speer plan, all such barge traffic would have been made to pass through the center of the new city of Germania via an underground canal. The Spree waters were to be diverted to encompass the great dome on three sides. This would have made for an artificial lake and a huge reflecting pool—a double image, an exaggeration of an exaggeration.

The architect recalled that, in 1940, Hitler had told him, "Speer, whatever our Kupferhalle actually costs, let's get Goebbels to tell American correspondents that it cost exactly double. Nothing in this world impresses Americans as much as bigness and money. They'll flock here in droves; we can even charge admission. Everybody thought King Ludwig the Second of Bavaria was a crackpot when he built his Neuschwanstein Castle. It turned out to be a gold mine for tourism."

In an earlier interview in his home in Heidelberg, Speer had shown me an original master blueprint of Germania, one of the few that had been salvaged. All these Brobdingnagian figures check out. In fact, I copied them directly from the plan. Speer also has in his possession a most curious, ominous souvenir, one of the first presents Hitler ever gave him. It is a small, postcard-sized sketch of the original Triumphbogen, basically the same design as reappeared in the 1940 plan. It was initialed A.H. Speer pointed silently to the date—1925.

I was amazed. Where, after all, was Adolf Hitler in 1925? That was one year before he published *Mein Kampf*. The thirty-six-year-old Adolf Hitler had just been released from a Landsberg prison cell and was knocking about at loose ends in Bavaria. But this malignant dreamer was planning his war even then. One does not build triumphal arches in anticipation of winning the Nobel Peace Prize.

Hitler may have drafted that sketch in prison or, just after his release, up in the clouds above Berchtesgaden. A line of the writer Ernst Juenger returned to haunt me. Hitler did indeed belong to "that very dangerous breed of men who dream concretely."

We continued on with our peripatetic dialogue. Since I first met Speer in 1969, on the occasion of the publication of the first of his two memoirs about the Third Reich and after, I had come to know him well. He is today a man upon whom much rain has fallen. At this moment, I could not resist needling him a bit, possibly because he had apparently shared with Hitler that unworthy little sneer about gullible American tourists.

I said, "Mr. Speer, one of your architect-team colleagues once told me that all of you spent many weeks, back in nineteen forty, wrestling with the acoustics problems raised by your huge copper cupola. He said that if a wandering tourist were to have dropped even a beer can or a tonic bottle, in all that yawning space, it would have set off a mighty, rumbling echo—a kind of indoor sonic boom. Is that true?"

Speer replied, "No, not really. We simply called in our best acoustics experts—from the Luftwaffe, as I remember it. They solved that problem in short order. It simply meant juggling the geometry of the dome's parabola a bit, and using rather expensive new soundproofing material. But we never did reach the point where we mastered a far more embarrassing problem—indoor cloud precipitation."

"That means rain," I said. "Indoor rain clouds in the

middle of a speech by Adolf Hitler? Mr. Speer, you must be joking."

On the contrary [Speer said], I am deadly serious. Even today I remember a moment in Spandau prison when I was quietly working in the garden, puttering about among my phlox, larkspurs, and dahlias. I was watching the summer clouds come and go. Glumly, I realized it was nineteen fifty. It was a rainy day. I began wondering if I could ever have completed that Kupferhalle under any circumstances. Only then did it really dawn on me what knotty technical problems all that architectonic gigantism had been raising—Hitler's megalomania, and my own.

Soberly, I came to calculate that body moisture and the throaty exhalations rising from such a massed Nazi audience, packed in so close together like sheep, would have slowly risen. Warmed air always does. Then, on a wintry day, up there under the cold, patined copper of the cupola, the steadily rising mass of warmed air would have met up with a compact, static layer of chilled air. This, in turn, would have led to small floating cloud formations and, ultimately, to precipitation.

On this truly giddy thought of the Fuehrer Adolf Hitler being rained out by clouds formed from his own hot air mixing with the beery sweat and throaty *Sieg Heil!* cheers of his frenzied followers, my last interview ended. In Berlin, the hourglass city, a city where it all could have happened.

Index

ABOUT THE AUTHOR

JAMES P. O'DONNELL is a native of Baltimore and a graduate of Harvard, where he majored in classics. He served as a captain in Signal Corps intelligence in Europe during World War II and, in 1945, became the first bureau chief for *Newsweek* in Germany. Among his many assignments for *Newsweek* and other periodicals were stories on the Nuremberg Trials, on conferences of foreign ministers in London and Moscow, and on the Berlin Airlift. In 1961, he joined the State Department and acted as special assistant to General Lucius D. Clay in Berlin. He is now a freelance writer in Berlin and has contributed to *Reader's Digest, The New York Times Magazine, Fortune, Washington Post* and other publications. He has also been co-author of five books on German and European affairs.

Mr. O'Donnell was one of the first Americans to enter Hitler's bunker after the fall of Berlin.

HOLOCAUST

"Those who cannot remember the past are condemned to repeat it."

George Santayana

The events leading up to, through and beyond the tragic years of persecution and resistance during World War II.

☐	13564	**HOLOCAUST** Gerald Green	$2.50
☐	06407	**A BAG OF MARBLES** Joseph Joffo	$1.75
☐	12527	**THE HIDING PLACE** Corrie ten Boom	$2.25
☐	12510	**THE LAST OF THE JUST** Andre Schwarz-Bart	$2.95
☐	11968	**MISCHLING, SECOND DEGREE** Ilse Koehn	$1.95
☐	12754	**THE UPSTAIRS ROOM** Johanna Reiss	$1.75
☐	13084	**THE WAR AGAINST THE JEWS** Lucy Dawidowitz	$3.50
☐	12930	**MILA 18** Leon Uris	$2.75
☐	11129	**THE MOON IS DOWN** John Steinbeck	$1.50

BANTAM WAR BOOKS

These action-packed books recount the most important events of World War II. They take you into battle and present portraits of brave men and true stories of gallantry in action. All books have special maps, diagrams, and illustrations.

☐	12657	**AS EAGLES SCREAMED** Burgett	$2.25
☐	12658	**THE BIG SHOW** Clostermann	$2.25
☐	13014	**BRAZEN CHARIOTS** Crisp	$2.25
☐	12666	**THE COASTWATCHERS** Feldt	$2.25
☐	*12664	**COCKLESHELL HEROES** Lucas-Phillips	$2.25
☐	12916	**COMPANY COMMANDER** MacDonald	$2.25
☐	12578	**THE DIVINE WIND** Pineau & Inoguchi	$2.25
☐	*12669	**ENEMY COAST AHEAD** Gibson	$2.25
☐	*12667	**ESCORT COMMANDER** Robertson	$2.25
☐	12927	**THE FIRST AND THE LAST** Galland	$2.25
☐	*11642	**FLY FOR YOUR LIFE** Forrester	$1.95
☐	12665	**HELMET FOR MY PILLOW** Leckie	$2.25
☐	12663	**HORRIDO!** Toliver & Constable	$2.25
☐	12670	**THE HUNDRED DAYS OF LT. MACHORTON** Machorton	$2.25
☐	*12668	**I FLEW FOR THE FUHRER** Knoke	$2.25
☐	12290	**IRON COFFINS** Werner	$2.25
☐	12671	**QUEEN OF THE FLAT-TOPS** Johnston	$2.25
☐	*11822	**REACH FOR THE SKY** Brickhill	$1.95
☐	12662	**THE ROAD PAST MANDALAY** Masters	$2.25
☐	12523	**SAMURAI** Sakai with Caidin & Saito	$2.25
☐	12659	**U-BOAT KILLER** Macintyre	$2.25
☐	12660	**V-2** Dornberger	$2.25
☐	*12661	**THE WHITE RABBIT** Marshall	$2.25
☐	*12150	**WE DIE ALONE** Howarth	$1.95

*Cannot be sold to Canadian Residents.

Buy them at your local bookstore or use this handy coupon: